THE INORDINATELY STRANGE LIFE
OF DYCE SOMBRE

MICHAEL H. FISHER

The Inordinately Strange Life of Dyce Sombre

Victorian Anglo-Indian MP and 'Chancery Lunatic'

HURST & COMPANY, LONDON

First published in the United Kingdom in 2010 by
C. Hurst & Co. (Publishers) Ltd.,
41 Great Russell Street, London, WC1B 3PL
© Michael H. Fisher 2010
Printed in India.

The right of Michael H. Fisher to be identified
as the author of this publication is asserted
by him in accordance with the Copyright,
Designs and Patents Act, 1988.

A Cataloguing-in-Publication data record for
this book is available from the British Library.

ISBN: 978–1849040006

www.hurstpub.co.uk

CONTENTS

v

CONTENTS

CONTENTS

ACKNOWLEDGMENTS

The research and exposition of this intricate book could not have been completed without the generous assistance of many institutions and scholars. I am grateful for funding for this research in India, Britain and America from a Franklin Research Grant from the American Philosophical Society and a Thomas J. Klutznick Fellowship and the Robert S. Danforth Chair from Oberlin College. The major repositories which have enabled me access include: the British Library, the National Archives of the United Kingdom [PRO], the Royal Geographical Society Library, the Wellcome Library, the Freemason's Library, the Institute for Historical Research, and the London Metropolitan Archives, all in London; the Stafford County Record Office and William Salt Library, Stafford; the National Archives of India, New Delhi; and the University of Texas at Austin Library. I have also presented parts of this project and received especially insightful comments at the Travel Writing Centre at the University of Nottingham, the South Asia Seminar at Oxford University, the Colonial and Postcolonial Studies Seminar at Emory University, and the post graduate seminars in History and English at Delhi University. The following scholars have proven particularly helpful: Helen Holmes, Ruby Lal, Gyanendra Pandey, Rosalind O'Hanlon, David Washbrook, and Tim Youngs. Manuscript reviewers Philippa Levine and Tony Ballantyne were particularly encouraging. My editor, Michael Dwyer, has made sage suggestions and improvements throughout this book project. As always, Paula Richman has been my greatest support; to her, this book is dedicated. Any errors are, of course, my own responsibility. Every reasonable effort has been made to identify and secure copyrights for reproduced materials; omissions, if brought to the publisher's notice, will be rectified in the next printing.

ABBREVIATIONS

DSAT—Dyce Sombre against Troup
Mary Anne Dyce Sombre, *Dyce Sombre against Troup, Solaroli (Intervening) and Prinsep and the Hon. East India Company (also Intervening) in the Goods of David Ochterlony Dyce Sombre, Esq., Deceased, in the Prerogative Court of Canterbury*, 2 vols, London: Seyfand 1852.

Dyce Sombre, *Refutation*
David Ochterlony Dyce Sombre, *Mr Dyce Sombre's Refutation of the Charge of Lunacy Brought against Him in the Court of Chancery*, Paris: Dyce Sombre, 1849.

Diary
Dyce Sombre's 'Diary', 'Private Memorandum', and *Pocket Book of 1846*, The National Archives of the United Kingdom [PRO].

IPC
India Political Consultations, British Library, London.

NDNB—Oxford Dictionary of National Biography, Oxford: Oxford University Press, 2004–

LIST OF ILLUSTRATIONS AND MAPS

(unless otherwise noted, they are the production or in the possession of the author)

LIST OF ILLUSTRATIONS AND MAPS

Separate Colour Illustrations

Genealogical Chart for David Ochterlony Dyce Sombre

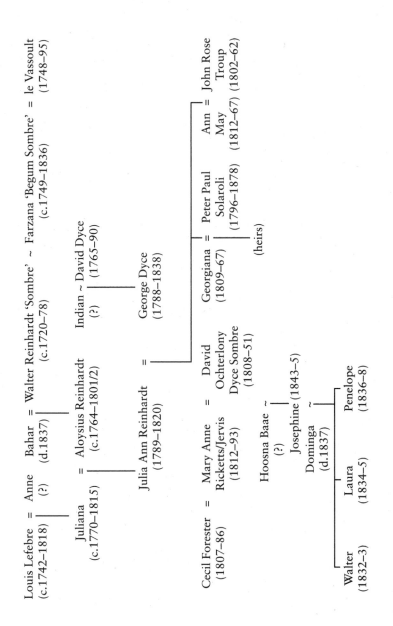

CAST OF OTHER MAJOR CHARACTERS

Combermere, Viscount, General Sir Stapleton Cotton (1773–1865) [NDNB], Napoleonic war hero, Commander-in-Chief in India, advisor to Begum Sombre and David Dyce Sombre.

Cottenham, Baron, Charles Christopher Pepys (1781–1851) [NDNB], Lord Chancellor (1836–41, 1846–50).

Drever, Dr Thomas (1797–1857), court physician to Begum Sombre then advisor to Dyce Sombre in England.

Lyndhurst, Baron, John Singleton Copley (1772–1863) [NDNB], Lord Chancellor (1834–35, 1841–46).

Metcalfe, Sir Charles Theophilus, Baron Metcalfe (1785–1846) [NDNB], Resident Delhi (1806–08, 1811–19, 1825–27), acting Governor General (1835–36), Lt Governor Agra (1836–38), Governor of Jamaica (1839–42), and Governor-in-Chief of North America (1843–45).

Mughal imperial family: Shah Alam II (r. 1759–1806), Akbar Shah II (r. 1806–37), Bahadur Shah II (r. 1837–58).

Ochterlony family: Colonel Sir David (1758–1825) [NDNB], Resident Delhi (1803–06, 1818–25); his mixed ancestry grandson and heir, Sir Charles Metcalfe (1817–91).

Prinsep, Henry Thoby (1793–1878) [NDNB], Persian Secretary to the Government of India later member East India Company Court of Directors.

Reghellini family: Major Antonio Giuseppe (1787–?), Italian courtier and architect of Begum Sombre, later manager of some of David Dyce Sombre's properties in India; Antonio's son, Stephan, travelled to Europe.

Skinner: family of mixed Indian and European ancestry, based in Hansi, includes Colonel James (1778–1841) [NDNB] and his son Captain Hercules (1814–66).

Sleeman, General Sir William Henry (1788–1856) [*NDNB*], anti-thug Commissioner (1839–42), Resident Gwalior (1843–49), Resident Awadh (1849–54).

Thomas family: George (1756–1802) [*NDNB*], Irish mercenary, who served and then saved Begum Sombre; his eldest son John Thomas, her courtier.

Trevelyan, Sir Charles Edward (1807–86) [*NDNB*], Assistant Resident Delhi (1827–31), Secretary to Government of India (1831–38), Assistant Secretary to Her Majesty's Treasury (1840–59), Governor Madras (1859).

Wellington, Field Marshall Arthur Wellesley, Duke of, (1769–1852) [*NDNB*], served in India (1797–1805), then in Napoleonic Wars (1808–15), Prime Minister (1828–30).

Wilde, Sir Thomas, Baron Truro (1782–1855) [*NDNB*], Dyce Sombre's barrister (1843–44), Lord Chancellor (1850–52).

INTRODUCTION

QUESTIONING CATEGORIES

When Colonel David Ochterlony Dyce Sombre, Esq., in August 1841 became a Member of the British Parliament, he had travelled far and crossed many boundaries, constantly defying categorization, his life ever inordinate. Fabulously wealthy, Dyce Sombre was the first Asian and only the second non-White ever to be elected to Parliament. His wife, the Honourable Mary Anne Dyce Sombre (daughter of English Viscount St Vincent), proudly observed his Parliamentary debut from the Strangers' Gallery. Other Members of the Commons included her relatives, close friends, and future second husband; the House of Lords included her father, her long-time benefactor (and widely-presumed lover) the Duke of Wellington, and Dyce Sombre's own patron, Napoleonic war-hero Viscount Combermere. All these English elites were already clashing over Dyce Sombre's racial identity—'Oriental' or 'European' or 'Anglo-Indian'—and his mentality—'lunatic' or 'sane'.

Only five years earlier, David Dyce Sombre had lived a world away, as the Catholic 'Anglo Indian' heir-apparent to the cosmopolitan but doomed principality of Sardhana, located near Delhi. In 1836, he had lost his Indian foster-mother, the infamous Begum Sombre, a Muslim courtesan-turned-Catholic princess who had ruthlessly ruled this small but prosperous state. Just before her death, she had transferred her vast personal treasury to him, but immediately thereafter the British seized Sardhana. Made homeless, Dyce Sombre journeyed across north India, to Southeast Asia and China, and then to Europe, where he soon married into the English aristocracy.

Following Dyce Sombre's expulsion from Parliament after nine months as a sitting MP, he faced an insurmountable challenge when his wife's family had him forcibly incarcerated as *non compos mentis*

1

(in popular parlance, a 'nincompoop') and his huge fortune sequestered. Only his dramatic escape from confinement to the continent
enabled him to wage an eight year long struggle to regain his property,
one that ended in vain. Indeed, he died at age forty-two on the eve of
the sixth inquisition before the Lord High Chancellor of England into
his mental competence. Thus, throughout David Dyce Sombre's strange
life, he transgressed boundaries and ventured through worlds where he
purchased prominence but never acceptance.

This book, written two hundred years after his birth, explores how
his contentious life illuminates larger issues of his day, and ours. Many
societies stress 'racial' classification and many commentators write
about 'the West' and 'the East', assigning essentialist characteristics to
each, but many individuals like David Dyce Sombre defy definition.
Nation-states presume that ethnicities and borders correlate, but root-
less cosmopolitans of all classes have become stateless and live as aliens
everywhere. Legal and medical systems still each seek to define and
diagnose insanity, but often themselves produce irrational anomalies
and contradictions. Gender relationships among men, women, and
their biological, adoptive, and marital families often deviate from
expected social norms. Once-loving couples separate, assert implausible accusations, and divide their formerly joint friends into feuding
factions. In the inordinate life of David Dyce Sombre, we encounter
someone who, by his very existence and often unprecedented words
and deeds, and by his cascade of violations of cultural norms wherever
he went, highlights the constructed and contingent nature of all these
categories which are so deeply embedded in both Asian and European
societies.

A Life in Brief

During the course of his tumultuous life, David Ochterlony Dyce
Sombre (1808–51) defied conventional classification. His diverse ancestry included a notorious German Catholic and an obscure French
Catholic mercenary, a Scots Presbyterian subaltern who died young,
and their secluded Indian Muslim or Hindu female partners (his Genealogical Chart precedes this Introduction). Far more famous than any
of his progenitors was his still-fabled adoptive mother, the Catholic-
convert Begum Sombre of Sardhana. She had risen from being a Muslim courtesan to become the powerful ruler of a strategically placed

cosmopolitan little kingdom, poised geographically, politically, and culturally between the wilting Mughal and burgeoning British empires. David grew up as the potential heir to the Begum's principality, displacing his father, George Dyce, as chief executive of her government and Colonel-Commander of her army. While David savoured the diverse pleasures derived from her power and riches, the Begum's state terminated with her death through annexation by the British. Now dazzlingly wealthy but exiled, David left Asia at age twenty-eight, never to return.

During the next turbulent thirteen years David Dyce Sombre rose high, empowered by his vast capital, but he never found social acceptance, wherever he vainly roamed. Despite his dark complexion and Catholicism, he soon married the much gossiped about daughter of an English Protestant Viscount, the former owner of hundreds of slaves in Jamaica and defender of slavery in the House of Lords. Amid escalating tensions with his low-church Anglican in-laws, Dyce Sombre bought election to the British Parliament, creating even more controversy on account of his blatant electoral bribery than for his uncertain citizenship and unprecedented origins. After Parliament eventually repudiated his scandalous election to the corrupt constituency of Sudbury (east of London), his noble wife's family had him arrested, convicted, and incarcerated as a 'Chancery lunatic'. Flight to freedom in France restored his liberty but not his full fortune. Repeated appeals for supercession of his lunacy conviction gradually restored much of his huge income but not his legal sanity in the eyes of the British Empire. He interspersed his judical campaigns with his ventures across the continent—as far east as Russia and south around the Mediterranean. Each of his half-dozen lengthy appeals, heard before three successive Lord Chancellors of England, set new precedents for international and medical law and were reported by newspapers throughout the Anglophone world. Each rehearing, held at a time when Britons increasing regarded Asians as essentially different from themselves, debated the unanswerable issue of whether he was a sane Indian or a lunatic European. Over the years, forty-five prominent European doctors declared him sane. But one English lay-jury and eight court-appointed British physicians judged him lunatic. Meanwhile jurists and physicians clashed repeatedly in public over their various inconsistent, ever-changing, and heatedly contested definitions of lunacy. In 1851, his abused body gave out suddenly. But his legacy, and even his corpse, remained in legal limbo for another two decades.

Evidence and Approaches

David Dyce Sombre's flamboyant life in Asia and Europe made him one of the most documented and controversial men of his age. Scores of newspapers and magazines throughout the British Empire and across the United States and European continent published a total of well over 700 articles about his strange predicaments: as wealthy Catholic heir to a former Indian principality, as an Asian MP expelled for the corruption of English voters, and as a legal lunatic in one jurisdiction who was officially sane elsewhere. Four decades of legal wrangling over his person and property, and seemingly interminable lawsuits against the East India Company over his inheritance, turned his private papers into official evidence, preserved by the many British courts in England and India that heard and tried to resolve these intractable cases. So infamous was he that scores of his European and Asian contemporaries, men and women of all social classes, gazed upon and judged him in their own publications. Further, hundreds of Europeans, Asians, and other people of mixed ancestry swore legal affidavits, often giving contradictory evidence in exchange for cash from contending advocates. Lawyers, judges, and legal textbooks still today cite dozens of different rulings from his various cases as precedent, wherever English law holds influence. Yet no clear categorisations of his racial or national or legal identities or of his mental condition emerged during his lifetime or since.

This biography, rather than seeking easy answers, explores how his life illuminates larger issues in Asia and Europe and shows how one distinctive individual actually lived in an early modern phase of globalisation. Part One contextualises David Dyce Sombre in the transition from the crumbling Mughal Empire to expanding British colonial rule in north India. During this volatile period, from the late eighteenth to the early nineteenth centuries, his European and Indian ancestors and foster-mother, Begum Sombre, necessarily made cultural choices, including language, religion, clothing, and comportment, which had imponderable political consequences. Rulers of Mughal successor states, like the Sardhana Begum and David (as he was familiarly known in India), her heir-apparent, dealt ambiguously with the often impoverished but still haughty Mughal imperial family and their high courtiers. She and David also sought to maneuver among imperious British officials and officers and the shifting colonial policies imposed on such remnant princely states as Sardhana. Other 'interracial' clans of Anglo-Indians in the region also related in complex ways with the Begum's fictive family. Moreover, wealthy young men of the time like David had various relationships with diverse women, based on their asymmetrical desires, interests, cultures, wealth, and power. By drawing upon extensive original records produced by and about the Sardhana court, including David Dyce Sombre's own private diary, this book seeks to demonstrate the intricacy and contradictions of his myriad social, cultural, political, and personal interactions.

Part Two follows David Ochterlony Dyce Sombre to Europe and the Eastern Mediterranean. English society of the 1840s was undergoing manifold realignments of its attitudes toward race, class, and gender in the realms of culture, politics, law, and medicine. Each category comprised challenges for and by Colonel D. O. Dyce Sombre (as he preferred to be known in Europe). For instance, his unconventional demands for duels against many gentlemen over his aristocratic wife's honour, and his shocking suggestion that she also challenge noblewomen to duel over his honour, appeared abnormal, as did many of his other extravagant attitudes and unbounded desires. During his numerous trials, public debates occurred across the globe that grappled inconclusively with how to identify and interpret him and what he represented. Drawing together the array of evidence by and about Dyce Sombre during his later life, including his own private papers and those of his associates and the hundreds of doctors, lawyers, acquaintances, and bystanders who repeatedly examined and diagnosed him, this book suggests how various parties drew their own multiple meanings from his inordinate life, revealing their own and wider Asian and European societies' often inconsistent principles of classification.

The Many Meanings of His Life

Given the controversial inconsistencies of evidence and interpretation about David Dyce Sombre's multiple and shifting identities, we must be ever cautious in applying to them our own terminology, approaches, and conclusions. He and those around him ascribed racial and ethnic labels in different ways. David himself often used the category 'native' to refer to other people born in India, but evidently never included himself in that category. Even living in England among native Britons he never described them as 'natives'. Yet, on occasion he proudly boasted of 'my Indian blood'. Further, his overall comportment fluctuated according to circumstance. He usually chose to don European-style clothing, but also wore what he called his 'Hindustani' dress on particular occasions, and sometimes mixed the two to the discomfort and confusion of some around him. His contemporaries in India and Europe with similar mixed biological origins made different cultural choices. Linguistically multivalent, he wrote and spoke in some contexts in English, in others 'Hindustani' (today called Urdu), and expressed his most intimate feelings in Persian. Seeking to construct various self-serving arguments about his 'essential' identity as Eastern or Western, his partisans and opponents differed among themselves as to whether he was really fluent in English or just 'faked' it. He himself assessed the cultural sophistication of Europeans, Asians, and people like himself based on their mastery of spoken Persian—the high-culture language prevalent among elites in north India but exotically rare in Europe.

In addition to his linguistic sophistication, he also used multiple names and identities. Following his own preferences, Part One of this book identifies him as 'David', although in north India he was also familiarly known as 'Davy' and, with increasing respect, 'Davy Sahib' or 'David Sahib'. 'David' was also his Protestant paternal grandfather's Christian name. His Catholic foster-mother had him baptised as 'David Ochterlony', after her friend and patron (and his possible ancestor on his father's mother's side), the famous American-born British officer and official: Sir David Ochterlony. In his twenty-sixth year, David himself added 'Sombre', the *nom-de-guerre* of a maternal great grandfather, and he later contemplated adding 'Reinhardt', the actual name of this infamous ancestor. Part Two of this book, however, uses 'Dyce Sombre'—the name he deployed in Europe. His wife apparently added the affectation of an acute accent: Sombré. She herself went from Miss Mary Anne Ricketts to the Honourable Miss Jervis to Mrs Dyce Sombré, but for consistency and clarity, and without disrespect, she is called 'Mary Anne' throughout this book.

No abstract theory, during his day or today, adequately defines David Dyce Sombre—his life was too inordinate. During his life, citizenship—a post-Enlightenment European concept central to the nation-state model—failed to classify him. He claimed himself a subject of Queen Victoria but was enfranchised nowhere in her Empire. Yet, he was himself elected to the British Parliament and voted there, at least until his election was later 'controverted' (annulled). But his right to membership in Parliament in the first place remained unproven due to his ambiguous natal status in the 'semi-sovereign' state of Sardhana, which was under British 'suzerainty' but not 'sovereignty'. Indeed, the standing of his foster-mother's rule remained undecided in international law for decades after his death. The English East India Company, whose own sovereignty remained moot, signed an international treaty with her but then unilaterally annexed her state. Later, to defend this annexation and confiscation of her private property, the Company (and then its successor, the British Government) argued, with only partial success before the Queen's Privy Council, that she was actually sovereign after all. Further, the British Crown, acting on behalf of his wife and her family, imprisoned Dyce Sombre (although he had violated no laws) and impounded his wealth, claiming to act in his own best interest. Even after he escaped to the continent and was no longer domiciled within Victoria's dominion, he was subject to seizure in England and anywhere else in the British Empire, except Scotland. In contrast, the French and Russian imperial governments extended protection to him against the British crown, although he was only transient though their realms. Overall, people and governments tended to take positions about his legal status based on their own interests rather than consistent principles of national or international law. He thus lived and died without any citizenship, either in India or Europe.

Some scholars have heuristically used 'hyphenisation' to denote binary identities, especially racial and national ones.[1] A related scholarly approach evokes 'hybridity' to describe how two or more separate ancestries or cultures come together or synthesise in an individual or single society.[2] During David Dyce Sombre's day, Britons applied to him—and to people of ancestry or enculturation similar to him as well as to people quite different—the labels 'Anglo-Indian', 'Indo-Briton', and 'Eurasian' (as well as many more impolite epithets).[3] Yet, both hyphenisation and hybridity both imply duality, fixity, and consistency, whereas real lives and groups often have multiple, fluid, and context-specific identities. The subcontinent of 'India' remained regionally and politically diverse rather than a nation long after David Dyce Sombre's death; 'Britain' was only gradually emerging as a nation-state during his lifetime; the Mughals themselves drew upon several Asian cultures in uneasy and inconsistent imperial syntheses; Sardhana, like many other Mughal successor states, created its own set of conventions.

Hence, while this book cautiously refers to 'Indian-style', 'British-style', or 'Mughal-style'—or even 'Indian', 'British', or 'Mughal' as types—it does not delimit David Dyce Sombre by any hyphenated or hybrid label but rather discusses his contested and contingent identities in each context.

Throughout his life, Dyce Sombre said and did things that jarred inordinately against social conventions and demonstrably contradicted empirical evidence available to him. He often reneged on his earlier assertions about what was true. As he himself admitted in his private diary, his carousing lifestyle harmed him and others, but he saw many wealthy men do worse and escape punishment. Particularly as his English aristocratic marriage broke down, he made accusations and acted toward his wife in ways that did not advance his cause among those close to him. Indeed, he often acted against what we might consider his own interests. For example, he generally (but not consistently) aspired to be accepted as European, although his own lawyers and advisors, and even his judges, deemed that his behavior was 'normal' for an Indian man but 'lunatic' for a European. Hence, his claiming he was 'Indian' may have meant exoneration for him, yet he refused to do so.

An inevitable question arises about whether Dyce Sombre was in fact 'insane', in absolute terms, on balance, or partially. During his lifetime and thereafter, many people, including dozens of prestigious medical and legal experts across Europe, simultaneously but contradictorily pronounced him definitively either sane or insane. Their clashing assessments, however, tell us more about their respective presuppositions concerning normality than about his actual condition. His actions and words in Europe considered by some as the strongest proof of his insanity were similar to deeds and statements he had made earlier in his life in India; he may not have changed to become 'lunatic' as much as his context shifted, which then made these actions 'lunatic'. Further, even over the single decade of his many public lunacy trials, the medical and legal professions each shifted from one dominant but incompatible theory to another. Dyce Sombre's case certainly shows how culturally constructed medical diagnoses of 'madness' and 'unreason' were, and are.[4] Hence, we should resist the temptation to attempt to psychoanalyze Dyce Sombre and his alleged 'delusions' based on evidence and assessments produced two centuries ago by people with ulterior motives. Any modern diagnosis of his medical conditions would also largely reflect our own presuppositions about 'normality' in the human mind and body.

Further, Dyce Sombre's social situation reflected changing British concepts about appropriate social and legal gender roles and boundaries. During this period, the rights of the bourgeois family were imperfectly displacing those of the autocratic male patriarch. Reflecting emerging Victorian ideas about masculinity and middle-class family responsibilities, the British state acted to empower Mrs Mary Anne Dyce Sombré over her husband, much to his dismay. As a wife, she could not herself directly control property (including her own) but she was nonetheless authorised by the British crown to control his body. During her widowhood, she regained legal power over her wealth, and much of his, only to lose control again by her second marriage. Yet, much British popular and middle-class sympathy favoured him, regarding her as a gold-digging aristocrat who had betrayed and perhaps even murdered a relatively innocent Indian. Her elite conservative family and supporters read the marriage in opposite terms: a corrupt Indian despoiling innocent English noble-womanhood. Across the globe, numerous newspaper editors and commentators interpreted the Dyce Sombres' tumultuous relationship in light of their own parochial perspectives.

Given how wide-spread were press and public commentaries on Dyce Sombre during and shortly after his lifetime, and the wealth of rich (albeit highly contested) evidence available, remarkably little has been written about him during the last century or so. His life fits into and advances the national narrative of neither India nor Britain, so scholars and other commentators have ignored him. However, Nicholas Shreeve's self-published books reflect an assiduous commitment to bringing to light the wrongs perpetuated against Begum Sombre and Dyce Sombre by their contemporaries as well as by trained historians.[5] Helen Clarey (later Holmes) researched and wrote a fine but as yet unpublished 1986 masters thesis on Dyce Sombre's wife: 'Lady Forester—A Woman of Wealth'.

Many other scholars, including William Dalrymple and Durba Ghosh, have kindly assisted me with valuable suggestions and key evidence and insights. Model studies of comparably complex historical problems have also helped me conceptualise this project including: Natalie Zemon Davis, *Return of Martin Guerre* and Partha Chatterjee, *Princely Impostor?: The Strange and Universal History of the Kumar of Bhawal.* Overall, this book presents Dyce Sombre's life history and contexts to reveal the complexity and contingency of his inordinate life rather than to judge him.

Part One

Asia

1

THE STATE OF DAVID'S ORIGINS

As soon as the dangerous and inauspicious first days had passed following David Ochterlony Dyce's birth on 18 December 1808, the aging Begum Sombre took him from his mother into her own keeping. The fabled Begum Sombre was only halfway through her improbable six decades of rule over the prosperous 625–square-kilometer principality of Sardhana, located strategically near the fading Mughal imperial capital of Shahjahanabad (Delhi) and even nearer the thriving British military base at Meerut (see Maps 1 and 2 below). The Begum's life of cross-cultural conflict and mistrust shaped her upbringing of David. She raised him at her feet amidst the churn of this complex transitional period as various Indian, European, and Anglo-Indian individuals, powers, and cultures vied for dominance. After many other men had failed or fallen away from her, she finally made David her heir. His life can only be understood by considering hers, and the state in which she raised him.

Through force of character and rare fortune, the Begum created various diverse families and prominent positions for herself throughout her turbulent life. From an unpromising childhood, she rose to make herself the favoured Indian mistress of a notorious German Catholic mercenary. Then, by dint of her own efforts during unpredictable circumstances, she managed to cling to the little kingdom of Sardhana that he had wangled through mercenary service to the Mughal emperor. Despite her disastrous marriage with a French Catholic officer under her command—which ended in a rebellion against her by Sardhana's army, his death, and her imprisonment—she survived and recovered power. For decades, she maneuvered skillfully through the volatile swirl of battles and politics that marked the fragmentation of

13

the Mughal Empire into clashing regional warlords and the English East India Company's aggrandizement of most of north India. While maintaining her ties to the Mughal emperor, Begum Sombre opportunely negotiated British protection in 1805, including promised postponement of the annexation of Sardhana, at least until her death. Over the next thirty years, she cached for her chosen dependents as much money and land as she could shelter from British confiscation. David would eventually emerge as her last designated heir. But the meaning of his cultural heritage would remain unresolved even at his death and the extent of his material inheritance from the Begum would not be fully settled until decades after that, by the highest courts in London.

Rise to Begum of Sardhana

Farzana—widely known variously as Begum Sombre, Somru, and Somroo—still stands out among the many contenders for power, position, and wealth in late eighteenth-century north India. She obscured her background and age but, during her long life, others surmised a variety of origins for her including as a dancer, courtesan, and slave, the impoverished daughter of a Kashmiri, Arab Sayyid, Georgian, or north Indian Muslim or Hindu family.[1] She herself may not have known the circumstances or the year of her birth (although her court much later declared it officially to have been 1749). Even today, she continues to be envisioned by various Indian and European authors of popular histories and fiction as alluring, arbitrary, despotic, exotic, nationalistic, pious, romantic, tragic, and/or vindictive.[2] Even her adopted heir, David, who grew up below her throne, found it difficult to comprehend her origins, motives, or policies.

Around 1765, teenage Muslim Farzana entered—by gift, sale, or mutual agreement—into the household of Walter Reinhardt (c. 1720–78), an older, German-speaking, Catholic mercenary, as his mistress.[3] Reinhardt had acquired the alias Sombre (variously spelled)—an epithet of uncertain origin, diversely attributed to his swarthy complexion, grave temperament, or possibly a mispronunciation of his German alias Somers. He was also David's great-grandfather and self-selected namesake.

Even among the diverse Europeans of Reinhardt's day who sold their purported military expertise to any Indian or European who would pay, he became particularly infamous. Eventually, a British consensus

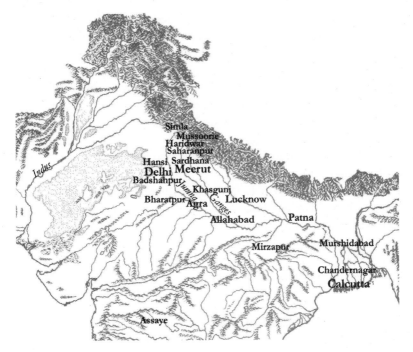

Map 1: North India and the Sites Relevant to David Ochterlony
Dyce Sombre

emerged that Reinhardt must have been of low birth—inconsistently
identified as a butcher, carpenter, or gypsy—who had left Europe as a
sailor and then deserted his French ship in India. Once there, he oppor-
tunistically profited while allegedly betraying all his employers, including the French and English East India Companies. His most enduring
condemnation came from his period of employment by Nawab Mir
Qasim of Bengal, who turned against his former patrons, the English
East India Company. After Mir Qasim's forces captured Patna city in
1763, Reinhardt, 'of a flint-like heart', and his men allegedly massa-
cred 150 helpless British men, women and children prisoners.[4] This
mass murder placed Reinhardt high on the British list of war criminals.
The Company then pursued him across north India, rousting him
through dire threats from his various Indian employers, including
Mughal Emperor Shah Alam II (r. 1759–1806).

Reinhardt's shift from one paymaster to another garnered him
wealth, various landed properties, and impressive mansions in Shahja-

15

hanabad (Delhi) and Agra. Most significantly, in 1777 Reinhardt gained from the Mughal Emperor the titles Zafaryab Khan, Muzaffar al-Daula ('Victorious Lord', 'Victorious of the State') as well as Sardhana as a *jagir*. While a *jagir* had customarily been a non-hereditary assignment of land revenue in exchange for service to the emperor, by the late eighteenth century many *jagirs* became virtually independent estates or principalities. Sardhana, located in the Doab (area between the Jumna and Ganges Rivers), contained rich and well-irrigated farmland, although it had long suffered spoliation from passing armies and robber gangs.

At Reinhardt's death in 1778, Farzana, emerging as Begum Sombre, asserted her own power over his *jagir*, other properties, consort, and son. Reinhardt's senior Indian wife (David's great grandmother), the mother of his heir, evidently suffered a mental disorder and lived quietly under Farzana's care, dying in 1837. Reinhardt's sole surviving son, Aloysius Balthazar Reinhardt (c. 1764–1801/2, David's grandfa-

Map 2: Sardhana in the Doab, with Other Landholdings of the Begum

ther), largely contented himself by luxuriating in the Mughal imperial capital on his allowance from Farzana. He displayed his mixed Indian-European biological and cultural heritage by boasting the same titles as his father—Nawab Zafaryab Khan, Muzaffar al-Daula—and also selecting as his poetic penname Sahib ('sir' or 'Mister', which increasingly but not exclusively was associated with Europeans).[5] Whatever affection Farzana might hold for Aloysius personally, she knew that, as her master's only biological and recognised surviving child by his most legitimate wife, he always represented a potential threat to her power and authority. Over the remainder of her long life, Farzana struggled to secure her precarious position and to find a worthy heir.

Ruling Sardhana in Tempestuous Times

For six decades (1778–1836), Begum Sombre sagaciously ruled and prospered notwithstanding perilous politics and warfare, although her quest to secure her legacy frequently failed. Effectively protecting the farmers of the rich lands of Sardhana from the depredations of various rival warlords, she collected growing land revenues and various other levies. Over time, she acquired additional landholdings at Dankaur, Jewar and Tappal within the Ganges-Jumna Doab plus Badshahpur west of the Jumna River (see Map 2). Her income from Sardhana and these other lands, plus occasional spoils of war, varied over these decades: estimates range from 600,000 Rupees to 1,600,000 Rupees annually (approximately £60,000 to £160,000, worth £5,000,000 to £16,000,000 today).[6] These sums enabled her to arm and pay her infantry, cavalry and artillery, totalling at different times 3,000–5,000 Indians with largely European officers, armaments, and drill. Her army not only defended her principality but also made her a force to be reckoned with, hired, or bought off by the various Maratha, Sikh, Rohilla Afghan, and Jat rulers who contended for power in her region. Her base at Sardhana, strategically located less than 100 kilometers from Delhi, enabled her to intervene rapidly in the imperial capital when she chose, but distant enough to avoid collateral damage during either the many assaults on that city or its frequent internecine conflicts. She occasionally led the Sardhana army into battle personally.

Begum Sombre generously donated to many religions but she officially converted to Roman Catholicism on 7 May 1781, three years after Reinhardt's death.[7] She accepted the religious authority of Catholic priests and the baptismal name Joanna Nobilis Somer, for example ordering it engraved in both Roman and Persio-Arabic characters on her official seal of 1200 Hijri (1785–86 C.E.). Significantly, she also reaffirmed her Mughal affinities by including Emperor Shah Alam's name centrally. Thereafter, she piously expressed her own personal adhesion to the Church, establishing Sardhana as a major Indian Catholic centre (a position it retains today).[8]

The Begum's Catholicism distinguished her from virtually all other Indian rulers. This conversion created for her another community of (putative) acceptance, that of global Catholicism, wherein faith rather than biological descent defined membership, at least theologically.[9] In practice, the strong Euro-centrism of this Catholic community meant that, by joining its communion under the European baptismal name Joanna, she alienated some Indians without gaining full equality or respect from Europeans. Her European priests frequently complained to the Pope that she retained various pre-conversion 'heathen' practices and beliefs while many British Protestants regarded her Roman Catholicism as anomalous and regressive.

At the time of her own conversion, she demonstrated her power over her master's son, Aloysius Reinhardt, by bringing him into the faith. She then arranged his marriage with Juliana (c. 1770–1815), daughter of Colonel Louis Anthony Lefebre, one of the French Catholic mercenary officers in her employ, and his reportedly Indian wife, baptized Anne. Thus, she continued to try to control the Reinhardt lineage, seeking her own potential heir from the next generation of that family, although they had no biological relationship to her and stronger legal rights to Reinhardt's estate.

Impression of the Seal of Joanna Nobilis Somer, 1200 H./1785–86 C.E.

As a Catholic Indian ruler, she proved especially successful in attracting and hiring French, Irish, Italian, Portuguese, and other Catholic European mercenaries as her officers and courtiers. Many of these men wedded women—Indian, European, or of mixed ancestry—of her court. In contrast, at this time, the English East India Company banned Catholics and also most men of 'foreign' or mixed ancestry from the senior ranks of its army. Around Sardhana, similar clans of mixed culture and ancestry won their own principalities, including the Skinner, Gardner, and Thomas families whose histories intertwined with hers (and David's).

Indeed, among the most famous of the Catholic soldiers of fortune who served Begum Sombre was the Tipperary Irishman George Thomas (c.1756–1802). Following years in her army, in 1787 he married one of her Indian Catholic goddaughters but then left to establish his own principality at Hansi, some seventy kilometres west of Sardhana.[10] Thereafter, he proved crucially loyal to her and then she supportive of his Catholic Irish-Indian family after his death, nominally adopting one of his sons, John Thomas.

In the welter of wars that wracked north India during the late eighteenth century, Begum Sombre sustained her power by strategic alliances with Maratha warlords, especially the most powerful of them, Mahadji Sindhia. Like her, he rose from humble birth. He made himself the dominant force in central India from 1771 onward; from 1784 until his death in 1794, he made himself the effective controller of Delhi and the emperor. Like her, he also depended heavily on European mercenaries, many of whom were French. She customarily addressed him in her correspondence as her 'Brother'.

Despite her obscure origins, Farzana also established and sustained deep and enduring ties with the Mughal imperial family. While the Mughal court at its seventeenth-century peak had excluded and alienated even powerful men due to their low birth, throughout the eighteenth century it was controlled by a series of self-made men who used the emperor for their own purposes.[11] In 1788, Farzana personally intervened to rescue Emperor Shah Alam from an assault by yet another would-be captor. In recognition of this and other services, he bestowed upon her the titles: Farzand-i Aziza, Zeb al-Nissa Begum, Umdat al-Arakin ('Beloved Child', 'Lady Ornament of Women', 'Support among the Pillars of State') and also the *altumgha jagir* (special hereditary landed estate) of Badshahpur south of Delhi. As the Emperor's symbolic daughter, she interacted in familiar but respectful ways with him, his wives, and his extended imperial clan. Even as the British kept Shah Alam and his two successors and their relatives as powerless and impoverished pensioners, she continued to provide the imperial family both ritual and monetary respect.

Precociously, Begum Sombre perceived the rising power of the English East India Company as it sporadically made incursions up the Ganges River. In 1791, she astutely gained good will from the British by brokering the ransom and release of one of their officers from his Sikh captors. She then nurtured this budding relationship through continued diplomatic exchanges, even as she served various Indian warlords who occasionally fought the British as well as each other.[12]

Her hold on Sardhana, however, was never secure. In 1793, as Farzana entered her mid-forties, she risked all by marrying one of her own French Catholic officers, M. le Vassoult (1748–95). Rightly sensing local hostility to this marriage, in 1795 she proposed to the British that the couple would abandon Sardhana in exchange for British protection, settling in the French enclave of Chandernagar near Calcutta. They transferred to Monsieur Joseph Evan—a Frenchman in Mirzapur who had earlier commanded the Begum's troops—enough of the Begum's treasury to sustain their retirement.[13] They also negotiated permission to leave Sardhana from the Mughal court in exchange for 1,200,000 Rupees and established for Aloysius Reinhardt in Delhi a permanent pension of 24,000 Rupees annually.

The Sardhana army and court refused to accept this desertion by their ruler, summoning Aloysius from Delhi to occupy the throne and chasing after Farzana and her husband. During the roadside melee as the couple were being seized, she was wounded and he killed himself. Cynical accounts of this disaster have her faking suicide in order cruelly to trick him into despairing death; sympathetic reports have her suicide attempt as sincere but ineffective.[14] Her subsequent nine month imprisonment by Sardhana's army only ended when her Irish former commandant (and rumoured lover) George Thomas responded to her appeals by rescuing and restoring her. The repentant Sardhana army officers swore loyalty to her.[15] Thereafter, she reverted to her earlier master's name, Sombre. Even decades later, David recorded that memories of her unfortunate marriage with le Vassoult remained disturbing within her court; David himself pondered how different his own life would have been had the flight of this couple not failed.[16]

Meanwhile Aloysius amiably returned to his courtly life of poetry and pleasure in Delhi. He died on the eve of the British conquest. His sole surviving child, Julia Ann Dominica Theresa Reinhardt (1789–1820, David's mother), lived quietly under Begum Sombre's care and became her means of creating yet another adoptive family, if she could survive the coming political crisis.

Uncertain Military, Political and Cultural Transitions to British Rule

Conflicts among martial contenders for dominance in north India created new threats to Begum Sombre's effectively independent rule and forced imponderable but vital decisions upon her. After the East India Company's aggression led to the Second Anglo-Maratha War (1803–05), events moved quickly. Driving across north India, British General Lord Gerard Lake seized Delhi from Maratha forces (16 September 1803), thereby capturing the feeble Mughal Emperor Shah Alam, a still prestigious figure despite having been impoverished and blinded. Meanwhile, most of the Sardhana army had marched 1,000 kilometers southwest to support the Marathas against another English East India Company army campaigning in the Deccan. Even as Begum Sombre in Sardhana diplomatically kept her options open by surreptitiously offering the services of her battalions to the British, the allied Maratha and Sardhana armies in the Deccan were outmaneuvered and

Battle of Assaye (British Perspective)

21

defeated by Arthur Wellesley, the future Duke of Wellington, at the hard-fought battle of Assaye (23 September 1803).

Like a growing number of other Indian rulers, Begum Sombre then strategically wagered that she would survive and fare best as an ally of the British.[17] Abandoning the Marathas and the substantial 900,000 Rupees that they owed her for the use of her troops, she rushed to present herself in person to Lord Lake. Her sudden submission before him, in the symbolic attitude of a daughter (although they were roughly the same age), obtained Lake's surprized sympathy and his gift of a diamond ring. She further garnered British gratitude by rescuing one of the Company's officials, Collector George Guthrie, from a surprise attack by Sikhs on Saharanpur. When letters purportedly from the Begum that schemed with the Marathas against the British were intercepted, exposing her apparent disloyalties, Lord Lake generously declared them to be forgeries, exonerating her. Protesting her innocence and fidelity to the British, she then passed on to them three unopened confidential letters to her from the ruler of Afghanistan. Thus, by her acute policies and fortunate timing, Begum Sombre gained access to the new British regime.

She subsequently conducted shrewd and well-timed negotiations with the British over the price of her submission. Seeking to consolidate territories under British authority, Governor-General Richard Wellesley insisted that she transfer Sardhana to the Company, in exchange for future possession of putatively equivalent but unspecified territories on the far more unstable borderlands west of Delhi. She protested, perforce agreed, but then procrastinated, without even beginning to leave Sardhana.

Meanwhile, she forged a congenial personal relationship with Lt Colonel David Ochterlony, posted East India Company Resident (political agent) in Delhi to solidify tenuous British gains in the region. As Resident, Ochterlony supervised the Mughal Emperor and also managed British relations with the surrounding Indian principalities under British power, including Sardhana.[18] Despite, or perhaps partially because of, Farzana's gender and rise from obscure origins, she established particularly sympathetic ties with the slightly younger Ochterlony (an American by birth) whom she customarily addressed as 'My Brother'.[19] Opposing Wellesley's policy to shift her from Sardhana, Ochterlony recommended that she would be a stronger ally of the British if she were permitted to retain her current *jagir* there.

Wellesley's sudden recall by London in 1805 (for excessive aggression against Indian rulers) strengthened her bargaining position. Further, the Company's negotiator was the same Guthrie she had rescued. Consequently, her treaty (ratified August 1805) put her army and foreign policy at the disposal of the Company but in exchange guaranteed her semi-sovereign rule over Sardhana for the remainder of her life.[20] Further securing the Company's good will, in October 1805 she loaned it 120,000 Rupees (at 12% annual interest, below the market rate) to help pay for its war against her erstwhile allies, the Marathas. The grateful Company promised in 1807 that, following her death, over 800 of her dependents would receive pensions totalling 90,000 Rupees annually.[21] (When she died twenty-nine years later, the Company repudiated this promise so her heir, David, personally paid these pensions.)

While the Begum ended her overt resistance to the British, she continued to maneuver for her own advantage, and that of her future heir, whomever he turned out to be. The 1805 treaty specified that all her lands 'within the Doab' would be confiscated by the East India Company at the moment of her death, although her legal heirs could keep her personal property. Since she had no biological children and was already in her mid-fifties, this treaty was a precursor of the 'Doctrine of Lapse' that the British frequently practised decades later: claiming authority to annex any Indian kingdom that lacked a male heir whom they recognised as legitimate. As the British did not notice at the time, but as Begum Sombre would later consistently assert, her *altumgha jagir* of Badshahpur was literally not included in this treaty since it lay west of the Doab and was technically her private property. Further, she defined as her personal possessions considerable materiél (including the armaments of the Sardhana army) which the Company assumed was official state property and therefore confiscatable. (Thirty-seven years after her death, the British Privy Council in London would judge her assertions accurate and the Company's assumptions illegal, as David had fruitlessly contended for the decades prior to his own death.)

Amidst this military and political instability, no one could guarantee continued British rule in north India, and alternative sources of power abounded. The Begum had seen first-hand how other invaders had also seized the Mughal emperor and his capital yet later were unexpectedly expelled. The defeat of a Company army by the Marathas in 1804 and the bloody failure of Lord Lake to capture the fortress of Bharatpur (250 kilometres south of Sardhana) in 1805, as well as the narrowness of some British victories, all proved they were not invincible. The nearby lands of the Punjab remained under the powerfully independent Sikh ruler Maharaja Ranjit Singh (r. 1799–1839); many other large kingdoms across north and central India lay under other autonomous and ambitious rulers. Further, in Europe, decades of wars against Napoleon brought news to the Sardhana court of British defeats as well as victories. Not until Waterloo (1815) did her old adversary, Arthur Wellesley, now the Duke of Wellington, finally triumph over the French, much to the disgust of French officers at her court.

Neither was a ratified treaty with the British absolutely reliable. While the British promised by formal treaty that Begum Sombre could continue to rule Sardhana, they had broken such written guarantees with other Indian rulers in the recent past; yet other treaties had been unilaterally amended for further British advantage.

Nor were British principals or principles consistent. Personal relations between Indian rulers and British officials affected official Company policies. As we saw, Begum Sombre's adversary, Governor-General Wellesley, was recalled in 1805, and the more congenial Lake, Guthrie, and Ochterlony reshaped more favourable policies toward her. To secure her personal influence, she proposed marriage alliances with British officials, for example, offering to wed one of her wards to the teenage son of the British Commander-in-Chief of India (who politely declined).[22] She later schemed to marry David to the daughter of General John Ramsay, Commander of the Meerut Division, and also made another British officer, Colonel Clements Brown, a well-compensated co-executor of her will. As rival factions within the Company or British governments gained the ascendancy, they often reversed their opponent's policies, including those toward Indian rulers. Each change in British official brought new policies, dangers, and opportunities for the Indians who dealt with them. Much attended to by the Sardhana court, in 1829, a young Assistant Resident in Delhi on his first posting, Charles Edward Trevelyan, successfully discredited and disgraced the far more senior Resident, Sir Edward Colebrooke, for taking bribes from Indian princes in exchange for political favours.[23] Trevelyan would later play crucial and continuing roles in the lives of David and his sisters, in India and England. In short, the future and extent of Begum Sombre's reign and estate remained unpredictable in welter of military and political forces that swirled around her, including during the first three decades of David's life. She also made fraught cultural choices.

Begum Sombre among Competing Cultures

As that rare specimen, a female Indian ruler converted to Catholicism, the Begum shaped her own evolving court by remixing cultures and developing her own distinctive clothing style and public persona. She nurtured her relations with the Mughal imperial family and their courtiers but served as intermediary between them and Europeans. She appreciated (and perhaps could herself read) Persian poetry, keeping a copy of the famous thirteenth-century Iranian poet Sadi's works always by her bedside.[24] We cannot know if she learned any German from Reinhardt or French from le Vassoult, but she evidently had at least some spoken English later in life since she conversed directly with her Anglophone guests. She also selected men with strong European affinities as her potential heirs. Her observation of seclusion went from full purda, even from her own subordinates, to gradually making herself visible to elite European women and men, then to her Indian courtiers, and then to her Indian subjects, even as she formulated a comportment that retained feminine modesty on her own terms. She also created both Mughal-style and European-style palaces, each designed for particular purposes.

Until his death, Emperor Shah Alam and his major wives treated her almost as a relative, embracing her as she entered their quarters. But, unlike them, she freely had access to the outside world by her own volition. She thus served as a cultural broker: conveying imperial wedding invitations from the senior Empress to European ladies and reciprocally instructing distinguished British women about imperial etiquette before personally introducing them into the Mughal public levees and private quarters, and interpreting for them once there. As English visitor Ann Deane noted, in late December 1808:

[The Begum] condescendingly [i. e., graciously] offered to introduce me to the [Mughal] royal family [in their] private apartments, which without hesitation I accepted... The following morning she gave a splendid breakfast, and I afterwards accompanied her to the royal residence... Before [the empty throne] the Begum made a profound *salaam*, and motioned me to do the same; I had determined to follow her example on all points of etiquette during the visit. We then ascended...to the zenanah ['women's quarters']... The Begum now led the way, through crowds of eunuchs... Here we were met by the Queen Dowager...an ugly, shriveled old woman, whom the Begum embraced... When we were admitted into the Royal Presence, the Begum Sumroo made three *salaams*, and I followed her example... [After presenting *nazrs*, 'submission offerings'] I then, agreeable to the lesson I had been taught, retreated backward to the edge of the carpet...sidling into the circle next to the Begum Sumroo.[25]

The Begum then translated the Emperor's questions to Ms Deane, answering for Deane about personal queries that she was too embarrassed or uncultured in imperial court manners to answer for herself. Thus, the Begum transformed an awkward cross-cultural encounter into a smoothed-over interview that conformed to both imperial court protocol and also English female proprieties. The Begum's deference to the Mughal family persisted; over the years, Begum continued to listen devotedly to the daily Mughal imperial *akhbar* ('newsletter'), although it consisted mainly of a repetitive recounting of imperial routines that most Britons ridiculed.[26]

Yet, she also prided herself on her status as a ruler, nominally subordinate to the emperor but much more autonomous. She was vastly wealthier than most of the imperial clan, the bulk of whom barely survived on their tiny pensions (at the time of the Begum's death, there were 795 such skimpily pensioned Mughal imperial family members).[27] Even the emperor periodically pleaded poverty to his British paymasters.

Most visibly, as a woman, the Begum had to decide in a changing environment how much to reveal herself among Mughal, British, and other men and women of various social classes. European accounts during the pre-1803 period described her personal seclusion from the public sphere. Yet, they also described her leading her army into battle. After her shift to political alliance with the British, she ceased practising the full purda in front of higher-class British officials and also before her own male Indian and European courtiers. In particular, she began appearing unveiled as she presided over generous feasts for Mughal male and also British male and female dignitaries—but did not herself eat in their presence, although she did drink wine and smoke her hooka. Later in life, she participated in public celebrations of her reign by openly receiving the salute as her army marched past, her band played, and her people cheered. Yet, her fascinated European guests also noted that she evidently dressed to preserve her current respectability, at least as they assessed it in allegedly 'Oriental' terms, by always keeping her head covered with a shawl and sporting a turban 'contrary to the practice of women in this country'—this fashion-conscious English noblewoman conceded it 'becomes her very much, and is put on with great taste'.[28]

Most Europeans combined feminine and masculine characteristics in their accounts of her. Typically, Ann Deane described how she looked in late 1808:

Her features are still handsome, although she is now advanced in years. She is a small woman, delicately formed, with beautiful hazel eyes; a nose somewhat inclined to the aquiline, a complexion very little darker than an Italian, with the finest turned hand and arm I ever beheld... A graceful dignity accompanies her most trivial actions [yet she was] frequently known to command her army in person on the field of battle...rallying and encouraging her troops.[29]

Similarly, Lady Nugent both called her in 1813 'a little, lady-like looking old woman' but also described her clothing 'more like a man's than a woman's—she wore trousers of cloth of gold, with shawl stockings, and Hindoostanee slippers; a cloth of gold kind of dress, with flaps to it, coming a little below the knees, and in some degree doing the office of a petticoat; a dark turban, but no hair to be seen; and abundance of shawls wrapped around her in different ways.'[30] Her sartorial style of the early nineteenth century is confirmed by the paintings she commissioned and exhibited.[31] [see colour Illustrations 1–2] In several, she had herself portrayed smoking an elaborate hooka, which may have suggested her intentional adoption of a more traditionally masculine royal demeanor.[32] Unlike most European women, the Begum did not customarily withdraw with the ladies at the end of the meal but rather remained as the gentlemen drank their port and smoked their cigars, while she sipped wine and smoked her hooka. In British eyes, she was exceptional, defying the social-class, religious, moral, and gendered stereotypes of the modern age, including what they expected of Indians.

Further suggestive of her cultural ambidexterity and desire for standing before both high-ranking Mughals and Britons, headed by the Emperor and the British Resident political agent, the Begum built two main palaces in Shahjahanabad (among many other houses and properties in Delhi and elsewhere).[33] David occasionally used each of these palaces, depending on his mood and the identity of his guests. The more traditional-style *Churiwala Haweli* she constructed in 1830, within in a dense residential *muhalla* ('neighborhood'), 350 metres southwest of the Jama Musjid, the imperial 'Friday' Mosque of Shahjahanabad. It was approachable only through a narrow *gali* ('lane') off Churiwala street, by palanquin, animal-back, or foot.[34] One entered her *haweli* ('mansion') through a magnificent gatehouse behind which

Map 3: Shahjahanabad with Begum's Palaces

Shahjahanabad / Delhi c. 1858

1. Red Fort
2. Jama Musjid
3. Chandni Chawk
4. Begum Sombre's Haweli
5. Begum Sombre's Kothi

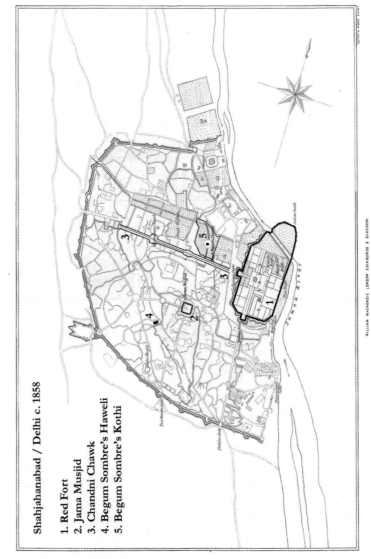

was a considerable closed compound of roughly 750 square metres. While the outer walls of the compound were windowless, this large inner open courtyard provided private space yet was open to the air. On two facing sides of this courtyard were a series of multipurpose rooms. Opposite the gateway across the courtyard was a large house with secluded, as well as reception, rooms. Such a *haweli* was typical of a Mughal grandee. Begum Sombre willed it to be used perpetually after her death for 'public assemblies of natives'.[35] (This *haweli* lasted until 7 August 1857 when, serving as a gunpowder factory in the defence of Delhi against the British, it blew up, killing almost 500 Indians.)[36]

Her European-style palace, called in Persian both a *kothi* and a *kamra* ('house' respectively from Sanskrit, *koṭhī*, and Portuguese, *ćamara*), Begum Sombre built in the middle of a huge garden of prime land on the north side of Chandni Chawk (the entire Red Fort was only seven times larger).[37] This Palladian palace was apparently designed by Major Antonio Giuseppe Reghellini, one of the Begum's European courtiers. [see colour Illustrations 3–4] A wide veranda circled the elevated main floor, overlooking the surrounding park. Large, glass-paned windows on each side linked the outer prospect to the spacious interior drawing, dining, reception, and sleeping rooms. Pairs of classical columns with Corinthian capitals supported a decorative frieze. Ornamental urns capped the corners of the rooftop balcony and the stairway posts. On the main front, the wide sweeping entrance road allowed horse-drawn wheeled carriages to carry dignitaries right up to its magnificent doorway. Indeed, the Begum herself owned 'an English coach…painted a bright yellow, with silver mouldings, lined with violet-coloured satin, embroidered all over with silver stars… [attended by two] postilions [who] wore scarlet jackets and caps, almost covered with silver lace'.[38] On the south of this palace, paired staircases swept up the pediment. Between this palace and Chandni Chawk was a row of shops which provided both income and protection from the noise of that major commercial artery; just 325 metres east, the Chandni Chawk terminates at the main Lahori gateway of the Mughal imperial Red Fort. Such a European-style palace was relatively rare in Delhi during this period; those built by high British officials, the Anglophile Mirza Babar (second son of Emperor Akbar Shah), and the Begum being the major examples.[39] (This second of the Begum's palaces became a British bank, was much damaged in 1857, and now, as Bhagirathi Palace, partially survives as the centre of a electrical goods market.)

Chandni Chawk, Looking West from Lahori Gate of the Red Fort

The Begum used this Palladian palace effectively to host influential Britons. One, Captain William Henry Sleeman, visiting Delhi (during his huge paramilitary crackdown against the Thugs, the alleged Indian cult of stranglers), described it thus early in 1836:

a fine building, agreeably situated in a garden opening into the great street [Chandni Chawk], with a branch of the great canal running through it, and as quiet as if it had been in a wilderness. We had obtained from the Begam permission to occupy this palace during our stay. It was elegantly furnished, the servants were all exceedingly attentive, and we were very happy.[40]

Impressed by the Begum's wealth and hospitality, Sleeman later avulcularly advised David, who appointed him co-trustee over David's sisters, gave him power of attorney over David's Indian properties, and named him co-executor of David's own will.

While the Begum both associated herself with the Mughals and yet also emulated some European customs, many Britons of her time moved in the other direction. The British power that its officials represented allowed some of them access to participate in Indo-Persianate court culture, thereby refashioning themselves as 'white Mughals'.[41] Most prominently, Begum Sombre's putative 'brother', Sir David

Ochterlony, KCB, twice held office as the Company's Resident in Delhi (1803–06, 1818–25). Ochterlony typified the 'Orientalist' life-style savoured by some of the more prominent Company officials of his age. While he controlled the imperial capital, he also personally adopted much of the Mughal way of life, boasting an Oriental fantasy of a palace, Mubarak Bagh ('Fortunate Garden'), and the title Nasir al-Daula ('Defender of the State'), bestowed by the aging Emperor Shah Alam.[42] While Ochterlony never married a European woman, he had several Indian consorts, recognising at least six of their children. Ochterlony made a son's son, Sir Charles Metcalfe Ochterlony (1817–91), official heir to his baronetcy and estates in Scotland.[43] This heir of Sir David Ochterlony, for a time, became the carousing companion to a man of comparable proportions of mixed ancestry, possibly his distant relative, and the Begum's final designated heir: David Ochterlony Dyce.

Recruiting Her Heir

In 1806. just before David Ochterlony lost his first posting as Resident in Delhi, Begum Sombre solicited his fraternal advice on how she could secure her succession (and thereby also obtaining implicit British official support for this objective). Specifically, she asked him to recommend a husband for Reinhardt's only living grandchild, a bridegroom who could also become her own heir. Ochterlony proposed a boy just leaving the Calcutta Military Orphan Asylum: George Alexander David Dyce (1788–1838), the only surviving child of a deceased Scots Presbyterian subaltern officer, Lieutenant David Dyce (1765–90), and an Indian woman (reputedly a descendant of Ochterlony himself by one of his Indian consorts).[44]

Accepting Ochterlony's advice, Begum Sombre invited the teenage George Dyce to Sardhana in February 1806 and then on 5 October married him with grand ceremony to her late master's seventeen-year-old granddaughter, Julia Reinhardt. Although Dyce accepted this wedding by Catholic rites as the Begum insisted, he himself refused to convert or fully submit to her will. The young Dyce thus suddenly rose from a youth of mixed ancestry and few prospects to the wealthy and relatively powerful Begum's chosen heir, soon empowered with the posts of Colonel-Commander of her army and chief administrator of Sardhana. Calling Dyce her 'son', she maneuvered to have the Mughal Emperor regrant the *altumgha jagir* of Badshahpur to him personally, thus hoping doubly to secure it from annexation when she would die. The British, however, scotched this transfer as beyond the authority of the Emperor and, further, refused to recognize Dyce as her officially adopted heir.

On his part, Dyce worked to consolidate power under his own control. He increasingly asserted his own right to rule Sardhana as legal husband to Reinhardt's sole grandchild, as the most prominent male in the Sardhana court, and as someone personally more congenial to the Company's policy-makers since he was Protestant, partially British by descent, and a British subject by birth in British India. Dyce's wife and link to the Reinhardt lineage, Julia, lived quietly, playing no prominent part in court politics or, apparently, in the lives of her children other than giving birth to them. However, Dyce and the Begum tussled intensely over each of his six children; David Ochterlony Dyce, sole surviving son and eldest of the three children who lived through infancy, became the particular object of their rivalry from the moment of his birth.

2

THE CHILDLESS BEGUM'S POSSIBLE HEIR

From his birth (18 December 1808) until age twenty-seven, David
Ochterlony Dyce was kept very close at hand by Begum Sombre.
Although he was raised almost as her son, their relationship remained
strained and unsettled until just before she died, in 1836. He consistently referred to her, even in his private diary, as 'H. H.' ('Her Highness'), suggesting his respect and unwillingness to presume intimacy
except on her terms. She insistently instilled in him devotion to her, to
the Catholic Church, and to the Mughal Emperor, and yet also trained
David to associate with Britons who would actually decide the fates of
Sardhana and of David himself. Unlike his father, Dyce, who resisted
her domination and also harshly demanded David's loyalty, he
remained dependent upon her until her death. Throughout their lives
together, his interests and those of the Begum were not identical, and
the goals of both inevitably clashed with many official British policies.

Uncertain Youth in a Cosmopolitan Court

David grew up attending on the Begum in her distinctively diverse
court. He saw Anglicans, Baptists, Catholics, Hindus, Jews, Scots Pres-
byterians, Shi'ites, and Sunnis all serve as her as officials and officers,
people whose mother-tongues included Armenian, English, French,
German, Hindi, Italian, Latin, Persian, Polish, Portuguese, and Urdu,
as well as regional dialects.[1] These courtiers of assorted ancestry and
culture composed poetry in Persian, Urdu, and English, as did David
himself. One chief secretary, Munshi Gokul Chand, penned a eulogistic
Persian-language poetic history of the Begum and her court and
courtiers. David also learned Latin and fitfully studied Italian. The

Begum annually hosted three-day festivals, often with fireworks, on the Christian Easter, Christmas, and Gregorian (solar) New Year as well as celebrated the two Muslim Ids and Hijri (lunar) New Year and the Hindu Diwali and Holi, among other special days. It became widely-known to Mughal, other Indian, European, Arab, and other tourists and dignitaries that they should stop by Sardhana to partake of her generous gifts and bountiful dinners, often accompanied by Hindustani *nach* (nautch, 'dance') performances. She also made rooms available in her various palaces, mansions, and houses in Sardhana, Delhi, and elsewhere to worthy, influential, or simply importuning guests of virtually any distinction. As David grew up, she increasingly tasked him with making these arrangements.

While she recognized the overlordship of the Mughal imperial family and deferred to the British crown, she also periodically demonstrated her own pretensions to sovereignty. Each year she presided over a military march-past and salute by her army while her band played 'God Save the Queen'. She also received a royal 101 gun salute (during the British Raj, 21 gun salutes signified 'perfect sovereignty' and only independent kings and queens received even that many, so the Begum's 101 guns appeared to British officials as particularly presumptuous).[2] Further, as was customary for sovereigns, she received *nazr* from her own courtiers in order and magnitude reflecting their respective ranks, and she bestowed appropriately hierarchic *khila'ts* (robes or other gifts of honour) on them.

Her hospitable court was open to a diversity of visitors, many of whom were distinctive even in her cosmopolitan court. In 1832, for example, Joseph Wolff—Bavarian-born but naturalized English, Jewish-turned-Catholic seminarian-turned-Anglican Christian missionary—met her and dined with David, received 500 Rupees and other gifts, but failed to convert them to the Church of England.[3] In 1835, appeared at her court 'The Effendi', son of the Qazi of Baghdad, who was scandalously travelling from Bombay across India accompanied by Mrs Mary Rich, the forty-six-year-old English daughter of a knight and the widow of the East India Company's Resident in Baghdad. The Begum sent this man and his female companion with David to a service at her Sardhana Catholic church and bestowed on him a substantial seven-piece *khila't* which he apparently accepted 'with great delight'.[4]

The Begum made grand donations to many institutions, both secular and religious, in Sardhana but also elsewhere.[5] For the people of

Sardhana, she built various places of worship for Muslims and Hindus as well as Christian Catholics and Protestants. For the British in neighbouring Meerut, she contributed one of the town's central bridges and handsome horseracing trophies and cash prizes. For the Church of England, she reconstructed the substantial Anglican church in Meerut seating 3,000 people and gifted some 750,000 Rupees to the Bishop of Calcutta and the Archbishop of Canterbury for their charities.[6] Indeed, Catholic priests at her court for decades complained to their superiors in Rome about what they regarded as her promiscuous donations to various other religions and personal participation in a range of heretical practices.

The Begum's adherence to customs associated with Muslim culture could prove frustrating to her Christian peers as well as her Catholic preceptors. In 1820, she suddenly postponed the elaborate wedding arrangements for one of her wards with James Gardner, eldest son of the prominent Gardner family. This family, like the Reinhardts, were descendants of a mercenary, in their case American-born William Gardner, who had carved out his own estate at Khasgunj (near Agra), transferring to British protection at the same time as Begum Sombre. At the height of the prenuptial preparations, one of Begum Sombre's courtiers died, so she entered a forty-day period of bereavement: wearing mourning clothes, feeding the many poor of Delhi, and even flagellating herself. Sir David Ochterlony, who had brokered this marriage alliance, participated selectively in the Begum's composite mourning rituals but confided 'the old Begum so mixes Christian customs with the Hindoostanee that though anxious to do what would please the old lady, he simply did not know what was required'.[7]

Overall, Begum Sombre made her most massive gifts to the Roman Catholic Church in Sardhana, elsewhere in India, and in Rome. She established several local charities for the hundreds of Catholics living in her capital, many of whom converted through her influence or were attracted to her court. As the largest material expression of her devotion, in 1820, she started erecting the vast, and vastly expensive, Sardhana Church of St Mary, modelled on St Peter's in Rome. Critics describe it as 'promiscuously mixed baroque and Mughal motifs, with a great classical dome rising from Mughal squinches decorated with honeycombed Persian *murqana* [prism-like] motifs'.[8] She lavished some 400,000 Rupees on its fabric and interior decorations, including an altar adorned by a mosaic of semi-precious stones. Identifying herself

Sardhana Church of St Mary, with detail of Altar

with her church, she ordered that her corpse be interred there. Although her church was consecrated in 1822, its official inauguration in 1829 was celebrated with even more ceremony. This was a landmark in the Begum's long-standing drive to make Sardhana a major centre of global Catholicism. Pope Gregory XVI responded to her 250,000 Rupee donation by addressing her as 'his daughter in Christ', elevating David to a knighthood in the Pontifical Order of Christ (complete with a diamond-studded cross as insignia), and promoting her Italian chaplain to bishop. This made her Sardhana church a cathedral *pro tem*, graced by the Pope with relics, including a purported piece of the true cross.[9] In contrast, many Anglican Britons disparaged her 'Popish' faith, judging it particularly incongruous in an Indian ruler.

While David, like the Begum, remained a practising Catholic all his life, he was more skeptical than the Begum about the virtues of the priests he encountered. David frequently caroused with one of her longest-serving chaplains, Monsignor, later Bishop, Giulio Caesario Scotti, known familiarly as Father Julius Caesar.[10] For one raucous fancy dress party, David himself donned the costume of a Catholic priest.[11] David also noted personal jealousy and vindictiveness among rival Catholic priests and squabbling monastic orders and was resentful of the bishop who threatened the Begum with exclusion from confession and the sacraments due to her charity toward Anglican institutions.[12]

From his earliest days David also learned from the Begum the comportment of the Mughal Persianate court culture that she respected and devotedly supported. He was known in these circles as 'Davy Sahib'. He conversed, read, and wrote prose and poetry comfortably in Persian as well as Urdu. But he also adopted a more cynical attitude toward the Mughals and their courtiers than did the Begum. Further, while he participated in the Catholic and Mughal practices of the Begum's court, he also sought to partake of the more Anglicised world of his father.

The Begum raised young David to become a crucial means of obtaining influence with the now-powerful Britons who would determine Sardhana's and his future in imponderable ways. Under her guidance and that of his father, David customarily dressed in European-style apparel. For instance, at one of the Begum's formal levees (Easter Sunday 1813), a touring British woman, Mrs Mary Martha Butt Sherwood, recorded what she and other Britons regarded as a quaint oriental tableau:

We were ushered into the principal tent, where her highness sat on a musnud, her shrivelled person being almost lost in Cashmere shawls and immense cushions of quin qwab [gold brocade]. Her superb hookah was set ready to one hand, and her glittering paun-box to the other, whilst very little of her person but her remarkably plain face was visible. Behind her, on the cushions, was perched David Dyce...a child of five or six years of age, in a full court suit—coat, waistcoat, and shorts of crimson satin—with a sword dangling to his side, and a cocked hat... Master David, in his crimson satin suit, was called upon to hand us out of the tent, which he did with the usual etiquette.[13]

David's European-style court costume and manners contrasted with the Begum's Indian-style dress and that of most other Sardhana courtiers.

David even wore his European-style uniform, cocked hat, and ceremonial sword while formally participating at the Mughal imperial court.[14] In private, he opted for Indian-style clothes for comfort. But on those public occasions when he chose to do so, he especially noted them in his journal as an unusual donning of what he called 'Hindoostanee' or 'native dress'.[15] Thus David largely stood as a public symbol of the Begum's gestures toward British culture, at least sartorially.

Other of her fictive children followed alternative cultural trajectories. Unlike David, they were trained to display Indian rather than British cultural traits. In January 1813, Lady Nugent described one of the Begum's levees in which a son of Major Antonio Reghellini (an Italian courtier married to one of her Indian wards) attended her in Indian court garb: 'His little boy, about three years old, seemed a great pet of the begum's; he was dressed in cloth of gold, with some handsome pearls as a band and loop to his hat'.[16] This boy, a couple of years younger than David and of similarly mixed descent, however, did not remain as close to the Begum after Reghellini fell from grace.

Next to David, the second most prominent child of mixed ancestry raised at her court was John Thomas, eldest son by an Indian wife of George Thomas, her former officer and later the agent of her release from captivity and restoration. When George had been driven by Sikh and Maratha forces from his nearby principality at Hansi in 1801 and died the next year, the Begum adopted and provided for John. He later married the daughter of her Iranian-Armenian household manager and lived as the Begum's courtier and an officer in her army. She recognised John after David as 'another of my adopted sons' in her official will.[17] Although John and David had comparable descent and both grew up as the Begum's adoptive sons, each followed a distinct cultural pattern. Begum Sombre's and John's habitual and usually elaborate Indian wardrobe contrast strongly with David's and his father's customary British-style garb, reflecting their respective roles within the intermingled cultural patterns at the Sardhana court. [see Illustration 2]

As David's star rose in Sardhana, he acted and wrote paternalistically toward his elder rival John Thomas. In particular, David noted in his private journal how he controlled John's relatively low-ranking career in the Begum's army, induced his father-in-law disgracefully to drink alcohol, and brought his wife and sister-in-law immodestly to attend and sing at all-night music parties in David's own living quarters, scandalously leaving behind garments on his bed when they finally left in the early hours. Thus, the children of the Begum's court vied for her affection, the vehicles of their parents' and their own evocation of different aspects of the cultural worlds around them, in her court and outside.

David's particular situation, as the Begum's occasional favourite and yet also as George Dyce's only son, led to his incomplete formal education in any culture. Under her direction, throughout his childhood, David studied Catholicism and Latin with the priests attending the Begum's court. Yet, when he was not yet five years old, his father prevailed over the Begum in hiring for him a Protestant tutor: John Chamberlain of the Serampore Baptist Mission Society.[18] Despite the Begum's antipathy to Chamberlain's low-church evangelism, she tolerated his presence at court. Chamberlain, however, only accepted the post so that he would be able to preach his fervent faith widely in the region. After less than twelve months of intermittently tutoring David, Chamberlain's public zealotry at the Haridwar Fair provoked the Company to force her to expel him for raising religious conflict.

Some six years later Dyce arranged for David to resume his formal education by living in the home of the Anglican Chaplain of Meerut, Reverend Henry Fisher. For the first four years of his teens, David took instruction at Fisher's school in the English, Persian, and Urdu languages and basic arithmetic, along with Anglican religious lessons. His classmates included other sons of mixed ancestry including the Skinners, a family with whom the Begum and David would continue to socialise.[19] While David respected Fisher as his teacher, he also resented being bullied by Fisher's own sons and other 'pure' European boys. Further, despite David's wishes, while away in Fisher's school at Meerut, he was only permitted to visit the Begum twice briefly during the week and then on Sundays; an unauthorised or overlong visit with her would lead to 'a royal beating' by Fisher or Dyce.[20] At one point, David's father proposed sending him to England for a more systematic and thorough education, but the Begum did not permit this.[21] Later in life, David often bemoaned his scattered and inadequate education: 'I thought seriously of myself, & saw the folly of the policy exercised over me, of not giving me an European education, which has done for [i. e, ruined] me in this world for ever...'[22] Yet he learned to keep a regular European-style journal recording his daily activities and his reflections on them in English—with only occasional Persian passages, usually of a poetic or erotic nature.

While David grew up as the Begum's potential heir, she also impressed deeply upon him how completely his life rested in her unquestionably arbitrary hands. He had to be ready to respond immediately to her sudden summons or risk her displeasure. She continually demanded he exhibit his loyalties and attentions to herself, enforcing her personal authority with assertions of command over him and the others in her court. According to one widely-circulated, notorious account, early in her reign, she had buried alive a slave women who had betrayed her by setting fire to a palace to cover theft and elopement. As John Thomas' father-in-law, who witnessed this execution, reportedly explained: 'the Begam's object was to make a strong impression upon the turbulent spirit of her troops by severe example'.[23] Similarly, Bishop Heber described her in 1824 when David was sixteen: 'She is a very little, queer-looking old woman, with brilliant, but wicked eyes, and the remains of beauty in her features... She is, however, a sad tyranness, and, having the power of life and death within her own little territory, several stories are told of her cruelty, and the noses and ears which she orders to be cut off.'[24] In later years, David himself recounted how in his youth the Begum had warned him not to deceive her, lest she poison him: to enforce her message, she had him watch the death agonies of a slave woman whom she had just poisoned simply as a lesson to him of her vital power.[25] She also instructed him that she had only survived through constant wariness so that he should not trust anyone else, even her longest-standing courtiers or his sisters' husbands, and he should anticipate poisonous plots and conspiracies against him at any moment.[26]

David's first political consciousness was of deadly conflict, inevitably fraught with unpredictability. His youth was punctuated by Britain's wars in Europe as well as against nearby and familiar Indian rulers. Not far from Sardhana, the British and the Gurkhas of Nepal fought a fierce war lasting from when David was aged six to eight. This conflict showed Begum Sombre and David that, while directly confronting the British might lead to defeat, the Gurkhas' subtle diplomatic maneuvering against them could preserve some autonomy thereafter. Continued struggles between Begum Sombre's erstwhile employers and allies, the Marathas, and her current protectors, the British, led to the Third Anglo-Maratha War (1817–19), which reinforced for David (aged nine to eleven) the lesson that direct opposition by Indian rulers to the British led to bloody losses and consequent exile. More distant from Sardhana, abrasive relations between the British and the King of Burma led to the expensive First Anglo-Burma War (1824–26). This conflict revealed to David (then aged sixteen to eighteen) how incompetent British generals could be, although their Indian soldiers eventually triumphed, leading to considerable annexations of territory on India's eastern frontier. Throughout David's youth, various Indian rulers were deposed or displaced—permanently or temporarily—by the British for a range of evident and inscrutable reasons. All this left surviving rulers like Begum Sombre unclear about how shifts in British policies and personnel would affect her and her legacy.

In an ongoing internecine struggle, young David had continually to choose between the Begum and his own father. He had from his infancy bonded to Begum Sombre but she constantly tested his submission to her. Dyce likewise worked to bring David under his authority, appealing to their blood ties. David was aware of these deep conflicts, adoptive maternal versus blood paternal, Catholic versus Protestant. He also had to balance the Mughals and the British. In his private diary, he expressed wariness at how his future might shift suddenly and decisively in one direction or the other due to factors he only imperfectly understood and could not effectively determine. Dyce's closer ties to British culture and officialdom made the Begum apprehend their support of Dyce as her rival for control over Sardhana and also David.

Displacing His Father

Over the years, George Dyce repeatedly offended the Begum by insisting that Sardhana really belonged to 'his' family: to his wife, to him, and then to his son, David. But a series of events weakened Dyce's claims. His mother-in-law, the widow of Aloysius Reinhardt, died aged forty-five, in 1815. His own wife, David's mother, died aged thirty-one, in 1820. Then, in July 1825, Dyce's long-time patron and putative relative, Ochterlony, had to resign reluctantly from the Delhi Residency. Mortally ill, Ochterlony retired to Begum Sombre's mansion in Meerut, where he soon expired. The new Resident, Charles Theophilus, Baron Metcalfe (just beginning his third posting to the Delhi Residency), received mixed signals from the Begum, reporting she 'ostensibly advocated [Dyce's] cause; but at the same time whispered in my ear "Don't let him have [Badshahpur]." This inconsistent conduct proceeded from her being at that time quite alienated from him, but in dread of his machinations against her.'[27] Dyce and the Begum further quarreled openly about appointments of officers in the Sardhana army (he favouring Protestants, she Catholics) and its deployment; Dyce was formally Colonel-Commander but the Begum was Commander-in-Chief.

As she struggled with Dyce, the Begum recognised how increasingly vital was British backing. Among the British officers with whom the Begum especially associated herself and David from 1825 onward was the English cavalry hero of the Napoleonic Wars, Stapleton Cotton,

Viscount Combermere, recently appointed British Commander-in-Chief in India, age fifty-two but still dashing. The Begum knew that the British had fallen into a particularly precarious position and needed Indian allies, although they could not be seen as depending on them.

British prestige had been shaken by its initial military reverses in the First Anglo-Burma War (1824–26). Furthermore, the conflict had provoked an open revolt, the 'Barrackpur Mutiny', when Indian troops in the Company's Bengal Army refused to serve in Burma. Seeking to restore the image of British invincibility, late in 1825 Combermere led British Royal and East India Company regiments to avenge their defeat twenty years earlier by finally capturing the massive fortress of Bharatpur. The Begum thereupon unilaterally and personally brought her expensively-equipped army in voluntary support; she also acquired a landholding at Pahari nearby. Although Combermere wished to make this victory a proof of British valour and so declined all offers by allied Indian rulers of military aid, after Begum Sombre arrived uninvited, she and he developed an especially warm and enduring friendship. Until he left India, the Begum repeatedly hosted him at Sardhana and made him promise to look after David following her death, perhaps arranging for an officer's commission in the English Royal Army; for years after Combermere left India, she and he exchanged correspondence, gifts, and portraits of themselves (in 1835, Combermere gave her a painting of Christ bound by soldiers, reputedly by Rembrandt, dated 1649).[28] Combermere warmly invited David to visit England in future and enjoy his repayment of hospitality there.

When Bharatpur finally fell to the British, conflicts between the Begum and Dyce came to a head. Dyce allegedly looted booty from Bharatpur, charges which, along with his loss of British influence, enabled the Begum to dismiss and exile him, along with other Protestants in his Sardhana faction.[29] To buy his acquiescence, she offered him 30,000 Rupees cash plus pensions of 100 Rupees monthly each for his two daughters, provided she retained custody over his son, David. The newly exiled Dyce refused to accept his dismissal or payoff, instead tenaciously lobbying for British support from Resident Metcalfe.

The Begum resolved to put Sardhana out of Dyce's grasp forever. Immediately after she dismissed Dyce, she verbally offered to Metcalfe that she would abdicate, surrender Sardhana to the British, and retire on a pension.[30] She had made the same proposal exactly thirty years earlier when her marriage to le Vassoult had alienated her from her court. Eventually, with the backing of his superiors, Metcalfe rejected Dyce's claim, earning the Begum's and David's eternal gratitude. The Begum then dropped her offer to retire and Metcalfe did not press her, vainly expecting to obtain Sardhana at her imminent demise (which did not actually occur until a decade later). Undeterred, Dyce continued to hover and scheme just outside Sardhana. He seized possession of her mansion in Meerut but she eventually winkled him out, which only exacerbated their implacable animosity.

On 7 August 1827, eighteen-year-old David suddenly awoke in the midst of a dramatic and nearly successful *coup d'état* by his father. George Dyce had enticed several of the elderly Begum's officers into his conspiracy and they briefly imprisoned her loyal officials. Dyce appealed for backing from the British. Instead, Colonel Clements Brown of the Meerut garrison supported the Begum, advising Dyce to withdraw and, as a British subject, throw himself on British mercy. Thereupon the coup collapsed ignominiously. Later, the Begum would make Brown the trusted and well-compensated co-executor of her will. For years afterward, David would recall these traumatic events and his own dangerous escape from retribution by both his repulsed father and the suspicious Begum, each of whom distrusted his loyalty.[31] David cautiously referred to his father elliptically, even in his private journal, as 'the old gentleman', 'the old rogue', or 'a certain person'.

Twice exiled, Dyce lurked just out of the Begum's jurisdiction in British territory. There, he was robbed, arrested, and shot at (the bullet passing through his palanquin), all, he repeatedly alleged, at the Begum's instigation. He brought multiple lawsuits against her for his claimed back-pay, and later against David over her will. He also worked secretly to turn his children against the Begum, writing covertly delivered notes to David, soliciting his affection and that of his daughters, Georgiana and Ann May, who continued to dwell in Delhi.

The British Resident in Delhi intervened to arbitrate the allocation of authority over David's sisters, delegating the youthful Assistant Resident, Charles Trevelyan, to scrutinise and interview them. Although the teenage sisters practised full purda, Trevelyan nonetheless insisted on his visual inspection to ascertain their identities. Reportedly, Georgiana was fairer-skinned, like her father, while Ann had a relatively dark complexion, like David.[32] Trevelyan reported what transpired: 'after some discussion and objection the Purdah was drawn up and removed but a chick or trellis work still intervened thro' which [I] directly saw and conversed with two young ladies bearing as [I] considered strong family resemblance to the said George Alexander David Dyce and his son... [Then] the said two ladies stated in answer that as they had been brought up by her... Highness the Begum Sombre, who had always been as a mother to them, they therefore preferred going to her at Sirdhana.'[33] On Trevelyan's recommendation, the Resident then ordered this done.

The Begum, having secured Georgiana and Ann May away from Dyce, recruited husbands for them, once again reconstructing her surrogate family. Years earlier, Begum Sombre had arranged the weddings of both her lover's son (Aloysius, who turned against her) and then only grandchild (whose husband, Dyce, had just revolted). Now, for the elder of Reinhardt's great granddaughters, Georgiana, aged twenty-three, the Begum arranged a wedding with an Italian Catholic, Peter Paul Marie Solaroli, aged thirty-five and newly arrived at court.[34] For the younger sister, Ann May, aged nineteen, the Begum found a twenty-eight-year-old, Scots Presbyterian, subaltern officer in the East India Company's Bengal Army, Lieutenant John Rose Troup (1803–62), a widower.[35] At the Begum's invitation, he resigned his Bengal Army commission, moved to Sardhana, and married Ann May, by both Catholic and Protestant rites. As Ann May later testified, 'My Sister and myself were kept in seclusion by the Begum previous to our marriage. We were frequently present when English gentlemen visited the Begum; openly so. I had seen Captain Troup at a distance, but never spoke to him before our marriage. It was the same with... my Sister.'[36] The sisters both married on 3 August 1831, but their husbands had differing careers. Solaroli advanced himself in the Sardhana administration, often challenging David's own rising authority. Troup, although well compensated financially by the Begum, garnered relatively little status in the Sardhana court. Solaroli's heir eventually obtained much of the Begum's fortune while Troup died childless.

The Begum's Will

As David entered manhood, the Begum, while suspicious of another betrayal, warily entrusted him with increasing responsibilities over the Sardhana administration and army. Unfortuneately in December 1828, early in David's administration, the Sardhana treasury was robbed of 105,400 Rupees.[37] Criminals had dug through the back wall of the treasury, absconded to Meerut, quarreled, killed one of their gang, and then been captured with the assistance of Colonel Clements Brown and his assistant Captain Patrick Craigie, although only part of the money was recovered. It emerged that the arrested miscreants were from families that had long served the Begum, one of whose mother was her pensioner. Under interrogation, they named David as part of their conspiracy. Suspiciously, while under David's authority, they escaped during their transfer by cart back to Sardhana. Dyce, Brown, and others accused David but could produce no tangible proof of his involvement.

The Begum was distressed by the entire incident and dreaded David's continuing relationship with his father, however cold it had become. Some of David's companions, including Captain Craigie, urged him to accept her offer that he leave Sardhana with 60,000 Rupees in capital to get him started, entering an agency house business in Calcutta.[38] After much uncertainty, David decided against taking this safer course and rather that he should risk remaining with the Begum and thereby possibly inheriting her vast wealth if not Sardhana itself.

Although she was aging grudgingly (she would finally die only in her late eighties or early nineties), the Begum, having 'settled' David's sisters through marriages with Europeans in August 1831, next resolved to announce the future allocation of her estate by drawing up her official will. On 16 December 1831, just two days before David's twenty-third birthday, the Begum signed this will (with Persian and English versions), making him co-executor and promising to give him almost everything she owned at her death, including her properties in Sardhana, Badshahpur, Delhi, Meerut, Agra, and Bharatpur. She also made him Colonel-Commander of her army (as she had done for his father twenty-five years earlier). Further, she directed David to append 'Sombre' to his name. The other co-executor, Colonel Clements Brown, was to be given 70,000 Rupees. She had Major Edward Bere and another British officer and her priest, Bishop 'Julius Caesar', witness her will, so it was immediately public knowledge.

This will was a decisive but revocable empowerment of David as overall manager of Sardhana and her designated heir. Aristocratically, the Begum decided not to divide her estate among David and his sisters or other dependents but keep it largely intact. For example, Ann May Troup only received 50,000 Rupees and Georgiana Solaroli only 80,000 Rupees while their husbands received nothing in their own names.[39]

While her will promised David virtually her entire estate, it also left him in limbo since she could unilaterally alter her testament at any point prior to her death (which would not occur for more than four years). He had to be always ready to respond to her imperious and increasingly petulant demands for his attendance and attentions. Thus, the will promised but did not actually ensure much.

This will also roused against David the animosity of his brothers-in-law, especially Solaroli, and others who had expected but would not actually inherit much unless they could get the Begum to modify her bequest or even repudiate David entirely (as she had his father). Further, no one knew if the British would honour her will when she finally died. Given the size of the estate, its unprecedented legal and political status, and the number of adamant claimants, including Dyce, even if the British Government of India accepted it, prolonged and rancorous civil court cases were inevitable. Hence, David needed to secure his inheritance before her death without offending Her Highness by seeming to anticipate that event.

In the following years, David overtly demonstrated his faith in her longevity by word and deed. In addition to constant attendance at her side, except for brief authorised or surreptitious absences, he voluntarily appended the name 'Sombre' to show his devotion to her will. He also undertook long-term building projects, including contributing a second steeple to her Sardhana cathedral. As a new home for them, he supervised the building in Sardhana of Dilkusha Kothi ('Heartpleasing Palace'), at a cost of some 100,000 Rupees, with a special mirrored bathroom for her and many bedrooms for him and his mistresses. However, unless the British capitulated and revoked their standing threat to annex Sardhana, David knew his position was temporary and much of what he built would be confiscated.

During this period (as before and after), British annexations of Indian kingdoms and principalities periodically occurred. The British had seized half of the nearby kingdom of Awadh in 1801, with only questionable legal justification. In south India, the British took over the direct administration of the large kingdom of Mysore (1831 onward) but kept the Maharaja nominally on the throne (and would restore his son to control in 1881). In the adjacent south Indian kingdom of Coorg, however, in 1834, they deposed and pensioned off the Maharaja and his family, even though his daughter converted to Anglican Christianity as Queen Victoria's goddaughter. Meanwhile, various

Indian deposed royalty sent their diplomats, or went themselves, to London to maneuver there for restoration or, at least, enhanced pensions and privileges (some thirty such diplomatic missions by Indians had reached London by the mid-nineteenth century).[40]

Thus it was obviously in David's personal interest to extract as much wealth as he could from the principality before the British annexed Sardhana, while avoiding provoking that annexation by offending any authoritative British official. He also had to assure the Begum of his loyalty, even though he would be the major beneficiary of her death. David tensely marked both the final preparations of Dilkusha Kothi for occupation and his own twenty-fifth birthday by carefully supervising the elaborate transfer of 3,548,270 Rupees from the Sardhana state treasury to the Begum's private one.[41] She urged him to sleep directly on top of this inner treasury so no other thieves could break in without alerting him. While he still had delicately to convince the Begum to actually hand over her money to him prior to her death, her public designation of him as her current heir apparent altered his self-perception as well as his status among the Mughals, the British, and the people of the court and land of Sardhana.

3

HEIR APPARENT TO A DOOMED PRINCIPALITY

As David's surviving personal diary for much of the four years between the signing of the Begum's will and her death reveals, he attended almost constantly on her: her intensifying infirmities and peevishness dominated her life, as they did his. Simultaneously, his increased income, tenuous administrative authority, and enhanced prestige as her officially declared heir all drew the personal interests and jealousy of diverse men and women in Sardhana, Delhi, Meerut, and elsewhere. David had to learn by experience what each of these people wanted from him, how he could satisfy his own desires toward them, and when he had exceeded the various limits they and the Begum presupposed.

As Begum Sombre's official heir, David increasingly enacted her political and social intercourse with various visiting dignitaries— Mughal, British, and others. While his personal attitudes toward each of these differed somewhat from the Begum's, he had ultimately to defer to her. Given her age and fading condition, and tentative indulgence in empowering him, David could not know how or when all this would end: whether she would change her mind, if the British would finally take Sardhana away, and what he could set aside for himself in the meantime.

David's Record of Life

David's private diary discloses his unusually intimate and detailed account of everyday life in a distinctive princely state, the Mughal capital, a major British garrison town, and the colonial capital of Calcutta. As probably taught by his Anglican teacher, Reverend Henry Fisher, David kept a daily (although not comprehensive) record of his actions, expenditures, and thoughts for much of his life; some of his journals, starting with his twenty-fifth birthday (18 December 1833) and ending with his arrival in London (7 June 1838), have escaped destruction.[1] Throughout his diary, his strong ego-centric voice enables us to recover his own candid perceptions and also how he constructed and then reconstruct his own history and circumstances. His impressions and descriptions of his actions often differ markedly from accounts by others. He often recorded one attitude toward an acquaintance in his diary but simultaneously wrote quite differently in his letters to or about that person. For example, he explicitly confided in his diary that he sent a letter 'with a humbugging paragraph of my regret' to an invitation from someone he intensely disliked and did not really regret avoiding at all.[2] Similarly, he even privately admitted that he knew he was in the wrong but also that he could never back down and admit that in public, losing face, but rather would hypocritically brazen it out: 'I & Troup had little bit of words, in wh[ich], I must confess, I was wrong... I had no right to say anything... but I made him ashamed before I quitted the subject'.[3]

Although David grew up multilingual (Persian, Urdu, and English), he wrote his diary predominantly in English, following the format he associated with that culture. For instance, he accounted for almost every day in chronological sequence, using Christian dates. Even if he had nothing to note, he wrote 'Nothing particular' or the abbreviation 'n.e.p.'. But in his idiosyncratic spelling of Persian names and terms, he often transliterated exactly (e. g., Mhmd not Muhammad since the short vowels are not written in Persian script), suggesting that he at least sometimes thought in Persian or Urdu first and then wrote in English. He kept a rough original record, updated daily or every few days, and then annotated and amended his entries, as well as periodically recopying the initial entries into a more polished version. His journal's occasional Persian phrases are of two sorts: poetic citations and sexually explicit remarks. Either he associated Persian with both elegance and sexuality or else he intended these remarks to be unintelligible to a chance or notional Anglophone reader.

He used his journal as a record of his expenditures, income, personal accomplishments and failures, as well as of auguries, and moral lessons to himself for the future. He believed in the larger significance of all that occurred to him, with the esoteric relationship between events revealed only in glimpses, which retrospective analysis of his own journal could provide him. For example, when he eventually learned about the death months earlier of one of his mistresses, Dominga, he reconstructed his own prescience of the event: 'on referring to my diary, I find that on the 27th [the day before she died], in the afternoon, I was very low spirited and cried at table'.[4]

His intended audience was explicitly himself, with self-exhortations, admonitions, and reflections scattered through the pages. Therefore, some of his accounts lack context. For example he baldly wrote 'I threw a cat over from the very top of this house, third storey, and I thought that it had died, but when I came down she has gone away', never explaining or mentioning this action again.[5] Similarly, he drew unexplained significance from evidently unrelated events: 'Had a request of 12,000 Rs [loan] from Captn [Richard Radford] Hughes, of the 62nd. Shaved off my eyebrows. From the above 2 facts, a philosopher should philosophy my future prospects in obtaining my fortune.'[6] He repeatedly but unsuccessfully vowed to control his costly gambling habit: 'Was very unlucky... lost not less than 22,000 Rupees [at billiards last night] I would not have bet so high'.[7] He regularly if futilely resolved to be more dutiful and prompt in his administration of Sardhana: 'I am ashamed to say, that from my neglect of public business, it is remarked in every office of mine, especially in the military office, the revenue, & the interior'.[8] He promised to lose weight: '19 st[one]. 9 lbs. [275 lbs., 125 kilograms]!!! Surely I do not look so much!'[9] Occasionally, he tore out pages or parts of pages for reasons we will never know, apparently ranging from his immediate desire for blank scrap paper to later self-censorship.

While he did not seem to have intended this diary to be seen by others, he did indicate that he considered his life of great potential interest to the public. For example, he recorded reading Samuel Warren's *Passages from the Diary of a Late Physician*. This popular multivolume novel, republished repeatedly from 1832 onward, colourfully recounted the lives of elite Englishmen and women, some of whom became lunatics or challenged each other to duels over points of honour. David identified himself with this author, a man his own age, and this fictional world: '[I] Forget lots; if I could write, or rather print my words, like the author of the Diary of the late Physician, oh! what I could dictate.'[10] He later read rapidly a similar work of fiction, Lady Caroline Scott's two volume *Marriage in High Life* of 1828, which recounted the tragic love of a rich banker's daughter for an English aristocratic and wayward husband, complete with threats of duels (although none were actually fought). David deemed this 'a stupid work, but went thro both volumes in about 6 hours; 600 pages; however, there were some passages in it that I could compare with my own case, only in a contrary way, for the book tells an unnatural tale' of a rich female's faithfulness.[11] If these novels informed David with a romanticised image of life in London, then he later lived up to it.

Frequently, his diary described his sex life, using the slang of the youthful British subaltern officers he consorted with and emulated. But he also made disingenuous gestures at disguising his references to sex with a suggestive '—'or'***' or in indirect terms: 'a certain thing', 'Did the business', 'Spent Sunday very ungodlylike', 'Instead of going to church... we went wh—g as did others. Shame, shame'.[12] Some of these remarks he later crossed out, nonetheless leaving them legible. Sometimes, his coy diction contrasts incongruously with the egotistical sexual activity that David recounted. For example, although he knew he had gonorrhea and his mistress was in advanced pregnancy, he demanded sex with her. But he noted mainly the pain he thereby caused himself: 'I think D[ominga] is enceinte, tho' I am so bad with the clap, & have the corde, but still I take my sly pokes, which gives me great pain afterwards.'[13] He thus interpreted his sexual exploitation of others as resulting in his own suffering.

Testing the events described in the diary with the same occurrences as recorded by other sources, we find that David valued factual accuracy, even if his interpretations of those events were idiosyncratic. He represented his own private motives as well as his construal of the personal motivations of others, matters that usually escape more formal historical sources about the diverse peoples and cultures in Sardhana, the Mughal capital, Meerut, and elsewhere.

Living in Sardhana

In the court of Sardhana, men and women rose and fell in position and wealth due to the Begum's shifting favour. While the Indian officials of Sardhana seem to have been more acquiescent—indeed, David mentioned them much less personally or often in his diary—the European ones proved consistently more challenging. In particular, Peter Paul Solaroli, a man a dozen years David's senior, with much more worldly experience, took umbrage at submitting to him. Solaroli, having married David's sister, Georgiana, because of her prospects from the Begum, rose high, serving as Sardhana state magistrate, thus exercising the Begum's judicial authority. David, after being named overall supervisor of Sardhana, deliberately and arbitrarily overruled some of Solaroli's judgments and also patronage appointments. Solaroli repeatedly resigned rather than obey but then grudgingly resumed office, perforce accepting the Begum's authority to delegate that authority to David and also desiring the consequent bequests that might ensue. David also responded badly to 'Georgiana's bluntness of manners' and her refusal to be godmother to one of David's daughters by a concubine.[14] David recorded how the Begum vainly tried to stop this squabbling, reportedly telling Solaroli 'that I [David] was the burra bahee [big brother], & to look up to me, & that I wd certainly have their interest always at heart'.[15] Solaroli, however, hated David's control over of the Begum's property.

In contrast, David's other sister's husband, John Rose Troup, lived relatively quietly. Although slightly older than David, Troup largely accepted David's directions. For example, when David warned Troup not to raise certain upsetting issues with the Begum, reportedly 'wisely he took my advice'.[16] In instances when Troup did not acquiesce, David blamed Solaroli for putting him up to it. In David's eyes, 'Master Troup' was almost childishly trusting and simple, and therefore far less of a threat than Solaroli. Similarly, Troup's childless wife, Ann May, was pitied by David as a 'poor woman' who 'had not the courage' to demand more for herself or her husband.[17] Despite the Begum's own gender, neither she nor David took as much notice of either sister as of their husbands, although both she and David wanted to ensure that Solaroli and Troup did not simply take advantage of the sisters.

David expressed his power by making repeated but vague assurances about how much generosity he would show to Solaroli and Troup, frequently and overtly patronizing them:

Solaroli seems to have pretensions that he has a right to be in H. H.'s secret; what a vain person!! At all events, he thinks that he ought to be considered the same as myself... nor [does H. H. approve] my giving so much power to Mr Solaroli, who certainly begins to show his teeth now; however, I've determined to give him a trial, & I mean to give him his present appointment of judge & magistrate of the zillah (excepting my jaghires) & to be of Sirdhana, besides superintendt of the revenue and customs; & if he is at all grateful for it, he shall have 1,200 Rs a month, the increase to be entirely from my jaghire revenue; also to Troup I will make up 1,000.[18]

But rhetorically to emasculate Solaroli and also to negate his relations with David's sister, David repeatedly referred in his diary to Solaroli as 'Mr Newter Gender' or 'the neutral gender'.[19] David also noted that Solaroli ranked far below him in the Freemasonic hierarchy. But, while David contested Solaroli's masculinity and distrusted his honesty, David also reluctantly felt he needed to have him manage David's interests and property in his own absence. Later in life, the tension between these men escalated and Solaroli's many children ultimately inherited much of David's estate despite his efforts to exclude them.

The Begum had long recruited British men as her courtiers, outsiders to whom insiders like David had to adjust and vice versa. Prominent among these was Dr Thomas Drever, born of a Scots gentry family who joined the Company's medical service and was stationed in Meerut in 1829. After his treatment of the Begum's many infirmities there, she hired him as her full-time physician in Sardhana from 1832 until her death. Drever, a decade older than David but no threat to his inheritance, tried to moderate and guide David's behaviour—with limited success. Given David's often self-abusive lifestyle, he frequently resorted to physicians, relying on them to restore his abilities. Indeed, David would most frequently trust doctors as legal as well as medical counsellors. Thus, despite sometimes resenting Drever's elder brotherly advice, David later gave him power of attorney, appointed him a co-trustee of his will, and, for a while, considered Drever one of his closest supporters in Europe. David convinced the Begum, who also literally entrusted Drever with her life, to bequeath him a generous 20,000 Rupees; reflecting his position in her official family, Drever would also join David, Troup, and Solaroli as her four pallbearers.

Despite his own somewhat haphazard management of Sardhana, David rejected the intervention of others, including the British. On their part, East India Company officials administering the surrounding districts resented Sardhana's autonomy. They repeatedly urged their superiors immediately to break the 1805 treaty and annex the Begum's territories, allegedly for the greater good of the people. Some British officials disingenuously condemned David for exploiting the Sardhana peasantry instead of making capital investments in irrigation and other infrastructure which would have long-term (i. e., post-annexation) benefits. They condemned him for being 'not very scrupulous as to his mode of enriching and aggrandizing himself'.[20] Yet, British actions were often self-serving. Major George Everest, Surveyor General of India, complained repeatedly in 1835 that David was blocking the progress of the Great All-India Trigonometric Survey. Allegedly in order to obtain a clear line of sight between two of its towers, the surveying party had unilaterally cut down trees on the land of Sardhana farmers.[21] Further, the survey's Indian workers had reportedly helped themselves to sugarcane and other provisions from these farmers without payment. The farmers resisted and retaliated by wounding some of Everest's men and dragged others before the Sardhana local magistrate. David supported his farmers and lodged claims for damages with British higher civilian officials. Recognizing the Begum's semi-sovereign status, they supported David and directed Everest to submit his men to David's authority while in the Begum's territories.[22] Even the famous Thug-hunter William Sleeman discovered that the police in British India falsely blamed crimes on David's allegedly lax administration since that was easier than taking responsibility themselves.[23] Following the Company's annexation of Sardhana, its officials had to admit that the farmers fared no better under British management than they had under David's.[24] Further, even after David left India, he continued to serve as patron and benefactor of the people of Sardhana until his death (and his English widow did thereafter).

From the time David had reached puberty and especially after being made manager of Sardhana and the Begum's designated heir, he became the object of the aspirations of many women and their families. They offered him sexual pleasure and children in exchange for money or position in the Begum's administration. He evidently took extensive advantage of these opportunities while, like many British men in India, reserving his official marriage for as highly ranked a European woman as was available.

By his twenties, David had already had acquired two regular concubines, Dominga and Hoosna Baae, keeping them in separate apartments in the Sardhana palace with the tacit consent of the Begum. David gave them allowances, several servants each, occasional gifts, and attention, but he also played each mistress off against the other in clear efforts to control them and demonstrate their dependence. They had to be ready to respond receptively whenever he showed up. Thus, they both submitted to his desires and occasionally abusive behavior in order to retain their tenuous positions in the Begum's household.

Dominga, a Catholic, apparently had (at least some, if not all) European ancestry. Hence, Sardhana's respectable Catholic families expected him to favor her and they occasionally acknowledged her socially. For example, David noted at the Sardhana Church one day, 'Mrs Derridon embraced D[ominga], and spoke to her, which is rather more than I expected.'[25] While he acted fondly toward Dominga, he more asserted his possession over her than seems to have been respectful. She had three children with David, all of whom died in infancy: Walter George (1832–33), Laura Celestina Roselia (1834–35), and Penelope (1836–38)—Penelope died on her way to England at the same time David emigrated there.

While David personally favored Hoosna Baae, a Muslim, over Dominga, he also recognised the relatively lower social status of the former, probably as a servant's child or courtesan. Hoosna had a daughter with David, Josephine Urbana (1834–35), but this child also died young. In addition to Catholic rites performed at Josephine's baptism and funeral, Hoosna also had Muslim rituals performed by a Qazi and also Hindu popular rituals performed by women servants.[26] David denigrated both her Islamic and her folk customs (including sacrificing a piglet to draw off her daughter's illness), but he permitted her to carry them out in her rooms.

Each of these mistresses had some emotional bond with David, yet he sought to ensure that they were also open rivals for his attentions. He noted egotistically: 'Poor D[ominga] begins to think of my being so fond of H[oosna], & quarrelled with me for almost nothing, in wh she was in the wrong.'[27] He occasionally ordered their beds shifted from one room to another in the palace, rewarding or punishing them by greater or less proximity to his own suite. He gave gifts and pensions to each, in proportion to their relative status and also current standing in his affections. When one became pregnant, she gained prestige as future mother of his child, but also lost out temporarily as his sexual partner. He apparently intentionally had sex with one within hearing of the pregnant other: 'H[oosna] & I very thick; when I did the 3rd time, I found myself more strong than the 1st and 2nd,... rather extraordinary; slept as usual over [pregnant] D[ominga]'s room.'[28] He also insisted on resuming sexual relations soon after each had given birth, for example, only sixteen days after Hoosna delivered their child, Josephine; his premature post-partum resumption of intercourse apparently caused her physical damage for which he confessed himself answerable.[29] Further, their positions in the palace diminished with the death of each of their children.

While David attended on the Begum, conducted his duties administering Sardhana, and moved around Meerut and Delhi, both Hoosna and Dominga remained waiting for him, ready to respond receptively whenever he arrived. They each had servants, friends, and families but David did not notice these in his diary and only indirect evidence about them appears in his financial accounts. Dominga appeared in public when she attended church, and David's brothers-in-law and most trusted male associates entered her and Hoosna's part of the palace. His mistresses' claims upon him, however, remained tenuous at best.

Further, David did not limit himself to these two women, even in Sardhana. Among others, David claimed flirting or sexual relationships with the daughters of numerous Sardhana courtier families, especially Catholic ones. He occasionally pressured them to allow him access to their women's quarters, generally barred to unrelated males. Since they had daughters whose marriage with David would bring wealth and increased status, they were placed in a difficult position to refuse his intrusion. For example,

I & [a British companion] Marshall went to call on old Derridons... I gave a hint to see Madame & he immediately consented to my going in with him... [Marshall had to stay out] for which I was not sorry... The Madame recd me very graciously, & kissed my cheek, & introduced me to her sister, & then afterwards to her daughters; Isabella, with whom I was rather in love with, was bashful; she has a boy about 2 years old; the rest of the daughters did not take my fancy. M[arshall] got impatient, & wrote me a note, saying that either to come out soon, or call him in...[30]

The next month, David tried less successfully to repeat the entry: 'Altho' I hinted [Derridon] to take us into his zenana, but he would not, & parried off my hint by saying that they are not ready to receive us, & the rain had completely upset them...'[31] A few months later: 'After church, I & Marshall went up to have a peep at the zenana, where [Derridon's] girls had gone too...'[32] The worried parents' anticipated reward for letting David have access to their domestic sphere was a wedding with him: 'The girls were again paraded before me'.[33] David was determined to enjoy this access but not to pay the price since he considered their aspirations for marriage with him 'impudence'.[34] Such intrusions thus became a contest between David and such families over his status: potential son-in-law or exploitative male intruder, patron who could not be denied or irresponsible libertine who should be excluded.

David's most consistently egalitarian relations were with elite north Indian families combining Indian and European ancestry and culture like his own. Among these, David grew up and remained on relatively friendly terms with the Skinners. David lent large sums of money to several Skinner men (including 60,000 Rupees to the patriarch, Colonel James Skinner).[35] He was respectful of the senior Skinner women. Yet, he also remarked unflatteringly on the personality and complexion of the Skinner daughters of marriageable age: 'quiet girls enough, but no gee in them... Miss Betsy or Elisa is very dark; poor Josephine will be very dark also...'[36] Whether it was their Anglican faith or personal features, he never (in the extant evidence) mentioned his possible marriage with that family.

David did, however, explicitly consider a marriage alliance with a Catholic French officer comparable in class to himself: General Jean-François Allard, a cavalry officer under Napoleon who, after Waterloo, went via Persia to Punjab, where he and other French officers served Maharaja Ranjit Singh as mercenaries for many lucrative years. In 1834, on his way to France, Allard stayed both at the Begum's court and with British officers at Meerut, receiving honour from each. The next year, her occasional correspondent, the French King Louis-Philippe, delegated the Begum to invest Allard with the Imperial Legion d'Honneur on his behalf (the French and Sardhana monarchs also exchanged portraits of themselves).[37] Throughout their exchanges, David felt an affinity for him: 'Monsr Allard came & was introduced to H. H. [the Begum]; he talks Persian pretty well for a foreigner'.[38] Allard's two daughters, who did not observe purda from David, reflected in their appearance their Indian mother(s): 'they both looked as if they had hill blood in them'.[39] Allard also impressed David by speaking admiringly about the latter's appointment as honorary Colonel from the French king: 'Genl Allard saw the French brevets I have got, & much approved of them, & said would take a copy to France with him'.[40] David and Allard kept up a warm correspondence and exchange of gifts for years, which included Allard reportedly proposing a marriage of his niece with David.[41] Later, when David first entered Paris, Allard introduced him into high French society (although Allard's death soon thereafter precluded further acts of patronage there).

Another French Catholic mercenary officer who prospered mightily under Maharaja Ranjit Singh and who enjoyed the Begum's hospitality was General Jean César Baptiste, Comte Ventura de Mandy. In 1834, Resident William Fraser introduced David to the older Ventura at the Delhi racetrack. Thereafter, David escorted Ventura, already initiated as a Freemason in Iran, to the local Meerut Lodge where he was quickly elevated to the second and then third degrees; David, as a Royal Arch degree-holder, remained his superior in the Masonic hierarchy.[42] Ventura and his Indian wife stayed several times in Sardhana, proudly displaying his fortune acquired as a mercenary and also 'the order of the Lion & Sun, given him by the King of Persia'. On Boxing Day 1834, Ventura had his mixed-ancestry daughter baptised in the Begum's Sardhana church. One of Ventura's accomplishments in coming to Sardhana was to find a suitable European at the Begum's court as groom for his sister-in-law, Helen Moses (as dowry, he gave 20,000 Rupees in gold and valuables plus 500 Rupees per month to the successful suitor, Captain Robert Dubignon de Talbot, who commanded the Begum's Household Guard). Three years later, the ever interested George Dyce induced Ventura to intervene on his behalf in claiming rights to Sardhana, although, as usual, to no avail.[43] Later in Calcutta and then Europe, David and Ventura resumed their relationship (it eventually degenerated, however, into bitter animosity).

In the culturally diverse Sardhana court, David accepted the benefits of attending on the Begum and worked to remain outwardly deferential to her, but he also tried to pursue his own pleasures and interests. He noted: 'H.H was very dull & sulky with me too, God knows why; but I managed to get her round....a whim of hers, for no one could be more attentive to her than I am...'[44] At the same time, he was trying to secure her backing in his contests with other courtiers and also to transfer millions of her rupees into his control. Rivals for her favour and inheritance resented his assertions. Others tried to attract him through marriage.

Moving among Mughals

Throughout David's youth, the sophisticated but impecunious Mughal emperor, court and capital retained prestige. The Emperor's authority could still influence British policy toward the Begum and her estate, especially since her *jagirs* of Sardhana and Badshahpur depended for their legality on imperial grants. Due to the Mughal clan's status as nominal sovereigns, they took symbolic precedence over the Begum.

Hence, Mughal princes, no matter how obscure, could expect in Delhi or Sardhana appropriately respectful submission from Begum Sombre as well as a generous *nazr*. Prominent Mughal courtiers socialised with the Begum as long-time allies and friends. Further, courtesans (from which class the Begum herself apparently arose) still oriented themselves toward Mughal courtiers, even if others paid more for their services.

Imperial Delhi, only five hours rapid ride away from Sardhana, stood as the nearest major metropolis, with a population of about 120,000. David and his guests availed themselves of the Begum's several establishments: the older *Churiwala Haweli*, the newer Chandni Chawk Palladian palace, and her other scattered houses and gardens. Even when the aging Begum became reluctant to make the journey, David often begged her permission to do so himself, seeking the excitement and stimulation of life there. When David visited Delhi, he paid his respects to the Mughals and other of their courtiers, negotiated with imperial Mughal officials—including the British Resident—to help secure his inheritance, and enjoyed the city's most stylish entertainers and sensual pleasure givers.[45]

David's maternal ancestry and his standing as the Begum's possible—then designated—heir gained him familiar access to the Emperor, his courtiers and some of their wives, including the Empress herself.[46] But Sardhana's wealth and their relatively impoverished status and clear suppression by the British meant that David did not hold the Mughal imperial family in the same degree of sincere regard as did Begum Sombre. In this attitude, David partly echoed that of the British: the Emperor and his large family survived with the barest deference, although the Company remained nominally his subordinate and continued to pension him and his clan. Thus, while David visited Mughal imperial princes in their homes, he disparaged their *hawelis* as well as their comportment: 'Mirza Jumsheed Bucht...lives in a damned place, in a hole, in fact... Went to see [Mirza Muhammad] Shah [eldest son of Mirza Babar and thus patrilineal grandson of Emperor Akbar Shah]... a d—d place also; the fellow was flying pigeons with his own hands, & seemed to pride in it; he was dressed in his father's English clothes!'[47]

Even Begum Sombre may eventually have found the Mughals pretentious and, over time, visited Delhi less. According to British gossip, later in life she bristled at her requisite public deference to Emperor Akbar

Shah II (r. 1806–37), allegedly avoiding Delhi rather than having to dismount her palanquin and bow when encountering the Emperor in procession.[48] When members of the imperial clan visited her in Sardhana, she was more gracious, controlling the etiquette as she did there.

The more prominent members of the Mughal imperial clan and court were long-known to the Begum and she welcomed them at Sardhana as honoured guests at her annual celebrations. As was customary, when they visited her, the Begum paid all their expenses and offered generous gifts as well. For example, Mirza Muhammad Shah visited Sardhana at Christmas in 1833, receiving honours from the deferential Begum including a handsome *ziyafat* (welcoming feast and gifts including 500 Rupees in cash), an eleven gun salute, *nazr*, and *rukhsat* (leave-taking ceremony and gifts for the road).

David, however, had to negotiate the mundane details of such visitations, which further decreased the status of Mughals in his mind. While not overtly offending protocols or decorum, he nonetheless regarded the imperial family as a relic from the past and impecuniously dependent on the generosity of the Begum and other real rulers like her. Thus, David denigrated Mirza Muhammad Shah as 'very foolish' for his committed devotion to flying pigeons and lack of interest in recent events. David disparaged him for not reading the *Jam-i Jahan Numa*, a Persian weekly newspaper from Calcutta, as David regularly did. David further derided this imperial prince's lack of an education beyond the *Quran* and Sadi's *Gulistan*, and called the quality of the *khila't* he bestowed pitiful. David recognised that mention of the attractiveness of an elephant's trappings by one of the Mirza's attendants subtly indicated that the royal visitor expected the gift of the entire elephant. But David rebuffed this prince's indirect hints for more presents, referring to such his visit as yet another 'begging expedition'.[49]

Similarly, imperial prince Mirza Jumsheed Bucht and his wife, Mootee Begum, visited Sardhana repeatedly.[50] For example, in 1834 and 1835 they received sincere and respectful receptions by the Begum who welcomed her friend, Mootee Begum, into her inner quarters. In contrast, David allotted the billiard room for the Mirza to stay in and disdainfully dispensed among his own servants the prince's *khila't*. To show off Sardhana's sights, David proudly conveyed this prince to a Catholic service in the new cathedral, but noted that the Mirza made a skimpy offering of only two rupees. To entertain the Mirza, David also escorted him to the Meerut horse-racing track for rounds of betting. Only when the Mirza explicitly pressed for them did David provide the requisite eleven gun salute, the present of a watch, and transportation. David vowed to himself 'Please God, next year, in the Salamitie [ceremony of paying respect] of H. H., I will take care only to call those that I know [to] come, & not any rag tag & bob tail...'[51] Thus, while David's public face showed sufficient respect for such imperial visitors, his private remarks revealed his sense of superiority toward them and resentment at the generous bestowal by the Begum on them of honour and money.

More welcome for David were the many troupes of Delhi-style courtesans whom he invited to Sardhana. In addition to their dances, David and other elite male patrons purchased these women's sexual services; conversely the women sought to extract money from these sexual clients. For example, David recorded the arc of his transitory relationship with one dancer, Moogloo. He saw her for the first time during a post-prandial nautch performance at the home of Jiwan Ram, the famous artist, in Meerut. David was just one of the many males in the audience and she was part of a troupe under the direction of a well-known impresario: 'Saw Mooglow there, the famous Jhujhur man's new pretty girl, but nothing extraordinary in her. I wd have taken a dig at her if I was not clapped, however I gave her 2 G[old] M[ohur]s...'[52] From her perspective, David's handsome cash present, without sex demanded in return, evidently distinguished him among her audience. His reputation as the leading man in nearby Sardhana would also have been known to her and her manager. Five weeks later, David reported encountering her during another nautch performance at a dinner in Meerut hosted by Colonel Stewart, a British officer acknowledged by David as 'a great connoisseur of Hindoostan...'[53] This time, although not yet cured of his fourth case of gonorrhea, David purchased her services as the party dispersed: 'Nucler Mogloo, one of Feiz Mhomed Khan's furd [collection], a very nice girl, I had [her] after they went away.' Periodically, each week or so for the next month, David recorded his sexual encounters with this woman: 'I had Moogloo, she is a d—d nice girl indeed'; 'I had a go with Mogloo, my favorite; this was the 3d one, tho' I am not quite well yet!!!'; 'I gave Moogloo 3 G[old] M[ohur]s; she is a great favorite of mine'; 'Had Mogloo at the bungalow, being almost alone'.[54] Finally, ten weeks after her first sexual encounter with David, she reported to him that she was pregnant: 'Mogloo in the family way!'[55] David then abruptly abandoned her, although he may have paid her a lump sum to see her off as he turned to the next such passing affair. While their relationship lasted, Moogloo had access to some of his cash but whatever temporary affective power she had exerted over him by her charms ended with her reported pregnancy. We can only speculate whether her report was true, about her intention or compulsion in making it, and the fate of her baby, perhaps David's only surviving child. David never mentioned her in his journal again nor included her in his will or list of pensioners, so while he admitted paternity privately, he did not do so publicly. Such asymmetrical and inconsequential (for him) liaisons characterised David's relationships with courtesans, as they did many of the British subaltern officers among whom he cavorted.

Moving among British Men and Women

In both Delhi and Meerut, David sought to ingratiate himself with nearby British colonial society. He often consorted with young British men, many of whom gained greatly from his inept gambling, generous (and usually never repaid) cash loans, lavish hospitality in the Begum's many mansions, and experienced guidance into local places of pleasure. David dined and drank frequently in the various regimental messes and also rose high in the secret society of Freemasons. Senior British officers and their wives, attracted by his wealth and princely position, invited him to dine and meet their daughters and other potential British brides. While David sensed himself never accepted by these Britons, at this stage in his life neither he nor they attributed his alienation to his mixed heritage or 'race', but rather to his idiosyncratic character and condition as the Begum of Sardhana's designated heir.

In Delhi, David met most extensively with Charles Trevelyan, Assistant Delhi Resident. On his part, David referred to him as 'jolly Trevelyan' and was gratified when Trevelyan had awarded the Begum custody of David's sisters.[56] But after Trevelyan rose in prestige and political power in Calcutta and then in Britain, he increasingly adopted what David resented as paternalistic, superior, airs. Trevelyan later publicly recalled David as awkward among Britons: David 'did converse and write in English; but it was not his native language; he had no readiness in speaking it, and was often at a loss for words. His letters to English people were written in English: but that was not the language in which he ordinarily conducted his business.'[57] On reading this, David in retaliation decried Trevelyan's lack of loyalty to himself and also to his chief, Resident Colebrooke:

I remember Sir Charles Trevelyan... when he first arrived as an assistant [Resident (1827–31)] at Delhi. I was with the Begum in Delhi at the time, and I soon became acquainted with him; we were about the same age, and naturally were more familiar than if there had been a great disparity of years between us. I found Mr Trevelyan... a well-read man; but what he means by my being a slow-minded and slow-speaking man, is more than I comprehend... it appears to me, on the contrary, that it was he himself who was considered, in spite of all his learning, a slow weak man, inasmuch that he would never have been allowed [promotion]... had he not taken the surveillance of watching the private life of an old official of the E. I. Company's service [Colebrooke],... being a guest always at this gentleman's table, and taking notes and other memoranda for the sake of meeting his ends. He succeeded so far, that the old gentleman was dismissed from the service; but Mr Trevelyan was not allowed to remain long in his comfortable position himself either... He was so disliked by the service for the part he had taken in this affair, that he was actually obliged to leave one of the best paid services in any part of the globe.[58]

David's mixed attitude toward Trevelyan also extended to one of Trevelyan's even more haughty senior rivals in the Delhi Residency, William Fraser.

Fraser, much older than David, met him socially but, particularly after promotion to Delhi Resident (1830–35), also proved annoyingly obstructive in the Begum's efforts to transfer Badshahpur and her other property to David. Other Indian rulers also resented Fraser's arrogant attitude, to the extent that Nawab Shams al-Din of Ferozpur had him assassinated (22 March 1835).[59] Fraser's brother, Hugh, notified the Begum and David by special messenger only hours after Fraser's death.

Despite their own resentment at Fraser's policies and attitude, both the Begum and David had internalised the legitimacy of British authority and also realistically feared being implicated in the plot. Fraser's assassination thus sincerely shocked David and the Begum. They immediately ordered newspaper advertisements publishing their sadness and regret as well as offering a generous 1,000 Rupee reward for the apprehension of his assassin, should he be captured in Sardhana. David also drew from this unexpected death the larger lesson of life's impermanence since he had met the deceased Fraser not long before in order to discuss the inevitable mortality of the much older Begum.

Attitudes in Sardhana toward Fraser in particular and the British in general were more mixed. Both the Sardhana Diwan, Narsingh Rai, and the Italian courtier, Major Reghellini, dismayed David by reportedly being 'rather glad' for the murder as the just 'reward of a tyrant'.[60] While shocked at their anti-British feeling, David concurred in part because Fraser has acted objectionably concerning Badshahpur and had also conspired with Dyce to undermine the Begum's authority. Meanwhile, Dyce and other of David's antagonists immediately spread dangerous rumours that David was part of the assassination conspiracy, which he urgently denied. For months, this striking breach in the British pretense of invulnerability fascinated David and many others; he futilely begged the Begum for her permission to attend the tension-filled but riveting public execution of Nawab Shams al-Din. Yet, even this assassination did not lead David to question the ultimate legitimacy of British colonial rule over the Delhi region. He and the Begum certainly sought to manipulate the British through subtle wording and interpretation of treaties, most notably with respect to Badshahpur, but they ultimately deferred to British power. Further, David continued to aspire to elite British society.

Throughout much of David's youth, the Begum spent each autumn at her Meerut mansion, hosting lavish dinners, especially for British officials, officers, and visitors, without necessarily receiving much gratitude in response. Europeans recorded their titillating thrill at gazing on their hostess, a woman they deemed so notorious. Many recounted romanticised versions of her infamous past, highlighting what they imagined had been her youthful beauty and plucky, as well as ruthless, rise to power. Some critiqued her morals or relevance, even as they enjoyed her largess. Reflecting these ambivalent attitudes was furloughed Second Lieutenant Thomas Bacon (who later became a barrister and then an Anglican priest):

When we recollect who the Begum originally was, the diabolical character of her husband, his perpetration of the massacre at Patna, and the many acts of crime and tyranny which she has herself committed, it is strange thus to find an enlightened British community, the victors of the soil, doing homage and seeking favour at her footstool, or even condescending to partake of her hospitality.'[61]

Yet Bacon himself attended on the Begum, boasting 'I have frequently been present at her durbars [levees], and have enjoyed the privilege of conversation with her highness, much to my amusement and edification.' He also approached David, in October 1834, soliciting the use of one of the Begum's several houses in Delhi, one at Raj

Ghat near the Jumna River: 'this I coveted as a residence during my stay at Dehli, and a note to my good-natured friend, Dyce Sombre, at once secured it to me. With his usual kindness and good-nature, moreover, Dyce sent extra servants over to Dehli, with orders to the mookhteya [agent] to get every thing in readiness for my arrival.' (But then Bacon ungraciously complained in print about the mansion's sparse, unaesthetic, and unclean furnishings.) Bacon promised that his father would repay the hospitality, should David ever get to the family estate in Devonshire. Further, Bacon asked David to loan him 2,500 Rupees on easy terms, which David uncharacteristically declined—advancing money to British men being one of the several ways that he tried to relate to them.[62]

Emulating his biological father, as a young man David most persistently tried to ingratiate himself with British officials and officers in the Company's service. Meerut, as a major East India Company cantonment, had substantial numbers of officers of both the Bengal and the Royal armies posted there or transiting through. This created a relatively open homosocial world where passable gentlemen were easily invited to raucous regimental officer's messes. Bawdy jokes and broad insults just short of duels passed for dinner table banter; discussion of women or horses had to be banned since they could provoke deadly confrontations. Drinking to inebriated levity or stupor was common. Since David could reach Meerut in less than an hour if he hurried by horse and could nap or recover from intoxication if he was carried more gently by carriage or palanquin back home, he could fit in quick pleasures there among his duties toward the Begum and the Sardhana administration.

Unlike David, virtually all these officers were 'pure' European by upbringing: the East India Company did not permit people of obviously mixed ancestry or culture in its regular officer ranks. Hence, these officers tended not to take him seriously or as one of their own. One subaltern of his own age recalled David as 'a heavy, over-grown boy, what in England would be called a Lout. He did not seem to have anything to say for himself.'[63] David admitted to himself that he was invited mainly because he was an easy source of money and access to Indian pleasures for the periodically impecunious young subalterns, not as a warm friend or companion. He resented their financial demands on him, but also feared their rejection if he did not continue to deliver. David, in his private diary, bemoaned his massive weekly gambling losses of hundreds or even thousands of Rupees, which continued to mount despite his frequent resolves to halt them. He also made large loans to British men, both high and low. Once they owed him money, he tried to hold that over them. As David openly asserted when urged to forgive a debt of honour owed him by a 'good fellow', 'I told him that if I wanted such a society, I could always purchase' it.[64] Conversely, his debtors avoided him, or kept him on the margins of their society, unless they wanted more of his cash.

Further, David remained removed from full participation in these military brotherhoods, even as he tried to emulate their manly conventions. As these British officers periodically marched gloriously to war, David stayed behind, seeing them off and then waiting to cheer their triumphant return and hear their tales of martial valour. Even after David acquired the title 'Colonel' from the Begum, these real military officers did not take his rank seriously.

Among British officers, personal honour was considered a matter of life or death. Hence, David characteristically refused to retreat, even when accurately accused of a lie or exaggeration. He admitted his errors not in public but in his diary: 'I know that I have not acted right, but he does not deserve it...[thus] I was obliged to deny [the truth] with a brazen face; what can I do?'[65] Thus, sticking stubbornly to his implausible position, even knowing its falsity, appeared far preferable to losing face by backing down. Such habitual practices hardly endeared him to his British counterparts.

One community that David craftily penetrated was the secret society of Freemasonry. Through David's initiation, aged twenty-three, into the 'Lodge of Hope' in Meerut, he entered a strongly British, empire-building, institution where men accepted the motto: 'Love the Brotherhood, Fear God, Honour the [British] King'. Only a year earlier, nine British men who were already members of Masonic lodges elsewhere (including Cameronian officer James Rogers, who had been initiated in Ireland), had organised this new lodge in Meerut and petitioned the United Grand Lodge of England for a chartering warrant. Without waiting the year before the warrant arrived (which recognised this lodge as number 596) they began recruiting new initiates into 'the Mystery of Masonry'—one batch of five in May 1832, then a second batch of seven, which included brothers-in-law David and Troup, that September.[66] In this all-male environment, the official bylaws tried to enforce a strict decorum that was apparently often lacking. As the

Meerut rules stated: 'as the innocent enjoyment of mirth is enjoined at the banquets of Masons, therefore no Member or Visitor of the Lodge shall, when the Lodge is closed, and the Brothers are assembled for refreshment, be permitted to sing improper songs, or do or say anything offensive, or that may forbid an easy or free conversation'.[67] David's admission early in the history of this particular lodge gave him seniority, and a clearly defined superior status over later British initiates, whatever their military rank or social station. Thomas Bacon, for example, was initiated two years later and thus had to defer to David within the lodge, if not outside it.

While the Freemasons addressed each other as 'brother' when they donned the ritual apron and other elaborate accoutrements, they also had clearly defined hierarchies. The craft ranking had three degrees: First or Entered Apprentice; Second or Fellow Crafts; Third or Master Mason. Some lodges added a fourth or 'sublime degree of Royal Arch', to which David was exalted at age twenty-five (along with Troup).[68] Further, not all Masonic lodges accepted people of mixed ancestry or 'pure' Indians; David's Meerut lodge accepted the former but not the latter during his day.[69] Of those lodges that did accept Indians, some admitted Muslims and Parsis but not Hindus, arguing that the Masonic creed required recognition of a single divinity that many Hindus could not be expected to avow. Thus within the separate space of a Freemason's meeting, David enjoyed a higher status than many of those who, outside it, may have looked down upon him as marginal to their society.

In north India, David apparently conceived of his possible intimate relationship with a European woman only through marriage. He believed that his position as heir to the Begum's fortune made him coveted by many respectable European parents as a son-in-law. After one dinner with General John Ramsay, Commander of the Meerut Division, David ran into 'Mrs Something, the late Miss Bishop, now a widow, to whom I was to be married once...', apparently referring to rumours that had paired them (although, since he could not remember her name, this affair could not have gone very far, nor did he renew his attentions with the widow).[70]

In high Meerut high British society, David regularly regarded himself as on trial as a groom. In 1835, he optimistically assessed his status among British elites:

Genl [Ramsay]... has always behaved in the most handsomest manner ever since I have known him. As a further mark of his kindness, he asked me to hand one of the ladies to the dinner-table in the eveng altho' there were 2 field officers, besides those that handed Mrs Ramsay & Mrs Brulton. I have very good chance of getting married, if I like, but I must not be in a hurry. Miss Fraser, who is not a bad-looking girl, I could get also; in fact, it was reported all over Meerut that I was going to get married to her; apropos the General read an advertisement in the *Meerut Observer* of a gentleman seeking for a wife! Many fellows called after breakfst; amongst them a Miss Woodcock, a guest of [Robert] Hamilton's; very dark girl for an European, but not bad looking, by all means.[71]

A few months later, the Begum discussed 'my marrying Miss Ramsay; I always suspected that'.[72] Such a marriage alliance between David and the Ramsays may have been considered appropriate only by one side: while it is clear that the Begum and David contemplated such a European marriage, there is no confirming evidence that the Ramsays entertained such an idea.[73]

For some members of the British élite, David's familiarity with north Indian Persianate culture provided comfortable access to women of the Begum's likely original class of courtesans. For the Ramsays and others, he arranged Indian dance performances: 'Had nautching, which Mrs Ramsay said was the first time they ever saw' it.[74] At such performances, David sometimes wore Indian clothes, hosting his British guests but also sartorially associating with the exotic performers: 'Miss Ferguson came ... & I sat in my native dress before her.'[75]

Often his male European guests did not conform to Indian cultural conventions, as David would have preferred. After hosting a dance performance for prominent English visitors at his home, David 'heard that after I left the room, Mr Sissmore & Mr Peterson were very troublesome with the Nautch women'.[76] To some small measure, David shared status with the procurers of these courtesans: he himself obtained the companionship of Europeans, which he valued, partly by providing them access to entertainment and sex with Indian women.

4

MADE ROOTLESS

As the Begum faded toward death, David's distraught attendance on her was infused with his sense of the impending termination of his own familiar way of life and need to secure possession of her money. When that long-dreaded event inevitably occurred, the British immediately implemented their annexation of Sardhana, seizing all state properties and papers, and displacing David as its manager and Colonel-Commander of the army. Having once run the entire state, he could not accept living under British authority there.

As soon as David extricated himself from the anguishing transition to British rule over Sardhana, he left on an extended getaway to the foothills of the Himalayas. He conceived of himself travelling alone, although he was attended by a huge entourage including Hoosna, Dominga, and his only surviving child, infant Penelope. After a brief return to complete his preparations to depart his homeland forever, he set out again to take his final leave of his long-time associates among the Mughals and other families like his own. Thereafter, although David retained financial and emotional ties to Sardhana, including with his dependents there, he became ever more alienated by time, distance, and diverging experiences.

As he descended the Ganges across north India to the imperial capital of Calcutta, he sought out his own family heritage, visiting people and sites from its past. Yet, wherever he went, his estranged father, Dyce, constantly shadowed him and claimed the family inheritance for himself. On David's journey, he also explored how other deposed or disempowered princes related to Indian and British cultures and peoples. He had insecure possession of a vast fortune in cash as well as property, but it remained legally disputed and could be snatched away by British judges or officials at any time.

Securing the Begum's Estate

Over the Begum's final years, as she herself recognised her growing enfeeblement and the uncertainty that her official testament would actually prevail posthumously, she moved haltingly toward the irrevocable act of transferring her legacy to David through means that she hoped the British would have to approve. She correctly anticipated that simply leaving her wealth to him in her will, which would retain her control over it until the moment of her death, was inherently uncertain (indeed, her will would be legally challenged for the next four decades by her would-be heirs and by the British). Hence, at the start of 1834, she decided to transfer the bulk of her wealth to David and designate him her official heir while she was still alive and able to enforce her acts. She devised the plan to create a Persian-language *hibbanama* ('deed of gift') which conveyed to him 3,600,000 Rupees— most of the cash in her treasury—plus ownership of her personal *jagir* of Badshahpur and other landholdings lying outside the Doab and therefore not legally subject to British seizure under her 1805 treaty.[1]

Inevitably, her plan further heightened tensions in her court and antagonism against David. The Begum repeatedly warned David that he 'had too many enemies', including his brothers-in-law, who might poison him at any time. Further, she also feared that British authorities might intervene since any money that she alienated during her lifetime would reduce the value to the Company of the coming annexation of Sardhana. Given these clashing interests, she and David could not expect disinterested advice from anyone.

Even after resolving on this course of action and repeatedly hinting about it to David, the Begum hesitated for months to announce and then complete it, terminating as it did her control over the fortune she had built up so devotedly during her six decades of autocratic rule over Sardhana. Over the early months of 1834, she incrementally and tantalizingly passed on to him the symbols of her authority, including her official seals, private keys, and personal jewelry and mementos, including one of her fallen teeth. Meanwhile, she suffered sores on her back and thighs, where even sitting chaffed, and painful bruises, when she increasingly lost her balance and fell. Everyone, herself included, realised her end was approaching. David frequently massaged her limbs and treated her ulcerated flesh himself. Meanwhile, regional newspapers published stories about her impending demise.[2]

On his part, David remained uncertain until the *hibbanama*, which she eventually dictated to him, was signed, approved by the British, and executed. He devised novel ways to assure the Begum of his devotion. He had already added 'Sombre' to his name in honour of her and his great grandfather and further contemplated adding 'Reinhardt' as well.[3] He informed her that he had drawn up his own will, leaving everything to her, thus restoring her control over her alienated wealth should he predecease her; he also willed that he be entombed at the entrance to her burial chamber in the Sardhana cathedral they had constructed.[4] He sought further ways to amuse her, for example, by presenting her with paper puppets, 'two fresh ones, with paper pullies, that made them act, such as one was a very jolly person, represented eating a roasting turkey, who cut his dish with one hand, & with the other he put into his mouth & his eyes turned as he performed the job. The other was a lady looking herself in a glass, and admiring her beauty; [H. H.] made me write for some more.'[5] We can only speculate about David's intent both in presenting to the Begum these particular toys—a feasting man and a pleased beautiful woman, but both paper puppets on strings—and in detailing their features in his diary. Eventually, David's preparations and anxious but indirect hints of the need to complete the *hibbanama* came to fruition.

She summoned not only all the prominent people of her court but also the most authoritative British officials who would attend. As David (having renamed himself David Ochterlony Dyce Sombre) anxiously hovered and dreaded the untoward, on 17 April 1834 the Begum signed the *hibbanama* on official British Government of India tax-stamp paper and supervised the witnessing of (and therefore acquiescence in) this document by twenty-one high-ranking male Europeans and Indians including: British Collector and Magistrate of Meerut, Robert Hamilton, and senior army officer, General John Ramsay; courtiers John Thomas and Dr Thomas Drever; and high Sardhana officials Rao Devi Singh, Munshi Gokul Chand, and Dewan Narsingh Rai. But David had to appeal to the Begum's authority in order to overcome the objections of his brothers-in-law:

I had a long dispute with Solaroli, in which I was rather harsh; he said he thought that himself and Troup ought not to sign the [*hibbanama*] paper tomorrow, & I said I thought you ought to be the first; & the only ground, he said, in support of his argument was, that he thought my sisters ought to be shown in equal rank with myself!! I wish he had told this to H. H., and then heard her answer.[6]

Finally, after much protest, even Troup and Solaroli signed.

In the Begum's heartfelt speech before these assembled witnesses, she proclaimed David her official heir, entrusted him to the protection of the British (saying David 'had nobody' else to look after him), and also commended his sisters and their husbands to David's care. Immediately on the signing of this *hibbanama*, David took official charge of the entire Sardhana administration, making transfers, promotions, and demotions as he saw fit to reward his friends and placate or punish his rivals. He also took over Badshahpur and other properties as his personal estate, adding some 100,000 Rupees to his annual income. His prominence rose even further in Sardhana and Meerut, buttressed by his even more lavish gifts, more generous loans, and more massive gambling losses.

But no one could predict the official British response. Ten months of silence passed while the Governor-General and his officials considered this *hibbanama*, punctuated by unsettling rumours heightened by inscrutable queries from the Delhi Resident. Should the Begum die suddenly, all these arrangements would come into question. Finally, early in 1835, David received official word that the Governor-General himself had approved the Begum's massive cash gift, although her transfer of the Badshahpur property remained unconfirmed.

Only after this did David risk asking the Begum for approval to take actual possession of the 3,600,000 Rupees. David begin sending under escort to Meerut huge loads of rupees. There, he arranged to have the cash converted into East India Company bonds, prudently registered in his own name despite Solaroli's protests and despite warnings from the Diwan of Sardhana, Narsingh Rai, not to trust the British—he predicted that they would stop paying interest after a while and might soon be driven from India.[7] These bonds not only paid 4% interest (144,000 Rupees annually) but David also hoped they were less likely to be dishonoured or confiscated by British authorities than almost any other kind of property. Indeed, David got the British Collector and Magistrate of Meerut, Robert Hamilton, personally to make the arrangements for the bond purchases. Hamilton only half jokingly solicited a 0.5% commission (18,000 Rupees) for himself. In exchange, Hamilton detailed to David exactly what Hamilton had been ordered by his superiors to do from the instant of the Begum's death: seize Sardhana and all its records and treasury funds immediately.[8] In a vain hope to reconcile David's 'very jealous' brothers-in-law, David promised to donate 100,000 Rupees to each of his sisters 'as a specimen of my good intention'.[9] He was also unsuccessful in striking a bargain with his father, Dyce, futilely offering him 300,000 Rupees if he would relinquish his own claims and keep his distance from Sardhana.

Despite her continued physical decline, the Begum remained alive for nearly two years after signing the *hibbanama*. The value of her 1831 will had diminished considerably by this 1834 gift, but she still retained legal possession of Sardhana and other extensive landholdings, mansions, and other property (worth some 2,000,000 Rupees) plus another 1,200,000 Rupees in cash. Revealing her continuing uncertainty about David's readiness to take over her full estate, she specified that he would only receive the interest from the bequests in her will until he reached age thirty, in 1838, with Colonel Clements Brown as trustee; only thereafter would David have full control over his legacy.[10] Thus, this *hibbanama* brought David's heritage much closer, but his future, and that of Sardhana, remained unresolved.

The End of the Begum and Sardhana

Finally, the Begum passed away on 27 January 1836. David was evidently distraught by her death, impending as it had been for some time; he wore mourning clothes throughout the following year. Immediately, Meerut Collector Hamilton rushed in, backed by Company troops, to occupy Sardhana and Badshahpur, take over her administration, and commandeer her army, demobilizing most of the soldiers and confiscating their weapons and accoutrements.

This was a shock to the Sardhana court when it actually occurred, despite being long feared. David did not resist, except to object when Hamilton confiscated the honourific gold batons of Sardhana's army officers. Crushingly, Hamilton retorted: 'I told [David] I was there to decide such matters; that he was a spectator, and that all orders would be given by me'.[11] Nonetheless, David recognised that Hamilton was only following orders and, despite the awkwardness of the situation, passed on a musical box owned by the Begum to Hamilton as a personal keepsake.[12]

Adding to the tension, George Dyce also suddenly showed up, seeking to intervene in the transition. David authorised Hamilton to offer his father 1,500 Rupees per month for life or 100,000 Rupees in cash, for relinquishing all claims.[13] Dyce rejected this offer, demanding more, but Hamilton firmly expelled him back to Meerut.

As soon as the late Begum's lying in state and grand funeral concluded, David appealed to Hamilton on three main issues. David asserted that the Sardhana army's equipment, much of which had recently been expensively purchased from the Company by the Begum, was her private property and therefore inheritable. Further, despite long-standing promises, the Company failed to pay the pensions of 800 of the Begum's retainers, alleging no authenticated list of them could be found in the Company records; David ended up paying these pensions personally. Most significantly, David argued against the seizure of Badshahpur since it was not included in the 1805 treaty, lying as it did outside the Doab.

David's protests over these three issues were all strongly rejected by an extensive confidential report by Sir Charles Metcalfe, Lt Governor of Agra, under whose authority Sardhana now fell. For example, concerning Badshahpur, Metcalfe conceded that it was literally outside of the 1805 treaty but that this British 'comparatively insignificant' and unintentional oversight, or clever obfuscation by the Begum, should not matter: 'It is possible that [Badshahpur] may have been omitted on the part of the Begum by design, taking advantage of our neglect; but there is no symptom that I am aware of, of an intentional omission on our part', hence he judged it legally annexable.[14] David's many appeals disappeared into Government officialdom, resurfacing only occasionally (they would not be resolved in his favour for thirty-seven years). Conversely, Hamilton complained that David did not immediately provide the funds necessary to pay the overdue salaries of the demobilised Sardhana army.

Fascinated news reports around the world echoed colourful accounts of the Begum's passing and legacy. The local *Meerut Observer* laid out the template that other newspapers followed, describing her great age, her half century in 'the most conspicuous position in the political proceedings of India', her long loyalty to the British, her great wealth left to David, and the curious mourning rituals of her court, including fasting, vigils, moaning and weeping from behind the purda by her maidservants, and the great pomp of her funeral by her Christian officers and clergy. Implied but not stated was that 'the celebrated princess' herself was Christian; no mention of her Catholicism appeared. Calcutta newspapers immediately republished this news. When this ship-borne bulletin reached London (2 August 1836) and then Washington (22 October 1836), national newspapers in these capitals rehearsed the essence of the story but garbled some of the conversions (for example, 'Jughire' was used as the proper name of her capital and the 'half a crore' of Rupees inherited by David was miscalculated downward by a factor of ten as only £50,000 rather than £500,000—still, however, a handsome sum).[15] Thereafter, David was associated globally with the exotic Begum and her fabulous and incalculable wealth.

Although the Begum's plan to transfer the bulk of her cash to David through the *hibbanama* helped, it did not fully secure even that money to him since he held Company bonds that it could unilaterally confiscate or cancel. Further, the remainder of her estate, conveyed mostly to him through her will, proved even less secure, especially until he turned thirty and could take full control over it. A range of disappointed heirs and dependents of the Begum, including Dyce, the brothers-in-law, and Major Reghellini, immediately challenged his inheritance.

Away from Home for the First Time

David now had vast wealth, but his life had no direction. Less than ten weeks following the apprehended but no less traumatic events of the Begum's death and the immediate annexation of David's homeland, he 'determined to march, set off' from Sardhana, beginning 'as I may style it, my travels'.[16] Despite the diversity of peoples who served or visited the Begum's court, David himself was relatively untravelled, having been tied to attendance on the aged Begum for virtually his entire life. As his first foray ever away from his homeland, he chose a long camping and shooting tour of the Himalayan foot-hills to kill tiger, cheetah, deer, and other jungle game. He also wanted to revisit people from his past, living and dead, and have time to consider his own future of having no career other than being a rich man (conditional on his securing his still uncertain but vast bequest). Never before in his life, from fear of being thought by the Begum to be neglecting her, could he wander freely according to his own impulse for as long as he wanted.

The Terai foothills of the Himalayas rose only some 200 kilometres north of Sardhana, but David had never visited them or shot tigers. For many Britons with whom he had long associated, tiger-hunting was a much vaunted proof of manhood. Elaborate protocols existed about the proper weapons and garb, where each hunter placed himself relative to the others, precedence in shooting, and rights of the man firing the first or the fatal bullet to trophies cut from the tiger's carcass.

David had often heard long and alcohol-stoked accounts and squabbles about all this but had himself never been able to participate. Even as he travelled away from Sardhana, he carried with him relics from the Begum that he depended on, including a fine rifle that Governor-General Marquis Cornwallis had presented to her in 1805, which David used for his inaugural tiger kill.

As he moved from camp to camp in the jungles, occasional male fellow travellers joined his camp and then departed, both Europeans and Indians (including the Anglicised son of the pensioned Nawab of Bengal). David's elaborate encampment offered them fine food, drink, and other comforts, but they provided the masculine hunter-model for him to emulate. David's aim was not always the best; many animals that he had only wounded then escaped or were finished off by others. He also bickered with his fellow-hunters as to whether his bullets had done sufficient damage to entitle him to the prized tiger skin.

David brought his mistresses, Dominga and Hoosna, along with him, providing a secluded set of tents for them. They, too, were removed from their network of friends and family but, unlike David, were constrained from exploring the countryside and forests. Further, since European and Indian gentlemen visited and stayed in his encampment, the presence of his mistresses had to be an open secret, known but unacknowledged.

During this trip David twice visited Haridwar, where the Ganges River debouched from the Himalayas. Most religious aspects of this Hindu pilgrimage site did not interest him but he did visit a Brahmin *purohit* ('genealogist') there whose records bore the signatures of his father, George Dyce, and father's father, Lieutenant David Dyce, which David noted closely resembled each other. Throughout this expedition David frequently and respectfully searched in the many Christian graveyards he passed for familiar names. But at the shrine to a Sufi saint and his four wives, David entered with his hunting boots on, was stopped by a shocked attendant, but then professed himself 'too lazy' to remove his boots and approach the graves.[17]

Led by whim, David bought animals as well as shot them. When he attended the great Haridwar Fair, he noted its masses of people but, disappointingly, saw 'no very great show of horses & other things' for him to acquire. He did see an already-captured elephant calf that he offered to purchase for 150 Rupees. When its owner would not sell the young calf alone, separating it from its mother, David refused to be thwarted and bought her too for an additional 650 Rupees. Along the way, he also purchased a bear cub and a young male tiger. To prove a British fellow-hunter wrong, David fed the heart of a shot tiger to the young one, showing that tigers would be cannibal. Indeed, David noted that his young tiger 'relished it very much!!!'.[18] Since David had no use for these expensive purchased animals, he quickly gave them away.

In India at this time, British and Indian elites would expect a welcome from their peers, even of distant or no previous acquaintance, when they dropped in without advance notice. David's wealth and ambivalent identity enabled him to draw upon several social circles. His lingering prestige as the Begum's adoptive son meant that many Indian officials, landholders, and royalty received him sumptuously, providing housing and food, and loaning servants, guards, and transportation as needed. David also received hospitality from Europeans whom he or the Begum had known, and often had hosted. When David stayed with them, he needed more than a single guestroom. His entourage required considerable space within the host's compound walls, an area secure from dangerous outsiders and also secluded enough for Dominga and Hoosna's tents to be modestly inconspicuous. Over feasts and entertainment, David and his Indian and European male hosts reminisced about his family and gossiped about the larger current and future consequences of Indian actions, British preferences and policies, as well as coming British-Indian wars.

Like most of David's lifetime, this was a time of uncertainty and danger for both Indian rulers and also the British. Emperor Akbar Shah was aging and the British remained undecided about the respective risks of allowing or denying succession to the Mughal crown. Further, the British were currently conspiring to re-enthrone an earlier but deposed incumbent as Amir of Afghanistan, Shah Shuja (r. 1803–09, d. 1842), who was living in exile under British protection. This would lead to the First Anglo-Afghan War (1838–42), by any measure a disaster for the British. Simultaneously, the British maneuvered to take advantage of the instability in the Punjab that would follow the expected death of the enfeebled Maharaja Ranjit Singh. This death in 1839 eventually led to the First Anglo-Sikh War (1845–46). David, himself no longer a political player, nonetheless followed these events closely and went out of his way to meet with deposed and pensioned princes, men similar in status to himself. For example, he gifted to Maharaja Ranjit Singh the late Begum's processional elephant howda and magnificent durbar tent, receiving in reply a terse thank-you note and a further request for an English horse (David, not reconciled to being a former princeling, privately complained 'the style [of Ranjit Singh's reply] was not very flattering in address, but probably that was not his fault').[19]

Moving further up into the mountains, at the hill-stations of Mussoorie and Simla David visited various Europeans from his past. Among them he sought support in his moral and legal contests against his father, Dyce (although he usually ignored their unwanted advice). For example, he repeatedly called upon and dined with Mrs and Reverend Henry Fisher, his old teacher. David gave her one of the Begum's diamond rings as a keepsake. David had obliged him by extending large loans (including one of 10,000 Rupees) plus giving him 8,000 Rupees to be distributed in charity.[20] David also met with their friend, the rising Bengal Army officer, William Henry Sleeman, who had recently visited Sardhana, just a week after the Begum's death.

On this two-month excursion, David repeatedly wrote in his diary about feeling 'alone, left by myself'. Nonetheless, he brought along Hoosna, Dominga, Penelope, and a staff of over 200 servants, guards, camp-followers, and locally hired guides and bearers. Over the following months—briefly back in Sardhana, on the road again, and then in Calcutta—he would haltingly pay off and dismiss every one of these dependents until he was truly alone.

Traversing North India

After returning to Sardhana for four months to wind up his personal and financial affairs, David paid his final respects to the Begum's tomb and left home for the last time on 3 October 1836. Sequentially, he took leave from the Mughal imperial family, the mixed ancestry Skinner family, and also European acquaintances. He visited for the first time the graves of his Reinhardt ancestors and properties that he had inherited from them. As David travelled down the Ganges toward the British colonial capital, he explored famous sites and measured his condition against other exiled or uncertainly placed Indian princes.

Despite David's repeated denigration of the Mughals in his private diary, he took formal leave from them as a significant stage in his withdrawal from his homeland. He distributed much of the Begum's equipage to her long-time friends in Delhi. For example, he presented her

Calcutta-made, English-style carriage and four mares to the Mughal Empress, the brass bed on which the Begum's corpse had lain in state to the Mughal Heir Apparent (later Emperor Bahadur Shah), and the tame young tiger he had purchased on his recent outing to imperial Prince Mirza Muhammad Shah.[21] He gave the Begum's state palanquin to the Maratha aristocrat Hindu Rao (settled in a mansion on Delhi Ridge) and then borrowed from him the use of a curricle in order to travel down to the Qutb Minar to take his formal leave from Emperor Akbar Shah. As David described this final audience authorizing his departure: 'the King sent for me at the Jumna [River bank palace], where the Begum [Empress] was also; it was a private Durbar, for besides the eunuchs, there was no one there, the King was affable, ... according to custom, gave me two pawns [betel-leaf condiments] as my congee, & the Queen a button...'[22]

David's own family continued to trouble him. His father constantly haunted him, abruptly appearing, sending letters (which David rejected, unread), and calling on friends of their family to reconcile father and son. David became so upset that he went to the Delhi Resident for a restraining order, to no avail. This part of David's past stalked him all the way down to Calcutta. Although David distrusted Solaroli, David felt compelled to appoint his brother-in-law as managing agent over his property in Sardhana. David's idiosyncratic management style was to occasionally accuse an employee or agent of malfeasance, with no evidence but vainly intending to frighten him into being 'more attentive to his [David's] business'.[23]

The family with whom David felt least uneasy was that of his schoolmates, the Skinners, people whose history was intertwined with that of the Reinhardts and Begum Sombre. But, in one of their fortresses, David was nonplussed to find artillery bearing the embarrassing name le Vassoult, dating from the brief time of his ascendancy over the Begum, which David wished to suppress. David visited the main Skinner family seat at Hansi (formerly the estate of George Thomas, friend and rescuer of Begum Sombre). As keepsakes, David presented one of the Begum's dining sets, worth 14,000 Rupees, to the family, valuable horses to the Skinner sons, and her own formal throne-like chair to the patriarch, Colonel James Skinner. Skinner's third son, Lieutenant Hercules Skinner, had recently returned from his four years of study at the Edinburgh Academy. The Colonel reportedly composed a poem in Persian advising David not to venture to England, perhaps knowing he was unprepared for what he would encounter there (although his son, Hercules, would later return to Britain himself, marrying and dying there).[24] David's parting from this family, having long associated with his own, was deeply emotional: 'The Skinners are very kind... the Col. gave me several letters of introduction, & an emerald ring, & at parting poor [eldest son] James & the Col. were quite affected, & so was I at seeing them'.[25] David and James would soon meet again (and carouse together) in Calcutta. Wishing David well, the Colonel detailed some Skinner's Horse cavalrymen as escort down the Ganges, showing solicitude for David's dignity and also providing protection on the still dangerous roads.

Rather than tour western India as he half intended, David passed from Delhi through his *jagir* at nearby Badshahpur (which he claimed but British officials confiscated and refused to return). As David set off, he reduced his entourage to a mere forty servants plus Hoosna, Dominga, and Penelope. David desired the attendance of his mistresses but he also felt somewhat embarrassed about them; he wrote Solaroli: 'I don't care if the people know that I have my Zenana with me, but... there is no use in publishing it to the world.'[26]

As he traversed down the Ganges toward the colonial capital, Calcutta, David stayed with and paid respects to prominent and influential British officers and officials, enlisting them in his support and against his father. For example, in Agra, David repeatedly paid his respects to and lobbied Charles Theophilus Metcalfe, whom he had known for thirty years at the Delhi Residency, who had risen to be acting Governor-General for a year, and who was currently Lt Governor of Agra province. David evidently did not know about Metcalfe's confidential report dismissing all David's legal claims, which concluded by condemning them as tainted by their illegitimate origins with 'Walter Reynard the Sombre... the sanguinary butcher who perpetuated the infamous massacre of the British at Patna'.[27] Ingratiatingly, David later arranged to make Metcalfe his future shipmate and then offered him a large cash loan on easy terms (neither of which Metcalfe appreciated).

As he travelled further from his familiar world of Sardhana, David encountered alienating rebuffs. When a junior British officer ordered him brusquely away from the gunpowder magazine of Allahabad fort, David explained away this unfamiliar insult: 'I excuse him; he did not know who I was'.[28] He then faulted his British hosts for exposing him to such embarrassment by not explaining in advance his bona fides.

On David's travels east across India during the winter of 1836–37, he also had mixed encounters with his family's past. In Agra, in addition to dodging his persistent father, David visited the graves of his grandfather, Aloysius Reinhardt, and great grandfather, Walter Reinhardt, the original Sombre. David wrote Solaroli ordering him to sell some of the family houses and gardens that Sombre had acquired there. Other inherited properties, including three gardens, David determined to keep. Later he stopped in Mirzapur to see the son of Joseph Evan, to whom le Vassoult had entrusted the Begum's retirement fund—money never returned after their flight failed.[29] Even later, in Patna, David observed with conflicting emotions the memorial to the 150 English people 'murdered by a certain person and was much disappointed in not finding any inscription on it. I could not help thinking abt them & him.'[30] Thus, even in David's diary he did not name his great grandfather any more than he used his own father's proper name. But he pondered his family's past as he encountered reminders of it.

One objective of his north Indian journey was to meet other Indian princes who, like him, endured various stages of disempowerment. When he visited each, David's response combined distancing—typical of European tourists—with sympathy for their dependent condition—comparable to his own. Most prominent among these were the current but largely puppet King of Awadh, the long-exiled Maratha Peshwa, and the pensioned Nawab of Bengal.

David spent a week in Lucknow, the capital of the largest princely state left in north India, Awadh. In 1819, the British had encouraged this dynasty to assume the title Emperor, thus rivaling the Mughals. David accepted this pretension, referring to the current ruler, Nasir al-Din Haidar (r. 1827–37) as 'H. M.', 'the King', and 'Jehan Punah' [imperial 'world refuge']. Yet, in David's diary and, presumably, conversations, he also subtly championed the superiority of Delhi over rival Lucknow in culture and sophistication, if no longer in wealth, including Delhi's superior dancing women.

Despite some broad similarities in David's background and experiences with those of the Awadh ruler, David approached the Lucknow court as a wealthy, respectable, but not royal or particularly Indian tourist; much of David's record of his impressions of Lucknow parallel those of a typical European visitor. The British Resident politely received David and directed him to view the usual sights of the city, including its oriental-style palaces, tombs, and vast royal stable. David judged it 'a large native town, but all filled with dirt... Everything in Lucknow...[is] a mixture of fineness and filthiness.' More than in Delhi, fancily dressed dandies passed down dirty alleyways. David, however, appreciated Lucknow's ubiquitous and excellent kabobs. He also savoured gossip about the notorious Nasir al-Din as a cross-dresser, in many ways the converse of British gossip about Begum Sombre as masculine in comportment. During David's first encounter in Lucknow's streets with Nasir al-Din's *sawari* ('cavalcade'), David 'was quite disappointed in not beholding H. M.'s face, who we heard was in the golden tonjon [palanquin] dressed in woman's clothes...'[31] But David later had his expectations partly satisfied by observing Nasir al-Din directly, although not in women's clothing but rather in Euro-peanised dress and possessing a European women—albeit not a par-ticularly desirable one. Just as David was departing Lucknow 'all at once... they said Jehan Punah was coming this way; and my [palan-quin] bearers dropped me down immediately, & I saw H. M. full in the face... he seemed to me abt 25 years age, rather good looking, & was dressed in English clothes, & had a star on his breast. There was a very fat European lady, on an elephant, behind him.'[32] David now felt emboldened to ask to meet Nasir al-Din personally through an introduction by the British Resident. But Nasir al-Din's retainers responded that he was otherwise occupied and turned David away. Rebuffed, David doubted the sincerity of this dismissal writing 'for [the King] was in his devotions, as he gives out, but I suppose he is enjoying himself in quite Eastern style' in his harem, likely with this 'very fat European lady'.

Implicit in David's account are comparisons with himself. Nasir al-Din was roughly David's age (David thought him age twenty-five, younger than David's twenty-seven, but Nasir al-Din was actually older, age thirty-four). Nasir al-Din possessed European women, and David aspired to do so. Nasir al-Din governed in an archaic manner, while David considered that he had administered Sardhana in a more modern way. Although ruling a much larger and more sovereign state, Nasir al-Din was subject to the disposition of the British, as David had himself just experienced first-hand. Only months after David left Luck-now Nasir al-Din unexpectedly died and his designated heir was imme-diately dethroned by the British in favor of their nominee, a half-uncle. Then, in 1856, the British deposed the incumbent and annexed the entire state.

Nawab of Bengal's Murshidabad New Palace

Next, David briefly paid his respects to another exiled prince, the long-deposed Maratha Peshwa, Baji Rao II (r. 1796–1818, d. 1853). As in Lucknow, David expressed a mixed sense of distance and sympathy: the 'poor man seems to be quite reconciled to his fate, but has certainly suffered inwardly of his misfortunes. We went in the Eastern style, with our heads covered & shoes off; & when he came into the room we took off our caps, & made him a bow, & put on our hats again.'[33] The doffing of shoes and donning of headgear was Indian etiquette; the doffing of headgear as a mark of respect was European. David also met Dandu Pant 'Nana Sahib', the young adopted son whom David assumed would inherit the Peshwa's title and pension but, like David himself, was ultimately barred from doing so by the British.

Early in January 1837, David visited the newly-completed palace of the pensioned and confined Nawab of Bengal in Murshidabad. David had already met one of the Nawab's Anglicised sons while on his earlier hunting excursion. Further, David's great grandfather, the original Sombre, had gotten his start serving an earlier Nawab. Once again, David pondered the issue of Westernisation. On touring the Nawab's nearly finished European-style palace, David had to admit its fine workmanship but he proudly noted that his comparable construction, Dilkusha Kothi, had only cost one-sixth as much. Further, David disparaged the capacity of the Nawab's womenfolk to be Anglicised enough to inhabit it: 'What a pity that such a palace will be thrown into the hands of people who know not how to live in it, unless the Nawab has the sense to keep this as his English palace, and not allow the women to live in it.'[34] Conveniently, David did not recall how he proudly installed the Begum and his own mistresses in Dilkusha Kothi. Further, to demonstrate David's own mastery of English conventions, he wrote a polite note in that language to the Nawab requesting an interview; the Nawab replied in the same language but admitted that official British permission was requisite before he could meet anyone, and that would take considerable time to solicit and obtain.

For all the Nawab's and David's Anglicisation, he also met with the Nawab's chief eunuch and chief astrologer, with both of whom he conversed in Persian. From consulting the latter, David learned: 'I will be a rich man, but will not know how to take care of my money! & that I could live to an hundred years age!'.[35] Only the first two of these predictions were prescient, however.

Finally, on 23 January 1837, David and his entourage reached the cosmopolitan colonial capital of Calcutta. On the road, he had celebrated his twenty-eighth birthday with a special camp dinner of turkey, plum pudding, and champagne. His expenses, just for the last two months of his trip (since Cawnpur), totalled a substantial 5,500 Rupees (worth some £40,000 today). In Calcutta, his costs, pleasures and risks would increase even more strikingly. The city's British officials and judges could secure for him his inheritance—including his claims for Badshahpur, the Sardhana armaments, and pensions for the many dependants of the Begum—or they could deny him all of these. Thus, ahead of him lay a new world of legal, social, and cultural challenges with which he was both unfamiliar and apprehensive.

5

THE LAST OF ASIA

In cosmopolitan Calcutta David remained unsure how he would be received in any particular quarter. Here he discovered for the first time that many Europeans considered him to be 'Black', but he also saw how much his cash could buy. Stubbornly determined to have his own way, he explored what he wanted his way to be. He tried to keep his diverse financial, social, legal, and personal activities separate, but often failed to do so. He struggled to disentangle himself from his past, restlessly moving houses and changing companions. For months, he plunged into a nearly continuous self-destructive binge of gambling, drinking, and whoring from which he repeatedly but ineffectually resolved to extricate himself. Nor did his extended tour of Southeast Asia and China stabilise him. So he finally left Asia forever.

Encountering Calcutta

Calcutta, a city of 200,000 inhabitants, already known as the 'city of palaces', exceeded in scale and complexity of power, wealth, and cultures anything in David's experience. Almost twice the size of Delhi, Calcutta centred on British officialdom and European 'boxwallas' (merchants) as well as Indian businessmen and landowners, rather than on the pensioned Mughals and their declining court culture. A port-city created by the British over 140 years earlier, Calcutta's extensive and diverse European population included social classes ranging broadly from the highest British officials of the supreme government of India to sex-workers of sundry European ethnicities. Much of the commerce between north India and the rest of the world, including both exports and imports of goods and ideas, flowed through Calcutta. In the vanguard of Indian society were the newly prosperous commercial and landowning classes, infused with an invigorating sense of how Indian and European cultures could compete as well as cross-fertilise. This innovative Indian spirit was then burgeoning as the 'Bengal Renaissance' of social and religious reform, but also creating cross-cutting cultural demands on rising Indian men and women. Further, exiled royalty and people from every other class and region and religion of India crowded Calcutta's streets day and night.

David, due to his anomalous background as well as his gold mohurs, silver rupees, and transgressive behaviour, both participated in many of these different worlds and also jarred against their developing moralities. Calcutta fostered an urban public life where anonymous exchanges of cash were beginning to prevail, as David suddenly experienced and soon tried to use for his own advantage. He already had lots of money to hand and, once he resolved his manifold legal difficulties, would possess an even huger stock of free-floating capital that would empower him in a system where almost everything was for sale (except race).

Being regarded as an unknown and untrusted stranger came as an unwelcome shock to David. Although he rented rooms in the leading Spence's Hotel, he had never actually stayed as an unfamiliar paying customer before, exchanging coin for hospitality instead of being welcomed as a houseguest. Similarly, on his first ever visit to a restaurant, he remarked how 'very stupid indeed' it was that the '7 or 8 people [there were] eating by themselves, & only now & then speaking to each other'.[1] In contrast, during the regimental messes or public dinners hosted by the Begum with which he grew up, people hitherto unknown to each other had joined in common conversation; it was the height of impoliteness to ignore someone dining nearby. But when David occasionally addressed someone in the hotel or dining hall, he met only a discomforting hostile repulse. Consequently, David soon created a more congenial environment by sharing a rented house with other rowdy young men of his acquaintance.

As a consumer on the city's streets, David discovered that merchants would not automatically recognise his worth. When first out shopping, he had not bothered to bring cash. To his dismay, 'I found no credit; nor even if I went so far as to deposit anything [of value] that I had by a chance. I even had not my watch with me [to deposit], wh I generally wear & I think it ought to have taught me a moral lesson, that without money in your pockets you are not welcome' in Calcutta.[2]

Dominga and Hoosna pleasured and attended on David in Calcutta but they also posed an embarrassment as he attempted to enter British society. He evidently did not even consider having them room with him in Spence's Hotel or later in his shared house. Rather, like many other rich men, both European and Indian, he used his money to distance and yet still control his mistresses. He quickly rented a house (at 35 Rupees monthly) with half-a-dozen servants across the Hooghly River for Dominga and Hoosna, immediately installing them there when their riverboats finally arrived. Thus he could access them at his whim but their existence would not have to be explicitly noticed by Calcutta high society. Such suburban mistresses were conventionally known as 'garden bibis'. But Dominga and Hoosna found this isolating life in Howra unsatisfactory and each strove to bind David to her, with mixed results. After much struggle, he would later buy each of them out of his life.

David arrived in Calcutta with access to several communities, but none of these proved particularly welcoming. As a high-ranking Free-mason, holding the exalted degree of Royal Arch, he had fraternity with important European (and a few Indian) Masons in Calcutta and throughout the Empire. Yet, while he once attended the Humility with Fortitude Lodge in Fort William, its membership disappointed him: 'besides 3 [Royal Army] officers of the Cameronians, all the rest were conductors [commissary agents], &c.', men of relatively low social status.[3] Hence, the craft in Calcutta did not provide a community which he felt desirable.

David's bonds with the Catholic Church were deeper and more enduring. In Calcutta, he frequently—but not regularly—attended Sunday mass. But notwithstanding the Begum's huge donations to the Church and his own status as a Pontifical Knight of Christ, he received little notice from the Catholic community. The Church establishment in Calcutta was currently divided, with the Irish Jesuit Robert St Leger as the Pope's Vicar Apostolic battling for control against Indo-Portuguese parish priests from Goa who had Augustinian affiliations.[4]

Perhaps reflecting these internecine Catholic conflicts, David never felt comfortable with the Church in Calcutta. Two days after he reached the city, David visited Dr St Leger about endowing a Catholic college in Sardhana but was coldly received, which David blamed on malicious gossip from his Italian brother-in-law: 'Oh, Solaroli! how you deceived me; it is all your doing, I know; I don't object to the measure, but why deceive me?'[5] Thereafter, David mainly attended masses presided over by men of Portuguese or mixed Portuguese-Indian ancestry (whom he called 'country-born'), but whose English-language abilities and manners he found lacking.[6] Nonetheless, Father Gondoli sheltered David's mistress, Dominga, and aided him in disposing of her.

During his time in Calcutta, he also explored other religious practices. He occasionally attended Anglican services, especially when his former teacher (and deep debtor) Reverend Henry Fisher presided. David once toured a Jewish service 'where I was very much amused for an hour. Saw some beautiful faces, & all well dressed; they read Hebrew, & every one had a "linen ephod" [vestment] on his shoulders; they were very polite, & invited me to sit down.'[7] Further, David observed a Scots Presbyterian wedding, remarking on the unfamiliar stark simplicity of the kirk and ritual.

David's Life among British and Indian Elites

On arriving in Calcutta, David soon called upon powerful Britons whom he had met in Sardhana, Meerut, or Delhi, assuming their influence would decide the fate of his fortune. The day after he reached Calcutta, he went to the home of Charles Trevelyan, his long-time acquaintance from the Delhi Residency who had subsequently risen high in the Company's administration. David characterised Trevelyan, a man his own age, as more grave and unpleasing than before but still willing to give David advice: 'he recd me very kindly; not the same jolly T—that I knew at Delhi, but a quiet man, grown very thin.'[8] David was particularly pleased that Trevelyan allowed him to meet his wife, Hannah Moore (younger sister of the influential Law Member of the powerful Governor-General's Council, Thomas Babington Macaulay), but noted she 'is a very plain woman, & now in a family way, near confinement.' Trevelyan also introduced David in official circles and showed him the wonders of the city, including its mint. David was fascinated, revisiting this modern invention that coined money by steam-power and pronouncing it was 'certainly the only thing that has pleased me in Calcutta'.[9]

Trevelyan, his wife, and Macaulay shared a house and invited David to dine. Apparently due to the slightly elder Macaulay's eminence, David belittled his appearance yet felt somewhat intimidated by him

Charles Edward Trevelyan and Thomas Babington Macaulay

and the other guests: 'he shook hands with me. He is a stout short man; there can be no doubt of his abilities; but when you look at him first, you would not take him to be the wisdom of the State; he is fond of talking, & he had a select small party at dinner; they were all strangers to me, of course.'[10] Dyce Sombre apparently did not know that Macaulay had earlier celebrated Begum Sombre's death in a private letter: 'An old hag called the Begum Sumroo is dead, and her death has put the government in possession of ten or twelve lacs [1,000,000–1,200,000 Rupees] a year.'[11]

Both Macaulay and Trevelyan championed Anglicisation: instructing elite Indians in the higher values of Britain. David, in their eyes, may have initially seemed a promising prospective example of their policies: Indian-born but Christian (albeit Catholic), of mixed ancestry but someone who dressed and spoke almost like a Briton. However, as David's legal troubles and disreputable personal reputation spread, the Trevelyans and Macaulay disapprovingly distanced themselves from him until they left Calcutta for England. There, Trevelyan eventually resumed his patronage of David.

To announce his arrival in an appropriate manner, David also immediately began dropping off his English-style visitor's card with the door-keeping servant at the home of each prominent European with whom he sought acquaintance. Among British gentlemen, a well established etiquette existed about 'dropping cards', including the bending of one or more corners to convey messages about how pro forma or serious this courtesy was meant. This custom placed on the recipient the onus of either inviting the card-dropper as welcome to call in person or else ignoring him without the mutual embarrassment of a face-to-face confrontation.

Among those homes where David quickly dropped his card was that of Henry Thoby Prinsep, long-time Persian Secretary to the Government (in charge of the Company's political relations with Indian states, including Sardhana), published historian, and also acting Member of the Governor-General's Council. They had met briefly in Delhi half-a-dozen years earlier when Prinsep, sixteen years older than David, had accompanied the governor-general on a tour. Prinsep invited David to his office (not home). Then, throughout David's stay in Calcutta, Prinsep particularly assisted him in his complicated financial dealings with the government: David was investing the vast sum of 3,950,000 Rupees in Company bonds but was also fighting for possession of them in Company courts, while simultaneously protesting the Company's seizure of other parts of his legacy. David cunningly hired Prinsep's elder brother, Charles Robert Prinsep, as one of his many attorneys. The East India Company, although heavily bureaucratic, also worked through personal relationships and hiring Prinsep's brother, David believed, would carry advantageous influence. Always sensitive to how familiar he could safely get with Britons, David particularly noted that, at a public banquet, Prinsep entrusted him with Prinsep's wife 'I handed [into dinner], according to his instructions, Mrs Thoby Prinsep, to whom I was introduced by her own husband, a very nice sensible pretty girl'.[12] Indeed, David met socially with five Prinsep brothers and their families in Calcutta.

Prinsep, however, opposed Trevelyan and Macaulay's Anglicisation policies and regarded David by ancestry as largely Indian and therefore qualitatively inferior to Europeans. Prinsep remembered David for his vast wealth but also for his personality, growing disreputable behaviour, and race: 'I thought him in India a man of jovial disposition. I saw less of him than might otherwise have been the case by reason of his being reputed a man of debauched habits... I looked upon him as a half native... He was always suspicious and mistrustful, as Indians are... I had [difficulty] in persuading him that the Government Agent would be safe... who would remit the interest to him, and obey any instructions he might send for the disposal of the principal' of his massive Company bonds.[13] Yet, Prinsep would later in England take an extensive interest in David and his estate.

Through Trevelyan, David soon obtained a formal ceremonial meeting with the Governor-General, Baron Auckland.[14] Even after this initial audience, David remained apprehensive about how he would be received personally: 'Went to the Choringhee Theatre, & there was the Govr-Gen there, & was in undress [casual European-style clothes], so rather shy in pushing myself forward.'[15] To David's relief, three days later Auckland's unmarried sisters, forty-year-old Emily and thirty-six-year-old Frances 'Fanny' Eden, sent him a formal invitation to their biweekly 'at home'. As David boastfully recorded in his diary:

Recd. an invitation... in the name of Miss Edens for their party this evening, & it ran thus in the postscript... "and on every alternate Tuesday eveng during your stay in Calcutta;" it was very flattering, & of course I determined to go... tho' I did not wish it at first, or else could have easily left my card at Govt House, & was sure to get an invite, this being the etiquette... The eldest Miss Eden did me the honour to sit near me, & had a few moments' chat...[16]

David described his gratification at the personal honour bestowed upon him by these most prominent British ladies and repeated such visits periodically. When he neglected to attend, he was pleased that both Miss Edens and the Governor-General himself noticed and commented on missing him.[17] David also pursued other pleasures, occasionally coming straight from a brothel to Miss Eden's salon: 'From a d-d bitch into the Govr Genl's compound in my phaeton, & then went into the "At homes," for an hour or so.'[18] In the close, gossipy world of Calcutta, David's disrespectable escapades were probably not as anonymous as he intended.

Throughout David's adult life, his obesity, habits, and the treatments for his frequent ailments weakened his body. He frequently consulted British doctors about his venereal diseases and also his skin conditions, including frequent boils on his legs and face that took years to heal. One of his most trusted physicians in Calcutta was Dr George Craigie, brother of Captain Patrick Craigie (whom David had known well in Meerut and who had now transferred to Calcutta; Patrick Craigie's step-daughter, the future Lola Montez, had already left for Britain, although David would later meet her for the first time in Paris at the height of her notoriety). At one time, David agreed to rent rooms in Dr Craigie's Calcutta home.[19] When facing legal difficulties, David sought his advice: 'he seems to be a regular man of the world, and on whose opinion I sh go much'.[20] In all, David gladly gave Dr Craigie 1,000 Rupees for his many treatments, for serving as a trustee in his legal affairs, but also 'more for his attention than anything else'.[21]

Not content with only one course of medications, David consulted other doctors, including James Ranald Martin (later his warder in London). David also self-medicated promiscuously. David's favorite therapeutic drugs included Morrison's patent pills; these came in two sorts, Number One and Number Two, consisting of different proportions of bitter apple (*Citrullus Colocynthis*), gamboges (a yellow resin), aloes, cream of tartar, and ginger. As homeopathic medicine, the pills were supposed to be taken in small doses, but David instead often quaffed twenty of them at a time, which produced powerful purging of his bowels. (Indeed, in 1834 in England, an intentional overdose of these pills had been used for murder.[22]) Other medications to which David was subjected by the many doctors he hired included mercury, blister plasters, hot-cupping, copious bleeding, and leeches. We can only speculate about the cumulative effects on David's body and mind of such a plethora of diseases and untherapeutic treatments.

The complex cultural environment of early nineteenth-century Calcutta, proved difficult for David to navigate successfully. Some Europeans there attributed to him an inferior biological racial identity, more strongly than ever before in his experience, disrespecting him as 'Black' and, for the first time, telling him so to his face. In Meerut, Delhi, and Sardhana, he had been the heir apparent to a principality, distanced by his origins and Catholicism from the British but not explicitly called racially distinct from them. In Calcutta, however, he recorded his discomfort at his first explicitly racial insult. A resentful European woman (of apparently middle or lower class) confronted him saying: 'O you blk bgr, if it was not for your money, no European would speak to you.'[23] This remark David both noted and also obscurely contextualised by marginalizing the speaker: 'I am very much struck by Jane's saying ['black bugger/beggar'] (who is not on good terms with me, for she can't make rice milk, but the fact is I don't like her)'. In public, David occasionally felt that every European was staring at him: 'to a concert (& all the ladies, wives, &c. of tradesmen), were pointing at me, never having seen me before'.[24]

Wherever he travelled, David always sustained his interest in Indian literature, carrying Persian and Urdu books with him. He endeared himself to Dr Burlini, Librarian of the Asiatic Society of Bengal, by donating the Begum Sombre's copy of the poetic collection of Persian poet Sadi 'always kept by H. H.'s bedside' and a rare early manuscript of that poet's *Gulistan*.[25]

David had became famous enough that he could read published accounts of how the British regarded him. For example, David's frequent guest in Meerut and Delhi, and fellow Freemason, Thomas Bacon, had written his own account of the Begum and David in his 1837 two volume *First Impressions and Studies from Nature in Hindostan; Embracing an Outline of the Voyage to Calcutta, and Five Years' Residence in Bengal and the Doab, from 1831–1836*. Learning that he had been described in print, David eagerly anticipated reading Bacon's book: 'I was much gratified to hear that Bacon, of the Horse Artillery, had spoken of me in his work...'[26] But, when he finally bought a copy, he read: David 'is a man of enormous bulk, though not more than five-and-twenty years of age, and though his complexion is very dark, he has a fine open countenance, expressive of mildness and intelligence. In disposition he is kind, and as generous as daylight; and he is a very general favourite with all who know him.'[27] Bacon also criticised the quality of the hospitality that he had received from David. David, apparently disappointed by this decidedly mixed portrayal, tersely noted in his diary: 'Read Mr. Bacon's 2nd volume, in wh he makes mention of me'.[28]

David's wealth made him attractive to some Europeans in Calcutta as a host. In May 1837, he was invited to join the fashionable 'Picnic Club'. He was surprised and skeptical, expecting some 'trick to shove me in "nolens volens"'. Indeed, he was soon instructed that his inauguration required him to pay for 'a large party at the Town Hall' due to, as he put it, 'the farce of my being entd into the Pic-nic Club'.[29]

Also complex were David's attitudes toward Calcutta's elite Indians, whom he treated with both reserve and sympathy. The Eden sisters invited Indian royalty and other prominent men to their parties along with David. While he prided himself on his own proper European sartorial expertise, many other invitees chose Indian dress or adopted European garb imperfectly, which David disparaged (as did many Britons). Conversely, David considered his own mastery of sophisticated Persian as the criterion for rating elite Indians. Reflective of these dual standards, David remarked that at the Eden sisters' drawing room he 'saw many natives well dressed, but without kumurbunds, some of them, wh looked very disrespectful. There was a Baboo, who pretends to be, I am told, a very clever man. I introduced myself to him, and talked to him in Persian, wh he talks pretty fair.'[30] If the leading Indian families of the Bengal Renaissance made overtures to include him in their movement, he made no mention of it in his diary or surviving letters.

Other exiled Indian princes, however, approached David, possibly as a source of moral support. David's own sense of alienation among elite Britons elevated his empathy but also wariness toward these other displaced royalty. For example, he both reached out to the pensioned sons of the late Tipu Sultan of Mysore in private but also felt uncomfortable with their overly familiar association with him in public. He presented one of the Begum's valuable antique copies of the *Quran* to Mysore Prince Gholam Muhammad, a man a dozen years David's senior. They also spoke comfortably in both Urdu and English together (Gholam Muhammad would follow his elder brother, Jamh ood-Deen, and David to London, arriving in 1854).[31] But at the formal Victoria Ball in Calcutta's Town Hall, David noted that Prince Gholam Muhammad 'tucked his arm in mine... I was not at all flattered. In the same manner, another of the Princes came up to me & said, "Pray sir, what o'clock?" imaging that wd lead to an acquaintance; poor devils, I dare say they feel it, they, like myself, are either sitting by themselves or walking alone.'[32] Similarly, after visiting a Parsi merchant, Rustamji, David noted 'he keeps a splendid house; but he is, like myself, not sociable with the Europeans, though he tries, like myself, to do his best.'[33]

In Seamy Calcutta

David also explored Calcutta's more sordid neighborhoods and rowdier people. Only two days after he placed Hoosna and Dominga in their Hooghly house, he began to cruise Calcutta's streets, looking for a 'decent-looking' woman from the legendary Calcutta demimonde to pick up and provide him with new sensual experiences.[34] Yet, he had difficulty determining how far up the social hierarchy he could go, so he tested which women were sexually available to him and which were not.

Unlike Moogloo, the courtesans and sex-workers of Calcutta that David paid remained nameless in his diary. When these women were not Indian, he referred to them by their ethnicity. In Calcutta's ethnic hierarchy, Armenian and Jewish women stood above many Indians, and he routinely preferred to hire their bodies.[35] But David at first approached English women hesitantly. He recorded: 'Saw a beautiful English girl at Mrs Maxwell's, in Bow Bazar, but she would not agree; saw her again at the theatre in the eveng'.[36] When he had sex for the first time with this woman, he did so on the urging of a European companion, noting carefully: 'he made me shag her; I believe she is the first European I have touched'.[37] Yet, he later hired various women, apparently including Europeans, at Mrs Maxwell's and Mother Brooke's, houses of ill-repute.[38]

In these unsavory incidents, his own identity became highly contested. He partied along with British men, but found that he had to be more discreet about his sexual practices than he had hitherto, trying to disguise who he was so as to escape public censure. He had several court cases ongoing, for which he felt he needed the good will of British judges. Calcutta newspapers delighted in exposés. David recognized that his relations with sex-workers were dangerous, but he felt his wealth and cleverness empowered him over them. He recorded that one day on the street, he 'saw a beautiful young maiden "taleem korowing" [literally 'greeting'] who I think I will make a bargain for'.[39] He then purchased her virginity from her madam: 'I went to the maiden girl's, where I had lots of fun, & after giving her 100 Rs, according to their bargain, found her to be a true [virgin] one…' Thereupon, he arranged a retainer of 100 Rupees monthly for further sex with her. David clearly commodified this woman, never mentioning her name but rather identifying her only by her purchased virginity. He also had a mixed sense about identifying himself to her and her madam. He wanted to use the prestige of Sardhana but feared giving them the power over him of accurate knowledge of his identity: 'they did not know me, tho' they called me once Sombre Begum's vakeel [agent]'. Ten days later, he reported that he went to her house but 'was told she was in menses; but I know it to be a trick, as she did not appear, for they want 100 Rs more than what I had promised for the month'.[40] To prove his power, he grabbed 'four gold jewels' from the madam of the house and started to leave 'with the hopes of inducing her to let me have another trial' with the young woman he had paid for. The women of the house followed him into the street, yelling at him, and had their watchmen stop his carriage '& one of them went to call the police jem[ada]r, when I gave up my booty before his arrival, & got my release'.

In addition to having an arrangement with the local police, another power these specific sex-workers had over David was the threat of scandal. Since his first visit, these women had learned his full identity, as he discovered to his dismay. He admitted 'Perhaps it was better that I did not bring it [the jewels he had taken] with me, for as they know me now, & my name also, they might have taken further steps about it'. On his return the next week, the 'd—d bitches had Chowkedars [watchmen] to pukkerlao [seize] me in their house, but I fortunately did nothing on which they could lay hold of me. So on coming down they saw that they had failed, so began to abuse me.'[41] Thereafter, David seems to have given up on further visits to these particular prostitutes, who kept the rest of his money he had paid in advance for their young woman's sexual services. While he was never overtly disciplined by the British colonial authorities for his sexual activities, many of them held his behavior to be excessively egregious.

Among the young men with whom David caroused most vigourously was twenty-year-old Sir Charles Metcalfe Ochterlony, the part-Indian grandson and heir of the late Delhi Resident, Sir David Ochterlony (Begum Sombre's friend and George Dyce's patron and putative relative). Although David and Charles were fellow Freemasons, they met first by chance as David was paying his respects to various British dignitaries soon after his arrival in Calcutta. While David politely mentioned his own connection with David Ochterlony, thus honouring Charles' grandfather 'to whom I told him the great obligations I was under', Charles Ochterlony appeared on first meeting 'very cold' toward David.[42]

Charles and David had comparable proportions of Indian and European ancestry but their upbringing and careers had been quite different. Unlike David, Charles Ochterlony had gone to Scotland, aged four, and been formally educated and enculturated at the Edinburgh Academy. There, he had been a classmate of Lieutenant Hercules Skinner (also a man of mixed ancestry well known to David). Despite Charles's part-Indian ancestry, his family had sufficient influence to obtain an appointment for him in the Company's civil service, and he passed through the East India Company's college at Haileybury. When he and David met, Charles was officially Assistant Magistrate and Collector of Ghazipur, the second highest ranking British official in that district. David had recently passed Ghazipur on his way down the Ganges, half way between Allahabad and Patna. But Charles had become disenchanted with serving in the Company's administration and left his post. Thus, they came together from opposite sides of the colonial frontier: David from an annexed principality, Charles from the Company's annexing administration. When David met Charles, he had just applied for leave and was awaiting approval to depart for Britain (as it turned out, never to return to India).

After they had repeatedly encountered each other at various dinners and theatres, they began to appreciate their mutual interests, common background, and became ever more friendly. Within a few months, Charles was sleeping in David's rooms, often after long and exhausting nights at Mother Brooke's and other brothels. Soon, it was Charles, although nearly a decade younger, who led David ever deeper into bouts of heavy gambling and other carousing: 'Shameful to say, did not go to church... but that fellow Sir Charles, took me to another place of a quite difft nature'.[43] David particularly appreciated that Charles 'always gives me the preference' of the women available in the brothel that night; David, however, almost always ended up paying everyone's bill.[44] In Charles' company, David's excalating gambling debts, running to hundreds of rupees each night, shocked even him, given their magnitude, but he addictively found it impossible to refuse an invitation to cards, billiards, or any other hazard: 'Young Och[terlony] goes out everyday now with me, he is a standing dish, & then at night again as usual...played at billiards & cards again, & lost a great deal. If I don't stop this, I am a ruined man'.[45] They agreed to share a rented house with other young men of their ilk. 'I & Charles, of course, together; he is a good boy; I like him, & probably will do something for him before I go to England'.[46]

Originally recommended by Dr Craigie as a ten-day pleasure cruise to restore David's health after a serious illness, he sailed to Saugor Island in late July 1837. Instead of recuperating, he instead almost continually gambled and drank with Charles Ochterlony and other cronies. Aboard the same ship, but condemningly aloof from their immoral company, was Trevelyan, who pitied David for being so obviously taken advantage of by his companions. David recognised 'Trevelyan cd not have had a great opinion of us, for we played cards all day long, & as the devil wd have it, more so on Sunday than on any other day'.[47]

Trevelyan claimed to have futilely tried to prepare David for social survival in Britain: 'I was so strongly impressed with [David]'s unfitness for European Society, and, considering his ignorance and great fortune, I felt such serious apprehension that he would be preyed upon, as it was understood he had already been at Calcutta, that I endeavoured, so far as the opportunities of my intercourse with him permitted, to prepare him for the new kind of life on which he was entering; and with this view I gave to him a selected list of books, descriptive of England and English Society, which I recommended him to read during his voyage'.[48] Yet David rejected Trevelyan's patronizing counsel and attempt at edification, directly refuting his account: 'As for Sir Charles Trevelyan lending me any books to improve my mind with, as he says, I remember the only time I received any books from him [was]... on leaving the boat, Mr Trevelyan offered me the loan of a book... "Glegg's Life of Warren Hastings". On arriving at Calcutta, I just glanced over the book, and returned it to him.'[49] As David struggled to find his way among these competing Calcutta cultures, he also faced legal barriers to his personal and financial freedom.

Legal Entanglements

From soon after he arrived in Calcutta, David entangled himself, and was enmeshed by others, in multiple legal battles. One set of these cases were his claims against the East India Company over the three issues of its seizure of Badshahpur, and of the Sardhana armaments, and about the Company's failure to pay the pensions to the Begum's dependents as it had promised on several occasions.[50] These lawsuits that would linger on for decades, long after David's death. Another set of suits were instigated by or against David over his inheritance from the Begum, brought by his father, his co-executor, General Clements Brown, and others. David finally settled these on the eve of his departure for England.

In addition to Charles Prinsep, David quickly hired several other rival teams of lawyers, including Mr Cochrane, Esq. Intending to spur them on, he constantly but inconsistently intervened, admonishing his lawyers by threats, insults, and new demands—'I wish I could bully them'.[51] Further, to David the cases were matters of personal pride that he did not really expect to be resolved quickly. Yet, the actual money at stake was vast and vital to his future. He often disingenuously played one set of his lawyers off against another, making empty threats of dismissal, which he never intended to carry out, believing thereby he could coerce them into working harder. He was sure that his many lawyers were deceiving him and secretly working for his enemies.

Among those who brought cases against him was General Brown, his co-executor of the Begum's will. David resented Brown, having previously tried to delete him from the *hibbanama* and will, which deletions the Begum explicitly vetoed.[52] On his part, the elderly Brown expected David to pay both their legal fees and make over the money due to other beneficiaries, since he largely controlled the estate's funds. When David initially refused, Brown sued him and had him arrested.[53] After much legal disputation and expense, David finally acquiesced on the cusp of his final departure from Calcutta; Brown died two months later at age 72.

Far more ominously, George Dyce filed several suits against David, the most substantial one for over 1,400,000 Rupees of the Begum's estate. David mistakenly thought that his many lawyers would protect him. Instead, late one Saturday evening (25 February 1837) two bailiffs, acting on Dyce's plaint, suddenly seized David. They threatened him with imprisonment until the following Monday at the earliest, when a judge would take the bench to hear his plea for bail. Rather than spend two shameful and uncomfortable nights in Calcutta's unsavoury jail, David persuaded the arresting officers to let him pause at the nearby house where Reverend Henry Fisher happened to be visiting. Immediately, Fisher sent off to rouse David's lawyers, who eventually located Henry Prinsep at the theatre. Prinsep sent an urgent messenger to awaken the Accountant General, who then had his assistant personally go to the Company's treasury and produce an official receipt for the requisite security of 1,493,400 Rupees using David's Company bonds as collateral. Dr Craigie also used his influence to help David escape being jailed. Through this tenuous string of personal interventions, David managed by 1:00 a.m. to secure his release, although he temporarily lost control over much of his fortune since it was held by the sheriff as his bond. On David's relieved return to his rented house early that morning, 'I spat upon Col. D[yce]'s door as I passed'.[54]

Seeing several overlapping conspiracies around him, David blamed his lawyers, imagining that they had wanted to tie up his money and publicly embarrass him for their own nefarious purposes: 'I begin to be afraid that my lawyers are not very honest; they can't help it, probably, for they could never have had such a client as myself. My arrest is announced in to-day's "[Calcutta] Courier"' newspaper, edited by George Prinsep, a brother of Persian Secretary Henry and lawyer Charles.[55] David. utterly convinced of the obvious truth of his own side and seeking to publicise what he considered to be the absolute absurdity of the cases against him, had fifty copies of Dyce's charges against him printed up and sent to influential people, characteristically not realizing how counterproductive this publicity would be to himself.[56] Throughout David's entire stay in Calcutta, he and his father continually squabbled in the courts as well as in the streets. Each made implausible accusations against the other, to the extent that David concluded 'he is mad, no doubt of it'.[57] Yet, David also admitted to himself that he was vindictive toward his father, but he also justified that vindictiveness: 'tho' God has given me more than enough, if I know how to manage it; but I am not happy; & God forbid that this should be owing to my conduct to the old gentleman; his to me has been a million times worse'.[58]

Divesting His Concubines

Before David could proceed with his life in European society, he felt he had to dispose of his long-term mistresses, Hoosna Baae and Dominga, and sole surviving child, Penelope. These women were vestiges of his Sardhana past; he felt they would not be appropriate companions for him during his new life in Europe. Yet he could not easily abandon his control over them and their bodies. Significantly, Hoosna and Dominga, who had been rivals in Sardhana, came together in Calcutta for their mutual benefit and support. Both women faced a common situation of removal by David from their home and support-base in Sardhana, and of unwanted (and unhappy) marriages at his arrangement. Not perhaps comprehending their fellow feeling and companionship for each other, David repeatedly noted with surprise on his tense visits to their respective homes that he found the two women in each other's company. Thus, these women had networks beyond David's ken and only indirectly evident to us in his diary.

Until nearly the end of his time in Calcutta, David only incompletely relinquished Hoosna. As a Muslim of lower social status than Dominga, Hoosna proved by one measure easier for David to dispose of. Yet, his greater personal desire for her also made it harder for him to let her go. In early March 1837, after three months together in Calcutta, David arranged a pension and passage for her back to Sardhana, and even sent her off by boat, only to change his mind despairingly several times and then abruptly summon her back the next day, feeling he could not live without her. Yet, since he believed he could not take her to Europe with him either, two weeks later David arranged for her to marry a Muslim of her own status. One of David's retainers, a twenty-five-year-old *khansaman* (steward) named Sayid al-Din alias Sheikh Edoo, who had worked for David for half-a-dozen years and whom he had originally intended to bring in his suite to Europe, proved willing to marry her, in exchange for appropriate compensation. They negotiated a pension, first of 150 Rupees monthly then, after further negotiation, 200 Rupees.[59]

Hoosna and Sheikh Edoo married on 25 March 1837. But David could still not bring himself to give her up. On her marriage night, David vainly tried to consol himself by hiring a sex-worker. The next night he lingered in the street outside the newlywed's house: it made my 'heart heave' to observe 'the light, where her bed is now; in my time this room was kept dark, as we slept in the verandah'.[60] Five days later, and periodically over the next month, David had sex with her again. Hoosna insisted that David escort her in public, openly displaying her continued association with him from his carriage, 'much against my will, but H. insisted', in exchange for her continued sexual favours.[61] David also considered promoting Edoo to superintend David's properties in Sardhana; David did not trust Solaroli but must have realised that he could not trust Edoo to guard his interests either. David, confiding 'Miserere mihi' and 'Misery; mortification; horror' in his diary, paid Edoo 2,000 Rupees in gold in compensation for this abuse of the marriage contract. Nonetheless, David continued his adulterous relationship for months, frequently noting in his diary how miserable he felt, both at his impending loss of Hoosna and also at his weakness in visiting her in her married state.

Dominga, as a Catholic and probably of part or all European ancestry, received somewhat different treatment. David initially proposed sending her back to Meerut with a pension (conditional on her not marrying without his permission). Since there was a smallpox epidemic there, however, she preferred to remain across the Hooghly River with a monthly pension of 60 Rupees, under the shelter of the Catholic Father Gondoli.[62] David insisted that he retain custody of their child, Penelope, but that he not be publicly seen with either of them. Then he decided, with her concurrence, that she should marry, as was appropriate to her status, a European. The priest located Mr Leyding, someone about David's own age and 'a gentleman earning 400 per month, but [he] wants cash in advance' of 10,000 Rupees in order to marry Dominga.[63] After extensive negotiations, Leyding got his money, while Dominga received a pension of 150 Rupees monthly, custody of Penelope until David returned from Europe, and various other gifts; she married Leyding on 28 April 1837.

Dominga's marriage also proved unhappy. David continued to visit, demand attention, and bestow costly gifts on her that must have added to the domestic tensions of the newly wedded couple.[64] When he saw Dominga and Leyding at the Town Hall concert, he felt somewhat resentful, even though David had procured their tickets for them. Indeed, throughout the five months of her troubled marriage, Dominga was often unwell, evidently from emotional and physical abuse from her new husband.

Touring Southeast Asia and China

Even as his private life was reaching a frantic pitch of debauchery, and despite the rising number and delicate state of his many lawsuits,

Map 4: India, Southeast Asia, and China

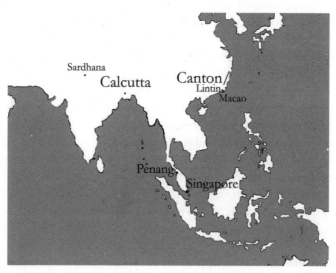

David determined to tour the Straits Settlements and China. Calcutta exported 2,320 metric tonnes of opium annually into China, so many ships from Calcutta sailed that way. Further, Dr Craigie encouraged this extended trip into the sea air and away from unhealthy Calcutta for the sake of David's health.

From a legal perspective, this was an inopportune time for him to leave Calcutta, but David was determined. His lawyers were unanimous in counseling against absenting himself, while the courts made him post a huge security bond, which cost him 50,000 Rupees in legal fees. Nonetheless, he felt it a matter of pride for him to go, demonstrating his independence from his many perceived enemies: 'I wd not please them, and so I determined on giving security & not leaving my passage... I wd rather lose 50,000 Rs than to gratify them... they cannot stop me from going.'[65] Further, he resolved to travel virtually unaccompanied, attended only by a hired Portuguese (or part Portuguese) servant, John, a man unknown to him but who had experience working for British gentlemen. He boarded the ship *George IV* on 20 August 1837.

David hoped the long trip east would restore his abused physical and financial health by ending the careening cycle of carousing and gambling he felt otherwise powerless to halt. As it turned out, David discovered philosophically the very day he left '...clapped again, I have had a good run with[ou]t getting it since I came to Calcutta, so I have no excuse to grumble'.[66] Thus, he spent the entire voyage being painfully treated for gonorrhea. Further, some of his most ardent British gambling companions shipped with him, hoping to continue to tap into his largess. He patronizingly paid his fellow passengers' local expenses, but resented their ingratitude.

Aboard ship, David had to position himself socially. This was the first extended period of time in which there were no Indians or people of mixed ancestry present except himself (excluding servants and seamen, whom the passengers did not count as part of their society). Although determined to make a good impression on the high ranking among his British fellow passengers, his usual habits got the better of him. On first boarding, 'tho I had not drunk much, but I abused my fellows [servants] loudly, not knowing that Mr and Mrs [Andrew] Reid on board, whose good opinion I was very anxious to get, for wh I have done the very thing contrary'.[67] Soon David was relieved and also disappointed to learn Reid was not a high official in the Company's civil service but rather an uncovenanted salt agent, much lower administratively and socially than David initially assumed.

David rented the prestigious and luxurious stern cabin of the *George IV* for 700 Rupees. After a quiet first week due to widespread seasickness among his fellow passengers, his cabin turned into the site of almost unceasing card playing: 'I have got into a very bad habit, wh I cannot break myself of'.[68] As usual, David lost heavily and, in the rare instances when he won, proved unable to collect what was owed him. He exchanged heated words with one of these gamblers, expecting to be challenged to a duel over this matter of honour: 'What a satisfaction wd it be to me to lose my life for the paltry sum of 5 or 600 Rs; but I wd rather lose it in a gentlemanly way than to be imposed upon. I reflected a good deal on it at bed.'[69] Eventually, even David became bored with the constant cards, much to the annoyance of his avaricious gaming companions.

Instead, David, reflecting his own ambivalent cultural interests, amused himself with Persian poetry and also European mathematical puzzles: 'such is my mania for arithmetic; but if it was not for that, I don't know what I would have done'.[70] Further, he grieved for his late Begum Sombre. Grappling with her memory, David consigned to the sea her official seal and also one of her teeth, which she had preserved among her mementoes and entrusted to him.[71] News of the death of King William IV and accession of Queen Victoria put him thinking about his own projected future: 'I wonder who her husband will be! & whether that will be in my favour in preference to the old King when I go to England'.[72]

During the long days aboard, so removed from his prior hectic life, he considered his past and future, reading over back years of his diary, recalling formative events in his life, and resolving to learn from his past errors. In this self-reflective spirit, he wrote up his third will during the voyage, giving most of his wealth to his sister Ann or, should she have no children, to Georgiana, with 500,000 Rupees to his own sole surviving child Penelope on condition she take the name Dyce Sombre in perpetuity.[73] He calculated exactly how long it would take his heirs to double his fortune to 10,000,000 Rupees (a million pounds sterling) if they practised fiscal discipline better than he had done hitherto.

After three weeks at sea, they reached Penang, the first place outside of India he had ever seen. This port was administered by the East India Company as part of the Straits Settlements, but it contained very diverse peoples and cultures. While David noted the unfamiliarly large number of Chinese workers and environment, he was most engaged by the French Catholic mission. Anxious to make connections and establish his own status, he asked the Father Superior 'if they had heard of the great Princess of Hindoostan, meaning her late Highness, and he immedly told me that he had, & talked of some of her charities'.[74] David especially admired the Catholic nunnery for orphan girls and the college there, thinking he should create a similar educational and religious centre at Sardhana: 'when these can support themselves, why should not the College of Sirdhanah flourish also, wh has friends [benefactors like himself]?'[75] Thus, in contrast to his uncongenial relationship to the fissiparous Catholic hierarchy of Calcutta, he felt more comfortable visiting Catholics in Penang.

Reaching Singapore, another of the Company's Straits Settlements, nine days later, he had his first exposure to a predominantly Chinese society. He noted with surprise, but had little interest in sampling, their street cuisine, as he understood it: 'they first begin by taking a small china cup of weak gin (China stuff), & then dipped also every morsel into this liquor, which they devoured most greedily; there was stewed pork & fowl, & some vegetables, which were dressed in their own fashion'.[76] He also visited the disappointing local 'Catholic priest, for whom I had brought packets of letters from Penang, & found another gentleman still more brutal looking, in a dirty hole, quite the contrast of Penang, & I was quite disgusted with them'. The priest's alleged familiarity with the Begum's fame, however, was gratifying and David made another donation for a mass in her name. Rather than try to find an Indian community, or explore the Chinese one further, he made a round of social calls on the Europeans to whom he had letters of introduction. He particularly noted those of mixed ancestry, 'country-born' as he called them, who were acquainted with similar families including the Skinners. Further, somewhat subdued by his current gonorrhea treatment, he only halfheartedly looked for women but found none sufficiently attractive.

Disembarking at the Portuguese colony of Macao, David for the first time in his life entered a land not ruled by the British, and therefore where different rules of race and law applied. As David described it: 'Here is a Portuguese Govt, who presides over the Europeans & country-born also; in fact, every one who uses European clothes; a mandarin over others; not like our country, where, till within late, we were disgraced for the sins of others, & in some respects still suffer'.[77] Here, David seems to have identified himself among the 'we' people whose mixed parentage unjustly caused dishonour in India despite their European comportment. He also sought out Catholics and found gratification at their putative recognition of the Begum and her charities. He again made donations to sponsor masses for her soul.

His two weeks in Canton and in Lintin, the nearby island and major European opium importing port, did not impress him. Tensions were high over relations between illegal British opium importers, their Chinese collaborators, and the Chinese imperial government that, at least nominally, sought to halt this drug smuggling trade. Indeed, the first Anglo-Chinese Opium war would break out less than two years later. David did not concern himself with these larger political conflicts but rather noted more mundane matters. Although he expected to find the women of China exotic, he was instead dismayed by their condition, especially the bound feet and long fingernails he observed on some of the female elite as they passed in sedan chairs. Given the constant genital pain and disability of his venereal disease, including his rising bubo, he was in no condition to explore Chinese culture further. He concluded: 'I am quite diapp[ointe]d; I wish I hadn't come'.[78]

Rather than carry on, David determined to return to India as quickly as he could, sailing via Singapore. He passed days aboard by solving arithmetic problems from Walkingham's *Promiscuous Questions* and listening to his two music boxes, one of which played Yankee Doodle.[79] He also contemplated his uncertain future: 'I dream & think of nothing else now but getting back to Calcutta; settling my affairs as much as I can;... & then going to Europe... I hope all will be right, & that I shall be protected...'[80]

Departing India

On 12 December 1837, a week before David's twenty-ninth birthday and just four months after he had left Calcutta, he returned. He calculated the expense of the trip as 5,100 Rupees, substantial but considerably less than if he had stayed put (indeed, his first four months in Calcutta cost him 28,832 Rupees). Some of the objects of his trip had been achieved. He had observed the Catholic communities and colonial cultures of Southeast Asia and China. He had nearly completed his treatment of gonorrhea (the large bubo in his groin burst the very day he returned). Finally, he no longer felt the insatiable desire to gamble wildly, although his sexual drive gradually returned. He now determined to settle his affairs in India quickly and set out for his new life in England. David only remained in Calcutta for two months before he left India, as it happened, forever.

Even as David was rushing back to Calcutta, parts of his past had finished while others required closure. He had received a packet of letters in Singapore that included news of three deaths. His maternal grandmother, the mentally weak wife of Aloysius Reinhardt, so long in the care of Begum Sombre, finally passed away in Sardhana. She evidently played little active role in David's life, his only surviving mention of her being a terse 'I also recd my letters from Solaroli, wh also informed me of the death of the old lady'.[81] Her passing thus had no financial or emotional repercussions. Indeed, a letter giving news of the death of Mughal Emperor Akbar Shah, 'the poor old man', evoked a tad more of David's sympathy.[82]

From other letters in the same bundle, he had also learned of the 'death of poor Dominga' from tuberculosis.[83] This news, about which he claimed prescience, reopened a painful problem. After he reached Calcutta, David felt he had to bury her and also deal firmly with her acquisitive husband, Leyding. Dominga, in her will, had left her modest estate to her one-year-old daughter, Penelope, with David as guardian. But Leyding, as her legal husband—however briefly and abusively— also claimed this estate, including substantial properties which he alleged she owned in Sardhana.[84] David's own mixed attitudes about control over Dominga, her corpse, and her legacy proved hard for him to reconcile. He had bought Leyding as a groom and therefore felt empowered over him, but because Leyding was European, David felt constrained against pushing him too far. Conversely, Leyding repeatedly threatened to publicise David's shameful part in this sordid arrangement at a time when David's other legal problems were peaking.

Eventually, after many reciprocal threats, David and Leyding split her possessions with David paying the cost of her burial at the Portuguese Church in Moorghatta.[85] David later retold the incident in a way that he appeared the hero, and also almost the victim of both Dominga and her husband:

[Leyding] turned her out of his house a short time after her marriage, & if it was not for me the poor thing would have been robbed and plundered; but, as he was the choice of her own, of course she could not blame me. I wanted her to marry Villa [David's European agent in Calcutta], who I must acknowledge is a prudent steady man, & I think if she had married him she would have been alive to this day, & happy together. Well, on my return from Canton, Mr Leyding laid claim to the whole of her property, which I was willing to give... not that he had a right to it, for when dying she had made a Will in favour of her child [Penelope], & appointed me as guardian... but I wanted to avoid mixing my name with a fellow like him... & as I could not bring upon myself to let her remains lie there, & be eaten by dogs and crows, so I had a decent monument put over her, for which I had to give the Padre 600 Rs.[86]

In this way, David sought to justify his own role, even after Dominga's death. He gave some of Dominga's jewelry, for which he had fought Leyding so hard, to his surviving mistress, Hoosna.

David also finally settled with Hoosna, regretfully dispatching her and her husband, Edoo, back to Sardhana.[87] Not surprisingly, they did not have a cordial marriage; they eventually separated, with each of them receiving a separate life pension from David. For weeks after her departure, he bemoaned his own loneliness and romanticised memories of Hoosna.

As soon as David returned to his old Calcutta lodgings, Sir Charles Ochterlony and his other carousing companions insistently drew him into their games. Reluctantly, David sporadically succumbed and partook of their gambling, losing 1,200 Rupees in three nights, for example. But David no longer had his former frenzied desire to bet. Further, he rented a separate house for himself in Alipore, near central Calcutta. He nonetheless remained fond of Charles, presenting him with an expensive phaeton (sadly damaged by a crash while David was driving).

Sir Charles Ochterlony finally left Calcutta soon after David, sailing to Scotland in 1839. There he eventually reformed himself; he and David evidently never met again. Although he was convicted in 1843 of 'criminal information' for challenging of a local landlord to a duel, he then rose rapidly to respectability, holding office as Magistrate of Forfarshire, marrying well, and leaving his five children a distinguished local reputation. David, whose life passed so differently despite their similar origins, nonetheless tried to leave Ochterlony £2,000 in his will, but this was later disallowed by British courts.

David also interacted with other men from his past, and future. For a time, Comte Ventura, who was visiting Calcutta, took over Charles Ochterlony's rooms in David's rented house. Ventura went out of his way to entertain David, inviting him for carriage rides, breakfasts, dinners, Indian-style nautchs, European-style balls, and Catholic church services. Ventura confided that he was about to bring his fortune and daughter to Europe, having pensioned off and left behind in the Punjab the Indian woman whom he had presented in Sardhana as his wife. Ventura justified himself to David by asserting that this woman was not really his wife, having only had an Armenian priest mumble a mock marriage ceremony to placate her, a ritual that Ventura did not consider legally or morally binding.[88] Ventura also enticed David to resume his sexual interest in dancing women.

David slowly recovered from his venereal disease. Dr Craigie had made a painful series of deep incisions and the insertion of a silver tube and seton to drain his bubo. David's weakened condition did not prevent him from recommencing his promiscuous intercourse, although it did slow him down a bit and he was occasionally subject to priapism. For instance, at one a Calcutta nautch: 'All 8 or 9 sets [of dancers] are not worth looking at even, with the exception of one Armenian girl, who I had known before (but not as a dancing girl) in Imambary-lane. Old Ventura even was cocky upon her, & took hold of her hands. I sent for her, but she refused; saying, it was not Calcutta custom to do this when they came to dance; probably it was better, in the [painful genital] state I am in.'[89] Further, as his larger legal cases climaxed, he sought to avoid distracting scandal. Ventura, in addition to presenting himself as a model for how David should treat women, also joined many other old acquaintances in exerting himself to convince David to accept reconciliatory notes from Dyce. David and Ventura would meet again in Paris, with the older man again providing patronizing advice that eventually led to bitter battles between them.

To strengthen his introduction into British society, David solicited and received letters of introduction from Governor-General Lord Auckland, for Sir James Rivett Carnac (Chairman of the Court of Directors), Sir John Cam Hobhouse (President of the Board of Control), and Sir Alexander Johnston (member of the Judicial Committee of the Privy Council specializing in colonial litigation, as well as a founder of the Royal Asiatic Society).[90] These letters suggest how Auckland regarded David, yet were couched in terms that David would accept since they were not sealed and David read them. Indeed, David copied the one to Carnac into his diary:

My Dear Sir,

Mr Dyce Sombre is about to proceed upon a tour of pleasure and instruction to England, & has earnestly requested me to give him one or two letters of introduction, so that he may not be more of a stranger in a strange land than is absolutely necessary. His history will be familiar to you. His father was a favorite with the late Begum, & he has been the person selected by her to inherit her immense personal property.

I am little acquainted with him personally, but I have heard him well spoken of for his excellent, tho' perhaps too easy, disposition, & it will be an act of kindness in you if you showed him favour upon his arrival in London, & so guide him as that his residence in Europe shall be useful & not injurious to him. This is the more desirable as he may probably return to India, & apply his wealth & his experience to the advantage of the country in wh[ich] his landed property lies.[91]

Auckland's expectations proved unjustified: David never returned to India and his life in England proved highly injurious to his fortune and health.

David also wanted to travel to England in the company of an influential man. He thought about asking to accompany overland the notorious adulterer and duelist, James Thomas, 7th Earl of Cardigan (who would later lead the famous 'charge of the Light Brigade' in the Crimean War). Rather than risk rejection from Cardigan, David instead delicately approached Sir Charles Metcalfe. Only when he was sure of Metcalfe's acquiescence, did he cancel his current reservation on one ship, the *Duke of Buccleugh*, at the loss of 2,000 Rupees, and book another on the ship, the *St George*, in which Metcalfe was sailing. Due to his late change of plans, David paid 3,000 Rupees for less comfortable cabins than he had anticipated, only able to reserve three for himself: 'one under the awning for reading-room, 2 below: sleeping and dressing'.[92]

While David decided to take his daughter, Penelope, with him to England, he also wished not to be publicly associated with her. At first, David arranged for them both to sail on the same ship, the *Duke of Buccleugh*, but then reconsidered. David's shifting to Metcalfe's ship thus had the added advantage to him that she would travel separately, on his earlier ship. Since she was less than two years old, she needed someone to look after her. David entrusted her to a British couple he knew slightly, Major Edmund Herring and his wife, whose passage David paid in exchange for their custody of his daughter. Sadly, she died (23 February 1838) just after the *Duke of Buccleugh* set sail, although he would not know about this for many months.

As David's scheduled departure from India approached, he finally fulfilled his long-promised provision for his sisters. Significantly, he chose the tenth anniversary of the failed coup by their father to create the trusts: 130,000 Rupees for Ann and 100,000 Rupees for Georgiana, providing a perpetual income of £500 for the former and then her prospective children and £385 for the latter and her children.[93] David named Dr Drever, Colonel James Skinner, and Major William Sleeman as trustees. In a tender letter which implicitly revealed David's distrust of his brothers-in-law, he entrusted his sisters to Drever's care: 'My Dear Drever, Pray take are of those poor girls; they have no advisers or guardians, and they know so little of the world. I have chosen you to be my representative, for I have confidence in your friendship, and I know you to be a conscientious man. I have no one else to depend on; both Colonel Skinner and Major Sleeman are excellent men, but they are not so near, so I have only you to depend upon, and I have made you guardian of those innocent beings. They have no father or mother to look to; they are both dear in every sense of the word, so you must be to them what I would have been if I was present.'[94]

Immediately, Solaroli demanded both more money and also his own personal control over the capital so that he could return to Italy and purchase a landed estate and title there, rather than leaving his family's share in trust in his wife's name. These demands both the trustees and David rejected, noting Solaroli 'has an eye to better himself, at the expense of my sister; this will never do, if I can help it.' Both David and his advisors, including Dr Craigie, felt that Georgiana, as 'an Asiatic woman', would only be secure 'in the country where she was born'.[95] This essentialist argument about Asiatic versus European natures, genders, and appropriate environments would inform British judgments about David's own later life.

Most of David's many lawsuits arose over rights to the Begum's huge legacy. At this point, David counted twenty concurrent court cases in which he was either defendant or plaintiff.[96] While almost all their mutual acquaintances made strong and repeated efforts to reconcile David with his father, not until nearly the eve of David's departure for England did he finally accept arbitration of their core disputes. David finally capitulated as the eminent Sir Charles Metcalfe took the witness stand to testify.

All David's life he had grown up admiring Metcalfe: as Delhi Resident, acting Governor-General, and then Lt Governor of Agra. We can assume that David knew about Metcalfe's three sons with an Indian woman, boys David's age or slightly younger, although they had been sent early to England for their educations (they would each return to Bengal about the time their father was retiring).[97] David had even joined the dockside crowd welcoming Metcalfe to Calcutta and ostentatiously subscribed 1,000 Rupees for his retirement gift of silver plate.[98] David did not know, evidently, about Metcalfe's damning confidential report about the Reinhardt family and opposing David's claims about Badshahpur, the Sardhana armaments, or the Begum's many pensioners. Therefore, David deferred to Metcalfe's advice, and that of so many others, that he finally settle with his father.

Only two days before David sailed, he agreed to arbitration of his disputes with Dyce. The mutually agreed upon arbiters, Metcalfe and Dr Craigie, quickly made Dyce drop his lawsuits against David in exchange for 1,500 Rupees monthly for life plus 10,000 Rupees cash plus reimbursement for Dyce's substantial lawyers' fees. This was far less than the 1,400,000 Rupees that Dyce had long sought, suggesting

Statue of Sir Charles Metcalfe, by Baily

that Dyce had been obsessively unrealistic about his legal claims for over a decade. Craigie served as trustee, receiving from David 450,000 Rupees in Company promissory notes as the capital from which to draw these funds.[99] Dyce only lived less than two months longer, however, dying (reportedly of cholera) on 4 April 1838. Since Dyce died intestate, each of Dyce's three children received an equal share of his modest estate of 43,845 Rupees (including 15,742 Rupees owing him from David).[100] This left David liberated from the conflict with his father that had lasted virtually since his birth, but he continued to clash with his brother-in-law, Solaroli.

As he packed up to leave Calcutta, David rapidly delegated responsibility for his Indian properties. He paternalistically left money to pay pensions for 76 of his dependents totaling some 900 Rupees. To manage all this, he gave power of attorney to Drever, Sleeman (currently visiting Calcutta), and Solaroli.[101] David's pangs of departure led him to a brief reconciliation with Solaroli on parting for England, but they soon resumed their quarrels by correspondence and when they met again in Europe.

On 15 February 1838, David finally embarked on the steamer that would carry him to his transoceanic vessel, the East Indian ship *St George*. He left India rich but virtually alone, attended by only a single servant, a hitherto unknown man he apparently hired just before his departure. David had expended a considerable portion of his inheritance, through his own dissipation and his gifts to his sisters, but he still had in liquid Company bonds and cash with his agents in India over 4,000,000 Rupees.[102] In addition, he had lands and mansions worth many hundreds of thousands more. He counted in his credit about a million more Rupees due from the Company for Badshahpur and the Sardhana armaments cases (which funds would never be paid during David's lifetime). In all, David's annual cash income of £20,000 put him into the upper brackets among the British elite, but its source reduced its prestige in some British eyes.

Part Two

Europe

6

TO BRITAIN

As soon as David boarded ship early in 1838, he moved away from
much of what he had learned and practised during his first three decades of life as the adopted heir of Begum Sombre. The confined British
company aboard ship conformed to conventions largely alien and
alienating for him, making him acutely conscious that they considered
him 'half-caste' and not fully a man. When he disembarked in England
fifteen weeks later, he started his new life as Dyce Sombre, a character
in many ways unprecedented in European society. Even his clothes had
to be remade since British customs agents seized his Hindustani garb,
while the made in India European-style clothing he had brought with
him proved unfashionable. Thus, he sequentially purchased two
entirely new wardrobes tailored for him in London, the first unsatis-
factorily according to his own ideas of what was suitable, but the
second under the expert instruction of his stylish elite British patron.
Transferring his vast capital into Britain, he explored the limits of what
his wealth would buy. He worked, not always successfully, to construct
a new gentlemanly persona, complete with honourific rank, coat of
arms, and aristocratic English wife.

But many people had difficulties accepting his novel self-representations. Like his British fellow passengers aboard his ship, Europeans
and also Indians in London also found him difficult to categorise. Further, Britons from his past affected his reception in London society, for
worse and better. While some blackballed him from their private club,
others introduced him into aristocratic society. Despite his aspirations
to be European, many found his oriental origins exotically attractive.
Indeed, he received the most personal of credentials when a fashionable English noblewoman quickly accepted his offer of marriage. Yet,

his transition from David Sahib of Sardhana to Colonel Dyce Sombre, son-in-law of Viscount St Vincent, came at considerable cost to all concerned.

Passage to Britain

Sailing from Calcutta to Bristol around south Africa, the East India Company's ship *St George* was an extension of British society. Dyce Sombre was the only person aboard of even part-Indian descent—possibly aside from some of the servants and crew who were virtually invisible to the paying passengers, including him.[1] He felt uncertain and isolated from the twenty-nine other passengers: British officers, officials, doctors, wives, and children. The only ones who knew much about his past were Baron Charles Metcalfe and his long-time private secretary, Lieutenant James Macaulay Higginson; Dyce Sombre rightly sensed that they knew more about him than he felt comfortable with. Further, for the first time in decades, convention required that he defer to the financial patronage of another man—Metcalfe—and not use his own money to purchase attention. Consequently, Dyce Sombre said little, drank and played cards sparingly, constantly feared making further faux pas, and read veiled criticism of himself into much he overheard. Throughout the three-and-a-half-month voyage around the Cape of Good Hope, Dyce Sombre felt excluded from the company of the other passengers and from the surreptitious sexual activity he sensed among them.

As soon as Dyce Sombre embarked, Metcalfe presided in introducing him to the nine British gentleman on the vessel. Awkwardly, Metcalfe did not introduce him to the four British ladies so, although Dyce Sombre dined at the same table with them about one hundred times, he could not bring himself to converse, as he privately bemoaned:

I am losing a hundred per cent. in the eyes of my fellow passengers, from not being able to speak, & I literally sit quiet. The fair sex have all cut me; Mrs H[igginson] never recognised me at all from the beginning, so of course I could not speak to her; Mrs C[urtis] I was never introduced to (at the time when Sir C[harles Metcalfe] introduced me to every body on the poop, the first day, there were no ladies there. Mrs D[ick] I had seen at Lucknow, & she made my acquaintance so far that I take a glass of wine with her every day, & this is the token of my acquaintance with the ladies. As for Mrs F[uller], I was never introduced to her, but having given some paper to her [three] little girls, she spoke to me one day herself, after wh we took wine; but sometimes she takes into her head, & never looks at me. Oh, education, what hast thou not lost to me. I am miserable, & my modesty or shame, wh shall I call it, makes me worst.[2]

Nor did he feel comfortable with the gentlemen. He played whist occasionally but for stakes he considered negligible. Hence, his usual practice of losing extravagantly at cards, which had in the past made acquisitive Britons eager to play with him, here meant that no one wanted him as partner. The consequent lack of wild thrill from gambling, he half hoped, might wean him from his past habits; he vowed 'not to touch a card while I am in Europe' but philosophically admitted from past experience 'how long I will keep this resolution God only knows'.[3]

For the entire voyage, the confined society of Britons made Dyce Sombre feel anomalous. His identity was not clear to him or them, neither European nor Indian, one of the passengers but not full participant in their society, male but not masculine. He thus shrank from social contact: 'generally speaking, they are all cold, because I am an outcaste, alias an 1/2 caste... who am nobody on board'.[4]

Hence, Dyce Sombre spent much time alone in his cabin practising arithmetic (as he had on his return voyage from China). He noted 'I am learning the decimal fractions by myself, by assistance of Hutton, & I am perfect master of vulgar fractions'.[5] 'Hutton' was not a fellow passenger but rather Charles Hutton, author of many popular instructional books including *Compendious Measurer, Being a Brief, Yet Comprehensive, Treatise on Mensuration and Practical Geometry With an Introduction to Decimal and Duodecimal Arithmetic, Adapted to Practice, and the Use of Schools*, first published in 1786 but in its 10th edition by 1829. Nor did Dyce Sombre even relate to his own hired servant enough to mention him in his daily diary.

Throughout the passage, Sir Charles Metcalfe presumed the premier role aboard as social and financial patron over all the passengers, including Dyce Sombre. In order to accompany Metcalfe, Dyce Sombre had hurriedly transferred to the *St George*, at considerable cost monetarily and to the quality of his accommodation. While Metcalfe sat at the head of the communal dining table, Dyce Sombre sat last (apparently due to his late booking). Increasingly over the voyage, Sir Charles behaved in ways that Dyce Sombre found equivocal and distancing. Initially, Dyce Sombre sympathetically projected onto Metcalfe his own sense of loneliness and intermission: 'Poor Sir C., finding himself quite alone, was actually dozing before dinner on his chair; it was a great reflection to me to observe, who had been in the habit of constantly employ for the last 8 and 20 years'.[6] Further, Dyce Sombre noted that only Metcalfe and he, among all the passengers, resisted seasickness. Early in the voyage, Metcalfe graciously offered Dyce Sombre the use of his large collection of reading matter, loaning him a copy of Lord Wellesley's recently published *Dispatches*. But Dyce Sombre hesitated to ask for more books. When he diffidently did, he was made to feel presumptuous by Metcalfe's dismissive private secretary, Higginson, a man three years older than Dyce Sombre but still only a Lieutenant, despite his long proximity to Metcalfe.

Indeed, Dyce Sombre constantly feared a direct personal rebuff from Metcalfe. Uncertain about the etiquette at table, Dyce Sombre initially waited each day until Metcalfe happened to look his way before saluting him with an offer to drink a glass of wine together. After careful observation of Metcalfe's response to his tentative approaches, Dyce Sombre found a time each dinner, 'between the removal of tart & bringing on of cheese', when Metcalfe did not seem to mind Dyce Sombre initiating this toast.[7] But, he also noticed that Metcalfe never called him by proper name, self-reflexively musing: 'perhaps he is puzzled whether to add Mr to it or not'.

In addition to apprehension about how Metcalfe would address him—as a fellow gentleman or not—Dyce Sombre was also unsure of the degree to which Metcalfe and the others considered him a 'native'. Over meals and in casual conversation, passengers frequently contrasted 'us' British colonial rulers with 'them... the native princes'; Dyce Sombre had never quite been included within either class.[8] During one dinnertime conversation about 'natives', someone remarked that 'they' did not take snuff. Based on his own commanding experience, Metcalfe stated 'I believe the Begum [Sombre] never took any' and then queried Dyce Sombre, as an informant, to support this declaration. Either confirming or contradicting it would be the awkward, but accurate, assertion by Dyce Sombre that he knew his adoptive mother more authoritatively than did Metcalfe. In Dyce Sombre's diary, he did not recount his own response.[9]

He also believed that, Metcalfe, having recently arbitrated Dyce Sombre's bitter dispute with Dyce, repeatedly singled him out for filial impiety. Metcalfe, who often preached on Sunday to the assembled ship's company and passengers, based one sermon on 'the 5th Commandment, "Honour thy Father," &c. I am aware it was a blurt upon me'.[10] Similarly, Metcalfe's humourous but pointed anecdote about a young nobleman anticipating his father's demise by prematurely taking his title, Dyce Sombre also believed, was a veiled lesson intended for him. Significantly, his long legal battle against Dyce having been resolved, this was the first time he referred to 'my father' in his diary (although Dyce Sombre did not know it, while he was as sea, his father died back in Calcutta).

Metcalfe asserted his authority over the entire voyage. He vetoed visiting Cape Town, much to Dyce Sombre's frustration. Metcalfe also insisted on paying all expenses of all passengers when they did pause for provisions at St Helena island. Dyce Sombre innocently offended Metcalfe's honour when he paid £1 for a carriage to visit Napoleon's tomb. Like many tourists, Dyce Sombre took leafy mementoes from the nearby willows, sending them to people he thought would appreciate them: Drever, Solaroli, Reghellini, Joseph Skinner, and Allard. While saying a Pater Noster prayer at the fellow-Catholic Emperor's grave, Dyce Sombre was flattered when the watchman mistook him for Metcalfe. Informed of this, Metcalfe neither welcomed the comparison nor saw humour in the watchman's error.

Dyce Sombre continued respect Metcalfe's superior status. In the circulated subscription list for the parting gift for the ship's captain, Dyce Sombre calculated that the others expected him to give £10 'but I wd not be guided by them. I gave £20; it was rather vain of me', since this was the second largest amount. But he did not dare openly exceed Metcalfe, at the head of the list, who gave £30.[11]

The long and idle months aboard this ship, like his voyage to and from China (when he was suffering from gonorrhea and its treatment), were the longest Dyce Sombre had gone without sex during his adult life. Yet, Dyce Sombre often detected furtive sex among other passengers: 'I think there was a little tête-à-tête today after dinner, in which I think all the fair sex were concerned...'[12] He noted the supposed adulterers' names in Persian characters: Metcalfe's officious private secretary, 'Higginson', and an allegedly abused wife, Mrs 'Curtis'. When any two adult passengers of opposite sexes were absent simultaneously, Dyce Sombre assumed they were having intercourse. For example, one Sunday, 'Mr Brown is missing... I was told he has not left "his room"; of course that was sufficient for me. I suppose he has been taking liberties with the European servant of Mrs Higginson, for she is the only person, if any, to take liberties with, after the L—[Lambert sisters].'[13] Dyce Sombre himself, however, was too intimidated to even speculate in his diary about his own chances for intimacy with any British women aboard. Only during the ship's brief stop in St Helena did he buy sex, at night easily finding an anonymous sex-worker: 'I took a ramble. I met a person who I wanted, & there went, &c., &c.'[14] Next day, he listed in his expense record: '6s[hillings] for ***'.

When it came to considering Dyce Sombre's future in Britain, Metcalfe proved discouraging. In one chilling conversation as they entered European waters, Metcalfe recounted how many people quickly perished when, having become accustomed to the Indian environment, they reencountered Britain's cold climate; as examples, he listed three prominent Britons whom he knew personally, including Lord Lake. This frightened Dyce Sombre considerably since he was not just accustomed to India like them, he was born and raised there. Further, he noticed Metcalfe's frigidity and immediate change of subject when Dyce Sombre broached the issues of the Company's illegal seizure of Badshahpur and the Sardhana armaments, and the Company's failure to pay the promised pensions to the Begum's dependents. Dyce Sombre still did not know about Metcalfe's authoritative but confidential report on these issues that dismissed Dyce Sombre's claims. Early in the voyage, Metcalfe had recommended that Dyce Sombre attend Cambridge University; later, Metcalfe advised private tutors and then purchasing an estate and title in Italy. Thus, Dyce Sombre understood Metcalfe would not stand as his patron in English society and refrained from even hinting again at this for fear of further repulse.

On landing in Bristol on 3 June 1838, Dyce Sombre found himself adrift. Evoking an Islamicate blessing on his new life, he exclaimed 'Bism Allah' [In the Name of Allah] as he stepped onto England's fabled soil. Noticing that royal customs agents were lax about opening trunks, he secreted his jewelry box in one instead of trying to smuggle it concealed on his person or that of his servant, as he had originally intended. But Dyce Sombre did not realise his extensive wardrobe of Hindustani clothing was subject to seizure and 30% duty on the supposed valuation, since all Indian cloth was officially deemed a threat to the British textile industry; it is not clear if he ever extracted these clothes from the mangle of Her Majesty's Customs. Seeing Dyce Sombre standing bewildered quayside, Metcalfe had Higginson summon him to stay in their hotel, the Bath Hotel Tap in Sion Mews, Clifton, and share dinner.

But Metcalfe parried any suggestion that they travel together to London. Dyce Sombre recognised this dismissive parting: 'Took leave of Sir Charles, who is a great humbug. He said, "Probably we shall not see you again"; I was foolish enough to say that we shd; not knowing that he hinted that he will avoid, as much as he can.'[15] Dyce Sombre soon tried to use his wealth to purchase some leverage over Metcalfe, however. He cunningly wrote to Metcalfe's younger, unmarried sister, Emily Theophila Metcalfe, that Sir Charles could not 'be so comfortable as his station in life entitled him to be, and as he [Dyce Sombre] had more than he wanted for himself, he would be too happy to make Sir Charles a loan of twenty or twenty-five thousand pounds [worth roughly £1.4–1.8 million today], payable in Calcutta, to be repaid at his convenience. And for which, I [Dyce Sombre] pledge my honour that I will expect no return of any kind whatsoever.' Metcalfe docketed this letter, 'declined with thanks'.[16] Nonetheless, Dyce Sombre, in his redoubled quarrel with Solaroli, would later repeatedly evoke Metcalfe's authority about many secrets the great man had allegedly passed on to him.

Overall in England, Dyce Sombre found he had trouble identifying the class of the Britons with whom he was interacting, particularly in assessing the sexual availability of the British women he encountered. On leaving Bristol, Dyce Sombre tipped the English chambermaid incommensurably, suggesting to himself that he might have purchased sex with her had he dared try: 'when the servt-maid, who was rather a nice looking girl, came to ask for a present, I gave her a sovereign [£1]. I wish I had known her, for paying so high; she was astonished to see the gold…'[17] This tip to his first ever native English servant was more than three times what he had recently paid the St Helena sex-worker.

On the stagecoach to London, Dyce Sombre noted two attractive young women passengers whose status he was uncertain about, but whose attention he awkwardly tried to buy:

[I] got in with an old gentn & two pretty girls, one especially, with whom I tried to chat, but wd not do; they were, or perhaps wanted to appear, very modest... I offered them oranges, wh I had bought on the road, but they wd not take it; I had only bought them for their sake, so I gave them away before them. I was very communicative with old gentleman till they were in the carriage, but afterwds I became dull... [At] Thumwell... these girls were handed out by a coarse-looking man, evidently master of the eating-house, saying 'Come out, my dears.' Here we left them.[18]

125

Thus, in his diary, Dyce Sombre showed how, rebuffed by these young Englishwomen, he diminished his proffered regard for them by giving away this expensive fruit in front of them. In his account, their departure into the hands of a crude inn-keeper further reduced their status.

During the stagecoach journey, Dyce Sombre kept seeking his place in this unfamiliar society. At dinner in a wayside inn, Dyce Sombre called for his customary champagne. When the innkeeper did not even have wine in stock, Dyce Sombre recognised himself as incongruous, excusing his faux pas by admitting (truthfully) to be a foreigner but (untruthfully) one familiar with Europe: 'I told [the wineless innkeeper]... I had never been in England, & that I was coming from India, but that I was brought up in France; so all passed off well.'[19] Dyce Sombre would continue until his death this uncomfortable process of seeking to locate himself among Britons and discovering what they would sell him for his cash.

Arriving in London Society

On entering London late on 6 June 1838, Dyce Sombre sought to began his new life. As a world city, London barely contained its two million diverse inhabitants, ten times the size of Calcutta where he had last lived. Despite all he had read or heard about the British imperial capital, it threatened to overwhelm him by its scale, diversity, wealth, and power.

Even as David's past life closed, he began his new life by trying to relate to people he associated with India. Further, London people—British, European, and Indian—identified him primarily with the Begum's legacy, both financial and cultural. Yet, as a former near-princeling with vast free-floating capital, he sought to recreate himself as a European gentleman, even aristocrat. His money bought him the services of Britons, from sex-workers to tailors to lawyers. But he fit into none of the various current social groups based on class, race, or nationality. Neither the Freemasons nor the Catholic Church nor gentlemen's clubs in Britain provided a congenial community for him. Instead, he frequently faced sudden and unanticipated alienation and slights, either intended by others or simply sensed by him, that kept him uncertain of his position and the way forward.

From letters awaiting him, he learned of two unexpected deaths: his father's in Calcutta and, more sorrowfully, his last child's aboard ship.

Had Penelope survived to join him in England as planned, his career would have been markedly different since she would have been a evocative public reminder of his earlier family. As it was, rumours of his Indian wives, concubines, and children would periodically appear to plague him in his newly burgeoning relationships with Britons. The night after his arrival in London, he took care of his immediate carnal needs through a surreptitious visit to an English common sex-worker, although he believed himself suspect for such incongruous behaviour for a gentleman: 'when I came out from a place of that kind, many people stared at my getting into a carriage'.[20]

Exploring the glorified imperial capital, he noted its features dismissively—perhaps defensively. London's rainy weather even in June seemed dreary and discomforting. Further, landmarks he had long heard fabled, from St Paul's Anglican Cathedral in the east to the Duke of Wellington's mansion in the west, disappointed. But he found impressive Queen Victoria's coronation ceremony at Westminster Abbey that he wangled a ticket to attend, referring to her fondly as 'our Sovereign'. To access London highlife, he also began hiring and meeting Britons whom he knew, or knew about, from India.

From Calcutta, he had already paid to be met in Bristol and then London by agents of artist and retired East India Company Army Captain Robert Melville Grindlay. Although personally unacquainted, Dyce Sombre knew Grindlay ran a flourishing agency to assist gentlemen travelling from or to India (later becoming Grindlay's Bank).[21] Since Dyce Sombre intended to settle, he transferred most of his financial assets to Britain, investing in East India Company bonds (worth £440,000, paying 4%) and stocks, plus British Government and railway bonds. In total, these investments yielded a princely cash income of £20,000 annually (today worth some £1,400,000).[22] Further, his capital was liquid, so he could spend it more freely than could men heavily invested in real estate or commerce.

Tensions over Dyce Sombre's own ambivalent social position reflected, albeit imperfectly, ongoing class conflicts between old and uprising elites in Britain. Prestige still tended to derive from established landed estates; aristocratic circles denigrated new mercantile or speculative money. Prior to 1838, all Members of Parliament were required to have a specified income derived solely from landownership; thereafter income from stocks, other financial instruments, or businesses also counted. Dyce Sombre had free-floating capital, which put him into

Coat of Arms of Colonel David Ochterlony Dyce Sombre, Esq.

the upper class by income, but no real estate; yet, he also claimed princely status from Sardhana, which made him more socially tolerable by some aristocrats and gentlemen among whom he aspired to move.

To facilitate Dyce Sombre's passage into London high society, he immediately adopted various honourifics and devices. He added 'Esq.' to his name. He assumed the rank 'Colonel' (based on his former position as commander of the Begum's troops and brevet commission from the French king). He petitioned the Earl Marshal of the College of Arms, paying to register of his putative pedigree and then the design and grant of his own newly constructed family crest: four quarters—two for Dyce, two for Sombre—complete with a royal umbrella and crown, tiger, martial flaming bombs, chain shot, battleaxes, and a fortress, as well as the motto: *Favente Numine*: 'God Willing'.[23] He sealed his letters in red wax using a self-designed signet ring of a crowing cockerel above the initials 'D.S.'. He attended, as a Esq., Colonel and honoured guest, the public examination of East India Company cadets at its Addiscombe Military Seminary on 11 June 1838.[24]

A particularly prominent aspect of acceptance in respectable society was membership of a gentleman's club. Within ten days of his arrival in London, Dyce Sombre had himself nominated for the prestigious Oriental Club by two founding members: Major Sir James Rivett Carnac, MP, Chairman of the East India Company's Court of Directors, and George William Traill, a retired Company civil servant. The Oriental Club had been created less than fifteen years earlier, in 1824, mainly by East India Company officials and officers, but was open to other 'gentlemen' who had lived in 'the Orient'. Its existence thus reflected the rise in numbers and respectability of British gentlemen with colonial connections. In 1831, the Club, located at 18 Hanover Square, had expanded its definition of 'gentlemen' to include selected Asians, but only as 'Honourary Members'. Then, in 1834, it elected a wealthy Parsi merchant of Calcutta, Sirkis Juhannas Sirkis, as a 'Full Member'. Indeed, the year before Dyce Sombre's arrival, Carnac had successfully nominated and secured the election to full membership of another Indian 'Prince' settled in London: Shahzada Shaykh Jahangir-i Zaman, Mahomed Jamh ood-Deen, a son of the late and notorious Tipu Sultan of Mysore and elder brother of Dyce Sombre's Calcutta acquaintance, Gholam Muhammad.[25] Other current members figuring largely in Dyce Sombre's life included: Lt Colonel George Everest, Hugh Fraser, and Richard Carr Glyn (each of whom he had known and conflicted with in India); Captain Robert Grindlay (the agent assisting his arrival); the Duke of Wellington (his future supposed rival

Oriental Club, London

in love); Lt Colonel James Law Lushington (repeatedly Chairman of the Court of Directors, whom he would challenge to a duel); and William D. Sherriff (his future warder).

When Dyce Sombre stood for election to membership in the Oriental Club, however, the votes against admitting him were decisive (10% was enough to blackball a candidate) so he was embarrassingly excluded. Such negative electoral outcomes were rare. Since those opposing him were anonymous, we cannot tell what facets of Dyce Sombre's personality or background deemed him 'unclubbable'.[26] His mixed ancestry may not have been decisive since, over the next few years, other men of similar descent were elected full members of this club, including his old familiars, Sir Charles Metcalfe Ochterlony and Lieutenant Hercules Skinner. To Dyce Sombre's great dismay and chagrin, he would also watch others he knew well be elected including Troup (his English brother-in-law), Dr Thomas Drever; and Sir Charles Metcalfe. Further, select Indian elites visiting London were admitted as Honourary Members, including: pretender to the Awadh throne (and dining companion of Dyce Sombre) Nawab Iqbal al-Daula Bahadur; businessman, banker, social reformer (fellow diner guest and future supposed lover of Dyce Sombre's wife) Dwarkanath Tagore; diplomat and author Mohun Lal; and deposed Punjabi Maharaja Duleep Singh. For the rest of Dyce Sombre's life, he continued to interact with members of the Oriental Club from which he had been rejected. Apparently to vindicate himself, he later sent 250 copies of his own, self-justifying book *Refutation*, to the club for distribution to its members (which its Secretary refused to do).

While Dyce Sombre was rejected by the Oriental Club, he persisted in seeking acceptance from other British societies. A year later, while visiting Scotland, he used his Masonic status as holder of the Royal Arch degree to gain election as a 'Knight Commander' in the Grand Conclave of the Religious and Military Order of the Temple ('The Knights Templar').[27] Far fewer members of this Edinburgh secret society knew him from India and, apparently, one who did (Captain Walter Scott, a 'Grand Aide-de-Camp' in this conclave) recommended him. This time he was not 'blackballed'. Having paid the various entry and membership fees, Dyce Sombre dressed in the elaborate Knight Commander's costume, complete with a red velvet cap, white woolen mantle and tunic adorned with the red silk tassels, fringes, and emblems of his rank, ceremonial sword, mystical badge, and esoterically engraved finger-ring. Thus, Dyce Sombre's entry into the society of British gentlemen proved uneven: his money could buy much, but not everything, that he wanted.

Indian Society in the Capital

At this time, Indians in Britain totalled several thousand, including men and women of all social classes, from seamen and servants to scholars, ambassadors and aristocrats. Among them, Dyce Sombre, as heir to Begum Sombre, held a respected if anomalous position. Most prominent of the Indians with whom he socialised was the claimant to the Awadh throne (mentioned above), Nawab Iqbal al-Daula Bahadur. This prince, exactly Dyce Sombre's own age, entered British high society just before him, in 1837, remaining in Britain for nearly two years. In addition to savouring all that London offered, he also came to lobby the British Government and East India Company for his enthronement as ruler of the huge princely state of Awadh, in place of his recently deceased cousin, Nasir al-Din. At Iqbal al-Daula's lavish apartments near Regent's Park, he and Dyce Sombre dined together, along with their European supporters. Most notably, Viscount Combermere championed both men in their legal battles. Dr George Gabriel Sigmond, personal physician to the family of the wealthy Sir Francis Burdett, also dined regularly with them.[28] The Nawab and many of his entourage were strictly practising Shi'ites, but Dyce Sombre had long experience socialising with Muslim royalty including the Mughal imperial family. He also met with a less orthodox Shi'ite Muslim, Mirza Ibrahim, an Iranian who taught in the East India Company's College at Haileybury as Professor of Persian (1826–44).[29] More experienced in Britain, these men explained to Dyce Sombre their understanding of the criteria for social success among the British elite.

Dyce Sombre's Patronage

Dyce Sombre also had an array of India-returned British acquaintances. Many of them owed him money or hospitality in return for what he had provided them in Sardhana, Meerut, Delhi, or Calcutta. While few actually repaid their financial debts, these Britons met and advised (often in contradictory ways) him about how to negotiate London society. Dyce Sombre repeatedly reminded them of their obligations to him, often at inopportune times.

General Sir Stapleton Cotton, Viscount Combermere

For a particularly experienced, influential, and prestigious guide to London high society, Dyce Sombre approached Begum Sombre's aging old friend, General Sir Stapleton Cotton, Viscount Combermere, Knight Grand Cross of the Order of the Bath and also of the Royal Guelphic Order, the once dashing cavalry commander under the Duke of Wellington, and former Commander-in-Chief in India. As we saw, the Begum had entreated Combermere, and he had vowed, to protect and guide Dyce Sombre after her passing. Over the eight years since Combermere's departure from Sardhana, he and the Begum had exchanged valuable presents, including portraits of themselves (such European-style paintings were a frequent object of exchange among elites in Europe and then in India).[30] The Begum had sent Combermere's second wife, Caroline Greville, an affectionate letter, addressing her as 'My Dear Daughter' and 'written in Hindustani on a piece of parchment, decorated with gilt stars and tied with gold cord'.[31] Later, she had also sent Caroline gifts of valuable jewellry. Combermere separated from this wife just before her death. At the time he began shepherding Dyce Sombre into London society, the sixty-five-year-old Combermere was courting his third wife, the Anglo-Irish Mary Woolley

Gibbings Grove, a woman two decades his junior, whom he married in October 1838.

The distinguished and querulous Combermere proved one of Dyce Sombre's most partisan patrons. Combermere gained Dyce Sombre entrée to many aristocratic circles that would prove central to his future in Britain and also bestowed emphatic advice on personal matters, including relationships with British women. Combermere was also a Masonic brother, currently Provincial Grand Master of Freemasons in Cheshire. Combermere knew the Duke of Wellington well from their much-celebrated service together in India and later Spain. Combermere also associated with fellow slave-owner Viscount St Vincent in the West India lobby of the House of Lords; they both received substantial financial reimbursement from Parliament for the loss of their 'property' when their slaves were freed.[32] In July 1839, the financially pinched Combermere asked Dyce Sombre to loan him the sizable sum of £10,000; this loan, while it never eventuated, led to much disputation later.[33] Both Dyce Sombre and also Combermere's enemies both assserted that the Viscount coveted Dyce Sombre's fortune and plotted to have a relative marry him.

Among Combermere's first acts was to outfit Dyce Sombre as a proper gentleman. When Dyce Sombre first arrived in London, he had immediately realised that he was unfashionably dressed: 'Can't go out anywhere, as I have no proper clothes'.[34] Although he had himself purchased new suits of English-style clothing immediately upon his arrival, Combermere disapproved of these as unstylish and so recommended Dyce Sombre into the exclusive clientele of one of London's most trendy tailors, a German named Stultz of Bond Street. Once Dyce Sombre had been dressed appropriately, Combermere introduced him to a good solicitor, the man he himself had long employed, Bartle John Laurie Frere, Jr., Esq., of Lincoln's Inn.

Frere advised Dyce Sombre in the next phases of his long legal disputes with the East India Company. Frere directed Dyce Sombre to make his three appeals against the Company's confiscation of his personal property more legally sustainable by declaring: Badshahpur's special status as an *altumgha* (permanently owned and hereditable) land-grant; the private rather than state ownership of the Sardhana armaments; and also the moral and contractual obligation of the Company to the deserving Sardhana pensioners. Dyce Sombre immediately wrote to the Company's Directors requesting that he be allowed to intercept and alter the Memorial that he himself had presented to Company authorities in Calcutta the previous April, as soon as it reached London.[35] The Directors did not reply for eight months and then curtly refused his request as 'contrary to the practice' of the Court of Directors—the tactics of silence and then vague claims of precedent they often deployed against Indian appeals. They also completely rejected his original Memorial when it finally reached London. Such frustrating refusals by the Company's Directors discouraged most Indian petitioners, but not Dyce Sombre.

In addition to the growing but unproductive correspondence with the Company, Frere also had Dyce Sombre file appeals against it in the London courts. Dyce Sombre later complained that all the best barristers, including Thomas Wilde, had already been retained by the East India Company. Nonetheless, Frere launched appeals which constituted the first stages of the numerous, protracted, and hugely expensive legal battles against the Company over these issues, cases that would

East India Company Court of Directors, 1844

be fully or partially won by his side only in 1872, long after Dyce Sombre's death and the Company's termination.

As with so many of his conflicts with the British authorities, Dyce Sombre regarded these disputes with the Directors as essentially personal and political. Consequently, he tried to cultivate influential British politicians and aristocrats whom he hoped would advance his interests amid the ongoing convoluted factional conflicts that characterised London politics. For example, in May 1839 Dyce Sombre confided: 'I hope the present [Melbourne] Ministry will not change, of which there is a talk about, tho' they have promised me nothing; but there are some good meaning people amongst them & I think they would not wrong any person knowingly'.[36] As his cases floundered over the decades, however, he continued to be convinced that political influence decided law cases, while his faith in the sympathy toward him of British politicians faltered.

In addition to recommending him to an exclusive tailor and a wily solicitor, Combermere also introduced Dyce Sombre to a distinguished patroness, the ninety-two-year-old but still imperious Lady Cork, widow of 7th Count of Cork and Orrery. She 'at once took [Dyce Sombre] under her fostering wing'.[37] In her drawing room, Dyce Sombre radiated exotic Oriental associations as former 'Prince of Sardhana'. He also sported gentlemanly credentials as a 'Colonel', bearing an attested coat of arms. Further, London newspapers proclaimed Dyce Sombre as the 'Croesus of India' for his fantastic fortune.[38] All this established him as one of the most eligible bachelors of the social season (albeit a man not to everyone's taste).

In early August, only two months after his arrival in London, at a soirée hosted by Lady Cork, Dyce Sombre attracted the attentions of one of London's most strikingly accomplished ladies: the Honourable Mary Anne Jervis (1812–93), youngest daughter of the second Viscount St Vincent. Their rocky relationship shaped much of the rest of Dyce Sombre's life.

7

A VISCOUNT'S DAUGHTER

Dyce Sombre's quick offer of marriage and the Honourable Mary Anne Jervis' rapid acceptance altered both of their conditions considerably. He immediately attracted fresh attention from the aristocrats among whom Mary Anne circulated. For her, his fabled wealth and exotic associations clearly overcame his corpulence, dark skin, and mixed origins. She, as an engaged rather than unattached woman, also gained new stature. Her family, while distinguished, had blemishes on its escutcheon and she herself had provoked much scandalous gossip, which Dyce Sombre would only gradually come to know about. Further, this was a difficult time for her personally.

The Future Mrs Dyce Sombre's Family of Repute

When Dyce Sombre first met the twenty-seven-year-old Hon. Mary Anne Jervis, known as 'Maidy' by her family, she had risen high in the British aristocracy. She had been born in 1812 as the more humble Mary Anne Ricketts. Her well-established landholding gentry family from Staffordshire had considerable slave and plantation holdings in Jamaica. Her father, Edward Lewis Ricketts, had qualified as a barrister from Lincoln's Inn, while his elder brother, William Henry Ricketts, became a Royal Navy Captain. These brothers married into the aristocracy and stood to inherit the title and wealth of the naval hero Viscount St Vincent. But her family also had created considerable notoriety through scandalous marriages and divorces and a widely-publicised lunacy trial of the family's heir apparent.

Mary Anne's paternal grandfather had enriched and elevated her family by marrying the sister of Admiral John Jervis, victor over a much larger Spanish fleet off Cape St Vincent in 1797. He rose to be First Lord of the Admiralty and Admiral of the Fleet, gaining the titles Baron Jervis of Meaford and Earl and Viscount St Vincent, GCB, as well as considerable wealth including annual pensions totalling £3,000 voted by the British and Irish Parliaments. He also made enemies, one of whom, another admiral, challenged him to a duel which only the intervention of King George III precluded. Admiral Jervis, however, had no children and his wife, Martha, suffered from mental disorders—although he avoided committing her to an asylum through constant confinement by hired nurses.[1] Nor did his only brother have any children. Hence, the several family estates, pensions and title 'Viscount St Vincent' would go to one of his sister's children, the eldest surviving Ricketts brother.

The elder Ricketts brother, William, married Lady Elizabeth Jane Lambert, young daughter of the 6th Earl of Cavan, in 1793 in fashionable St George's Church, Hanover Square. Although they soon had two daughters, only months after William sailed off on active Royal Navy service to the Caribbean, she took a handsome but poor lover, Royal Army Captain John Hargreaves. After William's return three years later, he obtained a legal separation from her and successfully brought a civil lawsuit against Hargreaves. Full divorce (*divortium a vinculo matrimonii*) at that time for Anglicans could only be obtained through a private divorce bill passed by both Houses of Parliament, an expensive and infrequent process (costing at least £700, only between four and ten such divorce acts were passed annually for all of England). William was to inherit the St Vincent title and estates, so there was much salacious public testimony, republished in newspapers and books, about every detail of his wife's sexual relations with her lover and with William.[2] Finally, both Houses passed William's private bill (39 George 3, c. 33) and the King approved the divorce on 19 April 1799.

Only six weeks earlier, the King had also approved the Parliamentary divorce act (39 George 3, c. 12) of the younger Ricketts brother, Edward. He had eloped with Mary Cassandra Twisleton, youngest daughter of the 10th Baron of Saye and Sale, when she was only in her early teens. Later, when she reached sixteen in 1790, they married in St George's Church, Hanover Square. Scandalously, in 1797, she betrayed Edward and their three children, becoming the mistress of Charles William Taylor, the rich, newly elected MP for Wells, Norfolk. This affair led Edward to obtain a legal separation from his wife fol-

Genealogy of Mary Anne Ricketts/Jervis later Dyce Sombre

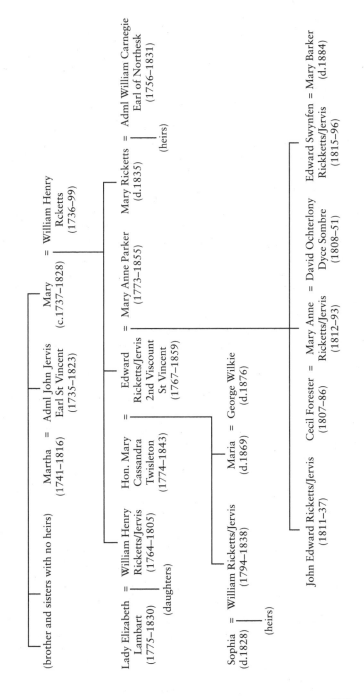

lowed by his lawsuit against Taylor in King's Bench Court for 'Trespass, Assault, and Criminal Conversation'. The judge excoriated Taylor for his immorality; the jury awarded Edward £5,000 in damages plus court costs. Immediately afterward, early in 1799, Edward petitioned Parliament for divorce. Although (or perhaps because) his wife's lover was an influential MP, his bill passed without opposition. Edward also kept custody of their three children. Now divorced, Edward distanced himself from this scandal by moving to Jamaica to manage the family's several prosperous sugar plantations, including their many hundred slaves.

After his elder brother's death by drowning in 1805, Edward moved back to England and, in 1810, enhanced his wealth through a second marriage, this time to his cross-cousin once removed, Mary Anne Parker. They soon had three children; they named their second child and only daughter Mary Anne. The eldest son, John Edward, remained unwell for most of his youth, dying unmarried. The youngest son, Edward Swynfen, eloped with Mary Barker, the daughter of a labourer. They married on 12 March 1838, without their parents' consent, in Gretna Green, Scotland—the infamous site for such unsanctioned weddings since it was the spot nearest England where Scottish law applied (allowing mutual consent by legal minors and requiring no banns).[3] This *infra dig* marriage, while legal, was never solemnised in an Anglican Church, bringing much stress to his family.

Mary Anne's half-brother, William, would have inherited the viscounty and family wealth. However, from his youth he acted erratically, unsettling his family. Despite the influence of his great uncle, Admiral Jervis, he abruptly quit his budding naval career. The next year, 1815, he married a rich childhood friend, Sophia. She served as his nurse-keeper, 'a lady, who had a great power over him, and kept him out of scrapes' through constant care.[4] Notwithstanding his eccentricities, as a gentleman of property he presided as a magistrate for Middlesex and contemplated using his wife's fortune to purchase election to Parliament from Chester.

When William's wife died suddenly in 1828, however, he launched into actions his family considered peculiarly embarrassing. He wrote improbable cheques, challenged prominent people (including King George III and Admiral Jervis, both long deceased) to duels on Wimbledon Common, claimed descent from King Edward III and inheritance of the British throne, confused his doctor with the Duke of

Wellington and proposed marriage to an aristocratic lady who was unknown to him. As bourgeois values permeated Victorian society, such transgressions, even by aristocratic men, became subordinated to domestic interests; his father thus determined to confine and legally disinherit him in order to protect the family's reputation and fortune.

First, his barrister father obtained authoritative diagnoses of William's lunacy from several leading 'mad doctors', including the famous Dr Edward Thomas Monro. (Monro's family had supplied four successive generations of physicians to Bethlehem [Bedlam] Lunatic Hospital; he would later judge Dyce Sombre likewise a lunatic for acts similar to those of William.) But William struggled to free himself, including by writing a £400 cheque to Monro, as William explained, 'because I desired to manage my own property... and wished him to go away'. Further, William wrote Lord Chancellor Lyndhurst applying for a *Writ of Habeas Corpus* to free him from his family's clutches and the jail in which he believed himself incarcerated, thereby making public his family's shame. Consequently, in 1829, William's father hired a Chancery solicitor to petition Lord Lyndhurst for a *Commission de Lunatico*

John Singleton Copley, Lord Chancellor Baron Lyndhurst

141

Inquirendo. This petition, if accepted by the Lord Chancellor, resulted in the immediate and private legal restraint of the alleged lunatic and the provisional sequestering of his property by his accusing family. (This same Lord Chancellor Lyndhurst would later preside over Dyce Sombre's lunacy case as well.)

Next, the Lord Chancellor (a political appointee, 'Lord Keeper of the Great Seal' and simultaneously presiding officer in the House of Lords) decided if a trial was justified. If he approved the petition, the Commissioners in Lunacy and a special jury would hold an open inquisition of the accused. If the allegation of lunacy was confirmed by a majority of the jurymen, this would eventuate in a *Writ* for permanent confinement as a 'Chancery Lunatic' and the confirmation of control over his or her property by the family. Since married women could not legally own property, two-thirds of such inquisitions were against male accused. The judge and jury were always, of course, all male.

During the early nineteenth century, the frequency of such *Commissions de Lunatico Inquirendo* rose to between thirty and fifty-five annually since they represented a potentially desirable solution to a family's embarrassment and financial peril.[5] This procedure thus provided a family with the means of legally confining an unruly relative at home or in a private asylum rather than either having to endure continued public embarrassment or to allow the state to confine the relation in a disreputable public insane asylum. It also enabled a family to preserve its financial heritage by removing all property from the power of the alleged lunatic to squander. Once confined, legal lunatics often did not undergo any medical treatment intended to be therapeutic or curative.[6] Nor could most convicted lunatics launch an appeal to reverse the *Writ*, confined as they were. In effect, the Crown authorised the family to reduce the convicted lunatic permanently to the legal status of a minor, incarcerated and deprived of property rights and custody of children without having committed any crime.

Yet, such open inquisitions also publicly broadcast the scandalous words and deeds of the alleged lunatic, temporarily increasing the family's shame. Such open hearings provided the accused with the opportunity to become the centre of attention and then to proclaim widely all of the supposed delusions and embarrassing accusations that had been hitherto suppressed by the family. The most prominent or salacious of these inquiries were reported widely in popular newspapers. As Suzuki explains: 'The enormous popularity of the commission of lunacy as a performance on a legal stage and a journalistic narrative was thus a part of the public's keen interest in matters relating to lunacy... Relish for comedy coexisted with the sober pathos of watching a tragic malady, and fascination with freakish delusions coexisted with earnest outrage against restraint.'[7] Bourgeois Victorian society found trials of aristocrats particularly entertaining in a period when it challenged their pretensions to hereditary privilege and superiority.

Nonetheless, the alleged lunatic, while temporarily the centre of public attention during the hearing, rarely had much effective agency. Unlike William, most accused lunatics were unable to secure lawyers to represent and guide them in court (Dyce Sombre would demand a lawyer but never receive one at his lunacy hearing). Further, many—like William and Dyce Sombre—vainly felt confident that they could personally tell their story persuasively as an incontrovertible revelation to the world, proving that they were actually more rational than their accusers. If the putative lunatic convinced the judge and jury of his or her mental competence, the family would lose all power to constrain its recalcitrant member. However, the system almost inevitably favoured the family: virtually all lunatic hearings ended in conviction and confinement.

The widely-reported two-day public inquiry into William's sanity before three Commissioners in Lunacy and a special jury was held in Gray's Inn Coffee House, London. Newspapers publicised many of his revealed transgressions in sensational detail. Curious and interested people, including fashionable London society, attended 'not only from the circumstances connected with it, but on account of the rank of the party', it being the most celebrated and expensive of such cases since the inquiry into the sanity of Lord Portsmouth six years earlier in 1823. The *Times* reported that William's divorced mother sat among the spectators, reminding its readers that Viscount St Vincent was prosecuting this inquiry against his heir apparent, the eldest son of his unsavory but aristocratic first wife.[8]

Among leading medical experts, the distinguished Dr Monro testified that William 'had become childishly acquiescent, seemed quite satisfied with having keepers about him, but was most anxious to have a cottage near Fulham, and free intercourse with the female sex. He was fond of writing checks.' Consequently Monro concluded that, in his expert assessment, William was 'decidedly of unsound mind'.

Contesting St Vincent's accusation were three lawyers representing William. He himself occasionally made lucid appeals for acquittal, the

Times reporting 'many of [his] answers were not only rational, but extremely well adapted to the questions asked. The alleged lunatic appeared to be free from agitation.' While William explained all his unconventional actions as resulting from 'a cold in my head' and drinking excessive brandy, his lawyers conceded that he may have been *non compos mentis* earlier but contended he had now recovered.

Throughout this period, in William's lunacy trial as later in Dyce Sombre's, controversy raged among leading medical and judicial authorities as to the nature of 'lunacy'. A generic term describing a range of mental conditions, in legal definition it still implied moonlike waxing and waning of the incompetence. In contrast, leading medical men (physicians, surgeons, and self-professed experts) had long dropped this moon-based concept. But they themselves publicly and in academic and legal forums debated whether lunacy was an absolute state or could be partial or temporary. Other moot issues included how doctors or law courts could objectively diagnose lunacy. Lacking any reliable definition or systematic data about causation or manifestation on which to build, prominent medical specialists in lunacy— 'alienists'—proposed a variety of disparate theories and treatments. These emphatic public disagreements detracted from the on-going efforts by these early psychiatrists to professionalise their discipline (as we would term it) and gain it the respect of a medical science. Further, lawyers, judges, and individual jurymen also each felt competent to decide such issues, insisting that they, rather than the disputing doctors, could authoritatively identify lunacy when they saw it. While medical men professed to seek the best treatment of the patient, legal men claimed to seek the protection of the life and property of the accused and his or her family.

William and his lawyers, despite the strong testimony of Dr Monro and other medical expert witnesses, indeed made arguments that persuaded his special jury to pause and demand further evidence. The jurors exerted their power to examine William themselves, once in open court and once privately for an hour. One juror had earlier served in another such lunacy inquisition, a hearing that led to one of the rare exonerations of an accused. However, William, by writing in his copy of Johnson's *Dictionary* that his judge, Lord Lyndhurst, was a 'coward' and part of a 'conspiracy' against him, did not help his own case.

Finally, although the 'verdict evidently caused some dissatisfaction amongst many persons in the room', on the instructions of the chief

Commissioner, the jury unanimously declared William a legal lunatic, decreeing that he had been so for the past 332 days (starting two months after his wife's death). Consequently, Lord Lyndhurst formally ordered William's property sequestered, excluded him from succession to the viscountcy and authorised his personal confinement by his family. The Lord Chancellor directed William's children, however, be raised not by William's father but rather by a relative of their late mother, Sophia. This led to further caustic legal disputes over their custody and property, provoking a challenge to a duel between the Solicitor General and one of the contending barristers.[9] Edward Ricketts' prominent position and considerable wealth, as well as his expert acquisition of a *Writ de Lunatico Inquirendo*, secured physical control over William until his death a decade later in 1838. The viscountcy and other inheritance skipped William and eventually went to his eldest son, Mary Anne's half-nephew, Robert Carnegy Jervis. Fourteen years later, her husband, Dyce Sombre, would also be declared a lunatic through the same legal process, under some of the same legal and medical authorities, at her family's request. Indeed, there were many similarities between the unconventional actions of her half-brother and those of Dyce Sombre, including alleged financial irresponsibility and supposed social improprieties like challenging men to duels inappropriately.

Thus Mary Anne grew up in a family with a mixed public reputation and internecine stresses. She had the prospect of distinction and even more wealth to be inherited by her father from the famous Viscount St Vincent. Yet, her legally lunatic half-brother, lower-class sister-in-law, alienated cousins, and her father's and uncle's shunned and divorced first wives all loomed around her, while her own reputation both suffered and rose from her public relationships with some of the most prominent men of her age.

Mary Anne Jervis Rises in High Society

As the daughter of a father with aristocratic prospects, Mary Anne received a fashionable if unsystematic education. She studied both privately, under governesses and in schools in the resort town of Bath and, briefly starting at age eight, in Paris. Indeed, while on one of several sojourns in Paris, she received a prize for being 'the best dancer in the school' from the hand of the newly-crowned King Louis-Philippe.[10] Her indubitable musical abilities and accomplishments would continue to bring her particular distinction as she rose into the British aristocracy.

At age eleven in 1823, she became 'the Honourable Mary Anne Jervis' on the death of her great uncle, the Admiral. As had been long expected, her father—on condition that he adopt the surname Jervis—inherited the reflected military distinction associated with title Viscount St Vincent, as well as considerable real estate and capital (worth some £30,000), in addition to the £3,000 annual pensions from the British and Irish Parliaments. Her own courtesy title and greatly enlarged family fortune brought her enhanced access to the highest English social circles, particularly those where her musical talents could shine.

At the time, aristocratic ladies of fortune could develop a respectable amateur musical avocation, quite discrete from the salacious world of professional women performers. Especially from age nineteen onward, the Hon. Mary Anne composed, arranged, performed, and published musical scores, in collaboration with the Right Hon. Lady Dacre among other fellow noblewomen. Her earliest published works included Italian-language duets, sentimental ballads (including 'Shall This Pale Cheek'), and songs (including 'Blow, Blow, Thou Winter Wind' from Shakespeare's *As You Like It*).[11] She wrote a 'Duet à la Ruse', which was later preserved by her first husband, Dyce Sombre, among his private papers. She dedicated various of her compositions to other female aristocrats including the Marchioness of Tavistock, Lady Augusta Vernon Wentworth, and Viscountess Falkland.

In 1831, she received lavish reviews in the *Morning Post* for her score of Pietro Metastasio's lyrics of the Orientalist opera, *Siroë*, sung by ladies of fashion in a proudly unprofessional performance at Covent Garden. An effusive reviewer proclaimed that her score, 'even in this age of prodigies is the most wonderful example of genius ever heard of, the young lady [Mary Anne] not having yet attained her twentieth year... the composition perfect and unique as the production of an amateur'.[12] At the next performance, two weeks later, she received equally fulsome praise plus a wreath of laurels from the recently abdicated Emperor Don Pedro I of Brazil. Her portrait was painted by the society artist J. C. Middleton, and exhibited in the Royal Academy. She and this portrait were also featured in the fashion magazine, *Court Magazine and Belle Assemblee* of 1834.[13]

Mary Anne's evident musical talents, celebrated and irrepressible vivacity, family wealth, and distinguished social standing raised her to the notice of some of the leading men of the day. For example, the promising young novelist and aspiring politician, Benjamin Disraeli,

Hon. Mary Anne Jervis

was urged in 1833 by a close friend 'to lay siege to Miss Jervis, which he thinks practicable, a great heiress and clever. She is pretty also.'[14] Although she and the future Prime Minister met at Lady Cork's, their personal relationship did not develop far, although they socialised occasionally for decades. One of her most ardent (albeit younger) suitors was Charles Manners, at the time Marquess of Granby but later 6th Duke of Rutland; his parents, however, vetoed marriage with Mary Anne.[15] Instead, she made herself among the most prominent of the young ladies attending on distinguished aging men who savoured the attentions of such devoted aristocratic women.

Unabashed by society gossip, Mary Anne attached herself in particular to the most eminent and controversial elder statesman of the era, the Duke of Wellington, Arthur Wellesley, a man already in his sixties. Living hero of the nation, he had defeated Indian armies (including that of Sardhana) and then Emperor Napoleon's armies in Spain and, finally, at Waterloo (1815). Wellington had gone on to make himself a frequent cabinet member, including as Prime Minister. His policies and his persona, however, made him reviled in many quarters. He had pushed through key bills including one that allowed Catholics into Parliament (1829). The controversy over Catholic emancipation led to

Field Marshall Arthur Wellesley, Duke of Wellington, as Prime Minister
(1828–30)

his well-publicised pistol duel against George Finch-Hatton, 9th Earl of
Winchilsea, 5th Earl of Nottingham.

The Duke also openly indulged himself in the company of attentive
young noblewomen, even before, but especially following, the death of
his uncongenial wife in 1831. Later that year, after hearing one of
Mary Anne's performances, he presented her, as 'Queen of Music',
with a gold crown emblazoned with his own initial 'W' in diamonds,
which he himself designed and commissioned from a leading London
jeweller. Wellington may have exercised dispassion on the battlefield
but he occasionally exceeded the bounds of propriety with young
women, Mary Anne among them.

Mary Anne's sentiments toward the Duke echoed those of many of
her female peers. She wrote in her diary:

We were enthusiastic about him. I can never utter his name, if I can avoid it,
to anyone who is not... I cannot be lukewarm about such a man as the Duke...
for nobody scarcely can feel and understand what he is. The generality of the
world contemplate him as the ablest of the politicians and the most glorious of
warriors, and so he is; arrayed in the wisdom of Solomon and crowned with
the glory of Caesar, but this they cannot comprehend, that he is to be loved,

almost adored, admired, venerated besides which no other mortal man could ever have merited in like degree, and now if anyone dare tell me my picture of him is too highly coloured, I will throw over it as many coats as they please of his beautiful simplicity that his highly finished mind and transcendent talents may not dazzle us too much.[16]

This wild adulation by Mary Anne and numerous other young English noblewomen offended many. For example, the Ottoman Turkish ambassador in London, Namik Pasha, ridiculed such open adoration: 'All the stupid, vulgar Englishwomen followed him about as a lion with offensive curiosity'.[17] Like many commentators on other cultures, this envoy assessed a society by the behaviour of its womenfolk, in this case unfavourably.[18]

Despite growing gossip against their relationship, Mary Anne and the Duke grew closer over the years. He bestowed upon her sentimental and suggestive Valentines, an expensive octagonal pianoforte, and other gifts including a costly bracelet with three rubies and 'a Garter in blue Enamel with the word "Wellington" over the Rubies' as well as 'a Ducal Coronet in small diamonds, with the Duke of Wellington's hair' at the back.[19] Their relationship became widely and scandalously known. It became customary for aspiring hosts to invite Mary Anne to dinners and house parties whenever they hoped to entice the Duke to attend.

Yet, jealous rival devotees simultaneously sneered suggestively about her immoral means of snaring the Duke. Another aristocratic intimate of his circle, the Marchioness of Salisbury, for example recorded in her diary of 1833 what she felt was the consensus about Mary Anne: she 'sings very beautifully and looks very mad'.[20] Three years later, this diarist quoted the Duke as confiding to her about Mary Anne after five years of her adulation for him: 'she is mad, but has talent and intelligence, though with less powers of conversation than any educated person he ever saw'.

While the Duke clearly relished Mary Anne's attentive company, as he did those of other adoring noblewomen, he also expressed reservations about making any substantial commitment to any of them. As the years passed, and Mary Anne clung to the Duke ardently, he began to admit openly the dangers of continuing their widely remarked upon relationship. By the late 1830s, he was trying futilely to reduce the frequency of their meetings and began repeatedly referring to her as 'the Syren on the road to get married' to him. He both invited her to stay with him and also feared being alone with her, as he wrote to another female confidant who could serve as chaperone: 'I spoke to the Syren about coming... I don't know what to do with her if you should be gone. If you should still be there, I shall be delighted to have her.'[21]

Further, the Duke and his male and female friends received anonymous letters in which Mary Anne was quoted as boasting of her prospects and sexual power over him, planning to entrap him into marriage by sharing his bed and conceiving his child. An anonymous letter to the Duke of 27 September 1837, which he showed their mutual acquaintances, asserted:

The lady [Mary Anne] is enragée at the sudden termination of her hopes. The [Duke's] castle once cleared of [other] guests, the day was her own, her victim clenched.—'If four-and-twenty be not an overmatch for sixty-eight, the devil's in't—'and thus she brawls like a billingsgate [fishmonger], and utters indecent threats with the audacity of a W[hore]. 'He is the best dangler in the world'.— she cried, '...never out of my bed-room, but when I am in his'—a singularly delicate boast from a lady, truly. 'Not let me stay! If I had no objection, why should he?—What's come to him? He was not wont to be so nice [delicate].— But no matter—I have a project, and will fix him yet—'
Fauth!—And the Duke submits to have his name thus degraded, because she can sing.[22]

While the Duke openly laughed at these accusations, he nonetheless was aware of the dire possibilities of a too public and regular association with her.

Even as the Duke vainly sought to create some personal distance between himself and Mary Anne, she also approached other leading older men. In 1837, she sought out for his autograph the Irish Catholic poet Thomas Moore, most famous for his lyrics for 'Irish Melodies' (1808–34) and for his poetic Oriental romance, *Lalla Rookh* (1817). Although he was long-married, Moore began to go out of his way to visit her and, over the following years, they sang together repeatedly, often for each other's enjoyment, occasionally for the pleasure of the Duke of Wellington or poet-banker Samuel Rogers.[23]

Indeed, she made herself a regular in the cultured circle around aging but unmarried Samuel Rogers, which overlapped with that of the Duke. As described by an eye-witness in August 1838:

Rogers ... was almost entirely occupied with the singing of his pet, Miss Jervis... To all appearance she is a gay, wild, audacious girl, who cares for nobody and gives full scope to that unmodified naturalness of manner which in society amounts to a very considerable degree of eccentricity. This makes some people say that she is half-mad, and others that she is as bold as a lion. But... Rogers assures me that she is in reality extremely timid... I can easily see what a charm there must be to the Duke of Wellington in a person who can be as free and playful as a child in her ways with him... Miss Jervis runs up, looks brightly in his old face, and laughs and chatters and coaxes him. When she sat down to sing, I thought there could not be a more formidable thing for a girl of three or four and twenty to undertake—a small room and a small audience, and a dead silence; the Duke planted before the piano; Sir Robert Peel, Lord Aberdeen, and others, the gravest of men and statesmen, stopped short in their conversations... But she began without a shade of anxiety for herself, sang the first verse of her song and then looked brightly over to the Duke and said, 'Do you like that?' and afterwards, when someone made her sing a song which she did not like herself, she seemed to have no difficulty in doing it, only saying, 'Now, Duke, you had better talk whilst I am singing this.'[24]

Her easy access to the Duke and other dignitaries thus received much notice, both admiring and envious.

For the Duke, her familiarity, flattering though he found it, began to appear to him ever more entangling as it persisted. In May 1838, he wrote: 'I hope that I shall not get into any scrape to render necessary my giving retainer to the great lawyers in such [breach of promise] cases...' Three months later he reflected '[I] should like to see the Syren married to Lord Lowther or anybody excepting myself—God bless her! ...I am old enough to be her great-grand father.'[25] While their degree of physical intimacy was probably exaggerated by her jealous rivals, she nonetheless had her name linked to his for decades. Nonetheless, she was losing the Duke's affections in 1838, just when Dyce Sombre appeared in the social circle around Lady Cork that Mary Anne frequented.

In addition to the rising dissatisfactions in her relationship with the Duke, at this moment Mary Anne also had other familial tensions thrust upon her. The previous year, her elder full-brother, John Edward Jervis, died; in February 1838, her eldest half-brother, William, the legal lunatic, died; in March, her younger full-brother, Edward Swynfen Jervis, eloped with a working-class woman. Apparently referring to these sibling stresses, Samuel Rogers wrote empathetically to her (8 September 1838):

Nerves like yours are not nerves of iron—and tried they were last spring, not a little... But pray, pray, keep your spirits up. You are the pride and delight of all who know you as I do. If there are some who envy you, it can't be helped, it's so much the worse for them.[26]

Thus, when she met Dyce Sombre at this stressful time, she had already achieved prominence during her twenty-seven years, but had yet to consolidate her position, as only marriage could do for a lady of her age.

After her engagement to Dyce Sombre, her social position altered for the better among her established acquaintances. She continued to meet her prominent male friends including poet Thomas Moore up until June 1839. Further, the Duke could relax about her intentions toward him as he continued to socialise with her for years. After her marriage, the Duke wrote about his own good fortune from 'the lucky coincidence of the Black Prince [Dyce Sombre] appearing' and terminating any moral or legal responsibility the Duke's reputation might have required from him toward her.[27]

Viscount St Vincent as Father-in-Law-to-Be of 'the Black Prince'

When Mary Anne told her parents about her serious interest in Dyce Sombre, they expressed very mixed feelings. His fabulous wealth clearly appealed to them. Indeed, Lord St Vincent made Dyce Sombre's 'good Fortune' his main characteristic when discussing among peers this budding relationship. Dyce Sombre's other characteristics, however, detracted from his value as a potential son-in-law.

One troubling problem for Mary Anne's parents remained Dyce Sombre's Roman Catholicism. St Vincent and his wife worked to advance the cause of evangelical, low-church Anglicanism. They were major patrons of a new parish church in their village of Stone, dedicated to that branch of the Church of England. These commitments made Dyce Sombre's Catholicism particularly distressing. Nonetheless, as St Vincent had earlier conceded in a speech in the House of Lords, even Catholics could be trusted if they put their loyalties to the English crown and country above those to the Pope.[28] Tensions over this sectarian difference continued, emerging occasionally over the course of Dyce Sombre's engagement and marriage.

Furthermore, Dyce Sombre's physique was hard to overlook. His portly figure (some 125 kg but only about 1.7 metres tall) would not have been a major issue except in terms of personal attraction. But his somewhat dark complexion, signalling his mixed, and entirely non-English, ancestry, repulsed the aristocrats among whom the St Vincents moved. Dyce Sombre was tagged by diverse European, Asian, and American journals variously as 'Black', 'Copper-coloured', 'Dark', 'half-washed Blackamoor', 'Indian', 'mixed breed', 'Negro', 'Orientalist', 'sable', 'Sambo', 'tawny alien', and repeatedly as 'Othello' to her as 'Desdemona'; French newspapers identified him as 'excessivement brun' and 'le prince noir'.[29] What his evident skin colour conveyed culturally, however, differed across British society. Compared to the British bourgeoisie, the aristocracy was often more open concerning racial and ethnic difference. But Britons with experience in the colonies tended to bring back with them the more rigid racial prejudices and discrimination established there. Indeed, for the next half-century, American newspapers—including *Albion, A Journal of News, Politics and Literature* (New York City, 26 July 1856), *Spirit of the Times: A Chronicle of the Turf, Agriculture, Field Sports, Literature, and the Stage* (New York City, 26 July 1856), *Daily Picayune* (New Orleans, 24 October 1895), and *Weekly News and Courier* (Charleston, South Carolina, 6 October 1897)—explicitly and specifically cited Dyce Sombre's marriage as further proof of the corruption of the British aristocracy which accepted such 'unnatural and unholy matrimonial alliances' between races, particularly between allegedly noble White blood and supposedly corrupt mixed-bloods or 'Negroes' like him. In contrast, the British and Foreign Anti-Slavery Society's *Anti-Slavery Reporter and Aborigines' Friend* evoked Dyce Sombre's dark skin more sympathetically as akin to the Africans they sought to aid.[30]

Viscount St Vincent, with his long years living in Jamaica as a slave-owning sugar-planter, was acutely aware of the colour gradations and cultural rankings denoted by different degrees of non-white ancestry. Jamaica had nearly as many slaves as the rest of the British Caribbean combined. After he returned to England in 1805, he closely associated with other absentee West Indian plantation owners. Following his elevation to the House of Lords in 1823, he made a series of speeches there highlighting his extensive experience in Jamaica to advance himself as an expert in the still hotly debated issue of slavery and its possible abolition. He consistently instructed the Lords that 'the West India islands formed a Paradise itself to the negroes in comparison with their native country'.[31] Further, he asserted slavery was necessary before 'negroes' could be useful and productive: 'in the fertile country of the West Indies, one day's work was sufficient to supply the negro with the means of subsistence for a week, and that consequently some greater stimulous than mere necessity was required to induce him to employ his time profitably to the country and his master'. St Vincent warned 'it was very much to be feared that if the British Legislature by a bold stroke dissolved the tie existing between the negroes and the proprietors, the slaves would no longer feel that respect and affection which they on many occasions evinced for their masters'. Thus, he concluded, compulsory emancipation of 'uncivilised' Blacks would be disastrous unless they were properly prepared for freedom: 'the cup [of liberty] offered to the negro was in fact the cup of Circe, which would have intoxicated and disordered his head, and have only introduced confusion and bloodshed in the colonies'.

For St Vincent, evangelical Anglicanism provided the solution. He argued in the House of Lords, while 'the negro' would be intoxicated by liberty alone, Christianisation first would make all the difference: 'The cup of which he could drink, the cup containing the living water [of evangelical Christianity should not be] dashed from his lips, but presented to him willingly by his master's hand'. Thus, he asserted that any slave who sincerely sought to become a Christian and subsequently wished to be freed should be allowed to do so. He supported his assertion by claiming Jamaica slave-owners had voluntarily and spontaneously emancipated nearly 4,000 slaves during 1820–23, after they had been made ready for freedom by Christian baptism. Mary Anne described her father as the evangelizing patron of his own slaves: '[he was] greatly beloved by the slaves on the Estate—If any of them behaved remarkably well, he would have them baptised and freed'.[32]

While, by 1833, St Vincent recognised the inevitability of abolition, given the widespread sentiment in Britain for it, he vociferously argued that the planters should not be victimised by unilateral appropriation of their personal property: their slaves. He and the other planters, including Lord Combermere, would acquiesce in emancipation only on condition that they were compensated by the state. Indeed, St Vincent received in 1835–36 about £4,000 compensation for his ownership (or part ownership) of 560 slaves (whose real value he claimed, however, was £9–10,000). Collectively British slave-owners (including him and seventeen other Peers) split £20,000,000 in compensation.

For Viscount St Vincent and his wife, Mary Anne's growing commitment to Dyce Sombre was troubling on several grounds. Nonetheless, she was approaching thirty years old, much gossiped about for her longstanding relationships with elder men who explicitly avoided marriage with her, and clearly had personal desires of her own. In the end, her father confided to Combermere that Dyce Sombre was 'a very honourable and good young man... and that there could be nothing against him but his colour, and that... was his Daughter's concern'.[33] Others in the family concurred: 'If it had not been for his Asiatic appearance there would not have been anything peculiar about him'.[34]

Mary Anne's own attitudes toward race seem to have been strongly overlaid by her commitment to social class distinctions. Among the former slaves whom her father had baptised, emancipated, and brought back to Staffordshire with him was his personal valet, incongruously dubbed (as were many former slaves) with an ironic honourific: 'Major' Jones. Mary Anne described Jones, strikingly not by his complexion but rather by his ludicrously fashionable affectations: 'He was a very smart fellow with his frizzy hair brought up to an enormous height and cut into the shape of a sugar-loaf'.[35] She continued by noting how he attracted white women of his own social class: 'all the [English] maids were in love with him—the Cook especially, who vowed she would drown herself if he did not marry her—She went to the basin, dipped her feet in, and came back, saying it was too cold.' For Mary Anne, the Afro-Caribbean emancipated servant's hairstyle and the English cook's timidity and lack of serious commitment to her love were both ridiculous, not due to their respective biological races but rather to the unsophisticated pretensions of their lower social class. The idea of (what today might be called) 'interracial sex' did not disturb Miss Jarvis, as long as it was between people of the same social class. She thus accepted Dyce Sombre as being of a social class worthy of marriage with her, and persisted in pursuing their engagement, despite ruptures, until it concluded in their wedding.

8

ENCOUNTERING THE EUROPEAN ARISTOCRACY

Dyce Sombre had long pondered when and which European woman he should marry. When he reached London he decided on an English one, and he could hardly have found a more aristocratic wife than the Hon. Mary Anne Jervis. She accepted his social standing as worthy of her and appreciated his attentions, exoticism, and wealth. Once their engagement had been agreed upon, neither was in a rush to wed. Each pursued individual interests for nearly a year. After they met again prior to their wedding, their clashing presuppositions about the other begin to surface. Even then, despite their deep differences, both determined to proceed to their wedding contract and then ceremony.

The Affianced Couple Apart

From their first meeting, Mary Anne and Dyce Sombre developed a strong mutual interest, soon exchanging correspondence that reciprocally used the endearment 'My Dearest Friendy'. Early in December 1838, after less than four months' acquaintance, Dyce Sombre proposed marriage to her, against the strongly stated advice of some he consulted (including Lord Combermere) but with the encouragement of others (including Dr Thomas Drever). She accepted.[1] Her family friend, Lady Hastings, helped her persuade her father to approve. At this time, Dyce Sombre turned thirty (on 18 December 1838), gaining absolute control of the last of the Begum's legacy (barring the parts under litigation).

But Dyce Sombre and Mary Anne agreed on an extended engagement. While averse to leaving his fiancée on her own, he felt he needed time to go to Rome and complete Begum Sombre's funeral obsequies.

Mary Anne desired to enjoy her approaching London social season. Before he left, he carefully explained his expectations for her in her new status as his betrothed, including that she never leave the shelter of her home unescorted nor be alone with any other man.[2] Dyce Sombre believed that she and her father understood and accepted these restrictions. He then left for the continent for a protracted stay.

Despite his strict injunctions, she continued in his absence her fashionable life of socializing and singing, now elevated in her high circles by her status as engaged, and supported by the prospect of sharing his fabulous wealth and romantic Oriental allure. She also continued to make music with and for Wellington, poets Thomas Moore and Samuel Rogers, and other of her old male acquaintances. During the months immediately after her engagement, the relieved Duke confided to a mutual friend about one of her continued visits with him:

I saw Miss Jervis at Dover, and asked her and Lord St Vincent to come and dine and sleep here. I did not perceive any difference in Her Appearance, But Her old acquaintances here thought she was looking ill. She was very good Humoured about singing, and I thought she performed better than ever. She told me that she was to be married... I understand that the Black Prince is a half-Cast man, very dark coloured. He is called Sombre Dyce, or Dyce Sombre. I wrote you what I could recollect of His Family in the East Indies.[3]

Since it had been thirty-six years since the Duke had fought at Assaye against Sardhana's army, it was not surprising that his memory of Dyce Sombre's family had become vague. The Duke went on to suggest that Dyce Sombre's wealth was his best feature.

Scandals among Mary Anne's social set abounded, many rumours reaching Dyce Sombre on the continent, doubtless enhanced by distance and malice. Gossip about adultery affected aristocratic women, enhancing or detracting from their reputations according to the circumstances. Duels, while illegal in England, were still prevalent among noblemen of high honour, even if the shots missed. Celebrated duellists during this period included men well-known to both Mary Anne and Dyce Sombre. Her long-time acquaintance (and, later, second husband), Captain the Honourable Cecil Weld Forester, MP, exchanged shots against another dandy captain in the elite Royal Horse Guards ('The Blues') in February 1839, the dispute arising from precedence at a funeral.[4] An even more famous duel was fought a year later by Lord Cardigan (whom Dyce Sombre considered accompanying on his journey from Calcutta). When charged by the local magistrate, Cardigan, as a peer, demanded a trial by the House of Lords, which unanimously acquitted him on a technicality.[5]

While Mary Anne finished her social season of 1838, and indeed began that of 1839, Dyce Sombre went his own way on the continent. But they exchanged intimate letters regularly. As a devoted Catholic, Dyce Sombre had headed across France and Italy toward Rome and the Pope.

On the Continent

Travelling as a Catholic 'Indian Prince' of wondrous wealth, heir to the intriguingly exotic Begum of Sardhana, and a Colonel, Dyce Sombre was received by the highest echelons of European society. In Paris the Begum's French friends, Generals Jean-François Allard and Count Ventura, débuted Dyce Sombre. Among other introductions, they secured him an audience with the late Begum's correspondent, the aging King Louis-Philippe (whom we will recall, although he probably did not, years before awarded Mary Anne a prize for her schoolgirl dance). Allard died later that year but Ventura met Dyce Sombre periodically in Europe over the next decade, first as his patron, but later as his bitter enemy.

As in London, Dyce Sombre's money enabled him to dwell, dress, and deport himself in a style commensurate with his received social status. The English expatriate newspaper, *Gagliani's Messenger*, proclaimed the arrival in Paris of 'Colonel Dyce Sombre', providing a brief history of the devout and munificent 'Princess Begum', which was duly echoed in the London *Times*.[6] Despite his ignorance of the French language, he savoured his reception and determined to see all the sights and to impress his aristocratic hosts.

In Paris, his indulgence in sensual gratification, especially through the purchase of food, alcohol, and sex, received even more acceptance as within the appropriate limits for a rich man than in London. Further, his 'Oriental' origins allegedly authorised even more licence. Baron Sébastien Félix Feuillet de Conches, one of Dyce Sombre's prime aristocratic guides into Parisian high society—and over the next decade his official government guardian—later characterised him as:

reserved in his behavior, discreet in his language, dignified in his appearance, according to the fashion of Orientals, rather silent than communicative, such he showed himself at the first... This reserved behaviour was not the whole

159

man. He had the fire of his country in his veins. Above all he was a sensual man, with passions that education, and his habits as a Nabob, drove into excesses with women... He was an Indian, out of his own country, lost, bewildered in the midst of civilization, supremely sensual, domineering, proud, haughty, prodigal of his person to satisfy a passion. Vegetating, rather than living and thinking; but who, full of intelligence and cleverness, would, rightly guided, have managed his affairs well, and have done good rather than anything bad.[7]

As with so many recollections about Dyce Sombre, this colourful representation was perhaps shaped by dramatic later developments in his life.

After a relatively brief first visit to Paris, Dyce Sombre journeyed south to crisscross Italy. Continuously received as an 'Indian Prince', he equipped himself with snowballing letters of introduction from the highest in European society, as one dignitary provided a letter for him to present to the next. Thus, Dyce Sombre gained access to aristocrats in Venice, Ferrara, Bologna, Rome, Florence, Genoa, as well as many villas and towns in between. Touring Malta, Dyce Sombre was received (3 April 1839) as a visiting Masonic dignitary by the Valetta Lodge of St John and St Paul.[8]

In his frequent personal letters to his former courtiers back in Sardhana, Dyce Sombre confided how inwardly tentative and overawed he felt in this sophisticated world. Once, he wrote his brother-in-law Solaroli: 'I can only plead my comparative ignorance of the world, and the way I was brought up'.[9] Experimenting by growing a long beard to enhance his appearance, he visited Reghellini's brothers.[10] Simultaneously, Dyce Sombre's mannered display of his wealth and also his patronage of the people he met reassured him of his own stature. As he luxuriously toured Italy, he had Solaroli send reminder notes to many British officers and officials in India about personal debts they still owed him. Indeed, he firmly instructed his former teacher, Reverend Henry Fisher, to buy a life insurance policy for 20,000 Rupees to cover his remaining debt since 'surely he cannot wish me to be a loser by it, in case of his death'.[11] Over the years, Dyce Sombre insisted that the Fisher family pay off their several loans in full, through as large installments as they could afford.

Particularly in light of Dyce Sombre's lavish spending, notable devotion to his foster-mother the fabled Begum, as well as his later notoriety, many expatriate Britons recalled meeting and speaking with him. Among the latter were two men his own age: William Gladstone (future British Prime Minister) and Dr Joseph Francis Olliffe (who would treat him later in life, witness his will, and often testify to his sanity), while sixteen-year-old the Hon. George Chichester, later 5th Marquess of Donegall, remained Dyce Sombre's occasional social and travelling companion for a decade.[12] The Reverend Thomas Farr journeyed for six weeks with Dyce Sombre in Italy and later repeatedly in Britain and on the continent. This Anglican clergyman particularly remembered how Dyce Sombre's 'feelings as regarded females were Asiatic to a most extraordinary degree... [He] stated... his intention, if he married [Mary Anne], of insisting on her living as his wife after the manner in which Eastern wives are accustomed to live, and of obliging her in a great measure to conform to usages and customs quite unknown to Europeans; saying also that his wife should never go out in a carriage alone, nor go to the Opera without him.'[13] Farr felt that this did not bode well for their future married life but delicately did not try explicitly to dissuade Dyce Sombre from the wedding.

Unlike many British expatriates in Rome, Dyce Sombre was a committed Catholic. His foster-mother the Begum's many handsome donations and extensive epistolary intercourse with the Vatican were well documented and much appreciated by the highest in the Church hierarchy. A painting of the Begum's dedication of the Sardhana cathedral (later reduced to a basilica) adorned the Pope's antechamber in his own Quirinal Palace.[14] One of her monetary gifts had persuaded Pope Gregory XVI to make Dyce Sombre a Knight of the Pontifical Order of Christ. Hence, soon after his arrival in Rome, he had a private meeting with this Pope in his personal chapel. A further donation from Dyce Sombre obtained a knighthood in the Order of St Gregario il Grande for his brother-in-law, Solaroli. Indeed, Dyce Sombre was surprised at the apparent cupidity of the Vatican. As he wrote to Solaroli, once the money was in hand, the only background check before bestowing the knighthood was a question from the Pope to him if Solaroli was Catholic since 'otherwise it would have been sacrilege to have made you [a Papal knight]'.[15]

As Dyce Sombre had sincerely promised the Begum before she died, he arranged a grand funeral mass for the woman he still reverently called 'Huzoor Mukbara' ('Fortunate Lord').[16] He negotiated with the Vatican to honour her in the Church of San Carlo al Corso, where a great wooden catafalque was constructed, over which an appropriately laudatory oration was preached by the rising priest Nicholas Patrick

Wiseman (Spanish-born but of Irish ancestry, later Cardinal and Arch-bishop of Westminster).[17] Dyce Sombre's commemoration of the Begum and her works was celebrated even in America, including by the *Catholic Telegraph* (Cincinnati, 24 January 1839). In contrast, Protestant journals for decades declaimed that the Pope was making her a saint, thus proving Romish corruption; these included newspa-pers not only in England but also in Ireland (*Belfast News-Letter*), Scotland (*Glasgow Herald*), and across the US (nationally, the *American Protestant Magazine*; in Boston, the *Christian Reflector, Littell's Living Age*, the *Recorder* and *Zion's Herald and Wesleyan Journal*; in New York, the *Spectator*; in San Francisco, the *Daily Evening Bulletin*; and even in the village of Bellows Falls, the *Vermont Chronicle*). Dyce Sombre's devotion to the Begum thus drew sustained international attention.

In addition, Dyce Sombre set his devotion in stone by commission-ing leading Italian sculptor Adamo Tadolini to create a vast and costly (£4,000) monument to the Begum in the finest Carrera marble. Dyce Sombre composed the inscriptions in Persian, Latin, and English for its

Cardinal and Archbishop of Westminster Nicholas Patrick Wiseman

Begum's Cenotaph by Adamo Tadolini, and Detail

pediment. He further posed for a full-length statue shown adoringly as first mourner, at her right foot. (This huge tableau's other three large statues were of Sardhana Diwan Rai Singh, Bishop Julius Caesar, and cavalry commander, Inayatullah; the cenotaph was eventually installed in the Sardhana basilica where it stands today.)

As Dyce Sombre informed his correspondents in India, the Pope most insistently and 'in a very flattering manner' invited him to extend his stay in Rome in order to be an honoured guest (along with the Kings of Naples and Bavaria, and recently abdicated King Dom Miguel of Portugal) at the canonization of six new saints. Dyce Sombre remarked that he found this Catholic ceremony 'very imposing' and quite different from the Anglican coronation of Queen Victoria which he had recently observed. Thus, although he complained of Italy's summer temperatures—'the heat is beyond bearing. I had no idea that I could have found it so in Europe'—and was anxious to advance his legal and matrimonial causes back in London, he did not rejoin his fiancée there until July 1839.[18]

The Intermittent Engagement

Officially Mary Anne's announced bridegroom-to-be, Dyce Sombre accompanied her as British high society dispersed to their country houses in England and Scotland. Tensions between the affianced couple arose over the next year as each tried to make the other conform to disparate expectations for their life together. Further, each felt alien in the other's social circle, where disparaging rumours and remarks abounded.

Immediately upon his return to London, Dyce Sombre faced embarrassing charges. On Friday, 5 July 1839, at 10 p. m., he had casually urinated against a lamppost on Weymouth Street, near Portland Place, and offended two respectable women. One, Janet Caldwell, a fifty-four-year-old milliner, accused him of exposing his genitals. They had heated words. She had him arrested for indecent exposure but then suddenly died of apoplexy from the incident. Lord Combermere and Reverend Farr came to the police station and then inquest to defend Dyce Sombre. Since Ms Caldwell's death was ruled natural and since the second woman had shrunk away and not actually seen the alleged exposure, Dyce Sombre could not be officially charged with either manslaughter or indecency. Newspapers, however, publicised this shocking incident, which did not ingratiate him with polite English society.[19]

Throughout their relationship, Mary Anne's aristocratic acquaintances found Dyce Sombre abrasive while his physical appearance and behaviour offended their conventions for deportment. Familiar with Mary Anne, they at best tolerated his alien presence. To dissuade her from this marriage, some informed her about his previous relationships (real or imagined) with Indian women, inaccurately asserting that he was still legally married and had a family back there. His response was denial and threats to shoot such rumour-mongers, backed by the pistols he always carried in his luggage and sometimes displayed. Overall, his evident discord with her and disconcerting words and actions led most of her circle to reject him, which they urged her to do too.

Some among his British mentors, most prominently Lord Combermere, and also many among Dyce Sombre's Indian and continental companions, questioned Mary Anne's virtue and the wisdom of his marrying her. Even before his return from Italy, Dyce Sombre had been hearing from assorted male associates colourful accounts of Mary Anne's immoral behaviour with her long-time elderly male friends prior to their engagement and during his long absence. On visits to her aristocratic hosts, he suspiciously observed evidence that confirmed these malicious rumours. The difference between socially conventional embraces, kisses, and prolonged face-to-face gazing during greeting and departure between female and male elites were evidently hard for him to distinguish from intimate and salacious exchanges and echoes or promises of sexual liaisons. Further, he was unused to conforming to the expectations and will of any woman except the late Begum, particularly one to whom he was giving so much money. He reportedly complained she 'was very clever—too clever for him'.[20]

Accordingly he repeatedly enjoined his future father-in-law to use his paternal authority to curb Mary Anne. Dutifully, the seventy-two-year-old Viscount St Vincent escorted his daughter to house parties that Dyce Sombre could not attend. Nonetheless, Dyce Sombre then strenuously objected to her going out at all except when escorted by himself; these strictures went largely unheeded. She continued to dine with Cecil Forester and sang for the Duke of Wellington. Along with her father, she even slept in Wellington's abode.[21]

On his part, St Vincent vainly appealed to sixty-six-year-old Lord Combermere to use his surrogate paternal influence over Dyce Sombre to make him relinquish his imputations about Mary Anne's unchastity. The thrice married Combermere instead repeatedly urged Dyce Sombre to abandon her as completely unfitting as a wife for someone like him. When the father heatedly defended his daughter, Dyce Sombre furiously felt his manly honour impugned.

Enraged, Dyce Sombre unilaterally broke the engagement. In a misreading of British aristocratic convention about when duels should honourably be fought, he threatened to challenge St Vincent to a pistol fight for inconsistently 'wishing to accept him as his son-in-law, and yet not sufficiently supporting him' in controlling Mary Anne's public behaviour.[22] Reluctantly, Mary Anne returned all (except one) of the fabulous jewels—many of them from the Begum's own collection—and other presents that Dyce Sombre had lavished on her. Combermere warned Dyce Sombre that this single remaining gift 'was only retained in order to afford her an excuse for opening a correspondence with him if she again changed her mind'.[23]

Distancing himself from Mary Anne, Dyce Sombre left in April 1840 for Paris and then Vienna. Combermere's warning proved prescient since she soon wrote Dyce Sombre post-haste, begging him to return and promising to amend her behaviour. Her letter eventually reached him in May and, persuaded of her sincerity, he rejoined her in England, restoring their engagement. Nonetheless, Dyce Sombre found their tempestuous relationship very disturbing. He felt so frustrated and upset, he even consulted the prominent alienist Dr Edward Thomas Monro (known to Mary Anne from her eldest half-brother's lunacy case). Dr Monro found it unusual for someone voluntarily to consult about his own mental imbalance; usually patients were compelled to do so.[24]

Another ongoing tension between the affianced couple was sectarian. In what he considered a concession, Dyce Sombre had agreed that, despite the doctrines of his Church, she could raise their future daughters as Anglican Protestant, although he insisted all sons be raised Roman Catholic. In the ongoing disquieted atmosphere, it either occurred to Dyce Sombre or was suggested to him that she might bear him only daughters. In this sonless circumstance, he now demanded their future daughters would be raised Catholic and vowed again to break their engagement unless she agreed. Since Mary Anne was still committed to the marriage, she conceded and restored the engagement despite her evangelical Protestant parents.

They had his own solicitor Frere draw up the substantial marriage settlement along lines conventional for wealthy Britons. Dyce Sombre quickly signed this nuptial contract (8 September 1840), without reading its legalese clauses carefully, trusting his advisor Dr Thomas Drever to do so on his behalf. This settlement transferred £133,333 in bonds and stocks—over a quarter of his capital—into an inalienable trust for her, with joint trustees Combermere and Drever representing him and her younger brother, Edward Swynfen Jervis, and maternal uncle, Thomas Hawe Parker, representing her.[25] Under British 'coverture' laws, as a married woman she could not personally possess any property or sign any contract independent of her husband. But this settlement guaranteed her the income from the trust, £4,000 annually, for the rest of her married lifetime, at the discretion of these four male trustees. Should Dyce Sombre predecease her (as in fact would happen), as a widow she came legally into personal possession of the capital in the trust, in addition to any of Dyce Sombre's other property he willed or British courts allocated to her. (Dyce Sombre later denied that he understood these intricacies of British law concerning such marital or inheritance issues.) In addition, he created a trust of railway shares and bank annuities that paid directly to her £300 annually as 'pin money'. He also presented her with much of his magnificent jewelry, valued at £7,000, mostly inherited from the Begum but also including his diamond and ruby encrusted badge as Knight of the Order of Christ, bestowed by the Pope. For her wedding ring, Dyce Sombre symbolically had some gold extracted from the late Begum's own signet ring, suggesting the extension of his loyalty to Mary Anne.

On the eve of their wedding, Mary Anne sent a long letter enjoining him to trust her 'in everything she might say or do'.[26] She also begged him to restrain his unseemly bursts of anger at European manners and conventions, which made him look 'terrific' (meaning terrifying) to her acquaintances. (She later destroyed this letter as too intimate a revelation of their relationship.) Her efforts to refashion him to meet the expectations of her social circle would prove as fruitless as were his efforts to alter her.

All these arrangements evidently having been successfully concluded, and dispensations for their intersectarian marriage from the Archbishop of Canterbury and the Pope authorised, they held a quiet Anglican wedding on 26 September 1840. The St Vincents reserved their parish church, the fashionable St George's, Hanover Square, London (undeterred by the inauspicious precedent of Viscount St Vincent's and his brother's first disastrous weddings there). In conformity with Dyce Sombre's faith, they also had a private Catholic wedding in St Vincent's house. Now legally bound in Anglican, Catholic, and

St George's, Hanover Square

English law, Mr and Mrs Dyce Sombre departed for their honeymoon, travelling across the continent bound for Italy, although they never arrived there.

Newly Married Life

Their honeymoon journey reached no further than Brussels before she became quite ill for eight weeks. It is not clear when he informed her about his many cases of venereal diseases or previous children and consorts or when (or if) they began marital intercourse.[27] Nevertheless, his constant attendance on her and her dependence on him and invalid inability to move about freely seem to have brought out the best in their relationship. Combermere and his third wife also joined them, with Combermere providing experienced advice to Dyce Sombre. He proudly wrote to Reghellini in Sardhana, asking for 'a handsome dress for my Wife' in the latest north Indian style, including a bodice of green and a tunic of sky-blue, pajamas made of blue gold-woven cloth, a scarf of pomegranate colour, also a pair of shoes worked in the shape of a peacock, and a kerchief with a draw-purse attached.[28] He suggested that the size should be Mrs Reghellini's, only with the legs of the pajamas a bit shorter. After this outfit arrived, Mary Ann wore and had herself drawn in it; Dyce Sombre proudly sent on a reproduction of this portrait of his adorned bride to the Reghellini family.[29] He also taught Mary Anne some loving phrases in Persian, the language he used to express intimacy, and recited what he said was an 'Indian Love Song'.

After their return to Britain in December 1840, their conflicting expectations resurfaced even as they entered the London season, what Mary Anne called 'constant and varied society, large dinners, and parties to the theatre', punctuated by visits to aristocratic country houses in England and Scotland.[30] In London, they took a semi-permanent suite of rooms in the Clarendon, one of London's most fashionable hotels. As the Honourable Mrs Dyce Sombre, Mary Anne now stood as a lady patron of concerts instead of being the sponsored performer.[31] The much sought after Hungarian painter, Charles Brocky, executed one of his high society portraits of Dyce Sombre.

Dyce Sombre also increasingly asserted his legal authority over his wife. He instructed Mary Anne to list all the people of her acquaintance so he could approve those she could visit. He also insisted that

D. O. Dyce Sombre by Charles Brocky

she inform him prior to all her unescorted trips away from him. Given the patriarchal nature of British society, Mary Anne conformed to his instructions, despite the strictures they placed on her customary movement through society. But Dyce Sombre proved still unsatisfied by her obedience and devotion to him.

At this point in their marriage, neither Mary Anne nor Dyce Sombre felt well. He had been taking quinine, Morrison's Pills, and other unspecified drugs. Their physicians urged a tour of the countryside, which meant visits to the rural estates of her aristocratic friends. Dyce Sombre may have been expressing resentment against her social set when he gave away to a passerby on London's Bond Street her Edmund Lodge's *Peerage, Baronetage, Knightage and Companionage of the British Empire*, a book she used regularly to brush up on noble families whom they were about to visit.[32]

During the summer of 1841, as the couple visited the country houses of the Duke of Wellington, the Marchioness of Hastings, and the St Vincents themselves, Dyce Sombre made an escalating series of explicit allegations. First confidentially and then ever more openly, he asserted his wife's immorality to his shocked, embarrassed and discomforted hosts: she was an opera singer and therefore a courtesan, had criminal sexual intercourse with men of all classes, and had committed incest with her father, all with the acquiescence of her mother. When Dyce

169

Sombre would not be silenced, Mary Anne's family and their friends felt he had overstepped bounds of propriety.

Disturbed, Dyce Sombre made a brief trip to Ireland, visiting a leading Masonic brother from Meerut, James Rogers, to whom he complained: '[Mary Anne] was a first-rate private singer, and very fond of having parties, which were very expensive, of a gay disposition, fond of talking with gentlemen… she turned him into ridicule… He regretted his marriage, and blamed Lord Combermere for it.'[33]

Meanwhile, the St Vincents considered how to remedy this distressing situation. After much private consultation, Viscount St Vincent composed a lawyerly repudiation of all these allegations for Dyce Sombre to sign:

Upon the fullest and most calm reflection I voluntarily disclaim, without qualification or mental reservation, every idea of casting any imputation whatever upon the virtue, modesty, and character of my beloved wife, whether in relation to her conduct before marriage or in relation to her conduct since her marriage; I also disavow all belief in every observation or insinuation which may have been made at any time to me by any one to her prejudice, and cannot ascribe any good motive or justifiable ground for it; I also disclaim every imputation on the character or honour of Lord St Vincent, for indifference at any time to the conduct of his virtuous and amiable daughter.[34]

When Mary Anne vowed to separate from her husband should he not sign, he did so on 7 June 1841, but reluctantly and without sincerely relinquishing his belief in her past and continued immorality.

St Vincent knew from his own first marriage that divorce, difficult to obtain in Britain since it required an act of both Houses of Parliament, was virtually impossible without proof of the wife's adultery. This declaration meant Dyce Sombre could not now make such a claim against Mary Anne. Evidently, Dyce Sombre did not comprehend the full legal implications of the document he had just signed.

Meanwhile, like Mary Anne's cousin, Captain the Honourable Swynfen Thomas Carnegie, Dyce Sombre decided to enter the British Parliament in the general election scheduled for later that same month of June. Although the St Vincents had long supported the Conservatives, Dyce Sombre inclined toward the Whig-Radicals. As he wrote to his brother-in-law in India, 'Mrs D. S.'s family are different from me in politics… Without being angry at it, my dear S[olaroli], I did not marry for the sake of interest; they knew very well what my politics were; & I go upon my own bottom, as the expression goes, tho' it is rather a vulgar one. I am too independent to be controlled by any one in anything and, after all, it is only then when you can dictate.'[35] Finding out how to proceed, including selecting and buying a constituency to elect him, however, required considerable political acumen and experience, which Dyce Sombre himself lacked.

9

DYCE SOMBRE IN BRITISH PARLIAMENT

Dyce Sombre, who had been excluded from the Oriental Club and shunned by his aristocratic wife's social circle, suddenly decided in June 1841, in the midst of his disturbing conflicts with Mary Anne's family, that he wished to become a Member of Parliament. This would enhance his social position in Britain, across Europe and throughout the British Empire. Furthermore, Dyce Sombre knew that personal political influence decided much in Britain, often overriding strictly legal rulings. Hence, being in Parliament, he felt, would advance his ongoing court cases against the East India Company, which had hitherto floundered before British judges. Relatively few Catholics, only one other person popularly considered black,[1] and no Asian had ever entered Parliament, but Dyce Sombre often ignored precedent and convention when he determined on something. Moreover, if others considered him black, Asian, or Indian, he thought of himself as fully qualified as a loyal and devoted subject of Queen Victoria. For Dyce Sombre, the substantial outlay of cash necessary to purchase his election to Parliament seemed worth paying.

Dyce Sombre Stands for Parliament

Since Dyce Sombre had little precise knowledge about the practical means or multiple implications of his desired entry into Parliament, he sought advice from various informed advisors. When elections were suddenly declared, in June 1841, he consulted, among others, Charles Edward Trevelyan, whom he had known well in the Delhi Residency and Calcutta administration, a man of his own age but one never hesitant to provide patronising advice. By this time, Trevelyan had made himself highly influential in the British government, currently holding office as Assistant Secretary to Her Majesty's Treasury and taking a prominent lead in civil service reform. Trevelyan counseled Dyce Sombre to become an MP: 'as he was a man of fortune and leisure, I thought he would do well to avail himself of any opportunity that might offer of getting into Parliament, and it would be a useful and improving occupation to him'.[2] Thus encouraged to run, Dyce Sombre then quickly needed an experienced and efficient political guide, as well as a compliant English constituency.

An anonymous 'West-end friend' (perhaps Trevelyan) referred Dyce Sombre to James Coppock, a solicitor and professional Parliamentary agent—the most notorious of the 'political partizans of the day'.[3] Coppock reportedly described Dyce Sombre as innocently 'chaste as unsunned snow', lacking any knowledge of British political practices, 'ready to conform to any politics', and being completely 'ductile matériel' in Coppock's skilled hands.[4] Crucially, Dyce Sombre was rich and willing to spend lavishly for the unpaid post of Member of Parliament.

In the decade following the 1832 Reform Act (2 William 4, c. 45) and its successors, the procedures and precedents of British politics were shifting substantially. Coppock and other political operators were becoming more professionalised in their manipulation of voters. Indeed, Coppock had in 1835 written an influential book on how to maneuver through the complex and untested election laws to maximise one's advantage: *Elector's Manual; or, Plain Directions by Which Every Man May Know His Own Rights, and Preserve Them*; many editions of this pragmatic guide followed over subsequent years. Coppock was already widely known (but not convicted) for his suspect electoral dealings. Further, he was central to the alignments and realignments of various allied factions among those politicians characterised as Whigs, Radicals, or Liberals. These factions were currently but sporadically moving toward an organised political party, in large measure through Coppock's firm guidance. As the base of his political operations, he used London's Reform Club, of which he was a founder, the solicitor, quondam secretary, and an honourary life member.

Even as Dyce Sombre placed himself in Coppock's experienced hands, delegations of various political stripes from many open constituencies were frantically seeking men with enough wealth to purchase their ballots. Following the defeat of the Melbourne Whig-Liberal government and its Radical supporters by a single vote, Parliament had dissolved on 22 June 1841 and an immediate election had been declared for the end of that month. This was the first general election in which reform laws subsequent to 1832 came into force. Hence, not even the best legal minds of the day quite knew which long-standing or novel corrupt practices would be tolerated and which would actually be punished, and to what degree.

The electors of the infamous 'rotten borough' of Sudbury in Suffolk, East Anglia, tended not to be swayed by principle as much as cash. Its six hundred qualified male voters had long used elections to make money by scandalously enticing rich candidates to bribe them, even after the 1832 Reform Act made such practices illegal. The constituency owned the right to elect two MPs despite its modest size: less than 6,000 residents, many of them impoverished silk and bunting weavers, originally Flemish but now long domiciled as British subjects. Sudbury had in the prior five elections returned seven Conservatives and three liberals (of various factions)—evidently based on the candidate's largess rather than ideology.[5] When an election did not seem to be hotly contested, and therefore when the bribes were unpalatably low, the worthy voters of Sudbury often desperately sought candidates who could be induced to contest, thereby creating lucrative campaigns. So contrary was Sudbury that, in the early 1830s, pranksters published mock advertisements that called for more 'idiot' candidates to stand from Sudbury, the 'Asylum of Idiots', joining the fictitious eight 'idiots' already declared (one being 'His Holiness the Pope'). Charles Dickens

Mock Election Poster for Sudbury, 1830s

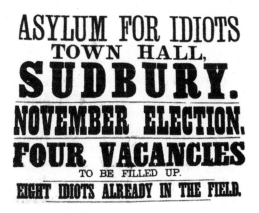

'The Election at Eatanswill' by Hablot Knight Browne 'Phiz'

reportedly based his riotous description of Eatanswill's venal election in *The Pickwick Papers* at least in part on the 1835 Sudbury election, which he had personally observed as a young newspaper reporter.[6] Nor were the amounts demanded as bribes modest; the expenditure in Sudbury's 1835 election purportedly averaged £35 per voter.

As soon as the 1841 election was in the offing, various Conservative delegations, including one from Sudbury, rushed as usual to the Carleton Club on London's Pall Mall, looking for rich men with their inclinations. They finally found two willing candidates: a wealthy Welshman named David Jones and youthful Charles Taylor, a resident of Sussex and the son of Sir Charles William Taylor, MP from Wells, Norfolk— incidentally, the convicted adulterer with Mary Anne's father's first wife. Despite being strangers to Sudbury, both candidates received assurances of an easy Conservative victory.

A rival Whig-Liberal-Radical delegation from Sudbury was simultaneously searching on Pall Mall at the nearby Reform Club. As one hostile, Conservative-sympathizing, provincial newspaper reported on the eve of the polls: 'Deputation after deputation has been dispatched to the Reform Club by the Sudbury Radicals, begging them to send

Reform Club, London

two candidates to contest the borough, but whether it was a distrust of the application; or a conviction of the utter hopelessness of the attempt, nobody has yet been fool-hardy enough to jump into the independent trap'.[7]

Mary Anne's would-be suitor, Conservative MP Benjamin Disraeli, more colourfully described in one of his political novels the desperate search by another Liberal-Radical delegation during this same 1841 election:

All this time the Liberal deputation... were walking about London like mad things, eating luncheons and looking for a candidate. They called at the Reform Club twenty times in the morning, badgered whips and red-tapers; were introduced to candidates, badgered candidates; examined would-be members as if they were at a cattle-show, listened to political pedigrees, dictated political pledges, referred to Hansard to see how men had voted, inquired whether men had spoken, finally discussed terms. But they never could hit the right man. If the principles were right, there was no money; and if money were ready, money would not take pledges. If fact, they wanted a Phoenix: a very rich man, who would do exactly as they liked, with extremely low opinions and with very high connections.[8]

While Disraeli singled out his political opponents for such ridicule, his Conservatives were equally culpable. Indeed, another friend of Mary Anne, Lord Forester, arranged for the heavily indebted Disraeli to switch for this 1841 election from Maidstone to the less expensive constituency of Shrewsbury. (At this time, Disraeli reportedly had over £22,000 in legal judgments against him and owed at least £6,800 more, mostly for election expenses.)[9]

Just before election day, Coppock and the Sudbury Whig-Radicals finally found one of its two needed candidates among the Reform Club's members: Frederick Villiers, Esq.[10] Although Villiers had considerable campaign experience, he also carried a motley past, personally and politically. The second illegitimate son of well-born, wealthy, but unmarried parents, Villiers had graduated from Eton and then Trinity College, Cambridge (where he was known as 'Savage Villiers'). Next, he had qualified as a barrister from Lincoln's Inn (like Dyce Sombre's father-in-law). Villiers later adopted his biological father's name, calling himself Frederick Villiers Meynell. Villiers had already been elected MP for Saltash in 1831 but then lost his seat when that constituency was disenfranchised as a 'Schedule A' rotten borough in the 1832 Reform Act. He had next been elected MP from Canterbury in 1835, but this result was controverted (reversed) three months later by Parliament on the double grounds of Villiers not having sufficient real estate income to qualify (£300 was required for a borough like Canterbury) and also of having egregiously bribed his voters.[11] Villiers stood yet again in 1837 from Canterbury but reportedly lost badly because he did not spend enough. Thus, he had much familiarity, mostly unsatisfactory, with the real politics of parliamentary elections. However, since Villiers lacked sufficient funds to bribe the Sudbury voters, Coppock and the Whig-Radical delegation still needed a second candidate with surplus capital.

The *sine qua non* of substantial cash for parliamentary campaigns was widely recognised. As one pamphlet of the age candidly explained:

In practice you [voters] do not choose your candidate... you must procure your candidate from one of the great metropolitan depots [especially the Carleton and Reform Clubs], where candidates are kept ready-made. Hence it is quite a chance what sort of a commodity will be sent to you; but the chances are against intellectual ability. Let us describe the lottery from which your prize will be drawn... [T]he primary qualification is money. The cost of every borough is known, and unless the would-be candidate is prepared to spend that sum, it is simply throwing away a seat to send him to the fight... Money and mind do not always co-exist, and, the former being the most essential qualification, the vast majority of candidates are men who have no other pretensions that wealth... You cannot win without money, and you must take the man who brings that recommendation, though he may be wanting in every other, or abandon the field.[12]

If Villiers provided the Sudbury Whig-Radical agents with experience in electoral connivances, Dyce Sombre provided cash.

As lawyers all too experienced with post-election challenges, Villiers and Coppock knew that Dyce Sombre needed certain qualifications, which recent changes in the law newly specified. After 1829, thanks to the Duke of Wellington, Catholics like Dyce Sombre were eligible to sit in Parliament (although Jews could not enter for another three decades, until 1858). After 1838, the requirement that the candidate's requisite £300 income for a borough like Sudbury was expanded from exclusively real estate to include personal income as well; Dyce Sombre more than met this revised requirement.

His birth, however, was a more vexed question. A decade earlier, Jeremy Bentham had reportedly proposed as a candidate for Parliament the social and religious reformer from India, Raja Rammohun Roy (who was then visiting England); since Roy did not stand, the issue of whether an Indian was eligible was never tested. Further, while Roy had been born in British-administered Bengal, arguably under British sovereignty, Dyce Sombre was born in Sardhana when it was itself legally semi-sovereign and outside of British India. Nor had Dyce Sombre been naturalised. Yet, his father's father had been Scottish. All these factors thus added imponderable complications for his potential candidacy.[13] Nevertheless, Villiers and Coppock apparently counselled Dyce Sombre to send for certified copies of his father's birth and wedding certificates from India (although these could not arrive in less than a year).[14] Thus, while Dyce Sombre was not qualified to vote in Sudbury or any other British constituency, lacking legal residency, he appeared to Villiers, Coppock, and the Sudbury Whig-Radicals as a passable candidate, particularly in light of his promising wealth.

The Sudbury Whig-Radicals, led by a local solicitor, John Francis Sikes Gooday, also briefed Dyce Sombre about its election customs. They specified how much cash he should send along as an advance payment and how many untraceable gold coins he should bring with him in a strongbox when he came to the town. The election itself allegedly ended up costing Dyce Sombre over £3,000, slightly more than the recent average for the seat but not an abnormal amount for such a constituency in those years.[15]

Later Parliamentary investigation disclosed that Coppock directed Dyce Sombre to write three cheques for £1,000 each. Although Coppock gave Dyce Sombre a receipt for the £3,000, Coppock's confidential clerk attempted to disguise the paper trail by forging one of the clerk's own distant relative's signature as the recipient of them and then cashing the cheques for anonymous gold. Coppock also advised Dyce Sombre and Villiers to go to Sudbury just before polling day and then seclude themselves from their future constituents.

Dyce Sombre also apprehended a personal problem: what to do with Mary Anne while he was away. His advisors, knowing the rowdiness of the polling to come, advised him not to bring her. Indeed, Dickens described how 'During the whole time of the polling, the town ['Eatanswill'] was in a perpetual fever of excitement... Exciseable articles [alcoholic drinks] were remarkably cheap at all the public-houses; and spring vans [ambulances] paraded the streets for the accommodation of voters who were seized with any temporary dizziness in the head—an epidemic which prevailed among the electors, during the contest, to a most alarming extent, and under the influence of which they might frequently been seen lying on the pavements in a state of utter insensibility.'[16] But Dyce Sombre also feared leaving Mary Anne unchaperoned even for the short time he would be away. On the advice of Combermere, he entrusted his wife to the elderly Lady Sophia (wife of Sir Francis Burdett) at their villa near Hampton Court, and turned his attention to getting elected.

In Sudbury, the Conservatives anticipated an uncontested election. But, while neither Villiers nor Dyce Sombre had yet arrived, their local agents, popularly known as 'Raps', had been gathering signatures to have them nominated, reportedly by distributing £1 each to about 200 voters.[17] On Sunday, Villiers arrived and Dyce Sombre, who had never set foot in Sudbury before, drove in after 3:00 a. m. on Monday, the very day of the nomination, accompanied by a servant and a small but exceptionally weighty strongbox. Such non-resident candidates were common in those years (about one-third of all MPs) but such last-minute arrivals were less so.[18]

That Monday, 28 June, the Returning Officer read out 'The Bribery Act' (2 George 2, c. 24), thus opening nominations. The agents of Dyce Sombre and Villiers, as well as the Conservative candidates, paid the approximately £100 in legal fees to this officer and various poll clerks and other officials. Then, the election was immediately held by a show of hands. Since the Conservatives were only paying 10 shillings per vote, half that of their opponents, this produced a visibly 'very large majority' for both Whig-Radical candidates.[19] Nonetheless, as was conventional, the losers demanded a formal paper ballot. Neither Dyce Sombre nor Villiers gave a speech nor even talked with any voters, leaving everything to their election agents. Indeed, this accorded with the sage advice of an insider's guide from that period which emphasised that experienced election agents 'should attend the candidate, and never leave him in the company of any persons whose devotion to his interests there is not an absolute assurance'.[20] Witnesses also testified that late that Monday, Dyce Sombre dispatched his servant on an overnight dash to bring more cash.

The Sudbury polls opened at 8:00 a. m. the next day, Tuesday. Supporters of the Radical-Whigs adorned themselves with yellow ribbons; the Conservatives besported blue. In addition to paying cash to voters, each party also promised to cover bills for drink, food, and lodging at local public houses, not only for the current election but also the outstanding ones dating from the previous election. Each election thus commenced by paying the hospitality costs of the previous one, locally called 'fixtures', and often ended leaving debts for the next, especially from the losing party.

Both sides furiously marshalled their forces. Commanding the Whig-Radicals was a stranger to Sudbury calling himself 'Mr Massey', later identified by witnesses as Coppock himself (although he denied this under oath, but later admitted it privately to friends). Working under Massey's battle-hardened direction were subalterns, unknown in Sudbury and later identified only by their hair colour: 'the fair-haired man', 'the dark man'.

When the polls opened in the market square, a crowd of up to two-hundred willing men pressed into the adjacent Black Boy Inn, one bastion of the Whig-Radicals. Despite men with staves hired with Dyce Sombre's money to keep order, eye-witnesses later testified that the crowd was so eager that the men broke the banister of the narrow and twisting stairwell to the right of the bar on their way upstairs. There, each voter received £2 in gold through a window from a locally unknown man, whose face was obscured and only his hand visible. The incentivised voter then passed out into the market square where

Sudbury, Black Boy Inn

he entered the voting 'pound' at the poll booth. There, his two ballots were publicly cast and recorded, giving the bribers evidence of fulfillment of the bargain. The voter then proceeded to the Swan Inn across the square, had his name checked off the growing list of cooperative electors, received a numbered cardboard ticket, marched upstairs, and submitted this card for an additional £4 in cash from another unknown agent, later only identified as the 'redhaired man'. Meanwhile, Dyce Sombre and Villiers openly sat in a downstairs newsroom, where it could be publicly noted that they were not the ones distributing the bribes. As Villiers and Coppock knew, no parliamentary candidate had ever been disqualified unless proven to be personally distributing or demonstrably connected with the bribes. As the 4:00 p. m. poll-closing approached, the vote tally stood so close that the last decisive 10–12 electors reportedly demanded £75 and received £50–60 for their votes. The Conservative candidates, who likewise had no prior connection to Sudbury, only paid about £2,000 from their less well-located haunt at the Rose and Crown Inn. Not prepared for such an expensive contest, they had brought less cash with them. Therefore, both Whig-Radical candidates were narrowly elected.

THE

POLL FOR MEMBERS

FOR THE

Borough of Sudbury.

CANDIDATES,

FREDERICK VILLIERS Esq.
DAVID OCHTERLONY DYCE-SOMBRE, Esq.
DAVID JONES, Esq.
CHARLES TAYLOR, Esq.

Note—Where no Parish is mentioned, the Voters are Inhabitants of Sudbury; those whose names are inserted in Italics are not resident at this Election.

		V. D. J. T.
1 Abbott, William	North-street	
2 Abbott, William	Newton-road	
3 Ablitt, James	Great Cornard	
4 Addison, Thomas Fenn	Chilton	
5 Albury, William	Croft	
6 Albury, William	Bures Saint Mary	
7 Albury, John	Bures Saint Mary	
8 Albury, John	Croft	
9 Albury, George	Cross-street	
10 Albury, Thomas	Waterside	
11 Alston, Peter	Cross-street	
12 Alston, Silvanus	Cross-street	
13 Alston, Sturgeon	School-house-lane	
14 Ansey, James	Cross-street	
15 Ansey, Thomas	Mill-lane	
16 Anderson, Robert	Sepulchre-street	
17 Andrews, George William	Friars-street	
18 Andrews, Thomas	Gregory-street	
19 Andrews, Samuel	North-street	

AT THE FINAL CLOSE OF THE POLL
THE NUMBERS WERE

For *Villiers*	284
Dyce-Sombre	281
Jones	274
Taylor	274

Number who voted	557
Number who did not Vote	30
Number deceased	16
Total on Register	603

Sudbury, Poll Book, 1841

When polling ended, Villiers had received 284 votes while Dyce Sombre took only 3 less, 281, enough for a bare majority (50.6%) of the 555 men who voted; their opponents each received 274, only 7 less.[21] Dyce Sombre's money seems to have been decisive rather than his ethnicity, which Coppock boasted he had craftily obscured from the electors despite suspicions by some among them that he was 'a Black man'. Since Dyce Sombre's money evidently only went to some 200 of the 281 men who voted for him, scores of electors chose him unpaid on the basis of party ideology (or, improbably, his qualifications). These higher-minded voters included the local contingent of teetotalling Quakers who voted the liberal ticket without compensation. Inadvertently allied with them in this election, however, were the poorer electors who also voted the straight Whig-Radical ticket, being most open to financial persuasion (Dyce Sombre's £7 each in bribes represented about 6 months' wages). In contrast, only four of the wealthier electors (who had relatively recently been enfranchised based on paying at least £10 in annual rents) voted Whig-Radical, while twenty-five voted Conservative. Some of the voters seem to have voted independently: one even chose Dyce Sombre and a Conservative candidate; three selected Villiers and a Conservative; one man relinquished

183

one of his two votes by only voting for Villiers and throwing away the other. Overall, what won the day were Dyce Sombre's money, the superior tactics of their local agents, and, for some, the liberal policies of the Whig-Radicals. Villiers got in as, what the *Times* called, Dyce Sombre's 'umbra' (shadow).[22]

As victors, Dyce Sombre and Villiers were 'chaired'—paraded through Sudbury behind a hired band of musicians in the former's rented open chariot, drawn by cheering (and suddenly £7 richer) townsmen. That night, Dyce Sombre hosted a feast in the Swan Inn in which Villiers' elder brother, Charles (also illegitimate), and the most prominent of their local supporters celebrated the election victory that Dyce Sombre's money made possible. Paying their own massive bill of £109 and 13 shillings at the Swan (but not bills due from other inns or to printers and other suppliers of election ephemera), Dyce Sombre and Villiers left Sudbury on Wednesday morning, never to return. The *Times* mockingly reported the Sudbury returning officer as 'Matthew Mammon', who purportedly informed Queen Victoria on behalf of the Sudbury voters 'on transmitting a black man as their representative,—

> 'Most gracious Mistress, we have done our best,
> 'And send a man no blacker than the rest.'[23]

Dyce Sombre was thus elected as one of Parliament's most distinctive Members.

As Honourable Member of Parliament

Seven weeks later (19 August 1841), the new House of Commons convened in its temporary building (the original having burned down in 1834; the reconstruction would take thirty years to complete). Over subsequent days, Dyce Sombre, Villiers, and Dyce Sombre's cousin-in-law, Captain Carnegie (just elected as a Conservative), along with the other Members officially entered the House by paying the £10 in customary fees to Parliamentary functionaries, swearing allegiance to Queen Victoria before the Speaker, and agreeing to rules forbidding having footmen or gaming in the lobby or stairs of the House. On 24 August he marched into the temporary House of Lords summoned by the Gentleman Usher of the Black Rod to hear the Queen's speech.

Among all the Members, Dyce Sombre stood out for diverse reasons. Still relatively unusual among MPs, he was Roman Catholic who took

Swearing Parliamentary Oaths, (Baron Rothschild as a Jew Refusing in 1850)

British House of Commons, 1843

a special oath, apart from the others, which explicitly denied the Pope's civil authority in Britain and vowed not to weaken the Anglican Establishment or religion. Unprecedentedly, he was the first Asian MP. Evidently, he was only the second Member widely regarded as non-white. Indeed, most commentators of the day noted him as distinctively 'Indian' and 'black'. For example, fellow MP (Mary Anne's friend and future husband), the Honourable Cecil Weld Forester, wrote: 'You seem to be very much surprised at Dyce Sombre (the Indian) being returned to Parliament. He was returned by his money, but there is a petition against him and I understand he is sure to be turned out, but that remains to be proved.'[24] To make Dyce Sombre appear more conforming, his official parliamentary biography dressed up his past, promoting his father to the rank of 'General' and the Begum to a 'sovereign princess' of India.[25] (Incidentally, this same source provided Villiers with a distinguished legitimate ancestry.) Conforming to an affectation favoured by Mary Anne, the Parliamentary record distinguished his last name with an acute accent, as Sombré.

Dyce Sombre's maiden vote in Parliament on 27 August was historic but set the tone for his futile career there. He and Villiers cast their first formal ballots in support of the old Whig government of Melbourne. While the Conservatives, thanks to Dyce Sombre, had been slimly defeated in Sudbury, across the country as a whole they surprisingly gained a dominant majority, easily defeating Melbourne 360 to 269. This forced Queen Victoria reluctantly to request Sir Robert Peel to form a new Conservative government, the first time in British history that the results of a popular election had defeated a government.[26] Facing this Conservative majority, the Whigs and Radicals (whose diminished memberships largely merged at this point) never won a significant vote during Dyce Sombre's nine months in office, although his vote brought them within one of stopping the reintroduction of income tax.[27] Other pressing issues of the day included the Corn Laws (government pricing policies that kept grain more expensive), which Dyce Sombre voted against, and issues about which he knew (or would know) much from personal experience: the Opium War in China, appeals by the deposed Indian Maharaja of Satara for re-enthronement, and the legal status of lunatics. As a new member, Dyce Sombre never rose to speak but the veteran Villiers did, most notably by opposing the Corn Laws. In all, Dyce Sombre cast six ballots identified by name in formal divisions plus presumably participated in anonymous acclaim votes. His last vote came only days before the termination of his Parliamentary career.

Ominously, the losing Sudbury Conservative candidates continued their contest in a sympathetic Parliament, dominated by their party, including Dyce Sombre's cousin-in-law, Captain Carnegie, who soon rose in the Conservative ranks. Among the welter of 62 election petitions against 73 MPs (12% of all the Members elected in 1841) were two against the Sudbury poll. Each petition had to come, at least nominally, from aggrieved voters willing to post a £1,000 bond as proof of their sincerity. One petition against Sudbury reached Parliament on 30 August 1841, another on 6 September. Officially each petition came from two Sudbury voters but they were actually financed by one of the losing Conservative candidates, David Jones, who still nursed a desire to enter Parliament.[28] The first of these petitions against the poll was withdrawn, sparking celebrations and church bell peals in Sudbury. But the second petition provoked a formal Parliamentary investigation.

Mounting such an election challenge, and also defending against one, would require considerable further outlays of money and energy, as Dyce Sombre found to his cost. It had become a widely-used tactic to prepare for such post-election contests during the election itself. As advised in a cynical pamphlet of the time, if a candidate appeared to be losing due to bribery, 'it is good policy to set a trap for the enemy by sending a trusty man to receive a bribe, which should be brought to you, and carefully preserved in specie for future production'.[29] The defeated Sudbury Conservatives either had one voter, blacksmith Samuel Shelley, carry out this gambit or else 'turned' him into an 'approver' later. Further, their assiduous agents soon collected extensive evidence of Dyce Sombre's money at work from voters willing (or forced by Parliament through immunity from self-incrimination) to testify and from female witnesses who could not themselves vote and thus were not incriminated. Following this 1841 election, allegations of bribery would result in findings of guilt in five constituencies, an unusually high number for the period.[30]

Nonetheless, from the time of his election to Parliament, Dyce Sombre enjoyed heightened esteem in society, both in Britain and on the continent. He also enjoyed the Parliamentary privilege of franking (signing his name in lieu of paid postage) on up to ten outgoing and fifteen incoming letters daily. Partially erasing his rejection by the Oriental Club, Coppock's Reform Club apparently admitted him as it did all liberal members of Parliament. From early after this Club's founding in 1836, it had elected Nonconformists, Roman Catholics, Jews, as well as 'Foreigners of distinction' including Asians and Africans into its membership, although often only on a temporary basis.[31] Dyce Sombre enjoyed dining in the grand new clubhouse, recently opened on fashionable Pall Mall; indeed, he allegedly purloined a sterling silver fork from the Club, proving he had dined there.[32]

He tried vainly to use his newly empowered position to influence the Board of Control (officially the 'Board of Commissioners for the Affairs of India') which served Parliament by supervising the East India Company's Court of Directors. Dyce Sombre wrote an official Memorial on Christmas Eve 1841 which provided no new evidence but extensively recapitulated all his arguments concerning the Badshahpur, armaments, and pension issues.[33] Dyce Sombre personally placed this Memorial in the hands of the Board's Secretary. While the Board showed respect, it refused to reverse the Company's official opposition to all his claims and directed him to address the Government of India should he have any fresh evidence.

Early during the parliamentary recess of 7 October 1841 to 3 February 1842, Dyce Sombre and Mary Anne toured the continent (including Belgium, Holland, Berlin, Dresden, and Paris) and Britain. In his honour, a freeman of Sudbury named his newborn son Edward Noah Dyce Sombre.[34] But while they received the respect due a MP and his wife, the public also gazed voyeuristically on the celebrated couple. Many Indians in London also recognised his unique status.

Dyce Sombre's Links to Indians and India

Apart from Dyce Sombre's relations with Britons of all classes, he also sustained connections and socialized with Indians who had settled or were visiting Europe, particularly with men close to him in class. Further, he kept up a regular correspondence with dependents and associates looking after his property and financial affairs back in Sardhana, Delhi, Calcutta, and elsewhere. In many of these epistolary or personal relationships with Indians and Indian-domiciled Europeans, Dyce Sombre stood as patron, using his wealth to induce or reward compliance with his directives.

By the early 1840s, a lively, diverse, albeit largely transitory body of several thousand male and female Indians of all classes inhabited

London. Dyce Sombre met repeatedly with the most prominent among them including Nawab Iqbal al-Daula Bahadur (the claimant of the throne of Awadh mentioned above) and Karim Khan—ambassador from Jhajjar, a small princely state near Delhi, who arrived in 1840 attended by a small suite. Karim Khan's daily Urdu diary recounts how he and Dyce Sombre exchanged at least five social visits (10 September 1840–5 July 1841), straddling the latter's election to Parliament.[35] They conversed comfortably in Urdu, with Karim Khan calling him both 'Davy Sahib' (his familiar name from India) and also the 'famous Colonel Dyce Sombre Sahib'. But Khan also inexactly identified him as the grandson (daughter's son) of Begum Sombre and Walter Reinhardt. Khan also passed on letters from mutual acquaintances in the Delhi region sent care of him but addressed to the more peripatetic Dyce Sombre.

Among the many middle-class professional Indians in Britain at this time was Sake Dean Mahomed, who repeatedly reconstructed his identity during nearly seven decades living in Ireland and England.[36] Dean Mahomed wrote and published the first book ever by an Indian in English, married an Anglo-Irish woman then bigamously also an Englishwoman, started the first Indian restaurant run by an Indian in London, went bankrupt, and then established himself and his sons as fashionable 'Shampooing Surgeons' (based on their interpretation of *champi*, a vigorous full-body therapeutic massage customary in India). Dean Mahomed thus manipulated British images of India in order to profit from them. Dyce Sombre ordered custom-made exercise equipment from Dean Mahomed and also regularly employed his son, Horatio, for shampooing. Indeed, Dyce Sombre in his 1843 will left a strikingly large £1,000 bequest to Horatio, who ran a bathhouse in St James's, London.[37] When the Mahomeds were not available, Dyce Sombre trained his servants and British and French sex-workers to provide thorough shampooing, much to the scandal of his landladies. As one male servant recounted, Dyce Sombre 'greatly preferred females' to do this to him.[38]

Further, Dyce Sombre continued his commitment to Persian literary culture, inaccessible to almost all his British associates. He proposed in 1839 bringing to Europe a scholar of Persian, Kullender Buksh 'Meanjee', whom Dyce Sombre had known in India:

If he has no better employment, perhaps he would not mind coming to this country. I would allow him 15 rupees a month for his trouble, & 5 shillings a day, & finding a lodging for him here. I want his assistance in some work I am doing for my amusement. Send him, if he is inclined to come, & let me know. Of course, I would pay for his passage out and back again, unless he took employment in England, in case I do want him to remain beyond a year; which, I was told, by Mirza Ibrahim, of the Company's College in England, a person might, with any common abilities; & then he need not be afraid of losing his caste.[39]

Dyce Sombre also frequently directed Reghellini and his other Sardhana correspondents to write him in Persian. This both evoked his earlier life there and also guarded the contents of these letters from his Anglophone associates and relatives.[40]

Dyce Sombre remained engaged with events, personalities, and property in Sardhana, writing to his brother-in-law, Solaroli, 'as you know I take a great interest in Sirdhana & its people'. Dyce Sombre chided both co-managers, Solaroli and Reghellini, for suspected pilfering of his money, as a matter of honour rather than need: 'however rich I may be, I do not like to be plundered, and one ought to be generous and liberal with his own [rather than my money]'.[41] He reluctantly agreed in May 1841 that Solaroli and Troup might bring their wives, Georgiana and Ann May, to Europe, leaving Dyce Sombre's affairs in India in the hands of Reghellini, who had quarreled again with Solaroli. Dyce Sombre also approved Reghellini's son, Stephen, to come to Europe and improve himself.[42] However, Dyce Sombre tensions with his brothers-in-law would only increase after they reached Europe and allied with Mary Anne against him.

Dyce Sombre's prominence spread in India, but both Indians and Britons considered his overweening aspirations inappropriate. Among north Indians, he remained recognizable for decades as emblematic of a man already elevated but whose desires remained insatiate. According to folklore (as recorded in a 1879 dictionary), when he had asked a mendicant for a blessing, this holy man replied with what became an Urdu proverb (which translates): 'Already on an elephant raised high, do you want a bamboo for a perch sky-high (like an acrobat)?'[43] To some Indians, then, his ambitions were limitless and insensitive.

Similarly, Britons in India and other colonies also responded badly to what they considered Dyce Sombre's pretentious and inapt achievements. British colonial power was becoming ever more dependent on strict racial separation, which his accomplishments threatened. Like all people of mixed European and Indian ancestry, his very being disproved this racial segregation.[44] Retorting with shock and horror at

Dyce Sombre's admission into Parliament, teenage Royal Army Lieutenant and fellow Catholic James Cumming fumed from Meerut (18 October 1841):

The election of a *black man*—a nigger—and one remarkable *for his want of attainments*, has set the white population of India into an uproar, and justly. It is an act that stamps disgrace upon England. *Dyce Sombre*... in Meerut... was considered a poor, mean spirited fellow. But behold, to our shame! what sordid mammon can effect in *degenerate England.*[45]

The *Agra Ukhbar* echoed: 'Shame and eternal disgrace on the abandoned mercenaries [of Sudbury] who could thus prostitute the great principle of popular representation—thus sell the people's palladium... to such a...half-washed Blackamoor...Alien...hardly able to speak English.'[46] The *Sydney Gazette and New South Wales Advertiser* (29 January 1842) likewise condemned Dyce Sombre's election. Many of these hostile attitudes toward aspiring Indians were seeping back from the colonies into English society.

Troubled Life in High Society for the New Member of Parliament

As a simultaneously prominent and distinctively unmatched couple, wherever they went Dyce Sombre and Mary Anne drew unwanted attention. Their international notoriety stemmed significantly from the often repeated story of the Begum's alternate excessive cruelty and generosity, his fabulous fortune, his scandalous Sudbury election, and even more from the unconventionally vociferous accusations Dyce Sombre made in ever louder voice about his wife's supposed infidelity.[47] Such rumours of her and his salacious conduct spread widely in Britain, feeding on widely-spreading envy, aspiration, and moral condemnation of both the English titled elite and also Asians. These rumours particularly resonated with deepening Victorian bourgeois stereotypes about European aristocratic decadence and Oriental despotic debauchery.

On his part, Dyce Sombre believed the shocking gossip against his wife, periodically wracking his brain to discover evidence of Mary Anne's adultery and the identities of her supposed lovers. Often when he had deduced, or had suggested to him, the name of one of these alleged adulterers, he wrote challenging a duel to defend her honour and avenge his own. Over time, the list of men he so accused grew, eventually including (but not limited to): the Duke of Wellington (a duellist, her long-time companion); Cecil Weld Forester (a duellist, another of her long-time friends, and, later, second husband); Lord Cardigan (a notorious duellist and rake); Comte Ventura (whom Dyce Sombre knew well in India and then Europe); Hugh Fraser (retired Political Agent from Delhi); Alfred Montgomery (former Private Secretary to Marquis Richard Wellesley); Sir Francis Burdett and Sir Willoughby Cotton (her old family friends); waiters at the hotels where they stayed; her servants; the doctors and tradesmen who served her; as well as her own father.[48]

Further, Dyce Sombre saw a conspiracy closing around him. He apprehended pitfalls in the London streets designed to injure him. His private papers, left in the keeping of the Clarendon Hotel while the couple toured the continent, appeared to have been interfered with. He appealed to Dr Drever to scout out and challenge his enemies.[49]

On her part, Mary Anne could find no way to dispel his antagonistic moods and evidently unreasonable accusations and behavior. He unpredictably interspersed his erratic allegations with periods of acts and words of devoted affection for her. She tried to conform to his strictures, unreasonable as they seemed to her, as best she knew how, but to no avail. She later testified under oath that, as early as August 1841 in Berlin, he had 'suddenly exclaimed "Mary Anne, I feel I am going mad; I shall die in a madhouse; it is in my family; I know it must be; don't you see the symptoms of it?"'[50] While Dyce Sombre later contradicted much that Mary Anne purported him to have done and said, he did not deny these prophetic words.

By early 1842, both Dyce Sombre and Mary Anne's family recognised the need to resolve their escalating marital discord, concurring on an informal investigation by an assemblage of mutual male acquaintances. Dyce Sombre invited his long-time supporters Lord Combermere and Dr Drever. As Dyce Sombre wrote to Drever 'if you wish to come forward as a friend, I was never in want of one more than I am at this present moment'.[51] Further, as he said, 'because I think it fair to Mary Anne to have her friends as well as mine', he suggested Lord Marcus Hill and Sir Francis Burdett join them.

On 31 January 1842, in Dyce Sombre's suite in the Clarendon Hotel, these men and others, including St Vincent family friend Lord Lowther, assembled to discuss the situation. They consulted a family physician, Dr Sir Charles Locock, who had risen in society circles as an obstetrician, appointed official physician accoucheur to Queen Victoria, and who also specialised in epilepsy. Locock gave evidence and then withdrew from this select assembly, recognizing he had no special expertise in marriage counselling or Dyce Sombre's particular condition.

To this assemblage, Dyce Sombre repeated his accusations of adultery and incest against his wife. The assembled men all categorically denied these and sought to reason with him. In order to document their faith in Mary Anne's virtue and also to excuse his apparent delusion as resulting from his Indian background and therefore unfamiliarity with European morality, all the men except Dyce Sombre, St Vincent, and Burdett signed a formal statement drafted by Lord Marcus Hill:

We, the undersigned, have come to a unanimous decision that the statements made by Mr Dyce Sombre against his wife have no foundation in fact. They seem to have arisen from feelings caused by ignorance of the manners of society in Europe, and we feel it to be due to the undoubtedly respectable character of his wife to declare that, by this investigation, we are convinced of her entire innocence and purity, and we feel entitled that the result of our deliberation should have the effect of dissipating all such illusions for the future; and we expect that the conduct of Mr Dyce Sombre to his wife shall in future be in unison with that ardent affection he has always expressed towards her, and with that regard which is due to an innocent and devoted wife.[52]

Her family carefully preserved this declaration by these Englishmen for any future legal action by or against Dyce Sombre, including divorce, separation, or petition for lunacy.

Dyce Sombre's invited allies, Lord Combermere and Dr Drever, signed this document, but for different reasons. In this assembly and in larger debates over him, each of these men represented himself as expert about Indian culture. While they concurred that Mary Anne was not immoral, they fundamentally disagreed as to the effects of Dyce Sombre's Indian origins and his reasons for sincerely believing her unchaste.

Combermere laid out a position, later widely circulated, that Dyce Sombre acted this way because he was essentially Indian. Combermere testified he was 'by birth three-fourths an Asiatic, and only one-fourth an European... He was entirely educated like other Asiatics, and according to Asiatic customs... the only instruction... at all of an English character was... by the Rev. Mr Fisher... but such instruction did not produce... any material or essential change in the mental habits, or in the Asiatic feelings, opinions and ideas in which [he] had been previously brought up.'[53] Claiming deep knowledge of all things Asiatic,

Combermere added Mary Anne must have offended Dyce Sombre: '[Combermere] is perfectly confident that Mrs Dyce Sombre must have repeatedly been in situations which would have annoyed her husband's feelings, and have amply sufficed to make him lose his self-possession, although there might be nothing in her character and conduct which would justify a suspicion, or occasion or give rise to a feeling of jealousy in the eyes of a European husband.' Thus, Combermere argued: Mary Anne had naïvely failed to adjust her behavior to the Indian values held by Dyce Sombre, as understood by Combermere. He and the St Vincent family had long been at odds, and they would emerge over time as the most prominent aristocratic adversaries in the struggle over Dyce Sombre and his fortune.

In contrast, Dr Drever argued the opposite position—that Dyce Sombre was essentially European but mentally disturbed. Drever presented himself as more authoritatively empowered to pronounce about Asians than Combermere, writing Combermere's 'knowledge of Indian customs and manners could not be considered great, as he is quite incapable of conversing with a native, in the language of the country, and his opportunities of knowing Mr Dyce Sombre were but slight'.[54] Drever declaimed that Dyce Sombre had been effectively Anglicised from youth in India: 'the society in which [he] moved was chiefly composed of the European civil and military servants of the said East India Company, at Meerut and Delhi, and others, and the language usually spoken amongst those admitted on terms of equality, except with her Highness [the Begum] herself, was principally English, and the manners much the same as those of English people in India...' Thus, Dyce Sombre's delusions had nothing to do with his Indian origins. Rather, Drever had recently come to believe that Dyce Sombre's mind was unbalanced. Nonetheless, Drever deferred to the consensus among the noblemen at the assembly, adding his signature to the formal declaration. European authorities would divide in their classification of Dyce Sombre as essentially either European or Indian, lunatic or sane, for the rest of his life.

Despite the contentions of all these men, Dyce Sombre refused to submit to their consensus and continued his allegations. When Drever asked Dyce Sombre, if he knew of Mary Anne's immorality from the beginning, why did he marry her? Dyce Sombre replied 'It is not unusual for us in India to marry women of bad character, singers and dancers.' Faced with what he considered this betrayal by both Drever and Combermere in signing the declaration, Dyce Sombre developed new doubts about their loyalty toward him. The next year, Dyce Sombre would evoke the Paris Jockey Club as a body equally qualified to assess Mary Anne's behavior as this British assembly was to judge his.

The very day that this assemblage met, Dyce Sombre wrote to Solaroli, directing him not to bring Georgiana to Europe, threatening to break with him if he disobeyed. Dyce Sombre went on 'I wish to keep up my connections with India always, and, as a matter of course, would wish your family to be permanently settled in India as well as my own, if I have any'. Although Dyce Sombre stated 'I will be candid with you', he did not mention that day's confrontation and disingenuously added 'Mrs Dyce Sombre joins in best regards to Georgiana'.[55]

News of the marital discord between Dyce Sombre, MP, and his wife excited London. For example, in early February 1842, a leading Conservative newspaper, the *Age*, published seven mocking and fictitious Valentines putatively from newsworthy noblemen to their partners (spouses or alleged mistresses). The identities of some of the principals were thinly disguised (thus avoiding costly lawsuits) but they were all prominent enough people that the paper assumed all its readers would recognise each of them. The culminating fictive Valentine poem was addressed 'To the Hon. Mrs Dyce Sombre' by one of her supposed British admirers:

> Never mind *Mungo*;
> But merely for fun, go
> To Twisleton Fines [Fiennes],
> (After soaking in wines
> At the Club where he herds)
> And ask, in what words
> He replied to the query
> Put by your dark deary?
> And you'll find, like a convict
> Who's been in the CROWN cast,
> That, besides being *half*,
> He likewise was *down* cast!
> A[lfre]d M[ontgomery][56]

The sarcastic poem thus highlighted Dyce Sombre's racial identity as a 'Mungo' (a common slave-name), 'half cast', 'dark deary' who was being helplessly and depressingly deceived and put aside by his amourous wife. Its public imputation of Mary Anne's alleged relationships with Alfred Montgomery and Twisleton Fiennes, men long suspected by Dyce Sombre of being her lovers, may have confirmed his suspicions. Just days before this mock Valentine was published, Parliament had reconvened, with Dyce Sombre resuming his place on the Whig-Radical back bench, although threats to his place there mounted.

Controversion of the Sudbury Election

The remaining Conservative petition against the validity of the Sudbury election was one of the sixty appeals against challenged elections that remained active, referred by Parliament to its General Committee of Elections.[57] This Committee recommended that Parliament appoint a Special Committee of investigation for each of the twenty-six more substantiated (and politically expedient) cases. During the long months of detailed investigations and extensive hearings by the Sudbury Special Committee, chaired by a young Catholic liberal member, Thomas N. Redington, evidence slowly mounted concerning the sordid history of the constituency's illegal or barely legal election customs and the particular actions of Villiers, Dyce Sombre, and their agents. To represent them in this delicate process, Dyce Sombre and Villiers hired James Coppock, who billed the former £911 in legal fees (given the disappointing outcome, his bill went unpaid for years).[58] The advocates representing the Conservative petitioners challenged Villiers financial qualification (as had occurred after his 1835 election in Canterbury).[59] While in Dyce Sombre's case they questioned his status as a British subject. The Special Committee summoned rival self-professed experts on India—Dr Thomas Drever and, with the permission of the House of Lords, Lord Combermere—to testify about Dyce Sombre's ancestry and the legal status of Sardhana at his birth.[60] Accusers charged that since Dyce Sombre was not 'the son or grandson of a father who was a natural-born subject of the sovereign of Great Britain and Ireland, was born out of the legiance of the crown of Great Britain and Ireland', and had never been naturalised, therefore he was 'an alien... wholly ineligible and by law incapacitated' from being elected to Parliament.[61] These personal charges against Villiers and Dyce Sombre, however, proved too complex, so the Committee set them aside. In addition, the petitioners never proved their further accusation against both Dyce Sombre and Villiers of 'intimidation' of Conservative voters 'by actual violence and outrage'. More persuasively, the challengers did provide testimony from witnesses alleging 'extensive bribery and treating' by Dyce Sombre's and Villier's election agents, although the candidates themselves were visibly not providing the bribes, and the identities of 'Mr Massey' and the men actually distributing them could not be proved.

On 14 April 1842, after five days of formal hearings and the public testimony of twenty-six witnesses, the Special Committee unanimously resolved that the Sudbury election be voided for 'gross and corrupt bribery... of the most open and notorious character—the most extensive and general system of bribery which could be supposed to exist'.[62] Further, given the unusually massive culpability of the Sudbury voters, the constituency should not be allowed to simply repeat the election as was customary. Such a finding on the basis of circumstantial evidence, without any direct proof of the candidates themselves offering bribes, was unprecedented, allowed only by a contested interpretation of recent law (4&5 Vict. c. 57). Most of the other ongoing Parliamentary investigating committees required that the identities of the actual bribe-givers be proved, which the Sudbury petitioners could not do. Nor was the alleged election corruption in Sudbury worse than in at least six other constituencies; for instance, the 182 electors of Harwich reportedly received some £47 each, while a Nottingham candidate allegedly spent £12,000, more than four times what Dyce Sombre had expended.[63]

Nonetheless, the next day Parliament voted to controvert Dyce Sombre's and Villiers' elections, expelling them from their seats but not expunging their votes to that point. Eventually, the Conservative-dominated Parliament would vote to expel seventeen members elected in 1841 on one grounds or another, an average number for this period.[64] Dyce Sombre and Villiers could well feel that their election had been singled out for unusual treatment but the new and broader standards of circumstantial evidence used in this Sudbury investigation would set precedents for future ones. While Dyce Sombre may not have been expelled primarily due to his Indian origin or mixed ancestry, the publicity around his expulsion did highlight these features.

Commenting on these election controversions, the English humour magazine *Punch* satirised the various 'tainted boroughs' including Sudbury specifically. Yet, it also noted that such actions by Parliament actually rested more on chance than principle. To illustrate, the article parodied a fictitious but stereotypical wealthy Indian MP (comparing him to a rich Jew) as a card-shark who would try to win by slight of hand but got caught doing so:

> ...if a RAMO SAMEE—who like Mr Dobree, the pawnbroker, has made a fortune by golden balls—were to be returned to Parliament... and were base enough (which we much doubt) to attempt to force or hide a card for party purposes, he might occasionally succeed; but... the Speaker... on the least evidence of legerdemain... would declare that he had 'caught the finger' of the very honourable member.[65]

Since Dyce Sombre was 'caught', lost his seat, and was the first and only Indian in Parliament to date, he may have been *Punch*'s inspiration for 'Ramo Samee'. The next Indian elected would be Dadabhai Naoroji half a century later in 1892, from Central Finsbury, after having run and lost in 1886; he was soon followed by Sir Mancherjee Merwanjee Bhownaggree, who won in 1895 and 1900.

Further, the electors of Sudbury to their dismay discovered the unintended disastrous consequence of their cupidity. The protests by the Conservatives and their collected evidence of widespread bribery in Sudbury were so powerful that they inadvertently caused the disenfranchisement of the entire constituency rather than the expected simple replacement in Parliament of Dyce Sombre and Villiers by Conservatives. The entire town was cast into mourning and witnesses who had testified against Dyce Sombre and Villiers were hung in effigy and had to be given official protection.[66] The respective politicos of Sudbury vainly proposed collaboration: a new election with only one Radical-Whig and one Conservative running unopposed and therefore above suspicion. When this and more than three years of Parliamentary maneuvering failed, Sudbury was disenfranchised (29 July 1844). Out of the many election challenges for the 1833–52 period, it was the only constituency disenfranchised; Sudbury was not allowed to vote again for four decades, until 1882.[67]

Newspapers in Britain and America brought the Sudbury election to the attention of their readers. The *Times* bestowed its fervent approval of the 'ejectification' of Dyce Sombre and Villiers and of Sudbury's recommended disenfranchisement as one of the half-dozen worst constituencies in England. It later highlighted how degrading for the English it was that Dyce Sombre,

> an alien of foreign blood and all but foreign language, should have been in a position to boast that he travelled down with his box of gold to a borough where his name had never been heard... as if he had been dropped down from

the moon, on the evening before an election—and that two days afterwards he travelled back... a member of a reformed Parliament—the very idea is intolerable... Bribery unsuccessful and exposed is its own punishment to the gentlemen whose pockets are the lighter for it, and who now find that their confiding generosity has only purchased for them a certain very unenviable notoriety—a position, we rejoice to think, in which they may be perfectly sure that not one of their undetected fellow criminals will 'bate them a single scruple of his very best indignation.[68]

The *Times* also inaccurately estimated that it cost Dyce Sombre £1,000 for every night he sat in Parliament.

Dyce Sombre's ancestry and wealth, as well as his curious political career, attracted international attention. Many American newspapers, including Washington's *Daily National Intelligencer* and Philadelphia's *Saturday Evening Post* published articles on his corrupt election, making it symbolic of British politics generally. The *Raleigh Register and North-Carolina Gazette* singled Sudbury out as a particularly corrupt constituency while the more sophisticated *New-York Spectator* demonstrated that Sudbury's corruption was typical of all elections to the British House of Commons. Indeed, New York's *Spirit of the Times* featured his expulsion among the highlights of the entire previous year: 'Mr. Dyce Sombre looks black by nature and blue by circumstances'.

Overall, the Sudbury electors, Villiers, Dyce Sombre, Coppock, and their local liberal allies had all misjudged the extent to which a seat in Parliament could still be openly purchased, while the Conservatives misjudged the consequences of bringing this evidence to light. This was a transitional period in British politics, so rules were particularly inconsistent. East India Company civil service officials and military cadets still openly, albeit illegally, purchased appointments. In the British Army, officers legally sold or purchased commissions until 1871. Thus, it was difficult for anyone to assess at the time what would pass and what would prove costly, what could be purchased legally (or at least without punishment), and what deemed corruption. But this expulsion, loss of parliamentary privilege, and international scandal came at a difficult time for Dyce Sombre personally.

10

LUNACY

By investing most of his money in Britain and by marrying an English aristocrat, Dyce Sombre subjected himself to untoward constraints on his fortune and person. Increasingly, English law courts enforced emerging Victorian social and cultural values about the primacy of the family and the requisite responsible role of the husband. Under law, the husband still controlled the wife's wealth but he could not simply dispose of family property as he willed without provoking possible state intervention. Further, behaviour that a wife or family deemed unmanly and anti-social could lead to the confinement of the errant husband, to the extreme extent of having him declared a legal lunatic and ward of his own family. Viscount St Vincent had already done this to his allegedly wayward eldest son and he saw no reason not to do the same to his son-in-law, Dyce Sombre. Dyce Sombre's brothers-in-law concurred. Only after Dyce Sombre's incarceration did the issue arise of cultural difference and the appropriate measure of 'normality' for a man of his origins. The debate about whether Dyce Sombre was essentially Indian or European gained force after he fled to freedom in France but had to leave his fortune behind in the hands of British authorities.

His Troubles Intensify

Throughout the period that Dyce Sombre was losing his parliamentary seat, his troubled relationships with his wife's family and British society generally were becoming ever more abrasive. Everywhere he looked, he saw enemies conspiring to defy his authority and deceive and entrap him, plundering his wealth and depriving him of his just and manly rights. Some of his suspicions that others were conspiring against him were true.

In addition to being singled out by Parliament for actions committed unpunished by many continuing Members, he felt frustrated by the double-dealing of the East India Company which cleverly played off the Company's dual structure and multiple jurisdictions against him. The Government of India in Calcutta told him to appeal to the Court of Directors in London. The Directors in London demanded that his Badshahpur, Sardhana armaments, and promised pensioners cases be heard in distant Indian courts in Delhi. Early in 1842, Dyce Sombre lost another one of the many legal rounds against the Company in India. He subsequently sent a personal challenge to a duel with pistols to Sir Richard Jenkins, former Chairman and current member of the Court of Directors. In June 1842, just after his expulsion from Parliament, the Board of Control refused to talk with him.[1] Further, his personal petition to the Prime Minister Sir Robert Peel, including sending unsolicited all the relevant papers, was tersely dismissed.[2] But Dyce Sombre's many expensive British lawyers launched yet other legal appeals, which would decades later (and backed by the political clout of his widow's second husband) result in the ultimate vindication of most of them.

Dyce Sombre also persisted in his ineffective efforts to control his aristocratic wife. She apparently took this as an attractive solicitude, remembering him declaiming: 'No great love could exist without jealousy!'[3] Mary Anne's honour, besmirched as he felt it to be, was after all what he claimed to be defending through his many duelling challenges to her male acquaintances.

On one hand, he continued to constrain her independence, supported by British law, but not her influential aristocratic friends. In March 1842, Dyce Sombre exerted his legal right as husband under British statutes to take personal charge of her income, including the £500 annual allowance provided by her father and the £4,300 paid by trusts he himself had established. He claimed to do this in order to prevent her hiring gigolos—something her family and friends found inconceivable. He secretly followed her when she went out, even in the company of her relatives and to church—which appeared awkward to all who caught him at it. He accused her of having lovers hidden about their apartments in the posh Clarendon Hotel, even introducing them into their bed as he slept—with no evidence that this ever occurred.

On the other hand, he constantly showered her with presents and willingly purchased anything she asked of him. For example, in April 1842, he escorted her to the massive auction of the estate of the late Horace Walpole (an author, diplomat, and fellow Freemason). There, because she expressed a desire for them, he paid over £180 for 800 letters to Walpole from the French literary lioness, the Marquise du Deffand. (Later someone, probably Dyce Sombre himself, diminished the value of these letters to collectors by cutting out the autograph signatures.)[4]

Trips by Dyce Sombre and Mary Anne to visit the scenic sites and aristocracy of Scotland (Edinburgh, Inverary, Taymouth, Inverness) and the continent (Berlin, Dresden, Belgium, Paris, Aix la Chapelle, and Holland) only exacerbated tensions between him and her social set. Among her friends, she felt at home while he felt alienated. He later complained, 'that she slighted him, and, together with those with whom she associated, turned him into ridicule; that she talked and sang, and accompanied others in singing, as he did not like... "She ordered me to do this and that—Dyce, come here—Dyce, go there—Dyce, do this or that."'[5]

Asserting his manhood and autonomy, Dyce Sombre redoubled his efforts to master her and also their social relations. He responded to what he perceived as outright insults to his honour, and that of her as his wife, with furious reposts. Revealing his self-distancing from her social set, Dyce Sombre confided to Drever, 'my Indian blood would not allow me to put up with slights' even 'from titled persons'.[6] At exclusive dinners, in private boxes at the theatre and opera, and in the street, Dyce Sombre was observed by distinguished members of high society acting and speaking antisocially. He continued repeatedly to threaten to duel the aging Viscount St Vincent, as well as sundry others. General Ventura, whom he had known from Sardhana, appeared first as a welcome companion from his past but later as yet another conspirator against him, therefore someone else whom Dyce Sombre should challenge to a duel.[7] Dyce Sombre also accused many of his hosts and hoteliers of putting poisons and drugs into his food, among other results making him impotent, a condition he found extremely frustrating.

At the same time, Dyce Sombre was attempting to keep news of his marital discord away from his Sardhana correspondents. He wrote to Solaroli 'I married when an opportunity offered, and I was pleased with the match' now 'What right have you to believe that Mrs D. S. and myself are not on good terms? You never heard me complain... it was indelicate as well as presumptuous on your part to write me [about my rumoured marriage problems].'[8]

By late in 1842, he was seeking portents and charms—including 'by freemasonry, sometimes by necrology, and sometimes by the rules of mathematics' according to Mary Anne—in order to learn the future and recover his control over it. He explained to Mary Anne how they should both adhere in daily alternation to the mystical rules of 'the Unity, the Trinity, and the Four Friends', each with a secret hand signal. Mary Anne sought ways to restore his composure, including through a course of treatment under Dr Harris F. Dunsford, the young but highly fashionable homeopath.[9] Conversely, Dyce Sombre sought ways to restore Mary Anne from her degraded condition. Among other methods, he urged her to challenge to duels the aristocratic ladies, including Lady Anne Beckett (a descendant of her family friend, Lord Lowther), with whom he claimed to have been flirting.

By early 1843, in order to spite his enemies in the Company's Court of Directors, he not only challenged several of them personally to duels, he also wrote Queen Victoria, promising to transfer all his legal claims against the Company to her since she would prevail where he apparently could not. In response, the Directors used their influence to post policemen outside his hotel and to follow him everywhere. Such surveillance only proved his conviction of a massive cabal against him.

Dyce Sombre also sought to recruit leading figures in British society to his cause. He abruptly asked Michael Bruce (famous for liberating Count La Valette from a French royalist prison in 1816) to liberate Mary Anne from her supposed warders as well.[10] After he had secretly trailed her to London's Conduit Street, he became convinced that she had been visiting the fashionable mesmerist, acupuncturist, and phrenologist, Dr John Elliotson in his living-quarters and office there. Consequently, he burst into Elliotson's office without appointment, demanding 'Make me have more of my wife's company'. Like Dyce Sombre, many Victorians believed (with fear or hope) that hypnosis could increase and direct a woman's sexual propensity. This tempestuous confrontation ended with Dyce Sombre challenging Elliotson to a duel for mesmerizing Mary Anne into promiscuity with other men instead of desire for him. The irascible Elliotson then wrote to her family urging that Dyce Sombre be restrained immediately as a public danger.

On her part, rather than follow the advice of her family by having him confined, Mary Anne suffered the accusations, threats, and even shoves of Dyce Sombre, but not without injury to her mental and physical health. Early in 1842, she had consulted a leading society physician, William Frederick Chambers, about her own health, but she also confided her fears that Dyce Sombre was insane (perhaps informed by her eldest half-brother's lunacy). Based on her statements, Chambers initially came to believe in Dyce Sombre's insanity, although this field was far from his own expertise. Chambers, son of an East India Company official, had spent his first seven years in India before returning to Britain for his schooling. He had risen to be official physician to the Company and physician-in-ordinary to King William IV and then Queen Victoria. A generalist, he had conducted some research on cholera but had little experience dealing with mental health issues. Arranging to examine Dyce Sombre directly, Chambers invited a specialist 'mad doctor', Dr Edward James Seymour, as a consultant. Seymour, a former Metropolitan Commissioner in Lunacy, had pioneered the heavy dosing of the mentally incompetent with opium for the rest of their lives as the only effective way to manage them. But when Seymour could not come, Chambers brought with him instead his younger colleague and fellow specialist in cholera and sanitary science, Dr John Sutherland.

After repeated examinations of Dyce Sombre over nearly a year, Chambers and Sutherland concluded in mid-December 1842 that his physical health was weak and that he was deluded concerning the infidelity of Mary Anne and aggressive in his language toward her. Yet these doctors also concurred 'that there were not sufficient grounds to warrant their signing a certificate of his insanity'. While they 'declared that though there was at present no decisive symptom of mental aberration, yet in consequence of the suspicions he entertained, the presence of Mrs Dyce Sombre kept him in a continual state of irritation, and advised Mrs Dyce Sombre to separate from him' lest his condition 'terminate in substantial insanity'. Their school of early psychiatry regarded emotional 'irritation' as a prime cause of lunacy—remove it and the patient might recover. Mary Anne, however, refused to heed this advice to stop nurturing Dyce Sombre and abandon him. She tried to cajole him out of his occasionally cold attitude toward her, for instance, presenting him with shirt studs made from her own hair stiffened by wire that would constantly remind him of her affection.[11] Further, she summoned other doctors for more congenial opinions.

In leading, if controversial, society physician Sir James Clark, the St Vincents found a doctor who would testify to Dyce Sombre's lunacy for the rest of his life. A Scottish butler's son, sometime Royal Navy surgeon, and specialist in tuberculosis, Clark had risen rapidly in fashionable society under the patronage of Queen Victoria who made him her physician-in-ordinary and a baronet. He was also an enthusiastic phrenologist but had no special expertise in mental health.

Clark first examined Dyce Sombre in February 1843 for heart pain. Over future visits, Dyce Sombre confided his accusations against Mary Anne, his conviction that good and evil spirits were battling over him, and other allegations that Clark found increasingly alarming. The latter consulted Sutherland, but disagreeing on their diagnoses, he then called in two physicians famous as alienists: John Conolly and Edward Thomas Monro. The celebrated Dr Conolly superintended the vast Hanwell County Lunatic Asylum in Middlesex (although he would lose that post in 1844 in a intramural factional conflict, reduced in a face-saving gesture to being only a visiting physician there). Indeed, Conolly made a lucrative practice out of appearing in Chancery and criminal lunacy trials, although, as Scull has judged: 'Not always scrupulous about observing the technicalities of the lunacy laws, Conolly was on occasion successfully sued for damages for false imprisonment. Nor did he make an impressive expert witness, being excoriated as all too prone to consign the immoral or merely eccentric to the ranks of the insane.'[12] Dyce Sombre refused to cooperate with Conolly, allegedly mistaking him for an agent of the East India Company and also a relative of a Captain Conolly whom he had known in India. Conolly later characterised him with Mary Anne 'not a bad representative of Othello with Desdemona'.[13]

Dr Monro of Bedlam Hospital had testified fourteen years earlier against Mary Anne's eldest half-brother, securing his confinement as a Chancery Lunatic. In Monro's examination room, Dyce Sombre asserted that Mary Anne had sex with another man in their bed while Dyce Sombre slept soundly, perhaps drugged. She again denied Dyce Sombre's accusations. Then, according to Monro, '[Dyce Sombre] placed Mrs Dyce Sombre on a stool and asked if she would deny it? she did so; and he then placed her on a chair and asked her would she now deny it? she did so; and he again altered her position, and asked if she still denied it? which she did.' On the basis of such symptoms, Conolly and Monro concurred in Clark's diagnosis and advice to order restraint, asserting that Dyce Sombre's actions were 'quite consistent with insanity' and dangerous to Mary Anne's life.[14] At the urging of the St Vincent family, Monro signed a certificate authorising Dyce Sombre's confinement at a lunatic. But Mary Anne, whose assent as spouse was legally requisite, hesitated to endorse such a decisive act, still hoping that he would regain his equilibrium.

Instead, Dyce Sombre's behavior became even less comprehensible to her, including: shaving off his eyebrows; battling with spirits from his Sardhana days; writing furious letters challenging gentlemen to duels for the slightest pretext; casting his wedding ring into the fire; and threatening to cut off her nose (as immoral women were treated in India). Mary Anne later deposed (using the third person) that Dyce Sombre 'seized this deponent by the throat, and said he would strangle her, but generally became very sorry afterwards, and said, although she had behaved improperly, yet it was unpardonable of him to treat her so, and would load her with caresses; and ten minutes, or sometimes an hour after, something would come across him, and he would begin again...' She continued that Dyce Sombre, fearing spirits in the night, 'appeared greatly alarmed; and always, for about four weeks after, kept hold of this deponent all night, for he said this kept the demons away.' He ritually lit candles and then made water to extinguish them, exclaiming 'Insult the light—insult the light.' Even during the day,

Duke of Wellington and Queen Victoria

Dyce Sombre regarded all around him as hostile. He wrote Drever a letter stating 'The maxim now is, to believe every one a rogue till he has proved himself to be otherwise'.[15]

Word spread through London society about Dyce Sombre's worsening condition, although it was not always sympathetic. The aging Duke of Wellington bemoaned his own plight when Mary Anne's accustomed attentions toward him were redirected toward Dyce Sombre. When Wellington had to arrange the annual performance of the 'Ancient Concert', he egotistically wrote on 27 March 1843 'god knows how I am to get on... If Mr Dyce Sombre was not mad, I should be under no difficulty' since Mary Anne would have managed for Wellington.[16] Two days later, Dyce Sombre faced a life-changing crisis.

On 29 March 1843, Clark examined him yet again. In the course of this examination, Dyce Sombre asserted that he would duel Mary Anne with pistols as soon as she returned from an ball he alleged (in the face of evidence to the contrary) was currently taking place elsewhere in the Clarendon Hotel, where she was dancing with Alfred Montgomery; if she would not shoot him, then he would shoot her. Finally, Mary Anne reluctantly consented to sign the long-prepared petition for a *Commission de Lunatico Inquirendo* which was immediately endorsed by the Lord Chancellor Lyndhurst (the American-born son of the East India Company agent in Boston who had helped Viscount St Vincent earlier by convicting his eldest son as a lunatic). The St Vincents had arranged for their solicitor, Frere, a doctor, and two muscular keepers to be on call for such an eventuality. In the middle of that same moonless night, these men entered Dyce Sombre's hotel suite and bound him into immobility. Dyce Sombre reportedly exclaimed 'I know what you are come for; you are going to shut me up in a madhouse' but made no physical resistance.[17]

While Dyce Sombre was later permitted some physical freedom inside his Clarendon suite, an experienced warder, veteran of India, and member of the Oriental Club, William Sherriff, led a team of keepers constantly supervising him. At first, Mary Anne continued to share Dyce Sombre's bed, but with the keepers on ready alert should anything untoward occur. As her husband, he retained the legal right to cohabitation with her. She also seems to have been devoted to helping him through this difficult period.

To protect Mary Anne and Dyce Sombre himself from harm, Sherriff removed all sharp objects from their room. However, this did not prevent Dyce Sombre from pulling out from his dressing-table two loaded and cocked (but not percussion capped) pistols, and aiming them at Sherriff and then Mary Anne before Sherriff eventually wrenched the guns away. Dyce Sombre later explained 'I merely presented the pistols to frighten him. It was not likely that pistols without [percussion] caps could do any injury. I did not draw the trigger, although I had plenty of time to do so if I wished.'[18] His act, as he intended, did indeed induce fear into Sherriff and Mary Anne. Simultaneously, Dyce Sombre was himself frightened by spirits which ordered him to kill a cat in a particular way, eat his own feces, and commit various other antisocial acts.

After a few days, she removed to her distant family home at Meaford, Staffordshire, while Dyce Sombre appealed to Lady Marcus Hill and other mutual acquaintances for her to rejoin him: 'Being in a very weak state of body, I appeal to the heart of M. A. to come back to me immediately, if she wishes to save me. I would go, but here I am kept under restraint.'[19] When this indirect appeal did not work, Dyce Sombre wrote Mary Anne directly, offering honourable reconciliation and pleas:

I have no wish to make you miserable; and any thing you may suggest, and which will not compromise my honor, I am ready to adopt, tho', at the same time, I am willing, and be delighted, to bring you back... Your coming back to me depends upon yourself. Now, I am ready to receive you; but it must be done in a fashionable manner now, since you have brought it on. I have given in already too much; and I see the folly of it now, when it is too late. However, I have a very high regard for you, and you may yet turn it into something better; but it all depends upon yourself now.

P.S. I am bound to say one thing, that your life is now become sacred to me.[20]

The St Vincents, however, kept Dyce Sombre restrained and Mary Anne in their care and protection from him. Her absence convinced him of her disloyalty.

Following nearly two weeks of this inadequate confinement in the Clarendon Hotel, Mary Anne's family arranged to sublet from the 10th Earl of Dundonald his elegant Hanover Lodge, a two-storied, Doric-pillared, nine-bedroom villa in Regent's Park (overlooking the Grand Canal, near the zoological gardens, and nearer where London's Central Mosque would later be built).[21] In 1840, this house had been occupied by Joseph Bonaparte, elder brother of Napoleon I and former King of Naples (1806–08) and of Spain (1808–14). But confined there from 11

Hanover Lodge and Regent's Park Plan

April 1843, Dyce Sombre repeatedly called it the 'Imperial Gaol' of Hanover Lodge.[22]

In Custody

Over the years since her father's successful lunacy case against Mary Anne's eldest half-brother, the number of *Commissions de Lunatico Inquirendo* had grown in England to an average of one per week.[23] As St Vincent knew, all that a family required to silence a troublesome member and gain control over his or her property was to petition the Lord Chancellor, laying out the details of the case, supported by a qualified solicitor, two agreeable physicians or surgeons, and the spouse. Such sudden private confinement appeared at this time as a very real fear among individuals at odds with their influential families, especially among adult men unused to such controls. Indeed, John Perceval, son of the assassinated Prime Minister, published in 1840 his extensive account of his brutal imprisonment for lunacy by his own mother, even after his recovery from his condition.[24] Such cases prompted change in the law (8&9 Vict, c. 100, Lunatics Act of 1845), only two years after Dyce Sombre's inquisition, making petition-based immediate incarceration slightly more difficult.

So remarkable was his case, global newspapers entertained their readers by reference to him as a character already well-known for his fabled origins and distinctive political career. For example, popular American newspapers like *Spirit of the Times* (New York City) echoed British ones, including the London *Age* and the *Satirist*, in noting his confined condition and sarcastically arguing that dealing with the irrational East India Company would drive anyone mad:

Mr Dyce Sombre's indisposition arises from a real or supposed injury inflicted on him by the Bashaws [Emperors] of Leadenhall-street [the East India Company's Directors], in regard to some property in the East Indies. If all the people whose property has been seized and appropriated, or who have been injured by that body, were to go out of their senses, not all the madhouses in the world would hold a thousandth part of them! It smacks of FOLLY to go mad on such grounds.[25]

Such public sympathy for him did not stop British authorities from proceeding according to the interests of the St Vincents.

Completely confined by Sir James Clark, Dyce Sombre nonetheless struggled futilely to exert his own powers. After less than a month of constant surveillance, questioning, and restriction in Hanover Lodge, he reportedly 'began to grow very impatient... and remained in bed until very late in the day, and only dressed in drawers and dressing-gown'. Clark took this as further evidence of lunacy.

Dyce Sombre, to spite his tormentors and control his fortune forever, redrew his will on 10 May 1843.[26] In this, he left £5,000 to the eldest son to be born to either of his sisters and the Begum's mansion in Delhi's Chandni Chawk to Mary Anne. To rival her family's patronage of low-church Anglicanism, Dyce Sombre left £1,000 to the Catholic chapel nearest the St Vincent estate in Staffordshire 'excepting that which may be on his Lordship's [St Vincent] or his Son's property'. However, he dedicated the vast bulk of his fortune to the creation and endowment of 'Sumroo's College', a new institution to be started 'for the education of the people of India in general, & that of Sirdhanah in particular'. Direction of this new college would be entrusted to four men: his long-time Mughal courtier acquaintances, Nawab Hissam al-Din Hyder and Mahomed Meer Khan, as well as a person nominated by the current Mughal Emperor, and a person named by the Anglo-Indian community. Dyce Sombre signed this will 'In the Prison of Hanover Lodge, Regent's Park'. The will's three co-executors were to be Colonel William Sleeman and the incumbent ambassadors to London from Russia and the United States.

To stymie Dyce Sombre, Clark arranged that no one witnessed this will. Dyce Sombre recognised that this lack of witnesses might invalidate it so he appealed to the executors: since 'I having been kept a close prisoner under the controul of Sir James Clark, from the morn[in]g of the 30th March 1843..., I have not the free means of getting this witnessed, but I appeal to their Excellencies' Honour and to the Honour and Sympathy of their respective Nations that this Will should be carried into full effect...' Further, Clark confiscated Dyce Sombre's letters to the American Ambassador announcing the will and appealing for assistance in regaining his freedom. Hence, Dyce Sombre added a codicil three days later replacing the American by the Wittenberg envoy. This codicil also shifted the £1,000 bequest from the Catholic Church to his regular, frequent, and expert shampooer, Horatio Dean Mahomed. When, the next week, the Wittenberg envoy declined to serve, Dyce Sombre replaced him with the ambassador from Prussia. Given the extremely uncertain situation of Dyce Sombre (an accused but not officially declared lunatic), his legal competence to make any will was extremely contestable; Clark ensured by the absence of witnesses that Dyce Sombre's will would certainly be set aside (indeed, Dyce Sombre never regained legal authority to execute any will under British law for the rest of his life).

For four months, the St Vincents used the Lord Chancellor's authorization of temporary confinement to have Sir James Clark assiduously collect and document every scrap of evidence about Dyce Sombre's delusions. All the paper on which Dyce Sombre wrote, even scribbles, Clark seized and scrutinised, marshalling evidence in support of his own diagnosis. Clark later had to admit under oath, in response to Dyce Sombre's cross-examination, that he intercepted, opened, and copied rather than mailed Dyce Sombre's sealed letters. As Dyce Sombre subsequently explained to the Russian Government: 'I was, under the pretext of being insane, kept under strict watch... my things were taken from me, trunks and boxes broken open, sealed letters, packets, letters, and even my will, which is reckoned a sacred thing in all parts of the world, were opened and read, and then given up to persons who may make whatever use they pleased of them'.[27]

Despite his antagonism towards Clark, Dyce Sombre allegedly confided to him, among many other delusions: that Begum Sombre 'had appeared to him and had witnessed his marriage again' with Mary Anne; that a 'Blue Spirit' appeared in the form of the letter 'T'; that another spirit, a man whom he had fatally imprisoned while managing Sardhana, harassed him; that by eating an apple soaked in brandy with bread, he would prevent Queen Victoria from holding a ball; that he had visited a madhouse, seeing there a lady dressed in Indian clothes and conversing with [the famously insane] King George III who had only one leg. The frequent examinations by Clark (who was simultaneously attending Queen Victoria during her pregnancy) and other fashionable doctors, and the complex legal process, were expensive but charged to Dyce Sombre's estate, now sequestered by Lord Chancellor Lyndhurst.

Over these four months, Mary Anne visited Dyce Sombre thrice. Whatever her motivations of affection for him, one school of medical experts in lunacy regarded this as a crucial test: provoking the delusion's power by exposure of the unbalanced mind to the major source of irritation.[28] Each moment of their stilted conversation was carefully transcribed. Clark reported, and Mary Anne confirmed, that Dyce Sombre revealed to her that 'the Queen had offered him a peerage if he would consent to "veil" his wife's irregularities, but that he had declined it'.[29] He then reportedly asked her mildly: '"Are you still living with Sir Frederick Bathurst? I saw you with him the other day in the carriage. Are you likely to have a child by him?" He examined her to see if there existed any appearance of her having a child, and then said he would take her back to live with him, on certain conditions... "First, let the Archbishop of Canterbury produce and furnish every requisite for [Dyce Sombre] passing a pleasant evening with a virgin of the same rank as the one now lost [Mary Anne]; second, let Mr E[dward]. Jervis produce another lady to receive the extinguisher of rank [sexual intercourse]; third, let there be a duel of three fires [shots] at the place in Hyde-park; fourth, let the Viscount St Vincent produce a roan horse, well broke for the occasion; and, fifth, when the ground has been consecrated by the duel, I shall re-consecrate it with Madam [Mary Anne], and bring her back home on the horse."' If they separated, Dyce Sombre assured Mary Anne that already a 'lady of high rank [hugely wealthy and haughty Lady Frances Anne Vane, Marchioness of Londonderry] had offered him her daughter [Lady Alexandrina Vane] in marriage' as compensation. In short, Clark found much to record and report that reconfirmed his own diagnosis.

Yet, when Lord Combermere visited, he declared Dyce Sombre 'in perfect health, and when conversing upon indifferent subjects he was perfectly sane in every respect, and when conversing on the subject of his wife he manifested precisely the same sort of opinions as those he had expressed [before].'[30] Thus, except on this one topic, Dyce Sombre always appeared to Combermere to be sane and sensible. The latter took no legal action to free him however.

For the person accused of lunacy during this period there were few recourses until the formal inquisition eventually took place. Mary

Anne's eldest brother, as a long-time magistrate, had known to file for a *Writ of Habeas Corpus* and to employ the expert authority of barristers in order to challenge his confinement. Yet, in the end, he succumbed to the almost inevitable outcome of such an inquisition: conviction as a Chancery Lunatic. The virtually isolated Dyce Sombre, in contrast, railed futilely against this deprivation of his liberty and property. His long-time solicitor, Frere, decided to support Mary Anne against him, leaving him with no familiar legal advisor to consult. Increasing his frustration, while he endured enforced celibacy, he heard his warders in the next room having noisy sex with the maid servants, all of them paid out of his estate. Over these weeks, Clark, Conolly, and other examiners appeared unexpectedly to ask him probing questions and note down his answers, without him having access to their account of his words.

Mary Anne's family, in addition to collecting evidence, also awaited the arrival of Dyce Sombre's sisters and their husbands, Solaroli and Troup, who had been slowly making their way from India to England. Over the preceding period, Dyce Sombre had become ever more suspicious of these two men, regarding them as maneuvering to take control over his fortune. He referred to them ironically as 'those precious and inestimable jewels of my brothers-in-law'.[31]

On 29 May 1843, the day after they reached England, they called upon Mary Anne, discussed their mutual and respective interests, and made plans for the disposition of Dyce Sombre and full confiscation of his estate. The following day, Solaroli visited Dyce Sombre, refusing to wait until Clark could attend and record their words. Dyce Sombre took offense and 'ejected' Solaroli, who thereafter publicly maintained that Dyce Sombre was indeed insane. Solaroli and Troup then asserted to Frere that Dyce Sombre had destroyed documentary evidence which would have given their wives full rights to Badshahpur. Solaroli and Troup also advised Mary Anne that young Stephen Reghellini, who had just come to England and visited Dyce Sombre in Hanover Lodge, and his father 'were highly mischievous and dangerous persons'.[32] The St Vincents arranged to send Stephen back to India immediately. Further, Solaroli, supported by Troup, encouraged Mary Anne to proceed with the inquisition, advised her to have Dyce Sombre incarcerated in a madhouse, and advanced their own claims to be appointed to the Committee that would manage Dyce Sombre's estate thereafter.

Finally on 27 June 1843, overcoming Mary Anne's reluctance to take this momentous step, the St Vincents' lawyers presented the long-prepared request for a *Commission de Lunatico Inquirendo* in her name to Lord Chancellor Lyndhurst. His subordinate, the newly created Commissioner in Lunacy, barrister Francis Barlow, would personally preside over the inquisition.[33] Barlow then authorised subpoenas for key witnesses (who were paid for their testimony), the assembling by the sheriff of the special jury from respectable men living nearby (who were paid a guinea per day), and the date for the hearing, a month later. Mr Calvert of Chancery Bar, the advocate working for the St Vincents, arranged to use the large drawing room in Hanover Lodge as the courtroom. To secure more evidence, Mary Anne's lawyers confiscated Dyce Sombre's box of private papers and opened them in the presence of Solaroli and Troup and prevented Dyce Sombre from consulting them prior to the public hearing.

Another Indian on Trial

Distinctive as it was, Dyce Sombre's lunacy case was not unique for the time. Earlier the same month as his trial, London newspapers had reported a quite parallel case: another lunacy petition brought by English in-laws against another person of mixed Indian and European ancestry, born and raised in India, who had reported delusions about a spouse. On 3 July 1843, Mrs Jane Cheetham was taken by her husband's family before the same Commissioner in Lunacy, Francis Barlow, and a special jury, in the Green Man Hotel in Blackheath, a southeast London suburb.[34] This lunacy inquisition was intended, as all were, to be a rapid disposal of an embarrassing family member for the supposed protection of self and property. As with most such trials, it lasted barely a day but determined the rest of the life of the putative, and then legal, Chancery Lunatic.

Ms Cheetham had been born in 1811 in Bengal Presidency, the elder daughter of young Captain Samuel Houlton of the East India Company's Bengal Army and an Indian concubine mother. Her father, from a long-established landowning Wiltshire family, had raised Jane as a Christian lady, providing her amateur training in European-style classical music. When she was twelve, her father had married a British woman, making her and her younger sister into embarrassing reminders of his youthful indiscretions. At age seventeen, two years after her father's death, Jane had married (7 December 1829) at Dinapore, Bihar, with a young English officer in the Bengal Army, Lieutenant John Edward Cheetham, a subaltern from a modest craftsman's family.

After the emotionally devastating death of their infant son, Jane's husband had brought her to London in 1834. When his leave expired a year later, he had returned to India, leaving her alone in rooms rented from a milliner on Judd Street. Although his family lived in suburban Woolwich, they apparently wished to keep her at a distance. Friendless, Jane was evidently treated badly by her landlady. After six years away in India, her husband died there (6 May 1841), official news of which reached her four months later.

According to her in-laws and the medical testimony of three doctors, Jane acted conventionally except in one regard: she refused to believe her husband dead. She continued, as she had for their half-dozen years of separation, to write him letters. Further, she claimed to have caught glimpses of him in 'different disguises' around London. Taking responsibility for his absence upon herself, she claimed he would be restored to her should she expiate 'some [unstated] offence against religion'. Her husband's family in Woolwich finally agreed to take her in. Although the family did not hire a professional warder, they never left her unsupervised. Finally, they petitioned Lord Chancellor Lyndhurst for a *Commission de Lunatico Inquirendo*, which he approved.

Since she was Christian, had an English father and husband, and was educated as an English gentry woman, her Indian mother's race and her first twenty-five years in India appeared only incidentally in her trial. Newspaper reporters rehearsed the distinguished family of her father. They also sympathetically characterised her as 'a beautiful young woman' (she was thirty-two-years-old). Yet, no recorded testimony or juridical deliberation considered how her Indian background might or might not have affected her relationship with her husband during his lifetime or after his death. Rather, her current demeanour was assessed solely by English cultural standards. Newspapers described her as 'perfectly collected, and [she] frequently smiled as remarks were made on her conduct'. Nonetheless, based on her reported 'religious infatuation' and 'one particular delusion'—interpreted as her apparent failure of will to accept her widowhood—the jury and Commissioner Barlow declared her a lunatic, starting two years retroactively on 6 September 1841 (apparently the date when news of her husband's death reached her). Commissioner Barlow and Lord Chancellor Lyndhurst ordered her kept until her death under the supervision of her husband's family, with her modest property and pensions controlled by them.

While Jane's younger full sister, Louise, lived in India with her second husband, Jane remained in England confined by her husband's family for the next half-century. The £102 cash she received from the Bengal Military Fund and her pensions totaling £92 annually from the East India Company and Lord Clive Fund were enough to defray her expense to her in-laws; although her unmarried status as a widow would have given her legal power over her property, her status as a Chancery Lunatic removed that power from her. For the last few decades of her life, she stayed in rural Hampshire under the care and control of her husband's unmarried younger sister.

In this instance, the goals of the Chancery Lunatic process succeeded from the perspective of the state and her English in-laws. Although Jane committed no crime and posed no threat to any family property or herself, she was legally and permanently disposed by the Crown into the physical and financial control of her in-laws and thus to pass the rest of her life quietly in seclusion. Her half Indian ancestry and youth there did not play any part in the London lay jury's assessment of her behavior or beliefs. In the case of Dyce Sombre, the overall process started similarly, but his extreme wealth, male gender, and initiative in rejecting his confinement by his in-laws led to a quite distinct outcome: eight years of very public embarrassment and continued international conflict, especially within and between the legal and medical professions.

Dyce Sombre on Trial

As the date of Dyce Sombre's hearing (31 July 1843) approached, he found the entire procedure incredibly frustrating and incomprehensible. Nor was he allowed access to his private papers, sequestered as they were by the St Vincents, Solaroli, and Troup. While Dyce Sombre was entitled to legal counsel, Sir James Clark, Frere, and the other St Vincent lawyers assured him that this was not necessary. Nonetheless, Dyce Sombre requested Mr Cochrane, Esq., a lawyer who had worked on his complex cases in Calcutta and whom he recalled having met again in England just six weeks before. When Clark reported that Cochrane was back in India, Dyce Sombre stubbornly retorted in writing that he would rather represent himself than agree to any other lawyer. Ironically, although he was accused of being mentally incompetent, his decision to waive legal representation was accepted by Commissioner Barlow as valid. Lacking any attorney representing him, the Commission against Dyce Sombre was officially 'unopposed'.

When Dyce Sombre asked for a written statement of the charges against him, Clark responded that there were no charges and that this was a different type of trial. Dyce Sombre then suspected that either the East India Company or Mary Anne (both of whom he knew had erred) were either the objects or instigators of this unfamiliar inquiry. Unlike the St Vincent family, Dyce Sombre had evidently never seen a lunacy inquisition. Hence, he had no advance knowledge of the one-sided proceedings nor what would be alleged against him. Nor would he receive an opportunity to state his full case or call any witnesses, although he did sporadically cross-examine hostile witnesses and answer occasional questions from Commissioner Barlow and the jury. Overall, Dyce Sombre's interventions proved largely ineffectual or counterproductive to his case.

He had come to believe the entire hearing was a plot against him by his true enemy, the East India Company's Court of Directors, which Parliament should remedy. Over the previous weeks, he had written repeatedly to prominent people explaining his discovery: 'whatever may be the ostensible reasons given out for deceiving the vulgar,... the Kings of India, commonly styled the Directors of the East India Company, are the persons who caused my confinement... but this not being India where the poor sufferer's cries could not reach the Conquerors of Hindoostan, I must not entirely omit the blame which is attached to Her Majesty's Principal Advisor represented by the Premier, who is at the head of Her Govt... I have already appealed the House of Commons.'[35] Since Parliament failed to free him, he concluded all its actions must be illegitimate.

Except for the embarrassing international publicity, the decisive one-day inquisition into Dyce Sombre's lunacy went largely as the St Vincent family anticipated. The same Commissioner in Lunacy, Francis Barlow, who had just presided over the successful inquisition of Jane Cheetham, served as judge in this trial as well. Like Ms Cheetham, Dyce Sombre had no legal representation. Yet, so celebrated were the social status of the St Vincents and Dyce Sombre's distinctive background, wealth, and recent parliamentary career that Hanover Lodge 'was crowded during the investigation by distinguished personages'; Dyce Sombre believed he recognised among the crowd the recently returned Governor General Lord Auckland (who had written Dyce Sombre letters of introduction and whose sisters, Emily and Fanny Eden, had hosted and chatted with him at her soirées in Calcutta).

Indeed, leading newspapers published detailed transcripts of the inquisition for the amusement and edification of their readers. American papers in particular identified him as a 'half-caste', captioning their articles 'Extraordinary Infatuation', ambiguously questioning Mary Anne's interracial love for him and his obsession for her.[36]

Even before Dyce Sombre had entered the courtroom, Calvert, the Chancery solicitor working for the St Vincents, opened and set the grounds for the inquisition. (He would continue to be lucratively employed by Mary Anne against Dyce Sombre for years thereafter.) As published widely by leading newspapers, he erroneously asserted that Dyce Sombre was 'the son of General Sombre and the Begum or Princess Sirhind [sic; some reporters heard it as Scinde]. At an early age he came over to England, where he remained until the course of education laid down for him was finished; when at the age of nineteen, he returned to India'. Since Dyce Sombre had earlier objected that it was insulting to expect him to be dressed and ready by 11:00 a. m. when the hearing opened, he was not yet present to correct the record. Indeed, only when the jury requested that he have the opportunity to appear was he brought into the courtroom. Many in the audience and other witnesses knew that Calvert's misidentification of Dyce Sombre as long-educated in England, as well as of his European paternity and the name of his birthplace, were all wrong. But the judge and jury did not and therefore did not consider how his Indian life until age twenty-nine might have informed his actions and attitudes.

Six of the British physicians who had examined Dyce Sombre over the past year testified—Clark, Chambers, Elliotson, Drever, Conolly, and Monro—albeit with inconsistent diagnoses. But the first four, as we have seen, had no special expertise in mental health issues. Each of these men repeated his earlier diagnosis, although they still did not fully accord. The professionalisation of 'alienists' into what would later become psychiatry, had not yet proceeded very far in Britain and so no special qualifications were required before doctors trained in other specialties testified authoritatively about mental illness.

The most socially prominent and influential of the doctors in this trial and in Dyce Sombre's future was Sir James Clark. He presented the most extensive and damaging evidence that the man in question was of 'unsound mind'. Dyce Sombre, after he was finally brought into the courtroom during Clark's second time on the stand, challenged Clark whenever he could. In fact, he scored an immediate but inconsequential legal victory when he rightly pointed out that Clark was testifying a second time although he had not yet been resworn as a witness. Dyce Sombre also appealed directly to the jury against Clark's ungentlemanly interference with his private papers and mail.

In contrast to Clark, Dr Chambers testified that he and Dr Sutherland (who did not testify himself) concurred Dyce Sombre had 'no decisive symptom of mental aberration'. They agreed with Clark that Dyce Sombre was deluded about his wife's infidelity and exhibited violent conduct based on his unfounded beliefs. But, while they determined him incompetent to act legally in his own interest, they also judged him 'not positively insane'.[37]

Also prominent but with a very different reputation was Dr John Elliotson, the famous but controversial mesmerist and founding editor of an widely-read journal of alternative medicine, *The Zoist: A Journal of Cerebral Physiology and Mesmerism*. Elliotson only had a single tempestuous meeting with Dyce Sombre five months earlier, when Dyce Sombre had burst into his chambers making accusations about Elliotson's mesmeric misleading of Mary Anne, followed by yet another challenge to a duel. Elliotson's ardent advocacy of hypnotism for a broad range of medical treatments had long put him at loggerheads with many in the establishment, but mesmerism and phrenology were quite trendy in Mary Anne's aristocratic social circle.[38] Less than a year later, a leading lawyer, the King's Sergeant-at-Law and former Attorney-General, Sir Thomas Wilde, MP, would assert in open court that 'Dr Elliotson, with his ideas respecting Mesmerism, was, in his opinion, quite as *insane* as Mr Dyce Sombre'.[39] A distinguished Church of England minister had recently called mesmerism 'the intervention of evil spirits' (presumably evoking different spirits from those Dyce Sombre perceived).[40] Elliotson, like Mary Anne, became a convinced practitioner of spiritualist séances. In the inquisition, Elliotson testified that Dyce Sombre was 'perfectly insane' but he explained that he meant Dyce Sombre had not a 'general insanity' but rather 'certainly seemed insane about his wife'. Some physicians of that time, following the French alienist, Jean-Etienne-Dominique Esquirol, termed this 'monomaniacal lunacy' ('in which the intellectual facilities are unimpaired, except with relation to some particular topic'), a diagnosis that had become widely fashionable for these few decades before it disappeared from modish medical jargon.[41]

In court, Dr Thomas Drever briefly recounted his long-standing personal relationship with Dyce Sombre. He read out Dyce Sombre's private letters to him which suggested the gradual and inconsistent onset of the disturbance of Dyce Sombre's mind. A signatory of the 1842 declaration of Mary Anne's purity, Drever nonetheless reemphasised his long-stated conviction that there was nothing in Dyce Sombre's Indian background that would rationalise or explain his delusions about his wife. Drever concluded Dyce Sombre was currently of 'unsound mind' although he remained competent to manage his own business affairs if relieved of irritating influences.

The other two doctors testifying were reputed specialists in lunacy: Dr John Conolly and Dr Edward Thomas Monro. Although they otherwise disagreed vehemently with each other about the validity of phrenology and the causes of *non compos mentis*, in this case they concurred. Conolly and Monro both asserted that Dyce Sombre's actions were 'quite consistent with insanity'.

While Dyce Sombre himself asserted the hearing should really be aimed at justifying his repudiation of his wife by demonstrating her immorality, four lay witnesses spoke of his anti-social behavior and her virtue. Dyce Sombre's warder, William Sherriff (employed by the St Vincents), provided evidence that he was dangerous, citing the pistols incident. Alfred Montgomery (a man often supposed by Dyce Sombre to be Mary Anne's lover), Lord Marcus Hill (a long-time friend of the St Vincents), and Edward Woodville Ricketts (Mary Anne's first cousin once removed) each spoke on behalf of Mary Anne, who did not herself testify. Dyce Sombre attempted to cross-examine Montgomery on details but with little effect. The three socialites provided evidence of Dyce Sombre's unjustified accusations against her and his promiscuous and inappropriate challenges to duels. The 1842 declaration by these and other men was introduced in support of Mary Anne's chastity and Dyce Sombre's failure to respect and appreciate it due to his groundless suspicions. These witnesses, however, disagreed as to whether Dyce Sombre would actually do violence to Mary Anne.

The solicitor representing the East India Company, Edward Lawford, presented correspondence in which Dyce Sombre threatened duels to quondam Chairmen of the Directors Sir Richard Jenkins and Major-General Sir James Law Lushington as well as to General Ventura and Sir Hume Campbell (the latter for allegedly looking peculiarly at Dyce Sombre's hat when passing on the street). Lawford also entered into the record Dyce Sombre's letter to Queen Victoria, entrusting his claims against the East India Company to her, as proof of his lunacy.

While the law had to decide if Dyce Sombre was a 'lunatic' or not, medical professionals were currently very divided about what that, in practice, meant. In Dyce Sombre's hearing, the six doctors divergently used the inconsistent terms: 'unsound mind', 'mental aberration', 'positively insane', 'perfectly insane', 'general insanity', and 'monomaniacal lunacy'. They also contradicted each other about whether he was legally incompetent without being insane or legally competent while being insane. Conolly himself wrote: doctors 'have sought for and imagined a strong and definable boundary between sanity and insanity, which has... been imaginary and arbitrarily placed'.[42] Another doctor had admitted only three years earlier:

All attempts at the legal definition of what constitutes unsoundness of mind have hitherto proved unsuccessful... Medical men have been subjected to much ridicule in our courts of law for the great variety, and sometimes total dissimilarity, of opinions entertained by them with reference to a correct definition of insanity. The great fault consists in attempting to define with precision what does not admit of being defined.[43]

On their part, Conolly and Clark also 'thought it an unsatisfactory and improper thing to determine the soundness or unsoundness of a person's mind by the opinion of an ordinary jury' of untrained laymen or lawyers.[44]

The legal profession, as well as the general public, also held their own conflicting views about what 'lunacy' entailed. Doctors found lawyers and judges adhered to archaic definitions which only confused the matter. Indeed, the most authoritative legal scholars, seventeenth-century Sir Mathew Hale and eighteenth-century Sir William Blackstone, had established for English civil law until the mid-nineteenth century only two possible categories of *non compos mentis*: 'an idiot', someone permanently incompetent, and 'A lunatic... one that hath lucid intervals; *qui gaudet lucidis intervallis*; sometimes enjoying his senses, and sometimes not, and that frequently depending upon the state of the moon.'[45] One doctor wrote in 1840: 'Nothing can well be more erroneous than [the current legal definition]. It assumes a theory connected with the disease, which, though believed at the time of Blackstone, is disbelieved now, and which renders the definition of no authority whatever.' Other doctors concurred: 'Legists have thrown much confusion in the matter of lunacy, and the opinions of the first authorities rather tend to puzzle the question than elucidate it'.[46] But doctors admitted: 'The attempts of medical writers to define insanity, have not been more successful than those of legal authorities to define what constitutes unsoundness of mind.'[47]

Conversely, many judges and juries in criminal, civil, and chancery trials discounted the testimony medical professionals, particularly since they failed to agree among themselves. Therefore, Commissioner in Lunacy Barlow, a trained barrister, frequently intervened to judge Dyce Sombre's condition for himself. In particular, he directly questioned Dyce Sombre about his unconventional and unmanly demand that Mary Anne challenge ladies to duels. In response, Dyce Sombre explained his explicitly altruistic reasoning: 'I wished her to challenge any lady she might select, because she might be jealous of the ladies as I am of the men, and I wished to afford her every satisfaction'. Unconvinced that Dyce Sombre was living up to his socially expected role as protecting Victorian husband, the Commissioner pressed further: 'But if the lady accepted the challenge, would you expose her to the risk of fighting?' Dyce Sombre retorted gallantly: 'Oh no; I should, of course, have taken all that part of the affair upon myself'. British society at this time was developing new ideas about manhood, including when, how, and by whom duelling was appropriate. Prominent men, including many of Mary Anne's and Dyce Sombre's acquaintances, would conduct widely-publicised duels in Britain for another decade, despite condemnation by various others.[48] However, Dyce Sombre appeared not to conform to any of these variant interpretations of the rules of honour then current in British society; he issued many challenges, on diverse grounds, expected his wife to challenge ladies, but he fought no actual duels. To many Britons, Dyce Sombre's actions thus appeared simultaneously both unmanly and also a mocking parody of true British proofs of manly honour.

Dyce Sombre also particularly piqued Commissioner Barlow's curiosity by his assertion that Parliament was now illegitimate since it had not acted to free him. When Barlow questioned this, Dyce Sombre explained 'It is no delusion... I thought the least [Parliament] could do was to have an inquiry [into my confinement] at once. Had I made an application in India, the sittings of the Supreme Court would have been continued until something was done, and I should not have been confined for months.' Barlow objected: 'That would not make the acts of Parliament illegal'. Dyce Sombre responded: 'That is a question for the jury to decide'. The Commissioner clearly saw lunacy in Dyce Sombre's thinking patterns and directed the jury to do likewise.

The jurymen also directly questioned Dyce Sombre, believing they themselves would recognise lunacy when they saw it, whatever the conflicting testimony from the six doctors. According to reporters, 'the rambling and incoherent nature of his answers' to their questions convinced the jury unanimously and quickly to decree that 'Mr Dyce Sombre was of unsound mind', hence a 'Chancery Lunatic'. By law, the jury also had to determine the exact moment when Dyce Sombre had entered *non compos mentis*. Precise dating was crucial since his legal competence terminated at that point. Yet, each witness dated the onset and full incompetence at a different moment. Calvert, representing Mary Anne's interests, strategically asserted: 'It was shortly after his marriage that the first symptoms of mental aberration manifested themselves, and they gradually increased until an inquiry was rendered imperatively necessary'. Calvert knew that, had Dyce Sombre been lunatic before his wedding, his generous settlement contract and marriage with Mary Anne could be invalid. Yet, Calvert also knew that Dyce Sombre had to be lunatic before she signed the petition for a lunacy commission for it to be valid. Other witnesses argued for various other times. For example, Drever dated the onset of his suspicions from Dyce Sombre's letter of 24 November 1841 but his conviction of Dyce Sombre's insanity from the January 1842 assembly. Perhaps because Lord Chancellor Lyndhurst had issued new 'General Orders in Lunacy' which altered the administration and supervision of Chancery Lunatics on 27 October 1842, the jury declared that Dyce Sombre's lunacy began on that exact date, 277 days earlier.

We can see how the medical and legal professions were currently constructing and reconstructing concepts of insanity, in dialogue, and often at cross-purposes, with other parts of British society, particularly with regard to non-Britons. At this first inquisition, none of the doctors or other witnesses raised the possibility of Dyce Sombre's condition being consequent from either the many cases of venereal diseases he had contracted or the many powerful drugs and other treatments he had received. Rather, lunacy appeared variously as a moral disease, or a condition caused by an emotionally irritated mind, or a spirit unbalanced by excessive consumption of alcohol and rich foods, or 'a morbid condition of the animal fluids... in the blood', among other contending theories.[49] Dyce Sombre's delusions also appeared to stem from his failure of will to understand both Mary Anne's chastity and also the other British conventions he violated, like the gentlemanly etiquette of duelling. Further, in this first inquisition, there was a marked absence of discussion about his racial or ethnic origins, or his evident culture-shock on entering Britain, or what he would know or not know about British marriage and duelling based on his education and enculturation in India. These alternate explanations arose only peripherally when Drever noted but dismissed them as irrelevant. Significantly, this very issue of his essential nature, European or Indian, which was ignored in this decisive first trial, would later become central to widespread popular, medical, and legal discourse about his condition in the many subsequent hearings about him.

Although he had neither committed a crime nor squandered his property, Dyce Sombre was now legally a Chancery Lunatic, one of 217 people in Britain at that moment so designated (out of about 20,000 official lunatics of all sorts); by the time of his death in 1851, there would be 530 Chancery Lunatics.[50] His one-day inquisition, however unbalanced against Dyce Sombre it might have been, was meant to silence and quarantine him forever. Indeed, it proved impossible for him to reverse. Yet, Dyce Sombre's later flight freed him, but not his fortune, from British authority. Once self-liberated, his virtually continuous appeals over eight years to supersede this decree, conducted by a costly and diverse range of lawyers and other advocates, raised new and awkward issues in a highly public and universally discomforting way.

In and Out of the Lord Chancellor's Charge

As a legal Chancery Lunatic, Dyce Sombre lost control over his person and his property, and was reduced to the legal status of a minor and ward of the Crown. Under the normal procedure, the person bringing the successful *Writ de Lunatico Inquirendo*, Mary Anne, would next petition Lord Chancellor Lyndhurst to appoint two committees.[51] The Committee of the Person, customarily including the person bringing the *Writ*, arranged for the perpetual physical care of the confirmed lunatic. The Committee of the Estate, also usually including a family member but not the spouse, would serve as trustee for the lunatic's property. Since disputes between Mary Anne and her husband's brothers-in-law over control of Dyce Sombre's money delayed her petition to Lyndhurst, the St Vincents continued to manage Dyce Sombre while the Lord Chancellor managed his wealth.

While Solaroli and Troup advised putting Dyce Sombre in an asylum (joining some 10,000 British men and women currently in them), Mary Anne preferred to confine him in Hanover Lodge or another private house under fashionable Sir James Clark's supervision. The leading medical experts in lunacy of the day disagreed fundamentally about both the nature of salutary treatments and whether lunacy was curable at all. Some doctors advocated and practised radical interventions, including physical purging and close confinement. Others (like Dr Seymour mentioned above), prescribed and practised heavy sedation with narcotics. The most progressive medical experts, inspired by Dr John Conolly's views, rejected coercion and recommended the 'moral cure': as limited restraint as was possible while strengthening the physical body through healthy diet and salubrious air. Clark became convinced of the virtues of Conolly's methods (Clark in retirement wrote a laudatory biography of Conolly).[52] Hence, under Clark's direction, Dyce Sombre continued as he had before his inquisition to have limited freedom within Hanover Lodge, to meet people there, and to be escorted on outings to nearby London parks.

One gentleman caller was Charles Edward Trevelyan, who had already offered Dyce Sombre patronizing advice in Delhi, Calcutta, and London. Like Combermere and Drever, but siding with the former and opposing the latter, Trevelyan represented himself as an expert on Oriental culture and incompletely Anglicised Orientals like Dyce Sombre. Over the preceding months, Trevelyan had followed reports about Dyce Sombre's engagement and then scandalous marriage but personally judged him only 'a raw, good-natured, easy, and very rich man, no Blue Beard or charlatan, as he appeared to be considered, but, nevertheless, with habits of thought and feeling so entirely different from those in which an English lady of rank and fashion is brought up, that such a marriage... could not fail to be unhappy and most disastrous.'[53]

Then, on reading extensive newspaper articles about Dyce Sombre's famous conviction as a lunatic, Trevelyan wrote a memorial (19 August 1843) to the East India Company's Directors about the 'great national injustice' of Dyce Sombre's conviction. Trevelyan supported Dyce Sombre's sanity, characterizing him as 'a slow-minded, slow-speaking young man, but perfectly good natured'. Trevelyan blamed Dyce Sombre's dislocation from India to England for his troubles. In India, Dyce Sombre 'possessed of sufficient sense to acquit himself well in the position in which he was then placed and to conduct his private affairs with discretion, according to the modes in use in that country'.

But, Trevelyan continued, Dyce Sombre was naturally unprepared to live happily in England or marry satisfactorily to an English noblewoman since 'his Asiatic manner of viewing things was so diametrically opposite to the manner in which the same things are viewed in European society'.

In his letter to the Directors, Trevelyan specifically analyzed three areas of British culture where Dyce Sombre had tripped up: dueling, the supernatural, and women. First, 'the customs with respect to duelling which prevail in a certain portion of English society are not founded on the nature of things, but are the accidental result of barbarous institutions which have long ceased to exist... Mr Dyce's conduct in this respect was a bad imitation of a bad artificial [English] national custom, which is not easy to understand, even by the natives of countries in which it prevails.' Second, Trevelyan argued all Indians, like rustic English county folk, believed in 'spirits... dreams, philters, etc.' so it would only be expected that Dyce Sombre would do so. Trevelyan also derided British false faith in mesmerism and Dr Elliotson, which Dyce Sombre had learned in London. Third, Trevelyan argued, like Combermere, that Mary Anne must have inadvertently violated Dyce Sombre's expectations for 'the female sex which he has in common with all his countrymen... which must have harrowed her husband's feelings to the quick, and have amply sufficed to make him lose his self possession'. In India, 'Mr Dyce would have been adjudged to have been a deeply injured husband; the line of conduct pursued by him would have been regarded as extremely moderate and humane; and his wife's conduct would have been considered so totally at variance with the most received and best established notions of female delicacy and propriety, that it would have been regarded as capable of being accounted for only on the supposition of her not being in a sound state of mind'. This theme from Trevelyan, Combermere, and others, that Dyce Sombre was acting rationally based on his native culture, would become vital to Dyce Sombre's advocates in future.

Additionally, Trevelyan argued that he, rather than Dyce Sombre, was capable of explaining all this to British authorities and further that he, Trevelyan, was competent to understand India while ordinary Britons could not. Although Dyce Sombre 'has learned, by mixing with English society, the common forms of conversation, the circumstance of his having to express his ideas in a foreign language gives to his speech an awkwardness and an oddity which, to persons before whom he appeared the character of an alleged lunatic, was likely to confirm the idea, as it really appears to have done, that he was not of sane mind...' Further, 'the commission and jury who tried the case were, from their exclusively English feelings and habits, totally incompetent for the proper discharge of the extremely important duty which devolved upon them'. Trevelyan went on that 'the answers returned and the observations made by [Dyce Sombre] during the inquiry, when they are interpreted by a reference [by Trevelyan] to Asiatic feelings and modes of thought, are by no means indicative of unsound mind'. He warned 'if this decision remain unimpeached, the management of his large income will be permanently entrusted to others—he will be condemned to an imprisonment for life of a most grievous and irritating kind, and he will probably soon really become what he has been judicially declared to be'. Hence, Trevelyan recommended that the East India Company, as guardian of all Indians in Britain, intervene 'in order to obtain the liberation' of Dyce Sombre as 'improperly confined'.[54] Claiming to speak for Indians collectively, Trevelyan asserted they would be upset at his unjust imprisonment 'entertaining suspicions in the highest degree degrading our [British] national character'. The core of Trevelyan's arguments, which had not been raised in the one-day inquisition, would form the most telling grounds for Dyce Sombre's future appeals against his conviction as a lunatic.

Nonetheless, after Viscount St Vincent's friend, Lord Marcus Hill, arranged for Trevelyan actually to meet Dyce Sombre in person in Hanover Lodge in early September 1843, Trevelyan suddenly judged that Dyce Sombre's condition had become irremediable. Trevelyan then wrote: 'the irritating circumstances and violent conflict between European and India, or Asiatic habits of thought... had wrought in him a state of mind which appeared to me to make it desirable' that he be kept in confinement since he had undoubtedly become 'a decided monomaniac'. Further, since Dyce Sombre indicated 'no intention of returning to India' and was already 'in humane and trustworthy keeping', Trevelyan recommended that everything should remain as it currently was.[55] Six years later, however, after much had transpired, Trevelyan would revert to his arguments as detailed in his earlier long memorial, retrospectively asserting that Dyce Sombre should have been returned to India and freed there.[56]

Once a Chancery Lunatic, Dyce Sombre was universally expected to continue his seclusion routinely for the rest of his life. Even after Clark was called away a month after the inquisition to attend upon Queen Victoria during her continental tour, his prescription for Dyce Sombre continued. During Clark's temporary absence, the St Vincent family hired James Ranald Martin, a retired Presidency Surgeon of the East India Company's Bengal Establishment.[57] Martin had met and treated Dyce Sombre in Calcutta and knew enough Urdu to converse with him in that language; indeed, Dyce Sombre suggested Martin's name as a possible medical attendant. This appeal to a British authority on India, its peoples, and cultures, seemed to Mary Anne's family a way to soothe and control Dyce Sombre's mind. When, after six weeks, Martin recommended that Dyce Sombre travel, he nominated as additional travelling medical supervisor his younger friend, John Grant, who also had experience serving as a medical officer of the East India Company and also knew Urdu.

Despite the centrality of Hanover Lodge's location in Regent's Park, the dampness of its location overlooking the Grand Canal made its unhealthy. Dyce Sombre's keepers took him on outings in London's other parks, limiting and recording his behaviour. When a more extensive trip appeared appropriate in order to occupy his fretting mind, Drever suggested sending Dyce Sombre to tour distant America, but this proved to be too complicated legally since, once off British soil,

Adelphi Hotel with Lime Street Railway Station in Rear, Liverpool

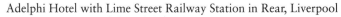

229

the Lord Chancellor's authority to confine him was unprecedented.[58] Instead, Martin, Grant, a medical attendant, and two servants took him on a tour of England for 'a change of air and scene'.

Setting off on 9 September 1843, they visited Bath, Bristol, Gloucester, Birmingham, and, finally, Liverpool (18 September). There Martin left them, ceding charge to young Grant. They took rooms in the fashionable Adelphi Hotel, near Lime Street railway station. As long as Dyce Sombre behaved 'in a very rational manner', as his keepers reported he did, he was able to walk the streets and converse with passers-by. For his amusement, he proposed purchasing a pleasure yacht for trips on the Mersey River. As negotiations for this purchase were ongoing, Dyce Sombre disappeared around 4:00 a.m. on 21 September 1843.

Aghast, Grant and his men frantically alerted the police to join their futile search. The police apprehended 'a tall and handsome man of colour', but he turned out to be an Indian steward of a vessel in Liverpool's King's Dock, and had to be released. Meanwhile, Dyce Sombre was long gone.

11

LUNATIC ONLY IN ENGLAND, SANE ELSEWHERE

Dyce Sombre had fled to freedom on the continent, but his immediate problem remained that the English judicial system still sought to incarcerate him and still had his money. People all around him were alienated by his actions but larger developments, well beyond his control, also shaped his situation. The European medical and legal systems were shifting as their practitioners professionalised. Within British society, classes contended over wealth, power, and position, and the appropriate roles for men and women. In the face of rival European powers and local resistance, the British empire expanded over peoples whom Britons judged Oriental and black, like him. Dyce Sombre's indeterminate legal, cultural, and social status and his inheritance of Begum Sombre's legendary legacy meant that people in Britain, on the continent, and around the globe judged him variously from their own diverse perspectives.

Legally, Dyce Sombre remained in limbo. The European medical and judicial professions both failed to resolve his condition, despite their evolving claims to rational and scientific universality. Once his original inquisition declared him lunatic, he found it impossible to disprove his insanity in England. He never underwent, nor was expected to undergo, any medical treatment. Yet, no English Lord Chancellor would supersede his original conviction without clear proof that Dyce Sombre was no longer a lunatic, or had never been one. No consensus existed among English doctors or jurists about what lunacy was or how one could diagnose its absence. In contrast, on the European continent from France to Russia, Dyce Sombre was legally sane, as dozens of doctors whom he hired attested and several judicial bodies affirmed. Since his behaviour remained relatively consistent in India, Britain, and the continent, his celebrated case demonstrated publicly then, as it does now, how culturally constructed and contingent were current standards of mental illness.

Further, Dyce Sombre held citizenship nowhere. Although he had been elected to the British Parliament, his colonial origins meant that his place in the English nation-state remained moot. Queen Victoria's government claimed he was subject to its authority, but the French and other continental governments extended protection to him against extradition. Anomalously, the English Lord Chancellor temporarily exempted him from seizure during each of the repeated rehearings of his case. He could have spent his life travelling freely anywhere outside English jurisdiction, but the English government had sequestered his property and he determined to recover it and his right to live there.

Dyce Sombre's social and cultural identities alienated him from virtually all groups in Britain. But his difficulties largely arose from his marriage which provided his English aristocratic wife's family with power over him and his fortune. They portrayed him as violating evolving Victorian bourgeois domestic values and proper behavior as a husband and gentleman. They thus obtained his confinement allegedly to protect his wife and his fortune. Many British men of all classes acted similarly, or worse, but most did not face as influential or assertive in-laws.

Given his wealth but also its origins, his social class remained moot. Many of his supporters were European noblemen who considered his possessive treatment of his wife and idiosyncratic disposal of his wealth as perfectly appropriate for a rich man. Some of his bourgeois advocates resented the titled pretensions of the St Vincents and Mary Anne's long rumoured relationships with British noblemen as well as her massive financial gain from her wedding.

During this period, concepts of racial identity also shifted. Since Dyce Sombre came from India but also from mixed ancestry, various people identified his race according to their own standards. Indians living or settled in Britain also had difficulties placing him. Many American journalists projected their own binary classification, called him 'Black' since he was clearly not 'White'. More sympathetic European commentators regarded Dyce Sombre as an innocent Asiatic unable to cope with the mendacity of his wife's family or with the complexities of European civilisation.

Ironically, British popular opinion was coming to regard all Indians as distinct from Europeans in culture and even physical bodies. Hence, most Britons who believed Dyce Sombre sane were those who identified him as essentially Asian and felt he should be judged only by alien Asiatic standards. Dyce Sombre, however, generally (but not consistently) aspired to be treated as European. Nonetheless, most English authorities judged that, measured by English standards, he was mentally and morally incompetent and therefore should be confined. Dyce Sombre's blatant disrespect toward English authorities and moralities demonstrated his resistance but did not aid his cause.

The material stakes in his case were enormous for all parties involved. Dyce Sombre, his wife, her family, his brothers-in-law, countless employees and dependents of each of them, the East India Company, and the British Government all had direct but conflicting claims to his enormous capital (mostly in Britain) and properties (mostly in India). The fate of the legendary Begum Sombre's fable fortune drew fascinated public attention across Europe, Asia, and Americas, heightened wherever Dyce Sombre travelled or whenever a new redaction of his convoluted cases arose. Hence, he had liberated himself from confinement in England and could live anywhere on the continent, dedicated to pursuing his own pleasures. But he also vainly persisted in trying to recover full control over his fortune and refuting his many accusers, whatever the cost.

Dyce Sombre's Dash to Freedom in France

Immediately on hearing from the chastened guardian Grant about Dyce Sombre's sudden disappearance in Liverpool, Mary Anne and her family feared both for his safety and also the legal and financial implications of his abrupt absence. Leading newspapers across Britain reported 'speculation, mingled with alarm' at his mysterious vanishing, hazarding he had been kidnapped by 'crimps, who are keeping him locked up until his gold shall have been exhausted'.[1] Then, a week later, word reached London from the British embassy in Paris that Dyce Sombre had reappeared in high society there.

In a swift flight that Dyce Sombre celebrated as a crafty victory over his enemies, he had boarded a night express-train from Liverpool's Lime Street Station to London. After four hours there, he changed to another rapid train to Southampton port. Catching an over-night steam-packet to Le Havre, he entered France despite having no identification papers, reaching Paris the evening of 22 September 1843. Only forty-four hours after he left Liverpool's Adelphi, he took rooms in Paris' Hôtel du Rhin. While Dyce Sombre had only limited cash with him, he sold the pocket watch of his servant, Pierre Daniel Roulin (which he had absconded with), the diamond buttons from his shirt (a present from the Marchioness of Hastings), and his solid gold pencil-case.[2] As with so many famously wealthy men, he charged expenses to his account, borrowed from acquaintances, and so was able to manage. He then resumed his social intercourse in Paris society, high and low.

Mary Anne proclaimed herself 'willing to undergo everything rather than fail in what appeared... to be her duty to him, by contributing what might be in her power towards his relief and recovery' and desired to hasten to Paris.[3] Dissuaded by her fearful family and French authorities, she then immediately dispatched solicitor Frere, a surgeon, and a medical warder to recapture her husband. Frere went to the barrister serving as official Counsel to the British Embassy in Paris, Mr Charles Henry Okey, to arrange the extradition of the fugitive but he refused to cooperate.

Dyce Sombre wrote triumphally about his self-liberation and confounding of his British enemies, gloating to Mary Anne: 'Madam, Perhaps by this time you are made acquainted that I have not waited the result of the good intentions of the Lord Chancellor, or of his representative, Mr Grant, to whom, by the way of remembrance from me, ask him if "John Bull has his own way at all times?"'[4] Similarly, he explained to Reghellini (who had managed his properties in India since Solaroli had come to Europe), that he was retaking charge of his fortune there: 'Strange events have happened since you last heard from me... You of course are aware that a mock trial was got up and I was pronounced insane or in other words mad and not capable of management of my own affairs, by which means the property I had in England was put under the Lord Chancellor and a pretty good hole they will have made in it before it is returned to me! ...I am no more mad than I was at Sirdhana and pray [you] do not attend to any instructions... either from the Lord Chancellor (Lord Lyndhurst) or his representatives.'[5] Dyce Sombre also suggested disingenuously (or sincerely but obtusely) that he had continuing influence over the East India Company's Directors, promising Reghellini that he was in the process of securing a Company cadetship for his son, Stephan.

Among Dyce Sombre's associates in Paris who quickly supported him was the powerful Baron Sébastien Félix Feuillet de Conches, Chef du Protocole, Department for Foreign Affairs of France. He and Dyce Sombre had over the past six years socialised frequently in Paris and England. Further, France had interests in India opposed to those of the British and always sought allies among India's princes, or even former near-princes. The Baron officially announced to Frere and Okey that extant treaties made no provision for extradition of men like Dyce Sombre who had committed no crime in either Britain or France. Further, the Baron arranged for the Paris Police Prefect to provide him an official escort, both to report on Dyce Sombre's activities and also to preclude his being kidnapped by the English. In frustration, Frere returned to London, as Dyce Sombre bragged, 'much disappointed he was, I am told, at not taking his prey back'.[6]

The Baron and the Prefect quickly assembled their own panel of distinguished doctors to examine Dyce Sombre including: Louis Jule Béhier (Quarterly Physician to the King); M. Bourneau (Physician to the Hospitals of Paris); and Sir Robert Alexander Chermside (Irish-born, Scottish-trained Physician to the British Embassy in Paris, Knight Commander of the Royal Guelphic Order, Knight of the Order of St John, Knight of the Prussian Red Eagle, and Member of the French Légion d'honneur).[7] Sir James Clark sent fellow Briton Chermside a long letter detailing topics that they should particularly probe to uncover Dyce Sombre's cleverly concealed madness and strongly advising the panel not to contradict Clark's own professional opinion that Dyce Sombre was lunatic. British authorities also made some of Dyce Sombre's own revealing private papers available. Just three weeks after he suddenly appeared in Paris, this illustrious panel met for three hours on 13 October 1843 in the office and with the active participation of the Police Prefect himself. Baron de Conches observed. Okey represented the British ambassador and translated the questions and answers since Dyce Sombre did not know French.

Dyce Sombre acquitted himself well before this eminent panel (none of whom had any special training in mental health). He denied ever abusing his wife, either verbally or physically. Appealing to the panel's fellow Catholics, he explained many of his actions as jokes and quips misunderstood by the obtuse and humourless English. Like Combermere and Trevelyan, he argued that his conduct was appropriate and normal by Indian standards according to which he should be judged. As the panel officially reported: 'Mr Dyce Sombre... related that being brought up in India, he had different and completely Indian notions, and which were diametrically opposed to our easy European manners, respecting the life married women should lead; that he had communicated those ideas to Mrs Sombre previous to their marriage... that they had been faithfully observed for some time, but afterwards, through the intervention of indiscreet friends and relations, they had been less scrupulously kept.'[8] Dyce Sombre admitted to his healthy sexual appetite which Victorian English prudishness had tried to suppress. He subtly indicated that the perfidious English East India Company's persecution lay behind many of the trumped-up charges against him. He also explained that, in the Begum's court, murder and intrigue were prevalent and therefore he had naturally expected to find them in England as well.

Although these doctors confided that they had originally expected to find Dyce Sombre a lunatic, they were completely convinced by his explanations. They attributed his un-European motivations to 'Oriental indolence, and want of education'. Further, their faction of French medical science had clear and exact rules about the symptoms that revealed the lesion in the brain that—it was convinced—caused lunacy. As self-assured medical experts, they concurred that Dyce Sombre did not exhibit any symptoms of such a brain lesion. They authoritatively asserted that no true lunatic would or could have acted or conducted himself as reasonably as he had done under their scrutiny. They most assuredly believed that their rigourous and extensive medical examination would have revealed any lunacy, had it existed. To prove their point, they described how Dyce Sombre confided that he had been physically unwell during the days prior to his original inquisition in London, but he deprecated the panel's trick suggestion that his warders in Hanover Lodge might have been poisoning him. The doctors stated rhetorically: 'Where is the lunatic... who, after three hours conversation on subjects most irritating for him... would have been so reserved in his accusation... and the idea of an attempt on his life being once mentioned, would not dwell further on that subject?' Overall, they found Dyce Sombre was 'altogether becoming, calm, and moderate' as became a 'proper gentleman' whereas 'the generality of deranged subjects... are reserved, anxious, and suspicious' people.

This official panel therefore unanimously declared to French government authorities that they 'absolutely have not seen or discovered anything which can lead them to recognise the least derangement in the mental faculties of Mr Dyce Sombre, who appears to them as enjoying complete lucidity and clearness of understanding'. They strongly recommended that he be permitted to remain free in France, protected against interference by the English. Even Okey had to agree that Dyce Sombre had displayed no unusual behavior in Paris before, during, or after this examination except for criticising Mary Anne for refusing to practise purda. Dyce Sombre explained to Okey: 'I asked her to cover her face as women do in my country, but she would not... my sister does, and I don't see why my wife should not'.[9]

The St Vincents, Sir James Clark, and the British government did not accept this panel's judgment, however. They upbraided the French doctors for being so naïvely deceived and redoubled their efforts to recover control over Dyce Sombre.

Over this period, Mary Anne and Dyce Sombre kept up frequent correspondence, solicitous and intimate on her part, intermittently cold and distant or warm and inviting on his. She referred to herself with their intimate pet name for her: 'yr little Dan', offered to visit him and repeatedly requested a lock of his hair and a picture of him as a child as mementos. In her absence, she begged him to 'say your prayers, and ask the Almighty to point out to you that you are wrong, and ask Him to let you see the truth as it is... and then I may still have happy days with you yet, after all the miserable ones I have spent alone without you, and quite forsaken and desolate.' She also warned him against his usual overindulgence in 'Morphia, Opium, Brandy, and liqueurs'. Further, she evoked the late Begum on her side, writing 'Ah, I wish she was here with me, she wd see the thing as it is, and you wd believe her'.[10] Mary Anne also awkwardly attempted to recall the endearing Urdu phrases he had taught her (although her memory of them was garbled and she thought them Persian), writing:

A mari tabré bemuse tré humi both offsorwa!
Hodar chatré tum geld ache troughi Humhushivé tum hary annsé!
You see, tho' I am obliged to write it in an English way, that I have not quite forgot what taught me, Boht hub, Persian hub; you must say Wah, Wah.

Evoking their former physical intimacy, she confided 'Yr great Bear skin coat I have on the sofa of my bed-room, to wrap around me and keep me warm, and I go to sleep in it, and it reminds me of you'.

In contrast, his letters addressed her coldly as 'Madam', initially indicating she should stay under 'your father's roof' while St Vincent (currently age seventy-six) should come to Paris for a duel.[11] (She replied that she hoped he would not force her 'Old Daddies' to duel him, not wanting her father to be killed.) He warned that he still set spies on her to catch out her bad behaviour. Further, Dyce Sombre repeatedly proposed that they refer her and her alleged lover's behaviour to the arbitration of the members of the influential and highly male Paris Jockey Club; these fashionable gentlemen would constitute a panel to 'trot out' the identity of her lover and dishonour him. He found she bridled at this proposal. As Dyce Sombre's lawyer later pointed out, this procedure simply echoed the assembly of gentlemen called by her family in 1842 to judge him.[12]

Simultaneously, however, Dyce Sombre sought to regain his husband's authority over her. He indulgently mailed her a lock of his hair; he sent her the Parisian bonbons she desired. Further, he invited her, her beloved dog 'Fiddelle' (pet-name 'Fidi', who would soon after be dog-napped and ransomed by Mary Anne for two guineas), and her maidservant to come to live in his Paris apartments.[13] Soon thereafter, however, he began writing of their irreversible incompatibility and inevitable separation, although not yet divorce.

What particularly rankled Dyce Sombre was his dependence on Mary Anne for money, funds which he had originally given her. While the Lord Chancellor and the Committee of the Estate refused to pay him anything, she doled out money to him according to her judgment about what was necessary and what not. With her wedding settlement of £4,000 annual income (allowed her by the Lord Chancellor) plus allowances from her father and Dyce Sombre's trust, Mary Anne was quite wealthy. She requested Okey to advance money to her husband at the rate of £10 weekly pocket money which, after his good behaviour, she gradually raised to £28, plus approved expenses. She still wanted Dyce Sombre to live as a gentleman, sending him an English valet, coachman, horse, and carriage. She wrote: 'I would wish you to live not only respectably, but in style, if you are true to me; but, of course, I am not going to pay for my own dishonour or your follies'.[14] These gender role reversals exacerbated Dyce Sombre's animus toward his wife.

To buttress his position, Dyce Sombre hired a second panel of physicians to reexamine him in Paris over three days in mid-December. He had his advisor, Lewis Goldsmith, Notary to the British Embassy in Paris, attend to attest to the panel's proper procedure and judgment. This group, unlike that of two months earlier, included doctors recognised as France's leading specialists in lunacy: Félix Voisin (Principal

Doctor of Lunatic Hospital of Bicêtre); Jean Pierre Falret (Principal Doctor of the Lunatic Hospital of the Salpétrière); Guillaume Ferrus (Consulting Doctor to the French King and Inspector General of the Lunatic Hospital); Dr Etienne Luc Bertin (late Physician to the French Embassy in London and member of the British Royal College of Surgeons); Robert Verity (late physician to the British Embassy in Paris); and his old acquaintance from Italy, Joseph Francis Olliffe (Irish-born, Paris-educated President of the Parisian Medical Society, future Physician to the British Embassy in Paris). This panel met at Dyce Sombre's lodgings and, after many searching questions, concluded (14 December 1843) that he was in 'full possession of his intellectual and affective qualities... That the movements of jealousy, the tenacity of which is revealed in several expressions of Mr Dyce Sombre, do not appear to exceed the ordinary limits in the feelings of an European, and with much more reason in those of an Oriental.' These distinguished doctors thus suggested that a man's origins as European or Oriental determined how he would and should feel and behave concerning jealousy of his wife. Such biologically based ideas would burgeon in French as well as English psychiatry over subsequent decades.[15]

This second panel therefore reconfirmed Dyce Sombre's unprecedented medical and legal situation: two French panels of unimpeachable medical experts contradicted the British Commissioner in Lunacy and special lay jury of ordinary Englishmen appointed by the Lord Chancellor. In England, Dyce Sombre was legally a lunatic, sentenced to confinement, while in France he was officially a sane and free man. Doctors and lawyers in Britain, the United States, and wherever else British precedent applied would debate the implications of his case. For example, New York's *Albion, A Journal of News, Politics and Literature* recounted this latest chapter in Dyce Sombre's fascinating and unpredictable career, highlighting these English-French clashes of authority. On his part, Dyce Sombre felt once again vindicated: 'I never was what they tried to make me out, a madman; and nowhere else [than England], I should think, such rascality could have been allowed to have taken place, under the very protection of the head of the law itself, the Lord Chancellor'.[16]

While these international legal conflicts continued, reciprocal stresses also escalated within Dyce Sombre's family. He expressed increasing resentment against his brothers-in-law.[17] In London, Troup accused solicitor Frere of acting deceptively in drawing up Mary Anne's generous marriage settlement which alienated almost a quarter of the Begum's fortune. Solaroli alleged—personally to Dyce Sombre in Paris and then on oath to the Lord Chancellor—that Frere and Mary Anne had tried to bribe him into support for her legal position. Solaroli also advanced Dyce Sombre a much needed £603 (reluctantly repaid by the Lord Chancellor out of Dyce Sombre's estate five years later); as much as Dyce Sombre needed the money, this reversal of roles rankled.[18] Trying to assert his own authority, Dyce Sombre wrote the Lord Chancellor objecting to either Solaroli or Troup having any role in controlling his estate, reemphasising that he had already given his sisters £20,000 plus £10–12,000 in jewels—all they would ever get from him. His suspicions and hostility toward Solaroli in particular intensified. Among other allegations, he accused Solaroli of kidnapping Dyce Sombre's daughter Penelope and then circulating false claims that she had died. Dyce Sombre gradually concentrated his accusations to exclude Solaroli from the Begum's and Dyce Sombre's family by asserting the illegitimacy of Georgiana as only the daughter of Dyce's concubine, Basanti, rather than his wife, Dyce Sombre's mother. These crosscutting legal and personal quarrels, impelled by the Begum's legacy, also pitted Mary Anne against Solaroli and Troup on some issues, even while these three stood as uneasy allies on others.

Within the British expatriate community in Paris, Dyce Sombre had his supporters. Dr Olliffe, who had met him earlier in Italy and then recently served on the panel of prominent doctors who had examined and cleared him, now became his regular personal physician and would later witness his will.[19] Okey provided funds from Mary Anne and covered Dyce Sombre's debts, although not without chiding him for extravagance, as when Dyce Sombre purchased on credit an £80 watch and £40 watch-chain.[20] When Mary Anne begged Okey to serve as Dyce Sombre's full time escort and guardian for the next six months, offering him £1,500 plus expenses to do so, Okey refused, saying he did not want to leave his family behind and also did not want to expose them to Dyce Sombre's 'frightful language and threats' when frustrated.

Dyce Sombre Enjoys His Sanity in Paris

Having secured himself from extradition and reconfinement in England by the unanimous declarations of two panels of the leading medical men in Paris, Dyce Sombre worked to advance himself both socially and legally. Among his predominantly male French and expatriate British companions, he presented his case as one of an erring wife and an unjust English legal system. Despite his lack of access to his wealth, he further finally secured the services of Britain's best legal minds to make his case, a case he himself had been ineffective in presenting during his one day inquisition.

Settling into continental society, Dyce Sombre began to study French, although his mastery of the language would never be complete.[21] As he had on his arrival in London less than six years earlier, he wore bespoke eveningwear of the latest fashion and elegantly embroidered court uniforms of his own design.[22] Baron de Conches and other elite connections obtained his reception by King Louis-Philippe at the Tuileries.[23] French newspapers announced him as the 'Black Prince Sombre', an Indian Nabob of the highest distinction, with millions in the bank and the physiognomy of Othello, who is welcomed in aristocratic salons.[24] Even people on the streets pointed him out as 'an Indian prince'.

Despite his shortage of ready cash, Dyce Sombre enhanced his prominence among the haute monde by inviting a select five hundred elite men and women to a grand dinner and ball that he hosted under the sponsorship of a controversial but wealthy widow, Lady Dorothea Louisa Campbell. The English satirical magazine *Punch* used Dyce Sombre's social triumph to lampoon both the French and the British:

The Triumph of Reason

Application having been made to Louis Philippe, to the effect that he would be pleased to cause Mr Dyce Sombre—who escaped his keepers to Paris—to be straightaway sent back to England, his Majesty, with his characteristic acumen, begged first to have the reports of half-a-dozen French physicians, touching Mr Sombre's implied madness. The physicians one and all declared that Mr Dyce Sombre showed the strongest symptoms of sanity (for an Englishman), for he was throwing about heaps of money for the encouragement of French ingenuity and French commerce. If, however, any doubt could remain of the gentleman's mental health, that doubt was wholly set at rest by him a few nights ago, when he gave a most magnificent supper to upwards of five hundred people. The French authorities very properly considered this to be the triumph of reason. Mr Dyce Sombre remains in Paris.[25]

Indeed, laudatory news of Dyce Sombre's lavish dinner-ball was publicised even by American newspapers, including Boston's *Emanci-*

pator and Weekly Chronicle. However, the *Cincinnati Weekly Herald and Philanthropist* editorialised this bountiful entertainment 'don't prove he is not a lunatic'.

Among other expatriate English gentlemen, Dyce Sombre cultivated his mutually beneficial association with Lewis Goldsmith, a famous albeit controversial anti-establishment author, journalist, sometime secret agent, and Paris 'character', a member of both the Illuminati and the Freemasons.[26] Like Dyce Sombre, Goldsmith did not conform to the usual model of a British gentleman. Although born in England, he was of Portuguese Jewish descent. Goldsmith swore in two separate affidavits in January 1844 that for more than three months he was 'in the constant daily habit of seeing the above-named D. O. Dyce Sombre at all times and in all hours, and in conversing with him on all subjects'.[27] Goldsmith gladly attended the second panel of French doctors who examined Dyce Sombre and concurred with them that Dyce Sombre 'was in the full enjoyment of his intellectual faculties'. Further, he introduced Dyce Sombre to his many distinguished friends and invited him into his family circle for dinners and conversations; they all found it shocking that anyone could have misjudged their new acquaintance to be a lunatic. Particularly encouraging for Dyce Sombre was the fact that Goldsmith was father of Lord Chancellor Lyndhurst's current wife.

Dyce Sombre's flight to freedom brought to light something Lord Chancellor Lyndhurst admitted was 'culpable negligence' by his office: no Committee of the Person or of the Estate had actually ever been appointed. Mary Anne's lawyers had never applied for this to be done and Dyce Sombre's brothers-in-law had demanded inclusion themselves. Thus, while the Lord Chancellor had informally entrusted Mary Anne to supervise Dyce Sombre's wellbeing, Lyndhurst's office still held custody of all Dyce Sombre's personal papers and also his funds but, in the absence of a Committee of the Estate, had to confess this money was 'at present without any protection'. Seeking to understand the case better, Lyndhurst proceeded to read all the relevant papers, including Dyce Sombre's will and intimate pre-marital correspondence with Mary Anne, which Dyce Sombre took as a personal affront.[28]

Not until 8 February 1844 were these Committees officially appointed: Mary Ann and Thomas Hawe Parker (her maternal uncle) constituted Committee of the Person, with Calvert, who had led the prosecution of Dyce Sombre, as their permanent attorney; John Pascal

Larkins (a fellow Freemason and retired senior merchant of the East India Company in Bengal) served as the Committee *ad interim* of the Estate. Under the Lord Chancellor's authority and with Mary Anne's acquiescence, Larkins then collected, had fully assessed by a professional auctioneer, and took legal possession of all of Dyce Sombre's jewellry, clothing, carriages, assorted books in English, Persian, and Urdu, maps, pictures, exercise weights, bed linen, and other personal items. In addition, Larkins exerted sole management over Dyce Sombre's real estate and capital in Britain and India, even over the Begum's unfinished cenotaph in Italy.[29]

The Lord Chancellor ordered Larkins to provide Mary Anne with her annual £4,000. The Lord Chancellor, however, only authorised minimal repayment to Dyce Sombre of his essential expenses, and only if verified by a precise receipt. This led to Dyce Sombre demanding receipts and every sou in change from waiters and cab-drivers, much to their mutual annoyance; for his opponents, this penny-pinching also became proof of his obsessive behaviour. Dyce Sombre believed Larkins only intended to harass him further by requiring such niggling accounting.

Dyce Sombre dismissed Mary Anne's power over him: 'Madam, From what I have heard of late,—in fact I always thought so,—that you are my enemy... Nevertheless, I am told you are appointed committee or guardian of my person. Pretty guardian you are when you refuse the paltry sum of 80 Napoleons to pay the doctors' bills [for the second examining panel]! Now if these very doctors had decided me mad, you and your confederates would have been too glad to have paid this sum.'[30] Further, he noted that London newspapers published her continued attendance on the Duke of Wellington and her other elder male patrons.

Unable to extradite Dyce Sombre, Mary Anne's and Larkins' agents shadowed him, seeking evidence for future legal hearings over control of his person and his wealth. These agents recorded all he was doing. They also paid for legal depositions from virtually everyone with whom he interacted, from his aristocratic acquaintances, his landladies, and even the cab-drivers and prostitutes he frequented. All this legal evidence made Dyce Sombre one of the most documented men of his age.

On his part, Dyce Sombre hired leading solicitor James Leman, of Vizard and Lehman Lincoln's Inn Fields, to advise him professionally about how to have his British conviction as a Chancery Lunatic revoked and his fortune and freedom restored. Leman initially had trouble getting a barrister willing to take up this unprecedented international judicial challenge; one leading barrister first accepted but, on further consideration, returned his fees. Finally, they briefed the expensive but highly successful Sir Thomas Wilde (himself appointed Lord Chancellor only six years later). Nonetheless, Wilde's reputation was mixed: one of his colleagues judged him 'a most honourable and simple minded man—indeed, his simplicity at times would have been deemed by the world—stupidity.'[31] In addition, Dyce Sombre's ally Lewis Goldsmith, well-connected with the British legal establishment, also seems to have advised on how to proceed. In March 1844, Dyce Sombre's advocates formally applied in his name to Lord Chancellor Lyndhurst for *supercedas* ('setting aside') of the declaration of him as a Chancery Lunatic.[32]

First Appeal and Rehearing for Supercedas in London

In this lengthy rehearing of Dyce Sombre's case, far more extensive than his first official one-day inquisition, various self-proclaimed experts and self-interested parties staked their claims to his estate and person in terms of the heated medical, legal, and cultural issues of the day. For doctors, his case presented the public with blatant contradictions among leading physicians about his condition. Since he received virtually no treatment in Hanover Lodge, and certainly none in France, the argument did not rest on the efficacy of any cure or change in his condition but rather on the authority of diagnosis. For jurists, Dyce Sombre's situation raised unprecedented jurisdictional problems that are still cited today internationally in case law: he was legally insane under English authority but simultaneously sane under French. Commissioner in Lunacy Barlow, appointed under English law by Lord Chancellor Lyndhurst, had ordered Dyce Sombre's confinement largely for violating English norms of rationality. Yet, two panels of unquestionably distinguished doctors constituted in Paris had ruled him sane, citing his normality according to Oriental values. But, various European 'Orientalists'—self-proclaimed experts in 'the East' and 'Asiatic' peoples and cultures—clashed over what allegedly oriental values were, particularly concerning gender, and also where Dyce Sombre should be located in terms of his ancestry, education, and comportment. Each of these vexed issues of medical authority, international law, and rising concepts of Orientalism played out confusingly in the first English rehearing of his case.

Lord Chancellor Lyndhurst, perforce unable to enforce in France his order for confinement or secure extradition, nonetheless decreed that Dyce Sombre should be seized whenever he should enter English jurisdiction. While untested in court, it appeared that the Chancellor's order for Dyce Sombre's immediate seizure prevailed in all British colonies, including India. But the Lord Chancellor's authority did not run in Scotland, so Dyce Sombre would probably be free there, although this remained unproven.

Lawyers for the Committees of the Person and of the Estate, led by the pugnacious Richard Bethell (later Lord Chancellor Westbury, notorious among his colleagues for being 'tricky and unscrupulous'), argued the Lord Chancellor should dismiss this appeal for supercedas.[33] They asserted only Dyce Sombre's personal appearance before Lyndhurst and a determination from court-appointed British doctors on English soil would be legally sufficient to overturn the conviction. These Committee lawyers continued that, as long as Dyce Sombre was in France, these preconditions were impossible to fulfill so his petition

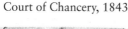

Court of Chancery, 1843

should perforce be rejected. Wilde, working for Dyce Sombre, argued the opposite: French law and French doctors should be sufficient to override his earlier sentence, even in England. Lyndhurst, unwilling to have his authority overturned by the French government, ruled that Dyce Sombre must in fact personally appear and be cleared by physicians appointed by him on English territory. Yet, Dyce Sombre reasonably refused to enter England where he would be reincarcerated.

This led to the anomaly of the Lord Chancellor giving Dyce Sombre, a legal lunatic, unprecedented temporary exemption from confinement to return to England and move freely about during his rehearing. But, should his lunacy verdict be reconfirmed, he would have to leave immediately or be reconfined. Since the concept of a Chancery Lunatic was founded on the Crown's obligation to protect an alleged incompetent and his property from himself, the illogic of the Lord Chancellor's ruling raised questions for many: how could Dyce Sombre have been so evidently and legally acting reasonably in France, and now be granted autonomous freedom in England during his rehearing, if he was still officially judged incapable of rationality and freedom by the Lord Chancellor's office? Further, the lawyers for the Committees of the Person and the Estate fought bitterly, allegedly in Dyce Sombre's own interests, against the lawyers he hired in his own interests as he regarded them.

To pay for Dyce Sombre's ticket and other costs to cross the channel from Boulogne where he waited and to live in London as befitted a gentleman during the hearings, the Lord Chancellor ordered the reluctant Committee of the Estate to send him £100 per week but warned 'there ought to be no extravagance practised'.[34] Such meager doling out of his own money by the Lord Chancellor clearly perturbed Dyce Sombre. Further, the embarrassed Committee of the Estate, Larkins, had soon to explain in court how he had ill-advisedly lost £5,000 of Dyce Sombre's money in an English bank failure.

After Dyce Sombre entered England on 28 May 1844, and over the four summer months while he awaited determination of the heated arguments over his future, he took lodgings on Half-Moon Street in London's Mayfair. He could read in newspapers of the day how another celebrity Chancery Lunatic of his own age and also of uncertain nationality, the part-Russian part-English Princess Catherine Louise Maria Frances Bariatinski and her more than £40,000 fortune and estates in Russia, were currently being fought over before the same Lord

Chancellor, with some of the same doctors testifying contradictorily about her sanity.[35] Ominously, Princess Bariatinski was ultimately found lunatic; she and her fortune were awarded to the custody of her aristocratic English in-laws over the protests of her Russian relatives.

During the period of his rehearing, Dyce Sombre also amused himself by roaming London's fashionable and tawdry streets and alleys, although shadowed constantly by plainclothes policemen and assiduous agents of lawyers opposing his appeal. Passers-by noticed this strange procession; many knew his striking story and stared, further alienating him from the surrounding society. On one of London's more stylish streets, Dyce Sombre gladly encountered someone searching for a person like him. Recently retired East India Company official Henry Thoby Prinsep, whom Dyce Sombre had known well in Calcutta, was currently canvassing for his election to the Company's Court of Directors. Prinsep knew Dyce Sombre owned sufficient East India Company stock to cast two crucial votes. In the past, Dyce Sombre had appreciated being lobbied by various candidates for a Directorship, recognizing the highly political nature of these elections and the significance of a seat on the Court of Directors where factions battled over the dispensing of patronage and the setting of Company policy over India and Indians. When Dyce Sombre lost control over his property, including his £6,000 in East India Company stock, he was upset that his name was therefore removed from the Proprietors' List and he could no longer cast his votes, even though the stock remained technically his.[36] Hence, Dyce Sombre had to admit embarrassingly to Prinsep that he could not help get him elected (the overly ambitious Prinsep lost this election and at least four elections for Parliament, winning a fifth in 1851 but then having it controverted).[37]

Prinsep remained Dyce Sombre's supporter for the rest of his life. Although he declined Dyce Sombre's request at this time to recommend a more effective solicitor, he did write to Lord Chancellor Lyndhurst urging that Dyce Sombre was sound in mind, fully capable of managing his finances, and should therefore receive more of his estate's income. Thereafter, Prinsep and Dyce Sombre maintained constant correspondence, Prinsep trying to use his growing influence on Dyce Sombre's behalf. Indeed, the latter for a while sent his debts to Prinsep who forwarded them to Dyce Sombre's London banker.[38] (Years later, in July 1850, Prinsep would finally succeed in getting himself elected to the Court of Directors which improved Dyce Sombre's attitude

Henry Thoby Prinsep

toward it, to the extent of making Prinsep co-executor of his will with handsome bequests to the other Directors personally.)

As the hearings on Dyce Sombre slowly unfolded before Lyndhurst, opposing lawyers carefully constructed arguments concerning Orientals generally, and Dyce Sombre in particular, that supported the interests of their respective principals. By this time, most Victorian Britons had come to presuppose that Oriental cultures and peoples differed fundamentally from Western ones, particularly concerning issues of gender. Various Europeans then took opposing stands on what these relative differences entailed versus what factors were universal to all men and women. In Dyce Sombre's case specifically, the contending sides respectively located him primarily in either Asiatic or European culture, thus determining which standards for rational behaviour he should be measured by.

As presented by his advocate, Sir Thomas Wilde, Dyce Sombre's appeal for supercedas used as its central argument that his unusual actions has always been 'but the result of his Indian birth and upbringing'. This theme, which had barely appeared in his first inquisition, emerged powerfully in the arguments of Combermere and Trevelyan, and then in the determinations of the two medical panels in Paris. By

248

shifting the implicit terms of Dyce Sombre's case from his alleged inadequacy of moral will in conforming with universal norms of behavior (as presupposed by Commissioner Barlow and his lay English jury) to a different argument for disparate European and Asian races, cultures, and measures of normality, Wilde cleverly recast the case in stereotypes that Britons were coming to presume. Dyce Sombre's legal team stressed how his conduct

was, in fact, nothing more than an Eastern prejudice against anything like a want of female delicacy... [in] a man who came from a country so strongly imbued with superstition... [Dyce Sombre] was three fourths an Asiatic, his father having been a half-caste, and his mother a native... If therefore you judge his delusions by an Asiatic standard, there was nothing particular in them; but, if measured by an European one, then the case would be altogether different... [Wilde] then proceeded to read extracts from the [ancient Brahmanic Sanskrit prescriptive text] *Institutes of Menu*, to illustrate what were the interpretations put upon some of the acts of married women... The great evil was not that Mr Dyce Sombre was insane, but that he had brought from India notions respecting women which were totally inapplicable to this country. He had applied his eastern tests to English women.[39]

Thus, Wilde argued, as virtuous as Mary Anne might have been, her actions would inevitably jar against Dyce Sombre's 'Oriental education and notions... different in clime and degree' from those of Europeans. Dyce Sombre's lawyers continued 'if this jealousy were the fruits and results of his Indian education, the question ought to be decided by those well acquainted with such customs—namely, an Indian jury'.

Supportive of this notion that Dyce Sombre acted rationally in accordance with Oriental customs was the testimony of Lord Combermere, who had long presented himself as an expert on the East:

[Dyce Sombre] to a person who had never been in India, or who had not been acquainted with the customs of Asiatics as to their treatment of women in general, and of married women in particular, would have seemed most strange, and even ridiculous; yet to any one familiar with Oriental customs, the complaints and charges which he made against his Wife, however groundless, and however absurd in the estimation of an European, would have certainly been considered as in fact they were, the necessary result of his India education, and the natural feelings of an Indian husband when placed in a society so different from what previously had been his own... [T]he point of honour among Asiatics rests on the habits and conduct of their wives and women, as it does among Europeans upon the preservation of a character for truth and uprightness, and all their most sensitive and cherished feelings of delicacy and propriety and personal reputation may be said to be centered on that point.[40]

Wilde wisely did not call Dyce Sombre as a witness since he both derided Combermere's knowledge of Indian culture and also often (but not always) presented himself as European.

The lawyers opposing Dyce Sombre also argued (like him) that he was European or at least Europeanised so none of his behaviour could be justified as based on Oriental values. Mary Anne's lawyers stressed his English education under Reverend Fisher. They also had her provide a timely affidavit that Dyce Sombre: 'possessed a perfect knowledge and understanding of the English language... She scarcely ever saw any English person write with such facility and rapidity..., and that the errors he sometimes committed in writing are wholly the result of inattention and the aforenamed rapidity with which he conveyed his ideas to paper.'[41] She later added that he was not 'of Asiatic extraction' since his father was 'a British officer'.

Similarly confronting Combermere's claims to expertise was Drever's testimony. Based on his own years of living in Sardhana, he swore:

[Dyce Sombre] was master of the English, Persian, and Hindostanee languages, and was... formerly remarkable for the absence of jealousy in regard to women... and during a time when he cohabited with a native woman, he freely admitted this deponent and other friends into the Zenana... [Thus] neither the education and habits of [Dyce Sombre], nor his Eastern parentage, can account for the delusions entertained by [Dyce Sombre], but that the same arose from insanity...[42]

While Combermere was more social prominent, Drever undoubtedly had more experience living in Sardhana.

While Mary Anne's lawyers compared Dyce Sombre to a cannibal, they argued that even a sane 'savage' would recognise reality:

If you bring a savage and see him sit to consume human flesh, it would be no evidence of insanity; but, if that savage were impressed with the belief that he had had a conversation with the Queen of England when he had not, the whole would be a delusion, and that man, whether Indian, African, or American, would be mad... Had [Wilde] shown that it was an Indian habit for father and daughter to cohabit together [Dyce Sombre's accusations of incest against Mary Anne might be explained. But] all books on Indian customs showed, that after the husband, the father was always considered the guardian of the daughter... [Hence] Mr Dyce Sombre's notions respecting women were very different to those entertained by natives of the east, for he was never in the habit, like them, of shutting up the females in seraglios and zenanas, but without feelings of jealousy allowed them unrestricted intercourse with his friends.[43]

Hence, they argued, if Dyce Sombre both had what would be delusions in any culture and also did not conform to Asiatic customs (as they represented them), therefore he must be a lunatic. Further, they asserted, Dyce Sombre had been normal in India but became progressively more lunatic after he arrived in England and wed.

Many spectators toured this fascinating and celebrated trial, including the claimant as Nawab of Surat, Meer Jafur Ali Khan Bahadur, and his large Indian entourage. They had recently come to London to plead for his title and estate. Newspapers throughout the British Empire reported the visit to Dyce Sombre's trial of 'his Asiatic Highness, who is a princely-looking personage, possessing features of a very fine cast'.[44] During the whole time this troupe visited the court, lawyers, judicial officials including the Lord Chancellor, and audience (Dyce Sombre was not himself present in court) all stared in fascination at these unquestionable examples of orientals. A member of the Nawab's entourage, scholar-official Lutfullah, described their respectful reception in this courtroom. Lutfullah's account was sympathetic but not fully accepting of Dyce Sombre as a countryman: 'an Indo-European, Colonel Dyce Sombre, an unlucky man, who had lost his large fortune by falling in love and entering into a marriage contract with an English lady of rank'.[45] But the Nawab and his suite did not meet or observe Dyce Sombre directly. Hence, Lutfullah represented his view of how the Lord Chancellor explained Dyce Sombre's anomalous case to these Indian guests to his courtroom. Lyndhurst may also have been cautioning these Indian guests against imitating Dyce Sombre's amour for an English noblewoman.

At this time, British medical practitioners, particularly alienists, were working to professionalise themselves in the face of a sometimes skeptical public. In 1841, they founded an official organization: the British Association of Medical Officers of Asylums and Hospitals for the Insane.[46] French physicians tended to be regarded (and resented) by their contemporary British colleagues as particularly advanced in the study of mental conditions. Dyce Sombre's case publicised how the most prominent of these alienists espoused strongly held but irreconcilable theories about the nature of lunacy. In strong support of Dyce Sombre's appeal was the undoubted medical authority of the two concurring Paris panels. Hence, his well-publicised case represented a challenge to struggling British medical men, exacerbated when even British specialists in mental illness vehemently and directly contra-

251

dicted each other in sworn affidavits before the Lord Chancellor and as reported to the public.[47]

Sir Thomas Wilde argued for Dyce Sombre that the recent decisions of the French panels showed either that he had never been insane or else that he had now autonomously recovered from that condition. But Bethell and other advocates for the Committees of the Person and the Estate reposted that Dyce Sombre's condition could only be determined by exactly the same doctors who testified against Dyce Sombre in his first inquisition, including Sir James Clark and Edward Monro: only these doctors could authoritatively declare that they had been erroneous in their earlier diagnosis or else discern his spontaneous improvement by comparing his past and present conditions. Wilde countered that those doctors were part of the problem: already prejudiced against him so that such procedure 'was calculated only to annoy, agitate, and irritate... the feelings of Mr Sombre to a high pitch, and furnish ground for a report that he was still in an unsound state of mind'.[48] Highlighting Dyce Sombre's foreign culture, Wilde argued that, while Dyce Sombre had lived self-sufficiently during his nine months of freedom in France, his 'imperfect' knowledge of the English language would embarrass, upset, and alarm him when examined by 'persons whom he viewed with suspicion'.

To settle this dispute, the Lord Chancellor proposed beginning with medical experts whom Dyce Sombre had never seen and therefore should not reasonably be suspicious of: two socially prominent Metropolitan Commissioners in Lunacy, Drs Henry Herbert Southey and John Bright. Southey (younger brother of poet Robert Southey) had written his thesis on syphilis, published on tuberculosis, and then risen to become Physician-in-Ordinary to George IV and Physician-Extraordinary to Queen Adelaide; he remained the Lord Chancellor's Medical Visitor in Lunacy, with a salary of £1,500, from 1833 until his death. Bright had become famous for advocating 'the controversial "Brunonian" approach to medicine (the treatment of disease mostly by alcohol or opium, according to whether the condition was classified as sthenic ["strong"] or asthenic ["weak"])'.[49] Southey and Bright were fellow Commissioners with Barlow, who had first convicted Dyce Sombre (as it turned out, they would never rule in his favour).[50] The Lord Chancellor arranged that Southey and Bright would later be joined in questioning Dyce Sombre by the doctors who had already decreed he was insane: Clark, Monro, and Conolly.

Further, Lyndhurst wanted to see for himself and judge Dyce Sombre directly. Since the principal parties did not participate personally in Chancery courts—rather they were represented only by their advocates and written affidavits—Dyce Sombre did not appear before the bench.[51] Unusually, Lyndhurst arranged to observe some of the court-appointed doctors' examinations, which he ordered held in his own home. Further, Lyndhurst later individually interviewed Dyce Sombre in private. Generally, Lyndhurst had the reputation among his fellow jurists of taking cases 'very indolently and easily, affirming almost indiscriminately the judgments brought before him on appeal. It was depressing to argue before a Chancellor whose heart did not seem to be in the business.'[52] Thus, Lyndhurst took a strikingly special interest in Dyce Sombre's unprecedented case.

Lyndhurst later regaled the House of Lords by recounting how in his personal interviews with Dyce Sombre

the Lunatic... appeared perfectly sane for some time, but afterwards got excited and said that he had been offered a peerage by certain Noblemen on condition that he would not expose overtures which had been made to him by Ladies of high rank and station (Laughter). By-and-by the Lunatic got more and more excited. He (Lord Lyndhurst) asked him the name of the Nobleman who has waited upon him, but he [Dyce Sombre] replied that the communication had been a confidential one, and that he could not venture to divulge it. As a matter of curiosity he (Lord Lyndhurst) then asked the Lunatic who the Ladies were (laughter) but the reply was—that this was a point of honour, and could not be disclosed (laughter).[53]

The Lord Chancellor thus used his privileged access to Dyce Sombre's notorious and unintentional parody of English gentlemen's honour to enhance Lyndhurst's own reputation as a raconteur.

Lord Chancellor Lyndhurst's efforts to dictate the terms of Dyce Sombre's case, however, were made more difficult in April 1844 when his father-in-law, Lewis Goldsmith, came to London from Paris at the height of these hearings to lobby on Dyce Sombre's behalf (and at Dyce Sombre's expense). We have no evidence about Goldsmith's meetings with his daughter or son-in-law, the Lord Chancellor, but his efforts to meet and bargain with Mary Anne failed. She strenuously avoided meeting him while their mutual friends found the situation embarrassing to say the least. She wrote that Goldsmith's actions were 'unbecoming a gentleman of any honourable or right feeling'.[54]

As the arguments raged in court, Dyce Sombre's lawyers further bolstered their case by privately employing many leading British doctors to examine him and write affidavits to his sanity. These included Dr John Ayrton Paris (President of the College of Physicians, former Commissioner in Lunacy) and four reputed surgeons. They unanimously declared him 'perfectly rational and proper', although he had declined discussing his wife 'as it made his head ache'. They concluded: 'The source of mischief, however, appeared to be jealousy operating upon the excitable character of an Asiatic... [I]f placed under restraint he would really become deranged, but that, with the qualification of a doubt respecting the nature and origin of the impression entertained by Mr Dyce Sombre on the subject of his wife... he was not of unsound mind; and [should] be restored to his liberty.'[55]

In contrast, the newly court-appointed doctors, Bright and Southey, judged Dyce Sombre much better than they had been led to expect from the reports of the earlier official doctors, but still labouring under certain delusions and not of 'sound mind'.[56] The earlier court-appointed doctors, Clark, Monro, and Conolly, as anticipated, only reconfirmed their standing diagnosis that Dyce Sombre was lunatic. In the face of their probing, he refused to repudiate his earlier assertions. Nor would they relinquish their earlier judgment that he was deluded. They argued that he might be clever enough to fool the French, yet was 'decidedly incompetent to the management of himself and his affairs'.[57]

Meanwhile, weeks of heated hearings continued before the Lord Chancellor. The British popular press expressed some sympathy for Dyce Sombre's harried condition:

If Mr Dyce Sombre is not mad, then never was there a gentleman, since a Commission of Lunacy first sat, who ever stood so sure a chance of becoming a Bedlamite... if we were Lord Chancellor we should come to the conclusion *ex pede Herculem* that the fortune-blessed *protégé* of the Indian Princess not alone was sane, but that he possessed a mind much stronger than the average of mortals, from the circumstance of his not raving like a Lunatic at the daily nay hourly, trials and subjections he suffers! His every movement is dodged by policemen, he is subject to examinations from a host of people who make a trade and living out of insanity, called 'Mad Doctors'.[58]

This editorial concluded that his vast wealth was the real reason for such interest in him, although it admitted that Dyce Sombre's accusations against the general immorality of all of English society were perhaps overstated.

The lawyers for the Committees of Person and Estate submitted many affidavits as to Dyce Sombre's past and current conduct to prove him a 'dangerous and confirmed lunatic'. Many allegations were simply recapitulations from his first inquiry. His former warder Sherriff, however, added that Dyce Sombre 'had very recently danced and shouted along Pall-Mall, and accosted every female he met with.'[59] This legal team produced affidavits they had purchased from 'loose women of London' asserting Dyce Sombre had over the past few days accompanied 'three or four of them of an evening to their homes'. The Lord Chancellor accepted these affidavits as evidence without the embarrassing necessity of reading them aloud into the record since they 'were certainly not fit to be read in public'.[60] Hiring one or more prostitutes was not illegal but it did not burnish Dyce Sombre's reputation to have done so blatantly during height of these hearings.

In contrast, Dyce Sombre's legal team also cited the latest theories in medical science by asserting that he might hypothetically be deluded but 'Delusions did not constitute insanity'. They also cited literary criticism, evoking another famous if fictitious Black to whom many compared Dyce Sombre, asserting 'Who that ever read Shakespeare would say, although Othello was guilty of all sorts of violence and absurdity, that he was a madman?' Further, they also dismissed Dyce Sombre's mistaken ideas of duelling as something only to be expected from an Asiatic. (Wilde may have been goading opposing lawyer Bethell who had notoriously nearly fought a duel quite recently.)[61] Wilde concluded with a gruelling sixteen hour closing argument.

Dyce Sombre's celebrated case also inspired British wags to attempt humour. In the heat of these hearings, the *Times* carried a fictitious exchange of letters allegedly between Dyce Sombre and Mary Anne, the former signed 'Othello' and the latter 'Desdemona'. Each letter conflated the arguments of their respective lawyers with Shakespeare's representations of these characters.[62] Catholic journals were generally more sympathetic to him.[63]

Even as this long hearing before the Lord Chancellor proceeded, the *Times* criticised Lyndhurst in a long editorial for unjustly concentrating on him.[64] The paper asserted that this case was so extensively considered only because of his money, dismissed as 'the accident of his being the present possessor of those hoards which formerly gave importance to some brown Begum in Hindostan'. In contrast, at that very moment, 16,500 British pauper lunatics simultaneously suffered confinement unheard. The paper inaccurately slurred Dyce Sombre for his supposed belief 'in all the incarnations of Vishnu' and simultaneous

disrespect for the Anglican Church. The editors ended by chauvinisti-
cally half-jesting: 'from the evidence in Mr Dyce Sombre's case,... there
must be a far higher standard of sanity in this country than there is in
France'. Thus, while widely known in Britain, Dyce Sombre also
appeared in the *Times* as an exceptional alien, favoured only because
of his exotic wealth, yet not alien enough to be excused for his un-
British actions and beliefs.

The Lord Chancellor, before he finally passed judgment, himself
extensively interviewed Dyce Sombre again. Then, on 8 August, he
delivered a three-hour judgment. Lyndhurst's summation, conducted
without reference to written notes (hence not always accurate on the
facts), was widely reproduced and considered by connoisseurs to be
one of his finest performances, celebrated in books and newspapers in
London, Edinburgh, Boston, and New York; the *Legal Observer or
Journal of Jurisprudence* and the *Times* featured it in full, the latter
devoting almost an entire page to his masterful oration.[65] In contrast,
critics satirized his 'Judgement' as 'strongly marked with manifest
injustice' due to Lyndhurst's deep 'conspiracy' with the St Vincents.[66]
Whichever the case, Lyndhurst's delineation of the legal issues would
remain salient for the rest of Dyce Sombre's life.

In Lyndhurst's summation, he struggled to reconcile the contradicting diagnoses of the British and Paris doctors. As a jurist, he presupposed the unscientific nature of the medical profession. His appointed
doctors 'by accident or otherwise have hit upon the weak point' in
Dyce Sombre. In contrast, the ones in Paris happened to fail to find
that flaw. Lyndhurst, however, generously excused their failure: 'they
had come to a wrong conclusion... not from an erroneous opinion
from the facts brought under their notice, but from the want of sufficient information upon the different heads of his disorder'. Lyndhurst
found it more difficult to reconcile the recent opposing diagnoses of
his appointed British doctors and the even more eminent British ones
concurrently hired privately by Dyce Sombre's attorney, who came to
radically different conclusions based on virtually simultaneous examinations and using the same background evidence.

Rather than rely on such unsound medical opinions, Lyndhurst
therefore proceeded himself to assess Dyce Sombre based on his alleged
Oriental race and enculturation. Yet, for Lyndhurst, Dyce Sombre presented difficulties in classification. On one hand, 'it was quite clear that
one of the prejudices, or class of opinions, existing among Asiatics

JUSTICE GIVING SHORT WEIGHT.

John Singleton Copley, Lord Chancellor Baron Lyndhurst'
and 'Justice Giving Short Weight'

appears to have taken deep root... jealousy with respect to female con-
nexions... which it was impossible... in consequence of his early habits
and associations to get rid of...' Even admitting Dyce Sombre was
'Asiatic by birth, education, habits, and feelings', however, this did not
fully explain all his delusions or his radically changed attitudes toward
Mary Anne before and after marriage. On the other hand, Dyce Sombre also had 'a mixture of European blood in his veins,... associated
principally with European people,... wore the English dress, [and]
became familiar with European habits and manners'.[67] Lyndhurst
decided that, if Dyce Sombre were fully and definitively Indian, he
might possibly have been judged sane. But instead, since he had sufficient European blood and culture, therefore his many deluded deeds
and beliefs must be indications of an 'unsound mind'.

Further, relying on the legal principle of *stare decensis*, Lyndhurst
concluded that, since Dyce Sombre was already legally a lunatic, definitive proof of sanity was required to overturn that verdict. The evidence
and conflicting opinions presented before him did not definitively prove
he was not a lunatic. Hence, Lyndhurst dismissed the petition for supercedas and kept Dyce Sombre in the legal status of Chancery Lunatic.

Lyndhurst wanted, however, to restore his own authority over Dyce Sombre. Recognizing the unprecedented nature of Dyce Sombre's legal condition, Lyndhurst had to reinterpret the rules. He retained Mary Anne on the Committee of the Person officially in charge of managing Dyce Sombre's welfare, but simultaneously and inconsistently advised that she 'should have as little interference as possible, as it might operate injuriously to the lunatic'. The Lord Chancellor's safe conduct guarantee meant that he could not order Dyce Sombre seized, but Lyndhurst insisted on having Dyce Sombre constantly attended by a medical warder (paid out of Dyce Sombre's estate) wherever he went.

Dyce Sombre rejected such medical supervision. Even while his lawyers negotiated with the Lord Chancellor, on 13 August he dramatically evaded the police and court officers assigned to shadow him, entering the Burlington Arcade at one end but never reappearing to his guards thereafter. The *Times*, *Observer*, and other British newspapers publicised this remarkable second escape from his warders 'although

Burlington Arcade, London

the most active measures have, doubtless, been taken to discover his retreat'.[68] Once again, Dyce Sombre cleverly evaded his keepers in Britain and reemerged safely in France.

As soon as he regained refuge at Boulogne, Dyce Sombre wrote a letter to the editor of the *Globe* explaining how 'the Chancellor having broken his faith, I took an opportunity of leaving my lodging unobserved by the police, who were placed to watch my motions'.[69] Now free again in France, he demanded that Sir Francis Burdett (seventy-three-years-old but, in Dyce Sombre's mind, one of Mary Anne's current lovers) meet him for a duel or else reveal himself publicly as 'as a coward and a man of no honour'. Dyce Sombre also decided that Wilde 'did not act very well for me' and dropped him as his barrister.[70]

The *Satirist* published a poem, attributed to Dyce Sombre, that celebrated his freedoms in France and ridiculed the Lord Chancellor, reading in part:

> To Lord Lyndhurst.
>
> ...I hate your dreary English land,
> Its clime and hearts so cold;
> Its mercenary altars raised
> To Mammon and his gold.
> I hate your dreary English land—
> Its scandals, trade and mist—
> Where e'en your women's lips are chilled,
> However warmly kissed.
> Give me the sunny land of Gaul,
> Its bright wines, its wild blisses;
> Give me the Paris Bacchanals,
> Dishevelled Locks and Kisses!
> Give me French hearts, as light and gay
> As their own glad champagne;
> Give me those lips that always smile—
> Those arms that always strain!
> Farewell, my Lord: when next you have
> Some spouse a 'madman' made,
> Don't let his keepers take him to
> The Burlington Arcade!
> For me, while France affords a home
> Your land, I'll ne'er regret it...
> —Dyce Sombre, Boulogne.[71]

Thus, almost a year since his first flight to freedom, Dyce Sombre resumed his life in France, although he did not remain there long.

On the Continent and in Russia

While Dyce Sombre's lawyers, the lawyers for the Committees of the Person and of the Estate, and the Lord Chancellor worked to sort out the consequences of his case and condition, Dyce Sombre amused himself in Paris. Finally, late in 1844, the London negotiations produced a compromise: Mary Anne and her uncle, as the Committee of the Person, would recruit a constant warder who would accompany Dyce Sombre everywhere. They hired a willing young medical man and hydropathy enthusiast, John Warwick, at £350 annually plus all his expenses. Then the Committee of the Estate, with the approval of the Lord Chancellor, would provide an allowance of £5,000 annually that Warwick would use to pay for Dyce Sombre's appropriate expenditures, including Warwick's own salary and expenses. In March 1845, Warwick eventually caught up with the reluctant Dyce Sombre in St Petersburg, winter seat of the Czar's court.

Ever eager for novel experiences and places, Dyce Sombre had conceived of a plan to travel slowly across Europe via The Hague, Amsterdam, and Hamburg to Russia and seek political and medical backing there.[72] Although he was uncertain of his reception by young Czar Nicholas I, Dyce Sombre reached St Petersburg safely in November 1844. He confided to Reghellini in India by letter 'I do not know if I could be able to find my way to the German frontier if the Emperor was to order me to quit this Capital, if he considered me dangerous, which they do in England'.[73]

Czar Nicholas kept strong control over the fledging field of psychiatry in Russia. Asylums were almost organs of the police and psychiatrists agents of the state. Hence, Dyce Sombre's relationship to the imperial government was deeply connected with his medical diagnosis.[74] To secure his welcome, Dyce Sombre wrote to the Imperial Minister of the Interior appealing for the Czar's protection from 'the intrigue of my enemies' who had imprisoned him until his dramatic escapes to France where he was proven sane. He proposed to 'endure a renewed examination, and through the favour of the Russian authorities to receive a certificate from the Medical men of the country, and with that document to return to England and reclaim the remnant of my once brilliant fortune'.[75]

Dyce Sombre's evocation of courtly intrigues, political imprisonment, and the superiority of French over British medical theory made sense to the Czar's ministers, although they also had him followed by imperial agents. Further, some Russian court factions were ardent to gain influence among India's princes, or former princes, and proposed using Dyce Sombre as an entree. In January 1845, the Czar's Medical Council had two of its members, both Councillors of State, begin a thorough examination of Dyce Sombre's mental condition. Learning of this new initiative by Dyce Sombre to reverse official British judgments, Sir James Clark supplied this Council with specific questions and areas to probe, all designed to reveal Dyce Sombre's encapsulated (as we might call them) delusions and reconfirm Clark's own diagnosis. These distinguished doctors probed his mind over months of intermittent examinations. They also asked many questions about political conditions in India. In addition, Dyce Sombre hired Dr Nikolai Fedorovich Arendt, private physician to His Imperial Majesty, to attend him and also testify on his behalf. Finally, after a joint examination by the entire imperial Medical Council of ten eminent doctors, they resolved unanimously on 20 February that he was 'in a perfect state of mind', showing none of the symptoms that they knew indicated lunacy. For example, they asserted 'It is well known that madmen have a very short memory; Mr Sombre, on the contrary, possesses a very good one.'[76]

During this period, Dyce Sombre had taken rooms in a boarding house catering to English gentlemen. Fortifying himself against the Russian winter, he purchased a sable coat and consumed much alcohol.[77] When an overindulgence in curaçao aggravated the 'disarrangement of the digestive organs', Dyce Sombre consulted an English physician based in Petersburg, Dr Handyside. After several visits, Dyce Sombre also requested Handyside to give a written attestation to his sanity, which Handyside, knowing of Dyce Sombre's long legal record, declined to provide.

While moving in elite Russian and British expatriate circles, Dyce Sombre and his affairs were the subject of much gossip. Leading Russian diplomat Count Nesselrode, recently back from London, passed on to Dyce Sombre that the Honourable Cecil Forester, famously 'the handsomest man in England' had been seen escorting Mary Anne about town.[78] This confirmed Dyce Sombre's suspicions in that direction and in March he sent Forester a challenge to a duel: 'It having come to my knowledge... that you are the person who were the cause of destroying my peace of mind, before it was necessary that myself and Mrs Dyce Sombre should be separated, and that you have since been cohabiting with her, I call upon you, as a man of honour, to give me satisfaction which the rules of society demand, and which you must consider due... I shall meet you in Berlin.'[79] Forester, who knew Mary Anne well (and would years later marry her), refused to respond to this accusation or challenge while Mary Anne, as usual, denied any impropriety.

Dyce Sombre devised a plan to carry on through Persia or the Ottoman lands to India, with Russian political support. But he admitted almost regretfully that the 'Russians have very little thoughts of invading India, so the English may sleep with stretched limbs'.[80] Instead, after nearly half a year in St Petersburg, Dyce Sombre slowly returned westward during summer 1845, now armed with the new certificates of sanity from the imperial Medical Council.

Dyce Sombre's official warder and paymaster, John Warwick, caught up with him just before he left Russia. Dyce Sombre rejected any controls by Warwick as insulting and also counterproductive to his own efforts 'to prove that I am capable of taking care of my property, I... rather I would sell my carriage... than take anything from him... a gaoler over me'.[81] Nonetheless, despite his protests, Warwick shadowed him, documenting all his misadventures for the Committees of the Person and the Estate.

Given Dyce Sombre's unrestrained lifestyle, he was frequently ill. After he consulted a doctor for his physical condition, he then customarily asked for an affidavit of his mental health. On his way west from Russia, he obtained numerous testimonials of his sanity from doctors, including six of the top Belgian and British physicians practising in Brussels.[82] One of these, Dr Jean Francois Vleminckx (Inspector General of the Service of Health of the Belgian Army and President of the Royal Academy of Medicine of Belgium), diagnosed: 'Eccentricity I witnessed, and excitement, never Insanity'.[83] Although he did not include this in the official affidavit that Dyce Sombre paid him for, Vleminckx later noted confidentially that Dyce Sombre was 'extraordinarily attached, or addicted to, women, whom he appeared to consider as formed only for the gratification of men... He would pass entire nights in a brothel, and be unsatisfied' due to priapism. Vleminckx was also impressed by the volume of betel nuts and cardamoms that Dyce Sombre constantly consumed; these Dyce Sombre imported by the seer (kilogram) from Sardhana.[84] In addition to affidavits from physicians, Dyce Sombre also obtained testimonials to his sanity from his bankers, stray gentlemen and noblemen he met, and even servants he employed.[85] Once, Dyce Sombre even calmly toured a Brussels luna-tic asylum, concluding 'however comfortable the arrangements might be, yet it was still a madhouse'.[86]

When Dyce Sombre had repudiated his appointed warder, Warwick, the Lord Chancellor had ordered his allowance reverted from £5,000 annually to £60 per week (although Warwick remained his official keeper, on the payroll of Dyce Sombre's estate, for over two years longer). Since the actual income from his estate was about £20,000 annually (minus the £4,000 that Mary Anne received), this assertion of the Lord Chancellor's control over Dyce Sombre's own money further angered him. Further, the Committee of the Estate still demanded weekly receipts for every expenditure. Dyce Sombre complained that this limited income prevented him from hiring the best lawyers and he had to settle for those lesser ones he could afford. Indeed, Dyce Som-bre, in desperation, entered a speculative agreement that would prove costly in financial and moral terms.

Lacking faith in his current legal advisors and short of cash, Dyce Sombre contracted with Dr Anthony Staghton Mahon (a retired sur-geon of the British Royal Artillery), whom he had met earlier and then perchance encountered again in Brussels during his extensive mental examinations there. Mahon loaned Dyce Sombre £600 and assured him that he could fix Dyce Sombre's lunacy conviction, in exchange for £10,000. In July 1845, Dyce Sombre agreed to this contingency con-tract, but specified that Mahon had to get him cleared of lunacy and again in control of his fortune by the end of the current calendar year.[87]

Mahon then took charge of the campaign, firing solicitors Lehman and Vizard and hiring Charles Shadwell (younger brother of Sir Lance-lot Shadwell, Vice Chancellor of England) as solicitor and Calcutta-born John Rolt, an Inner Temple barrister, to replace Wilde. Mahon also arranged for carefully managed medical examinations of Dyce Sombre, with affidavits from all the favorably inclined (and well-compensated) doctors accumulated for the next petition for superce-das.[88] Mahon's strategy was to restore Dyce Sombre's control over his fortune and then use that money to purchase a divorce from Mary Anne. Dyce Sombre even conceived of a plan to marry a daughter of Lord Chancellor Lyndhurst and thereby gain supercedas.[89]

As Dyce Sombre moved among the spas and cities of Germany, Bel-gium, and France, he occasionally encountered people from his Indian past. In April 1845, General Ventura had hosted a magnificent dinner,

Dwarkanath Tagore

his guests including both Dyce Sombre and 'Babu' Dwarkanath Tagore, the famous Calcutta merchant prince and social reformer. According to Ventura,

speaking in the language of India, [Dyce Sombre] asked [Tagore] if had seen his wife in London. The Indian having replied yes, Dyce Sombre asked him, 'Does she continue to sleep with everybody?' I interposed, to remonstrate with him, telling him it was scandalous to talk in that way, dishonouring his own name. Dyce Sombre said to me, nobody understands the Indian language here... Upon this the Baboo speaking in my ear, said, 'this man is decidedly mad'.[90]

Tagore, himself infamous as a rake, was soon thereafter spotted at the London opera, escorting a lady, according to newspaper reports, 'exactly resembling Mrs Dyce Sombre'. London's *Satirist, or, the Censor of the Times*, echoed by the American popular journal, *Spirit of the Times: A Chronicle of the Turf, Agriculture, Field Sports, Literature and the Stage*, salaciously chided Mary Anne about Tagore: 'There is a proverb which says something about being "off with your old love to be on with your new"; and it would seem to have some application in the case of a lady who, having lost one Asiatic husband, evinces a *penchant* for the society of an Indian Prince whose polite attentions to her are a matter of notoriety'.[91] Dwarkanath Tagore, however, died in Britain that year so his relationship with Mary Anne, if it ever existed, must have been brief. Nonetheless, Dyce Sombre often read or heard such rumours that reconfirmed his conviction about her immorality.

Ventura continued to patronise Dyce Sombre, who gradually began to consider him 'no friend of mine... a rascal and a coward'.[92] At Baden-Baden spa, they had a violent confrontation in which Ventura shouted at Dyce Sombre 'although they say you are mad, yet you are not always mad; and even if you are mad, still if you insult me by staring at me in the manner you did just now, I must employ means to bring you to your senses'. Ventura then repeatedly struck Dyce Sombre with his cane; they grappled until the police separated, detained, and deported them both. More confrontations, arrests, and expulsions followed as the two crisscrossed western Europe. Ventura challenged Dyce Sombre to a duel, but then withdrew it since, he said, he did not wish to offend public opinion by assassinating a mental incompetent.

According to Ventura, at one altercation in Paris, Dyce Sombre verbally assaulted him in the presence of Ventura's daughter, using 'every abusive term that the English, French, Persian, or Hindustanee language can furnish; in fact he ransacked the vocabularies of the four languages for filthy and disgraceful epithets'. Ventura reached for his pistol, threatened to throw his pocket liqueur flask at Dyce Sombre, and responded with comparable insults, including an Urdu phrase literally defying Dyce Sombre to show his manhood. This Dyce Sombre exposed to plain view, much to the shock of passers-by and Ventura and his daughter.

Dyce Sombre repeatedly wrote public and personal letters advocating his own cause. So persistent was he that the *Times* specifically announced to the world that 'we cannot publish the correspondence sent us by Mr Dyce Sombre'.[93] Undaunted, Dyce Sombre also sent multiple missives to various influential British noblemen and politicians personally, including the Foreign Secretary George Hamilton-Gordon, Earl of Aberdeen, and Prime Minister Sir Robert Peel, pleading for their influence with the Queen to overrule Lord Chancellor Lyndhurst. Dyce Sombre also tried to secure their support by promising to make these British cabinet ministers the well-compensated executors of his will, which would assign his estate to be used under their direction 'for the benefit of India'.[94] In April 1846, he reminded Peel of his alleged promise of a baronetcy to Dyce Sombre as reward for having offered to command an Indian Army regiment during the British invasion of Punjab. Peel did not concur; his government fell soon thereafter.

Indeed, the end of Peel's government in June 1846 included the resignation of Dyce Sombre's nemesis, Lord Chancellor Lyndhurst. The elevation of the new Lord Chancellor, Charles Christopher Pepys, Lord Cottenham, appeared to Dyce Sombre as a fresh opportunity to clear himself. Cottenham had the reputation in legal and political circles of being 'not brilliant' and further 'largely given to crush the facts of any case so as to fit any principle on which he professed to act.... [H]e had his Partialities, this was a most mischievous faculty, and worked great injustice... [H]is contemporaries... knew this his weakness or wickedness.'[95] Immediately, Dyce Sombre and Mahon had his new lawyers, Shadwell and Rolt, officially re-petition newly installed Lord Chancellor Cottenham for supercedas of Lyndhurst's declaration of Dyce Sombre's lunacy.

Lord Chancellor Charles Christopher Pepys, Lord Cottenham

As usual, lawyers for the Committees of the Person and of the Estate opposed this petition, saying the last inconclusive hearing had cost Dyce Sombre's estate £4,408 in court and lawyers' fees. Again, they demanded that any official medical examination be held on English soil by court-appointed British doctors. Dyce Sombre's legal team proposed another certificate of safe conduct so that he could cross the Channel to Dover and be reexamined there. Cottenham finally accepted this arrangement, with the same officially appointed doctors, Southey and Bright, conducting the examination on his behalf.[96]

Encouraged by this new opportunity, Dyce Sombre landed at Dover. His notoriety drew the attention of bystanders, but there was also a sense of tragedy about him. One gentleman recalled observing him: 'a tall, dusky, heavy shouldered, lumpish man—skipping pebbles into the sea for pastime'.[97] Thus, everywhere Dyce Sombre went, people stared and gossiped about him, a situation not conducive to his comfort.

In Dover, Dyce Sombre privately hired new doctors to examine him and write certificates to his sanity. Of these, the famous James Copland, who would examine Dyce Sombre repeatedly over the following years, asserted 'I could find no proof or sign of insane delusion... [Dyce Sombre] was of perfect sound mind, memory, and understanding.' Rather, according to Copland, Dyce Sombre behaviour resulted from his supposed race, culture, and the pressures he had undergone: 'circumstanced as he was for several years, and possessing as he did an Asiatic constitution and temperament, mentally and physically, [that he] should consider himself as constantly watched, and as the object of a conspiracy, especially when in this country, was quite natural; and, indeed, the reasonable result of communications made to him and of cautions actually imposed on him, by several of his friends.' The much-published Copland specialised in cholera, palsy, apoplexy, tuberculosis, bronchitis, and scrofula. He actually had no experience or direct knowledge of India (although he had spent considerable time in west Africa) but he nonetheless pontificated on the cultural origins of Dyce Sombre's earlier mistaken assertions that Mary Anne and her father had been intimate: 'incest (and of that particular kind [father-daughter]) is not so uncommon in India, or, as I regret to know, in this country either, and common passages of affection between a father and his child might, in such a mind as [Dyce Sombre]'s, give rise to the suspicion of infidelity...' Copland went on to describe many of Dyce Sombre's beliefs as no more misguided than Roman Catholic, and even

Anglican, doctrine: 'Who can draw the line of demarcation between prejudice, antipathy, articles of faith, and belief and delusion. Are not many doctrines inculcated by many, viewed by others as delusions? Is one of the oldest doctrines of the Romish Church, and one of the Articles of Belief by some of us, the "credo quia impossibile est", a sound doctrine or a delusion?'[98]

In early September 1846, as they waited anxiously for the next examinations by Southey and Bright to begin, Dyce Sombre and Mahon quarrelled. Angered by Mahon's hectoring advice on how to act and what to say, Dyce Sombre, with arms raised to strike and shouting abuse, rushed at him in front of his family. Mahon struck the first blow, blackening Dyce Sombre's eye. Dyce Sombre challenged him to a duel. Dyce Sombre also wrote privately to the Lord Chancellor complaining that Troup had offered Mahon £50 to strike Dyce Sombre but that Mahon had gladly punched him gratis.[99] On his part, Mahon immediately wrote Dyce Sombre a deep apology and appealed to their mutual acquaintances who patched up this relationship just days before the examinations.

Second Petition and Rehearing for Supercedas in Dover

During four days of reexamination by court-appointed doctors Southey and Bright in the Ship Hotel in Dover, Dyce Sombre largely, but reluctantly and incompletely, followed the advice of his lawyers and remaining supporters, especially Combermere. Southey and Bright were apparently not aware that Dr Mahon had been coaching Dyce Sombre based on Mahon's own professional knowledge of medical doctrine about lunacy. Nonetheless, the doctors reported that Dyce Sombre seemed insincerely to state whatever they wanted to hear rather than what he truly believed: 'his words were at some variance with his thoughts'.[100]

On the first day of examination, for example, Dyce Sombre repudiated his earlier frequently stated accusations against Mary Anne of incest and adultery with all classes of men. But then, in measured tones, he explained his discovery and current conviction that Mary Anne's lovers were actually only Cecil Forester and General Ventura. This was clearly not enough of an improvement. On the second day, after an evident overnight rebriefing by Mahon, Dyce Sombre altered his assertions of the previous day, saying that 'his notions of Mrs Dyce Sombre's infidelity were all delusions... [S]he is as virtuous and chaste a woman as ever lived.' He further explained that the many 'teazing examinations' he had endured over the years were 'enough to upset any mind'. While he still sought to justify his past behaviour, he also asserted that he had put those resentments and injuries behind him, ready to begin afresh. As Mahon knew, admission and then repudiation of past delusions indicated, in the leading medical theory of the day, proof of spontaneous recovery by a lunatic.

In addition to explaining carefully all the incidents already in his case file, Dyce Sombre was made by Southey and Bright to explicate the many controversial incidents that had occurred since he last met these doctors fifteen months earlier. Adding to the mounting record of his case, Dyce Sombre's elaborate self-justifications, though carefully couched, did not fully accord with the sworn affidavits of others. In reply to Ventura's accusations, for instance, Dyce Sombre denied culpability and explained how he had innocently enacted the literal instructions Ventura had given him in Urdu to expose himself. Dyce Sombre also refused to apologise to Mary Anne personally, still blaming her for all his legal troubles.

Despite the 'obvious contradictions' that Southey and Bright perceived between his spoken words and what they believed were his suppressed latent delusions, they reported progress. On the positive side, he no longer displayed any delusions about spirits or being poisoned. His manner had become 'mild and gentlemanly'. On balance, Southey and Bright concluded, 'he is still of unsound mind' at present but had demonstrated 'sufficient improvement to warrant the hope of his ultimate recovery'. They further admitted that he 'seems perfectly to understand the nature and extent of his property' so they recommended that his income be increased from its current £60 per week and should in future be paid without any of the annoying delays by Commissioner of the Estate Larkins that had hitherto irritated him.

Like many other jurists, Lord Chancellor Cottenham distrusted the opinions of physicians and relied more on his own personal assessment of sanity. This equivocal opinion from Southey and Bright apparently only reconfirmed his low opinion of medical expertise. In commenting on another case of aristocratic lunacy that he later judged (Joanna Dalrymple alias Gordon, Countess of Stair), Cottenham recalled how useless the medical profession had been in the Dyce Sombre case.[101]

Even during these Dover hearings, Combermere wrote to Dyce Sombre promising to get Mary Anne to agree to a Deed of Separation—not a legal divorce but one which terminated their conjugal relationship (both Mary Anne and Dyce Sombre rejected such a partial-divorce *a mensa et thoro*).[102] Combermere, as a co-trustee of Mary Anne's marriage settlement, managed her investments (with only mixed results); her family resented Combermere's many allegations against them.[103] On her part, Mary Anne refused to give up hope of reconciliation with her husband. She had long blamed Combermere and his associates for poisoning Dyce Sombre's mind against her. Indeed, she accused Combermere of wanting to free Dyce Sombre so he could marry a 'close connection' of Combermere himself, thus gaining power over Dyce Sombre's fortune by displacing her.[104]

Dyce Sombre found the promising but inconclusive report by Southey and Bright highly frustrating, particularly since he had compromisingly conformed to Mahon's directives that he repudiate what he still believed to be truths. Immediately on his return to Paris, he wrote identically to Prinsep, Troup, and Reghellini: 'Alas! Alas! the Doctors report [from Dover] has dished me again... [T]hey are blackguards and rogues as well as Liars—Pray see what Shadwell says—... put myself again in his hands and Mahon's.'[105] To Reghellini, he added that the doctors' report should be published in the *Delhi Akhbar* to prove and publicise in India how he was being persecuted; the editors of that newspaper, however, declined to publish it.[106]

Dyce Sombre also chided Combermere for having failed to free him. Combermere responded that Dyce Sombre had not fully followed instructions:

I am sorry that you seem to think I have not done all in my power to serve you. My having failed is no proof that I have not done all in my power to redeem the promise I made to the poor old Begum, to befriend you thro' life. Now, I am sure you will allow that I have, upon all occasions, given you the best advice, which, had you followed, it would have kept you clear of all the annoyances and difficulties which have beset you, and now deprive you of your liberty and the enjoyment of your property.'[107]

Aiding Dyce Sombre was often thankless and unproductive work, although many personally profited from it.

Since Cottenham's court-appointed doctors had not fully cleared him, the Chancellor resolved not yet to reverse Dyce Sombre's status as a legal lunatic but was open to letting him recover control over his fortune. Consequently, over the next eleven months, various lawyers representing the several concerned parties sparred before the Lord

Chancellor about control over Dyce Sombre's finances.[108] Lawyers for the Committees, acting against Dyce Sombre's freedom (but nominally for his own protection), opposed any increase in his allowance and demanded that the Lord Chancellor declare a moratorium on new affidavits from him. Mahon, mindful of his £10,000 reward for success, continued to assiduously garner, and had Dyce Sombre submit to Cottenham, testimonials from all the influential people, including aristocrats and leading physicians, whom he could induce to provide them.

Despite the unusually large and growing mountain of testimonials, affidavits, and motions, the Lord Chancellor wearily stated 'in cases of lunatics and children, he had always considered it his duty to look at all' of them thoroughly.[109] Advocates for the Committees then argued that classifying Dyce Sombre along with children meant that the Lord Chancellor was responsible for curbing his immorality by limiting the money available to him 'to expend in debauchery,... calculated to do the lunatic himself a most serious injury'. Scrutiny of Dyce Sombre's papers produced his expenses and remaining £911 debt from the Sudbury election hearings, as newspapers noted, re-evoking Dyce Sombre's past political corruption.[110] Weakening the force of the argument by the Committee of the Estate, however, was substantial evidence that Larkins continued to mismanage Dyce Sombre's funds.[111]

Shadwell countered that, since it was Dyce Sombre's own money and not illegal, the Lord Chancellor had no right to stop him from 'indulging in sensual pleasures to an inordinate extent, even to the undermining of his constitution.' Thus, Dyce Sombre should go from his current £60 weekly to £8,000 annually. Still, when Dyce Sombre re-petitioned in mid-January 1847, Cottenham declined to hold another hearing yet.

Then, in March 1847, Dyce Sombre personally wrote imploringly to Cottenham, asking for his Lordship's rapid decision in his favour, increase in his allowance, and protection against his solicitor, Shadwell, whom he alleged had been bribed by Troup.[112] Nonetheless, Mahon kept Shadwell as their solicitor and Rolt as their barrister; refreshed by regular fees, these men submitted motion after motion to keep his case active. Further, the medically-trained Mahon had Dyce Sombre sign a document in May 1847 that exonerated Mary Anne from all the charges he had made against her over the years. As Mahon knew, in British medical theory at the time, such an explicit repudiation of earlier delusions comprised strong evidence of the waning of the patient's lunacy and spontaneous recovery of morally responsible attitudes.

Third Petition and Rehearing for Supercedas in Brighton

Working behind the scenes, Combermere and his son-in-law, the Marquess of Downshire, both privately lobbied Lord Chancellor Cottenham in his House of Lords rooms, urging approval of the next petition for supercedas. These renewed efforts, and the skillful drafting of another new petition and new affidavits of sanity by Mahon and Dyce Sombre's legal team, secured Dyce Sombre yet another reexamination. On 14 July 1847, Lord Chancellor Cottenham again issued a safe conduct so Dyce Sombre could travel to Brighton to face Southey and Bright.[113]

Just before this new examination, Combermere wrote explicit instructions to Dyce Sombre, urging concealment in order to pass:

It now all depends upon yourself! Whether or not you are fully emancipated, everything has been done by us for you, and I have had great difficulty in stirring up Shadwell and Rolt... If you answer [Southey and Bright's] questions coolly and in a few words, they must declare you to be in such a state as to render you quite fit to have your liberty and property... I hope when you are examined, that you will say as little as you possibly can about Mrs D. S. You should, I think, say that whatever delusion you laboured under some time ago, has left you, as you became divested of your Eastern notions and feelings about women; and further, that there is no longer any danger of your being jealous of her, inasmuch as you have lost all love, admiration, and affection for her, and that no power upon earth should induce you to live with or go near her again. You should say also, that it is your wish to go to India, for the benefit of your health, and in order to look into and arrange your affairs.[114]

Indeed, Combermere brought his family to Brighton to advise and cheer Dyce Sombre on as well as protect him from Mary Anne's party: 'the enemy, [who will make] every attempt to excite and irritate you'.[115]

Similarly, on the eve of this rehearing, Combermere's third wife also personally wrote imploring Dyce Sombre to deceive the doctors about his true feelings:

Dear Col. Sombre,

I write to congratulate you on the happy turn your affairs have taken lately; be assured that we feel most sincerely rejoiced at the prospect of your speedy release from the constraint and persecution... Now, my dear sir, on your prudence in this emergency depends your fate through life. Guard every word and action, and whatever your opinions are, keep them to yourself, for there is no sort of comparison between the petty vengeance of expressing your suspicions,

and the far greater triumph of defeating your enemies now by your own liberation, and deferring to a later period the exposure of their evil intentions and
unkindness towards you...

Trusting that you will be prudent, and above all things, very quiet and abste-
mious, I wish you all the success you can desire for yourself, and in this hope,
as well as in every kind compliment, I am joined by Lord Combermere.[116]

Such extensive and explicit advice by both Combermeres to Dyce Sombre on what to say, and what not to say, seconded by Mahon, seems
for once to have been more or less heeded in his testimony if not his
personal behaviour.

In addition, the editors of some London newspapers including the
Times and *Standard*, were convinced strongly to advocate Dyce Sombre be declared sane. These papers cited the authority of 'the first medical men of St Petersburgh, Brussels, and... the joint affidavits of the
following four eminent English physicians in Paris—viz., Sir Robert
Chermside, [Joseph Francis] Olliffe, [Daniel Joseph] McCarthy, and
Berne, which fully coincide with the one given by Dr James Copland,
whose recent work upon mental disease ought to be a guarantee for such
an opinion.'[117] Dyce Sombre's team thus proved effective publicists.

Nonetheless, this third examination by Southey and Bright led these
doctors to an even more mixed recommendations on 5 August 1847.[118]
They were impressed by all the new evidence that doctors (secretly
directed by Mahon) had submitted. Further, as Dyce Sombre later
admitted, '[I] of course said what [Southey and Bright] wished me to
say, for they had often told me, in plain words in London in 1844, and
at Dover in 1846, that until I denied some facts, I should never be out
of Chancery'.[119] Southey and Bright thus concurred he was much
improved, having 'acquired much more self-control'—something
becoming highly valued by Victorian morality.[120] This, they asserted,
was proof of the accuracy of their own earlier diagnoses that he had
been insane but was now improving, and the error of the 'many physicians both foreign and English' who had contradicted them over the
years by contending he had never been lunatic. At the end of their
examination, they concluded with a series of double negatives: 'we are
bound to admit that we were unable to elicit any positive delusion
under which Mr D. Sombre labours though at the same time we regret
to add that we feel no confidence that he is entirely free from such
delusions... nor... can we therefore conclude that he is now perfectly
sane.' They asserted that finding no delusions did not mean none

existed. More positively, they added, he was undoubtedly competent to handle all his own property. Further, these funds would enable 'the tranquilizing influence of foreign travel' which they prescribed to speed his on-going spontaneous recovery. They implied that this would also keep him occupied far from the universally embarrassing British press.

Acting a month later on this equivocal recommendation from Southey and Bright, the Lord Chancellor judged Dyce Sombre 'on trial' but since his 'alleged insanity has been checkered with a lucid interval of so striking a character that, though still a lunatic according to law, he is deemed competent to take care of his fortune' without the supervision of Warwick or any other medical warder.[121] Cottenham thus ordered the Committee of the Estate to turn over to Dyce Sombre all the income from his assets, to manage and spend however he wished. (Larkins took another nine months before actually arranging for Dyce Sombre to receive his money.)[122] Should Dyce Sombre continue to improve and not relapse, the Lord Chancellor expressed his confidence that official supersession of the commission of lunacy would eventually follow, calling this 'a blessing in reserve, to be bestowed on the contingency of permanent sanity'. However, various newspapers, including *Atlas* and the *Times*, found 'Jobbing Chancellor' Cottenham's verdict on Dyce Sombre itself irrational: 'for perplexing and strange as have been the various judgments pronounced on the mental condition of this gentleman, nothing appears more perplexing than a decree for giving the rights of property to one of whom the law still takes cognizance as a lunatic'.[123] This outcome created even more public skepticism about the capacity of the medical and legal professions to define, identify and manage lunacy.

While in Brighton, Dyce Sombre provided his opponents (that is, the Committees of the Person and of the Estate officially assigned to guard his interests) with much evidence of his continued immorality if not irrationality. They took affidavits from the landlady of Pegg's York Hotel, where he resided during the examinations, which recounted his violations of British social norms. He reportedly: frequently brought female prostitutes into his room, quarrelling loudly over their demanded fees; used the water closet, located in the hallway for several lodgers to share, without fully closing the door, thus exposing his private acts and parts to his fellow and female boarders; entrapped the landlady in just such a water closet; solicited chambermaids to 'shampoo' (full-body massage) him in his room (one chambermaid accused another of having have taken his money for various intimate acts).[124] Further, he was served a debt notice and threatened imprisonment for the remaining bills owed to James Coppock from the Sudbury election hearings, which he refused to pay (although the Lord Chancellor later had them paid by Larkins).[125] So infamous was Dyce Sombre's case that his name became proverbial in Britain for an extreme anomaly such as the freak-show star General Tom Thumb.[126]

Despite his dutiful testimony in Brighton, Dyce Sombre clearly retained many of his suspicions of a conspiracy by his enemies closing in from every side. On the steamer from Brighton back to Boulogne, he spied Sir Richard Jenkins, former Chairman and current member of the Company's Court of Directors and a previous recipient of a dueling challenge from Dyce Sombre. When three boxes of Dyce Sombre's valuable jewellry disappeared en route, Dyce Sombre decided that Jenkins had purloined them. When Jenkins denied this, Dyce Sombre widened his accusations to assert that Jenkins had been skulking around Brighton, soliciting adverse affidavits from servants, guests, and the landlady of Pegg's York Hotel.[127]

Acting in the name of Dyce Sombre's property and at the explicit orders of the Lord Chancellor, in 1848 the Committee of the Estate instituted a lawsuit in the civil court of the Principal Sudder Ameen court in Delhi for Dyce Sombre's long dormant claims against the East India Company over the Badshahpur and also Sardhana armaments disputes. These twin cases thus became enmeshed in deep ironies: a retired East India Company official, Larkins, acting on the explicit orders of the Crown's Lord Chancellor, reactivated these suits against the Company in the name of Dyce Sombre; Dyce Sombre, who had been dispossessed of Sardhana by the Company and had originally instituted these claims, now opposed these lawsuits; he also twice attempted to transfer his rights in these cases to Queen Victoria, who declined to accept them; he later vainly tried to bequeath his rights in these cases to the East India Company, which would therefore have been suing itself; but the Crown disallowed this bequest, enabling Mary Anne and Dyce Sombre's brothers-in-law subsequently to sue (with some ultimate success) the Company (and later the British Government of India).

These cases provided several additional unparalleled legal dilemmas over the years. The Company claimed that the Mughal Emperor had not been sovereign enough to make the Badshahpur grant. However, the Company also claimed that the Begum was sovereign enough that the Badshahpur *jagir* and Sardhana armaments were state property, not private. The Company further contended that a private individual (Dyce Sombre) could not sue a sovereign government like itself over such seizures in a civil court. But the sovereignty of the Mughals, the Company, and the Begum were all highly disputed and unresolved issues. Finally, when Larkins initially filed this case in Delhi on 17 August 1848, the Company argued that the twelve year statue of limitations had expired six months earlier, since the Begum died on 27 January 1836. Thus, this case raised the unprecedented legal question of whether an official lunatic, prohibited in acting juridically in his own interest, should be subject to such a time limit or whether the clock stopped at the moment of his disqualification to act as a legal person. The Principal Sudder Ameen and then, over decades, several other levels of East India Company's courts of appeals in India upheld the position of the East India Company that the suit had expired. The Privy Council in London, however, eventually reversed those rulings and declared that these suits remained valid since Dyce Sombre could not be held accountable during his period of lunacy. This decision by the Privy Council, however, did not come until March 1857, six years after Dyce Sombre's death. Further, this Privy Council ruling only meant that the cases could begin all over again at the lowest level court in Delhi.[128]

Back in exile in Paris, Dyce Sombre circulated in high expatriate British society and kept abreast of its gossip.[129] Learning about the notorious brutality and misogyny of the nephew of the Duke of Wellington—William Pole-Tylney-Long-Wellesley, fourth Earl of Mornington—Dyce Sombre decided to spend some of his income, newly ordered partly restored by the Lord Chancellor, to buy trouble for that family. He gave a generous unsolicited donation to Helena Bligh Mornington to assist her in her lawsuit against her abusive husband.[130] Dyce Sombre knew that, as antisocial and irresponsible toward his family and fortune as this Wellesley had proven to be, he was never charged with lunacy as Dyce Sombre had unjustly been. But then tiring of Paris life, Dyce Sombre determined to go south again, albeit further this time.

12

TRAVELLING, PUBLISHING, CHALLENGING AND EXPIRING

Over the next four years, as Dyce Sombre regained much of his income and waited between further rounds of hearings on his lunacy, he pleasured himself through travel, choosing to explore the Ottoman empire and then each European capital. To prove himself right and all his expanding range of opponents wrong, he compiled and privately published a massive book and two pamphlets that he believed vindicated him and refuted his persecutors by exposing their immoralities and inconsistencies. He also struggled for recovery of his status as sane in England and of his full fortune through political influence and launching three more appeals to successive Lord High Chancellors. Although his legal prospects eventually improved, his body finally broke down from the accumulated abuses of his short life.

Exploring the Continent and Ottoman Empire

With £9,000 of his annual income reinstated, Dyce Sombre occupied himself with a tour of the Mediterranean. In late August 1847, he began to travel south from Paris through Alps via the Simplon Pass, Milan, Trieste, Venice, Corfu, Athens, and then the Ottoman Empire, accompanied only by one valet, Auguste Kastenbein.[1] As during his tour of Southeast Asia and China, Dyce Sombre was not a typical traveller, especially given his legal and cultural baggage. In Venice, he publicly insulted Solaroli, leading to Dyce Sombre's expulsion by municipal authorities; later, Dyce Sombre's pistols 'wh[ich] I had taken for Solaroli' would be confiscated by the government.[2]

However, like rich Britons, Dyce Sombre paid handsomely for first-class accommodation in ships and hotels established for high-class tourists, dined with European aristocrats and other elite fellow-travellers, paid to tour famous monuments and palaces, and called upon the services of British consuls in major cities. But, Dyce Sombre was Catholic, widely considered non-White, had an infamous reputation among many Britons, and had his origins in a heavily Islamic culture somewhat similar to Turkey and Egypt. Hence, his perspective both paralleled and diverged from that typical of a wealthy British man.

As usual, Dyce Sombre kept a daily diary of his life, mostly in English. But it differed from the many journals of his contemporary British male travellers in its methodology and points of comparison. For example, he occasionally shifted to Persian when detailing his sexual activities. Further reflecting his unconventional behaviour, he used a printed English *Gentleman's Pocket Book of 1846* to chronicle his impressions, actions, and expenses but for the period August 1847 to April 1848; consequently, the days of the week and sequence of months did not correspond.[3] Unusually, his original diary for this period survived Mary Anne's posthumous destruction of his most private papers.

In Constantinople, Dyce Sombre highlighted distinctive features familiar to him. He sought out kabobs and pilafs (finding them only 'tolerable', implicitly compared to those of north India).[4] He found Ottoman seraglios and palaces 'nothing to be compared to the Agra or Dehli Palaces'. He also deprecated the local religious and sanitary culture: 'The Turks are more than half Infidels now, the Butchers meat hangs nearly touching the ground, the Paria Dogs, of whom there are herds, are literally licking the meat and trying to eat off bits for themselves.' But, as in Calcutta, he did admire in Constantinople the 'Mint for Coining... better than one would expect'.

In Alexandria and Cairo, he appreciated being saluted by the Pasha passing on the street. He also admired that ruler's magnificent Ottoman and also European-style palaces, implicitly comparing them to the Begum's and the Nawab of Bengal's similar pairs of palaces.[5] But Dyce Sombre also noted the flourishing Egyptian slave market and Ottoman political oppression over the local population. Further, he recognized fruits from north India in Egyptian markets. He half considered continuing his journey on to Sardhana, but feared being seized and incarcerated as soon as he entered British India under the Lord Chancellor's sentence of lunacy. Besides, he unrealistically lamented, 'What shall I do there? I tell you, if I wished, the [British] Ministers would compel the Indian Govt. to give me an appointment in their covenanted Civil Service, but I have no wish to go back to India, if I can enjoy in Europe, but I dare say I will visit India yet; when that will be I cannot say.'[6]

Not feeling quite comfortable in Egypt, Dyce Sombre returned to enjoy Europe. But he unpunctually missed his steamer from Alexandria to Marseilles, which left on schedule, carrying with it his money, passport, luggage, and valet. Marooned, he philosophically reflected 'but what could I do, but to summon courage', managing, as he had after his first flight to freedom in Paris, by borrowing on his evident gentlemanly status enough cash credit to catch up with his things and servant a week later. Then, quarantined in Marseilles, he 'had an Egyptian for my Neighbour as he call'd himself, but I rather think he was Maltese for he wore the European Clothes & spoke French & Italian but we lived separate of course, he became very familiar with my Servant Auguste'.[7] Dyce Sombre thus distanced himself from another man of mixed culture whom he characterised as something of a fraud and associate of servants.

Pope Gregory XVI

Carrying on across Italy to Rome, Dyce Sombre negotiated with Pope Gregory XVI and Cardinal Fransoni, Préféct of the Propaganda de Fide, about obtaining a divorce on grounds of Mary Anne's failure to bear children and errant behavior. To the Pope, Dyce Sombre represented himself as raised as Eastern 'but having mixed a good deal with the English, & having a good deal of European blood in him, he has taken up their habits, & in fact considers himself to be one of them in every respect'.[8] Dyce Sombre claimed the East India Company had paid Viscount St Vincent £5,000 to entrap him as son-in-law. He also detailed for the Pope how Mary Anne had violated both European and Eastern morality. He cited as precedent the Pope's annulment of Napoleon's marriage with Joséphine and warned that, if he became Protestant, he could easily divorce. Dyce Sombre believed he heard the Pope privately hint to him in response that a divorce was possible if he promised to marry Mary Talbot, daughter of leading Catholic peer, Lord Shrewsbury.[9] Dyce Sombre knew, however, that Mary had in 1839 married Philip Andrew, Prince Doria Pamphili Landi, a man even wealthier than himself. Therefore, Dyce Sombre wrote challenging Prince Doria to a duel, but the Rome government intervened, ordering Dyce Sombre to keep away from the Prince. Ultimately, Papal authorities fobbed off Dyce Sombre by directing him to submit any petition for divorce through his local English bishop.

While in Rome, Dyce Sombre also spurred Adamo Tadolini toward finishing the Begum's huge cenotaph. To goad the sculptor, suing him if necessary to ensure quality, he hired for £200 a man he mistakenly thought was the impoverished Lord William Ward.[10] But this was apparently an imposter, not that really quite wealthy peer who inherited vast estates and later the title Earl of Dudley. Lawyers for the Committees of Person and Estate highlighted for the Lord Chancellor these unreasonable miscues about Prince Doria and Lord Ward as evidence of Dyce Sombre's continued lunacy.

Despite his teeth beginning to fall out and occasional illness (which Dyce Sombre concluded came from poisoning by Solaroli or other enemies), he toured Naples, Pisa, Genoa, and Nice.[11] Approaching Lyons by ship, he encountered: 'a madman who was on board holding a crucifix, who after we started became outrageous & cried for a full hour, with all the Vehemence & without interruption "Ah Notre Dame, prie pour moi, Oh Notre Dame, prie pour moi", and asking us all round to go down on our knees as he was doing & two of his female relations, trying to pacify him, at last he became exhausted & fell on his face & fell asleep, besides this he was not mischievous.'[12] Thus, as Dyce Sombre had in Belgium, he found lunatics fascinating and quite different from him.

As Dyce Sombre toured France, he encountered the 1848 revolution. His carriage was attacked when 'the Mob... with the Cries of "Vive la Republique"' mistook him for Prince Metternich.[13] Although Dyce Sombre had once aspired to be Prince of Sardhana, he convinced these Frenchmen that he was no longer an aristocrat (although he was not their fellow citizen either). Eventually, these revolutionaries lost interest in identifying who he actually was and let him go. Liberated, he carried on to Paris after an absence of 225 days.

Revolution and Refutation in Paris

Dyce Sombre had an ambiguous position amidst these tumultuous revolutionary events. On reentering Paris he faced further insurrections as the people periodically took over the streets. Having himself endured annexation of his own princely state, Dyce Sombre tended to sympathise with royalty. Further, some of his conservative supporters warned adamantly against social disorder. His current advisor, Henry Prinsep, warned him from London:

There will be no peace for [Paris] for years to come; this last Revolution being one that has set class against class, with so furious and cruel a spirit... [W]herever you go in France, the same violences will be acted everywhere. England, or Denmark, and Russia, are the only countries in which society continues bound together in the old bonds, and likely to continue so; wars of classes or wars of races prevail everywhere else on the continent. India is a model of peace and good government in these times.[14]

But Dyce Sombre could not align these epic events of 1848 with his own situation and campaigns to prove himself sane. He had himself already been deposed by this alleged model British Government of India and expelled from the British Parliament, yet still had faith in them to restore his full inheritance. He had aristocratic supporters, but also aristocratic enemies. He had been condemned to incarceration by the British Crown, yet constantly appealed to it for justice. Hence, he wrote 'Kings are going down by dozens... [S]o far the politics of Europe! but they do not concern us, beyond idle curiosity.'[15] Yet, he was often trapped in his rented Paris apartments, finding the 'Mob' in the streets too dangerous; on several occasional excursions out, he barely escaped assault again.

. Nonetheless, as during any insurrection, people like Dyce Sombre pursued their mundane personal pleasures. He requested Prinsep to send him an Indian cook, a man currently in London, since Dyce Sombre found that simply having his valet add cayenne pepper to all his French meals was unsatisfactory.[16] Perennially fascinated by mathematics, in mid-May 1848 he hired Professor Catherin John Henry Montucci—who had a doctorate from the University of Siena and an appointment as Professor of Industrial Arts and Commerce at the University of Paris—to tutor him in geometry and algebra. These mathematics lessons lasted only a few weeks but Montucci later worked extensively with Dyce Sombre in articulating and publicizing his case widely. As an Italian and someone who would eventually study all the documentary evidence that Dyce Sombre presented, Montucci regarded his suspicions of Mary Anne to be entirely reasonable: 'He was an Eastern in his notions respecting women, and the duties of wives; then, as comparing the habits of the East with Europe, England, and Italy, the remark would be made, that he was considered insane for doubting the chastity of his Wife, when in Italy, any Husband, without exception, would be laughed at loudly, and ridiculed, who should pretend to believe, absolutely, in the chastity of his wife.'[17] Although Dyce Sombre paid well, Professor Montucci found his pupil willful and not always respectful: 'He treated his servants as rich men commonly do, who are accustomed to be obeyed at a moment's notice'.

As Dyce Sombre sought progress in his case, Prinsep had come to vie with Combermere as his premier British advisor. Dyce Sombre confided to Prinsep: 'I am sorry to be obliged to come to such terms with Lord Combermere, but really he does not recollect what he says or promises & I was obliged to stop all communications with him'.[18] Dyce Sombre also quarrelled with Combermere's ally, Dr Mahon. Since Mahon had not cleared Dyce Sombre by the April 1848 contractual deadline, Dyce Sombre refused to pay him anything either in salary or in reimbursement. Yet, Mahon claimed he had incurred huge expenses in order 'to manage, conduct, and obtain the favourable reports of medical men of the first eminence'.[19] Indeed, Mahon claimed substantial success—tripling Dyce Sombre's income from £60 weekly to £9,000 annually. Eventually, Dyce Sombre would agree to arbitration with Mahon. Meanwhile Mahon and Combermere continued to work on Dyce Sombre's behalf, as they understood his interests. But he was not an easy man to support.

Lord Chancellor Cottenham's judgment of September 1847 had been encouraging. Thus, in May 1848, Dyce Sombre and Mahon directed the solicitor Shadwell to submit yet another petition for supercedas. To provide new evidence on which to base this appeal, Dyce Sombre underwent more private examinations which Mahon arranged in Paris by British Drs Charles Shrimpton and Thomas Davidson. They added to the long list of physicians who declared they could find no delusions and attested him fully competent to manage his affairs. Shrimpton, however, did not include in this affidavit that he had been personally offended by Dyce Sombre's 'licentious taste' in erotic art: a 'filthy piece of sculpture on the chimney-piece' in his apartments where they examined him.[20] (This pre-Freudian doctor did not consider whether the revealed erotic inclinations of his subject had anything to do with his mental condition.) On 17 June 1848, as soon as these latest examination results were in hand, Dyce Sombre had Shadwell assert in a formal petition to the Lord Chancellor that the Commission against him should be superseded since Dyce Sombre was now 'entirely free from any symptoms of insanity... [as] attested by the certificates of several eminent physicians of Paris'.[21]

Thinking to assist his case, the next day (18 June 1848), Dyce Sombre sent a handwritten personal note to Prime Minister Lord John Russell detailing his situation and the reasons why Georgiana was illegitimate, saying he knew Lord Charles Metcalfe, before his death in 1846, had privately entrusted Russell with a written statement to that effect.[22] Attached to this letter was a separable slip of paper on which Dyce Sombre had written '£1,000'—his offer should the Prime Minister take appropriate action. Instead, Lord Russell, who had heard nothing of the sort from Metcalfe and resented this bribe-offer, turned this letter over to an incensed Cottenham. Cottenham was all the more insulted since Dyce Sombre also wrote a personal note to Cottenham's own wife with an offer of £1,500 if the commission be superseded and Dyce Sombre also obtain divorce from Mary Anne. Further, Dr Bright and the wife of Dr Southey each received cards from Dyce Sombre offering £250 annual pensions should they recommend that Dyce Sombre had recovered fully.

Sir Charles Edward Trevelyan took these multiple bribery offers as further proof of his own contention that Dyce Sombre was essentially

Indian. He wrote, bribery 'was no more than would be expected from an Asiatic. What we call bribery, but which they look upon in a much more venial light, is habitual to Asiatics; it is difficult for even the most enlightened among them to conceive that any one would be entirely above taking a gratuity in a case which, according to their views, the ends of justice would be counteracted thereby.' Dyce Sombre's lawyers concurred that bribery was common in 'the East', pointing to the British political Resident of Tanjore, Captain Douglas, who was convicted for it in London in 1845.[23] Although the Lord Chancellor expressed his anger and resentment at these obvious efforts by Dyce Sombre to influence him and other British authorities, he once again ordered a rehearing of this unique case.

Fourth and Fifth Petitions for Supercedas in London

The Lord Chancellor, as had become customary for Dyce Sombre (but otherwise unprecedented), ordered on 9 August 1848 the creation of a medical panel and a temporary safe passage, so he could come to London for his reexamination in October. In addition to Southey and Bright, who represented Cottenham as usual, he allowed Mary Anne, as Committee of the Person, and the person, Dyce Sombre himself, each to nominate a qualified doctor. Mary Anne selected Sir James Clark, who had long argued against Dyce Sombre's sanity and would unalterably do so until his death. Dyce Sombre, learning of what he regarded as the adverse composition of three-quarters of the panel, confided in Prinsep: 'I am sorry the Lord Chancellor has named Drs Bright and Southey again, they are corrupt men and [with] Sir James Clark... there will be three to one in favor of the opposite party.'[24] Nonetheless, confident that this time he would convince them all of his sanity, he nominated his former warder, James Ranald Martin, to be his man on the panel. Martin, although nominated and trusted by Dyce Sombre, would instead advance his own views about India, Indians, and Dyce Sombre.

Protected by the Lord Chancellor's most recent exemption against arrest, Dyce Sombre settled into a suite in Mivart's Hotel, one of London's most fashionable. There, to make him feel comfortable, Mary Anne sent him clothing (including 101 shirts), 94 of his books and artworks, his hair-curling tongs, and one of his carriages. Dyce Sombre also futilely instructed Shadwell to secure him naturalization as British, thinking this would 'be so very requisite in [my] case'.[25]

Even before the next reexaminations began, Dyce Sombre consulted Dr Martin about his various physical disorders. Dyce Sombre attributed his stomach-aches to poison, for which he suspected Solaroli, Troup, and Frere. Supporting the possibility of poison, Martin explained his view to the Lord Chancellor that poisoning with Datoora, a species of Stramonium, was a widespread form of assassination in India. At the same time, however, Martin thought poisoning unlikely in this case and rather diagnosed a more mundane cause: Dyce Sombre was 'immoderate in his eating, taking animal food largely at dinner, and also late at night, turtle soup, etc., and also in drinking, consuming much brandy... besides wine.'[26] The advice from Martin that Dyce Sombre moderate his consumption, echoing so many other doctors, failed to change his ways.

When reporting to the Lord Chancellor, Martin represented himself as an especially authoritative expert on Indian home life: 'very few European men have had the same opportunities I have had of becoming acquainted with the interior of the native houses... [including] Mahomedans, Hindoos and Christians'. Contradicting Dyce Sombre's own lawyers, Martin pontificated that Dyce Sombre's possessiveness and ill-founded accusations of Mary Anne's promiscuity and incest were not attributable to his Indian origins. Martin self-assuredly knew all Indians to be quite different, detailing his own stereotypes of those 'natives':

The natives of India are a remarkably reasonable, placid, temperate people, and not at all liable to furious excesses of jealousy or other passion. Neither are they so foolish as to apply the same rules of conduct to women in totally different circumstances... [T]hey feel towards our women great respect and treat them accordingly, perfectly well able to allow for the difference of customs and rules of conduct and to distinguish between the liberty arising from European habits and because the result of mind and wantonness. I never witnessed in a native Indian any operations of jealousy which would serve as a parallel to explain or justify Mr Dyce Sombre's suspicions against his wife, such as I have witnessed myself in him.[27]

Nor, Martin assured the Lord Chancellor, could Dyce Sombre's accusations of the illegitimacy of Georgiana be accurate: 'The natives of India do not live in such a state of promiscuous concubinage in their own homes as to render the parentage of the children a matter of doubt, on the contrary, their homes are regulated with a strict and most decent etiquette'. Thus, Martin unilaterally dismissed the arguments of Dyce Sombre, his lawyers, and many of his supporters.

Over three days in November 1848, the panel collectively reexamined Dyce Sombre thoroughly in his hotel suite. He, believing that he had been misquoted in the past, demanded a shorthand note-taker be present. When, after some consideration, the Lord Chancellor permitted this, Dyce Sombre claimed authority over the evidence by refusing to share the shorthand record with the doctors, insisting they take their own notes and he would correct them where they erred.

Over the three days the doctors probed him sharply about his more recent delusions. Despite their skepticism, he insisted Sir Richard Jenkins had indeed arranged his Brighton 'scrapes' and documentation of them. He insisted the East India Company was wrong about Badshahpur and the Sardhana armaments. He insisted Georgiana was illegitimate, citing the confidential oral confirmation of this from Charles Metcalfe (now deceased). Further, he justified himself concerning his misadventures in Rome.

While these new issues appeared to the doctors as proof of his current delusions, Dyce Sombre agreeably proved willing to disavow his past accusations against Mary Anne. He now explained his misapprehensions arose from his naïve unfamiliarity with 'European rules, and since he had been informed of the innocence of those acts... he now acquitted her of infidelity'. Nonetheless, Dyce Sombre insisted that they could never reunite, due not to her immorality but rather their temperamental incompatibility. He even, after much pressing by Clark, admitted that Clark, Commissioner Barlow, and the original English lay jury might have been correct in calling 'delusions' his beliefs about Mary Anne's immorality. While the doctors took this as a hopeful sign, they determined to test how sincere his improvement actually was.

A few days later, to try Dyce Sombre in yet another way, the Lord Chancellor agreed with the doctors to approve Mary Anne's proposal that she meet Dyce Sombre directly. She and he had not spoken for over five years, since September 1843. As she explained,

I sought that interview because I love my said husband and because I longed to see him again [hoping] it might bring him back to what he used to be and revive the former great affection which he entertained for me before he was placed under restraint and which he continued to evince afterwards by several of his letters... I hoped if I could bring back his former feelings for me that I might be the means of happily disengaging him from his enemies and my enemies who have for many years been making a prey of him and causing his destruction both of body and mind.[28]

The doctors arranged for her to come to Martin's nearby Lower Grosvenor Street home on 10 November 1848, where Dyce Sombre would be brought uninformed of what would transpire.

When, Drs Clark and Martin ushered Mary Anne unannounced into the room where Dyce Sombre waited, he initially did not recognise her. Assuming she was Mrs Martin, he advanced politely to shake her hand. As she extended hers saying 'Friendy ain't you glad to see me', he suddenly realised who she was, retreating in dismay. Suspecting another trap, he refused her invitation to sit nearby and told the doctors to remain. When they insisted on leaving the two alone, Dyce Sombre agreed only if they left the door open and positioned themselves to observe him; Mary Anne sat out of their sight. As with many estranged couples, they spoke at cross-purposes. She proposed 'I would rather you got better, and that we lived together'. He retorted that he was arranging for a divorce by the Pope. He also directed the conversation so she attested to Georgiana's illegitimacy and Charles Metcalfe's alleged assurance of that fact, which she did not contradict but also disavowed any particular knowledge. Conversely, her efforts to blame Combermere for their estrangement failed. When she proposed future meetings at her home, or even openly on the street nearby, he rejected these. Indeed, they never met again.

Drs Clark and Martin carefully noted this uncomfortable conversation and reported it to the rest of the panel and Lord Chancellor. When the four official doctors submitted their unanimous recommendation on 18 November 1848, they concurred Dyce Sombre had not improved, indeed he had worsened since the last examination: 'he is more obviously unsound in mind than [before]... he is quite unfit to be trusted with the management of his own affairs'.[29]

Cottenham accepted their diagnosis, although he did not reduce Dyce Sombre's allowance. Further, despite Cottenham's earlier promise to consider carefully all evidence and appeals from lunatics, children, and other wards of the crown, he deliberately tried to quash future supercedas petitions from Dyce Sombre. To do this, in a legal device that became precedent-setting, he delayed officially closing these hearings by not yet allotting court costs, a procedure he intended as 'sufficient security against any unnecessary and, therefore, improper repetition of applications without sufficient cause to support them'.[30] If he thought this would silence Dyce Sombre, he was much mistaken.

The parties supporting Dyce Sombre were disappointed with his performance. Soon after this unsatisfactory official report, Combermere wrote Mahon: 'I was much afraid that our friend would not stand a good examination; he is sane, but so exceedingly imprudent and obstinate that I really see no prospect of his emancipation'.[31] Undaunted, Mahon (who had still not been paid by Dyce Sombre), arranged and rewarded handsomely (about £70 each) for extensive examinations while Dyce Sombre was still in London by six of the leading medical experts then available: Dr Sir Alexander Morison (Physician to Bethleham Hospital and to diverse private lunatic asylums); Dr William B. Costello (Principal of Wyke-house Asylum, Brentford); Dr Thomas Mayo (Fellow, Censor, and later President of the Royal College of Physicians and author of an influential book on lunacy); Dr Robert Ferguson (obstetrician to Queen Victoria); Dr John Ayrton Paris; and Dr James Copland. The last two of these physicians had earlier examined Dyce Sombre and already testified to his sanity. While these six advocated diverse theories of lunacy, their unanimous professional opinion was that Southey, Bright, Clark, and Martin were all wrong about Dyce Sombre and outdated in their understanding of lunacy. Rather, these six concluded that Dyce Sombre suffered 'no unsoundness of mind, that the present commission ought to be superseded, and that the pressure and annoyance to which he was subjected by reason of the said commission might, if persisted in, lead, ultimately, to mental alienation and bodily infirmity'.

Taking a popular Orientalist line, the six doctors collectively contended his actions arose naturally from his Asiatic race, so evident in his complexion:

His parentage proves, and his aspect confirmed, the fact of the great preponderance of the Asiatic over the European blood in him... [H]e was essentially an Asiatic, having inaccurate, confused, erroneous or superficial knowledge of European Society... [H]is strong passions had been encouraged into sensuality by his Asiatic habits... [A]ll the eccentricities he had been guilty of were the fruits of his Asiatic education, and had no reference to any unsoundness of mind... Mr Dyce Sombre had been brought up in the East... where suspicions of treachery were invariably entertained toward any one in any way an enemy... Jealousy of women is an overwhelming passion of the Oriental mind, and seems in a high degree to have existed in his,... born and bred in countries where incest is common, and treachery habitual.'[32]

In particular, obstetrician Dr Ferguson specified that Dyce Sombre himself had been born and raised an Oriental despot, corrupted further by his ill-education in English:

The despotic power on the one hand and the Oriental servility on the other must have tended to render the will imperious and violent when it should meet with opposition... I found him illiterate and ill-read; his acquaintance with the English language was inaccurate and defective; enough, it is true, for the ordinary purposes of every-day life; but whenever I came on topics of nice scrutiny, requiring a precise knowledge of the import of words and phrases, I saw how vaguely he apprehended my meaning; and I was constantly compelled to vary my phrases to be certain that it was understood... As an instance, I found that a variety of meanings was attached by him to the word Confession, which he used sometimes as equivalent to not denying, and sometimes for assent when the person accused declined to answer... [H]is strong passions had been encouraged into sensuality by his Asiatic habits. He was readily influenced by flattery and by rank. He appeared good-natured, but his excessive vanity and his belief in the omnipotence of his wealth made him tetchy and quarrelsome on points which trenched on his notions of self-importance.'

While this served Dyce Sombre's cause, it also offended his self-image.

Hearing this part of their report, Dyce Sombre rejected their assumption that he was 'a native of India which I protest... I was born there, but don't own myself to be a Native.'[33] Fortunately for Dyce Sombre's lawyers, he made this denial of being 'a native of India' in a private letter to Prinsep. Nonetheless, the assertions made by these doctors resonated with deepening British stereotypes about the Orient and suggested that Dyce Sombre, due to his race, could never be properly Anglicised. The doctors used this to show he should therefore not be declared lunatic by being tested against racially incompatible British norms.

Further, medical theories about mental health also changed over the years of Dyce Sombre's several trials. These six leading doctors attacked the underlying presuppositions of all previous official panels about the very nature of lunacy as proven by delusions. Rather, several of the new panel denied that delusion necessarily indicated insanity. As Dr Paris stated 'the consciousness of having had a delusion, which has passed away, does (or may) abide and survive its departure, so as to leave a soreness of feeling, and a liability to irritation from a reference to it—a revival of the subject; its shadow, as it were, remains, and to an extent does cloud the mind; but that tenderness in the recollection of a past delusion is very distinct from the domination of the delusion itself'. Dr Morison concurred, adding that the Victorian moral power of self-restraint was what really mattered:

There may be madness without delusion, and delusion without madness; they are not synonymous; ungovernable passion may be unaccompanied by delusion; people may be insane by having no self-control... [A] man may retain in a sane state a delusion of which he was possessed when insane. He may have it, but he will not act upon it. That is the criterion: he may have a recollection of it, and not be under it, therefore not acting upon it.[34]

Since Dyce Sombre evidently managed his financial and social affairs adequately through self-possession during recent years, he should be allowed to walk the streets without external constraints, even if he still mistakenly believed his wife immoral.

Similarly, Dr Mayo concluded Dyce Sombre was 'a person having no regard for truth, rather than... insane,... a mind tainted with false-hood, not insanity—a bad man, not an insane man'.[35] Mayo added that Dyce Sombre, out of nervousness, had 'stimulated himself largely with [alcoholic] spirits' before the last official examination, hence displayed a temporarily drunken rather than insane condition. Indeed, in *London Medical Gazette or Journal of Practical Medicine* (1850), Mayo directly attacked the Lord Chancellor's outdated medical ideas.[36] He further based his influential Croonian Lectures at the Royal College of Surgeons in 1853 on his authoritative diagnosis of Dyce Sombre as self-controlled, able to manage his wealth and himself, and therefore no longer insane despite his continuing 'notional delusion' about his wife.[37] Not until the 1853 Lunacy Act did lawyers and politicians catch up with these newly fashionable medical developments.

Following these hearings, despite—or perhaps because of—Dyce Sombre's lack of legal progress, he recognised his need to settle his contractual dispute with Mahon before he left London. Unwilling to pay Mahon the £10,000 he had promised contingent on success, or even a large portion of that amount, Dyce Sombre nonetheless agreed to binding arbitration. He asked his current supporter, Prinsep, to represent him as one arbiter while Mahon nominated another. Princep, who was growing closer to Mahon, hinted that he felt Dyce Sombre not entirely in the right and later recalled suggesting Dwarkanath Tagore be selected as a more neutral arbiter instead, but Tagore had died two years earlier and could not serve. While Dyce Sombre's legal capacity to make any contract was highly questionable since he was officially mentally incompetent, all these parties accepted Mahon's unconventional contract as binding. Finally, on 24 December 1848, the arbiters awarded Mahon three years' salary, at £500 annually, plus his actual expenses, for a total of £2,140 7 shillings 6 pence.[38] Dyce Sombre agreed to pay this arbitration award. Further, just two days later, he renewed his contingency contract Mahon for the same £10,000 (minus the £2,140 7s. 6d. already paid) should he recover full control of his fortune and have his condemnation as a Chancery Lunatic reversed, extending the deadline for exactly one year more.

On his part, Dyce Sombre determined to demonstrate to the public the rightness of his attribution to Georgiana of illegitimacy and to Sir Richard Jenkins of perfidy. The same day he renewed his contract with Mahon, Dyce Sombre in the *Globe* republished (with a cover letter to the editor) private correspondence that in his mind proved his case.[39] First was a note to him from his old companion (and witness to the Begum's will) Major Edward Bere, about how Georgiana's illegitimacy was common knowledge in Meerut during her youth (Dyce Sombre, however, edited this note considerably from what Bere originally wrote). Second was one of Combermere's letters to Mahon providing detailed instructions on how Dyce Sombre should be coached to tactfully respond to doctors. His public revelation of these private letters was embarrassing to their authors and did not advance his contentions as he intended. However, after Dyce Sombre left Mivart's Hotel, his supporters solicited and received an affidavit from the eponymous hotelkeeper testifying that Dyce Sombre had acted in a 'quite orderly and gentlemanly' manner.[40]

After Dyce Sombre returned to the continent, Lord Combermere arranged in early January 1849 for many of his most prominent supporters—including Lords Downshire (his son-in-law) and Shrewsbury (father-in-law to Prince Doria) and Major Edward Bere—to join him in writing a private letter to Cottenham, appealing for reconsideration of the Lord Chancellor's verdict:

We positively affirm that Colonel Dyce Sombre never showed the least symptom of insanity before his marriage. That he is, like most natives of Hindostan, of a very jealous disposition, and also (though naturally a good-natured and quiet man) passionate when roused, and treated Mrs Dyce Sombre in a manner quite un-English, though justifiable in Hindostan, when a woman is suspected of infidelity. Some of the undersigned, who are acquainted with Mrs Dyce Sombre, are of opinion that her manners are such as to kindle unpleasant feelings in a breast less susceptible than that of Colonel Dyce Sombre's, and should make allowance for conduct towards Mrs Dyce Sombre which, in all probability, may never be experienced again, inasmuch as he is determined never to cohabit with her. The object of keeping him under the special control of the Court of Chancery was (so Lord Lyndhurst informed Lord Combermere) the protection of Mrs Dyce Sombre. This might be obtained by a deed of separation, which Colonel Dyce Sombre would at any time sign, and find security for his abstaining from, in any way, molesting Mrs Dyce Sombre, to whom a liberal allowance would be given... The undersigned know of no person more careful of his money, and more capable of managing his affairs, than Colonel D. Sombre.[41]

Soon afterwards, Trevelyan signed his own letter to Cottenham, repeating his earlier assessment that Dyce Sombre's actions were 'mainly attributed to the excitement caused by the remarkable contrast between his Asiatic habits of mind and the new situation in which he was placed' and that he was sane.[42] These influential authors clearly expected their prominence and prestige to sway the Lord Chancellor personally to reverse his official judgment.

Cottenham, rather than bow to this private lobbying, openly revealed and then condemned it from the bench as 'most irregular and improper..., of a character unexampled, I hope, in the history of this Court..., calculated to divert the course of justice'. While Cottenham deemed the letters 'high contempt', given the social eminence of the signatories and Combermere's distinguished war record, Cottenham only scolded rather than prosecuted the authors.[43] Frightened, Lord Shrewsbury apologised in writing to the Lord Chancellor, claiming he signed the letter in haste, out of deference to his peers, without reading it carefully or appreciating fully the implications of such a private communication to the Lord Chancellor about an on-going case.

Inadvertently adding further evidence of the irregularity of his side, once back in Paris, Dyce Sombre also wrote a personal letter to the Lord Chancellor naïvely documenting his unconventional agreement with Dr Mahon and repeating his extensive accusations against Sir Richard Jenkins.[44] Further, he accused Committee of the Estate Larkins of embezzlement. According to Dyce Sombre's careful calculations, his annual income should have been £16,000 (plus the £4,000 that Mary Anne received and £1,000 he provided the Sardhana pensioners) but he only received £7,000. He demanded that Cottenham tell him 'where does the rest go?' Coming at about the same time as the letter from Combermere and his friends, all this clearly offended rather than persuaded Cottenham.

Unabashed, Dyce Sombre also wrote personally to Queen Victoria, repeating his offer of six years earlier, that 'I do not consider myself entitled to claims [against the East India Company for Badshahpur and the Sardhana armaments] now, as having been made over to Your

Majesty by me'. Triumphantly, he also sent her his latest private medical report 'trusting that Your Majesty will condescend to read it'.[45] He also sent copies of this favourable report to Prime Minister Lord Russell, the current First Lord of the Admiralty, and his earlier acquaintance as Governor General, Lord Auckland, seeking their personal influence and intervention in his case.[46] All these dignitaries declined involvement.

Further, that same January, Mahon, in Dyce Sombre's name, petitioned for supercedas, the fifth such petition. In this instance, Mahon primarily evoked the permanent authority of the six British physicians who had recently examined Dyce Sombre. He also pleaded with the Lord Chancellor that such an unusually rapid reconsideration was deserving of the Lord Chancellor's leniency since a Chancery Lunatic, like an infant, was an incompetent entrusted to the care of the Crown and should not be held to all the formal conventions of the court. From Dyce Sombre's complaining letter to the Lord Chancellor, however, Cottenham knew Mahon had only a limited time left in his contingency contract with Dyce Sombre and also had full charge of Dyce Sombre's legal affairs.

Even some doctors had become wary of participating in this increasingly messy and well-publicised matter. In February 1849, Mahon asked four leading British physicians, Drs Seymour, Forbes Winslow, Lawrence (of Bethlehem Hospital), and Thomas Harrington Brett, to travel to Paris and examine Dyce Sombre. The first two declined doing so 'without obtaining the authority of the Court of Chancery for the investigation', which Mahon could not provide. The more compliant Drs Lawrence and Brett, however, agreed, pocketed the handsome expense account and consulting fee from Mahon, and provided supportive affidavits.[47]

Meanwhile, Prinsep engaged himself actively in monitoring the ongoing hearings on this latest petition. He also advised Dyce Sombre to follow fully and exactly the guidance of Mahon 'who has worked and is working with great zeal and effort... You are bound in honour therefore to do nothing except in concert with him, till he fails, which I hope he won't.'[48] Prinsep warned Dyce Sombre not to write anything further to the newspapers, dignitaries, or the Lord Chancellor since 'your opponents are looking out for ground of cavil, wherever they could find it; being driven to their wits' ends, especially just now, by not knowing how to meet the report and affidavits of the six first-rate physicians who have certified in your favour'. Dyce Sombre accepted this, reportedly confiding 'it was now incumbent on him not to allow himself to be carried away by his feelings, as what in others would not be considered insanity would be thought, or looked upon, as insanity in him'.[49] Prinsep, Mahon, and Dyce Sombre, however, were overly optimistic.

The January 1849 petition—putatively from Dyce Sombre but actually from Mahon—prompted months of hearings. These were all chronicled in Britain, Australia, and America by the daily press and periodical magazines, including various letters to the editor from the several sides.[50] In opposing this petition, Bethell raised, virtually for the first time, the argument that Dyce Sombre's condition arose from a physiological as well as moral cause, an 'inflammation of the brain' brought on by his 'life of the grossest licentiousness'.[51] On their part, Dyce Sombre's lawyers tried to recast the entire conflict as marital. They demonstrated that he had acted with even more 'eccentricities' and 'violence' before his marriage than after, so he had not changed and Mary Anne should have known what she was marrying.[52] Further, his alienation from her resulted from 'a mere matter of caprice... of [lost] love and affection [which] was not deemed by the law any proof of insanity'.[53]

Finally, on 20 April 1849, the Lord Chancellor delivered his precedent-setting judgment.[54] While the latest arguments made by leading British physicians indeed gave him pause to reconsider, he decided to ignore them since medical experts were capable of contradictions, easily bought, and unhelpful to jurists: 'I have seen enough of professional [medical] opinions to be aware that in matters of doubt, on which the best constituted and most informed minds may differ, there is no difficulty in obtaining medical opinions on either side of the question'. He both rejected the latest medical theories of Drs Paris, Mayo, and Morison that delusion was not proof of insanity and further scolded them for interfering in legal matters beyond their ken: 'When they tell me that notwithstanding there is delusion, the mind is sound, they appear to involve themselves in a contradiction; and I think they overstepped the duty they undertook when they presumed to give advice to me...' Additionally, the Lord Chancellor deduced that Dyce Sombre could not logically both be sane—as claimed by the petition—and also simultaneously request the leniency graciously extended by courts to a lunatic. Further, the Lord Chancellor took as strong evidence that Dyce

Sombre was 'reckless' with his fortune both his £10,000 contingency contract with Mahon (twice entered into) and also Dyce Sombre's offers of bribes to politicians, doctors Southey and Bright, and to Cottenham's own wife. He further expressly lauded Mary Anne's virtue and condemned with 'high reprobation' Combermere and his associates for their contemptible private lobbying and letters.

After much courtroom drama and reciprocal accusations among the various principal and supporting parties, the lawyers for Mary Anne, Solaroli, and Troup (supported inadvertently by Dyce Sombre's own letter to the Lord Chancellor) had convinced Cottenham that Mahon, not Dyce Sombre, lay behind this renewed petition.[55] Cottenham argued that if Dyce Sombre was not himself being assessed, but rather this paid medical advisor's constructed case, then the entire judicial process had been perverted by Mahon, who acted to 'plunder' Dyce Sombre. The Lord Chancellor later refused to permit Dyce Sombre's several lawyers to be paid out of his estate for their work on this latest petition, directing them to get their money from Mahon instead.[56]

Concluding that a higher standard of proof was requisite to overturn a Lunacy Commission than was necessary to establish one in the first place, Lord Chancellor Cottenham disallowed this fifth petition for supercedas. Nonetheless, he ended by encouraging Dyce Sombre himself, rather than his rapacious mercenary agent Mahon, to petition the court again in future: 'I have... one piece of advice to give Mr Dyce Sombre: he must not think the door is shut against him because this petition is dismissed. Any application made by himself shall be carefully attended to, and as soon as it can safely be done, the Commission shall be superseded. The only operation of the Commission now is to protect the capital of his property.'[57] His judgment left Dyce Sombre in the anomalous *status quo ante*: arrestable as mentally incompetent if he reentered English territory and legally incompetent to manage his property but fully competent to use his income (after deductions for Mary Anne and other items) as he saw fit, to live in freedom outside England, and to draw up his own future petition for supercedas. Indeed, Cottenham would hear much more from Dyce Sombre in future.

Living, Writing, and Publishing on the Continent

Despite his bruising battles in London and the disappointment at Cottenham's latest decision, Dyce Sombre remained impatient to regain his status as sane and to recover full control over his fortune. Taking literally Cottenham's advice of 20 April 1849 to petition for supercedas himself, Dyce Sombre wrote eleven days later to Shadwell ordering for him to compose such a sixth petition on his behalf. Immediately on receipt of this directive, Shadwell diplomatically replied that such a rapid reapplication was not 'prudent... it would hardly be respectful to his Lordship' and would 'injure you in his Lordship's estimation'. He advised, Dyce Sombre should 'only live quietly and respectably for a few months' to build up his case again. Instead, Dyce Sombre wrote Cottenham directly (9 May), sending him this correspondence with Shadwell and asking the Lord Chancellor's personal advice on how to proceed now. Receiving no satisfaction from Cottenham, Dyce Sombre wrote Shadwell again (25 May), this time directing him to petition the Lord Chancellor for permission to come to England and examine his financial accounts personally, asserting that Larkins was defrauding him. Again, Shadwell urged Dyce Sombre that this would not be a judicious demand at present.

Frustrated on this front, Dyce Sombre nonetheless continued to try to control his fortune forever. His earlier will (written 10 May 1843 while he was first confined in Hanover Lodge) had left the vast bulk of his estate to endow 'Sumroo's College' in Sardhana but Sir James Clark had prevented it from being witnessed. Further, Dyce Sombre's legal competence as 'sound in mind' to write such a will had been highly contestable. Six years later, while last in London, Dyce Sombre had discussed with Prinsep how he might draw up a legally binding will, lest he die intestate. Naïvely, Dyce Sombre asked Prinsep if a basic, pre-printed form would do.[58] Instead, Prinsep directed him to his own skilled solicitor, Lawrence Desborough, Sr, who began the long process of drafting an iron-clad will according to Dyce Sombre's complex situation, strongly-held (but inconstant) specifications, and sincere wish to fulfill the late Begum's intentions as much as he could.[59] But they had awaited Cottenham's judgment before proceeding to complete it, since, had that judgment overturned the Lunacy Commission, Dyce Sombre's legal competence to contract a will would have been resolved.

After Cottenham again frustrated Dyce Sombre's hopes in April 1849, he worked in Paris with the younger partner, Lawrence Desborough, Jr, to discover a way for him to write a legal will anyway. They spent much time drafting and revising it so as to make it reflect Dyce Sombre's current intentions. They also decided that it would be legal if witnessed by three prominent physicians who would attest to his sanity at the time of signing.

On 25 June 1849, Dyce Sombre finally concluded this, his final will and testament.[60] In it, he again left most of his wealth to create and endow 'Sumroo's College... for higher classes of natives of India, without any distinction of Religion, to qualify them for holding public and other situations of trust'. The students were to be admitted between the ages of 7 and 12. This time, however, he left the East India Company's Chairman and Deputy Chairman *ex-officio* as the College Trustees.

As evidence of Dyce Sombre's deep and continuing knowledge of the precise details of the people and property left behind in India, his will directed the particular distribution of his many buildings and parcels of land in Sardhana, Delhi, Meerut, Agra, and elsewhere, and also endowed the considerable pensions by name to his family's scores of retainers still there. Before her death, the Begum had intended pensions for some seventy-six such households. While the East India Company had promised (but failed) to continue most of these pensions, Dyce Sombre had himself been paying them out of his own income. In this will, Dyce Sombre endowed those pensions and also set aside another quarter million rupees for his own dependents. Replacing himself as trustee of further 262,500 Rupee endowments established earlier by the Begum for the Catholic church and clerical college, Dyce Sombre named whoever was the highest Catholic functionary there. He also endowed a fund as for the Sardhana 'blind, lame, or indigent... without any distinction of caste or religion'. Literally dedicating himself to Sardhana and the Begum, he directed that his heart be embalmed in a silver case and placed adjacent to the Begum's sepulcher in the magnificent church they had constructed, while the rest of his body be buried in the Sardhana Christian cemetery, facing south-east, under a bronze cross surmounted by a death's head.

In the first version of this will, Mary Anne received his jewellry, use of the Delhi Chandni Chawk mansion, and other properties in India, while his sister Ann received the interest from £2,000, but Georgiana received nothing. A codicil of 13 August 1849, however, disinherited Mary Anne and both his sisters entirely, revoking his earlier gifts including his marriage settlement for her and 230,000 Rupee trusts for them. Dyce Sombre also rewarded several of his British supporters with £5,000, including bestowing £1,000 on Combermere's youngest child and still unmarried daughter, Meliora Stapleton-Cotton.

Significantly, to ensure that even his enemies on the East India Company's Court of Directors would fight vigorously in support of this will, he assigned to its luminaries a total of £48,500 immediately plus substantial pensions. Specifically, should the will be found valid, he would leave £500 each to Sir Richard Jenkins' two daughters and £1,000 each personally to the 24 current Directors plus the next 6 incoming ones. In addition, the President of the Board of Control and the Chairman of the Directors would annually each receive another £1,000 and the Deputy Chairman another £500. As executors, who would receive £5,000 each cash plus £2,500 each of the Begum's jewellry, he named Prinsep, Mountstuart Elphinstone (former Governor of Bombay), and Sir Henry Miers Elliot (whom he had known as Collector in Meerut), all distinguished men with long careers in the upper ranks of the Company. He thus cleverly secured the Directors' personal interest in directing the Company to deploy its formidable financial and political corporate resources in defence of his will (as they would do, following his death, at the Company's considerable cost for years to come). Further, implicitly, should this will be sustained, the huge lawsuits against the East India Company over Badshahpur and the Sardhana armaments would become part of his estate and the Directors could cancel them. Thus, Dyce Sombre (and many other Indians) had very mixed attitudes toward the Company's Directors, both regarding them as arbitrary oppressors and also legal protectors.

As witnesses to this will, Dyce Sombre and Desborough selected three doctors of unimpeachable probity and professional prominence who had examined him over the years: Drs Daniel Joseph McCarthy, Charles Shrimpton, and Joseph Francis Olliffe (with Dr George Gabriel Sigmond replacing the absent Olliffe for witnessing the codicil). These doctors all swore on oath that Dyce Sombre was perfectly sound of mind and body at the time of signing.[61] This procedure raised unprecedented legal issues about whether someone, still legally a lunatic in England (but legally sane in France), could have a sane interval sufficient for him to sign his will on French soil, and, if so, who had the authority to declare this will valid.

Even as he prepared and signed this will and codicil, much of Dyce Sombre's time from March to August 1849 was also spent in compiling his massive 591 page book: *Mr Dyce Sombre's Refutation*. He had his mathematics tutor, Professor Montucci, do much of the anonymous editorial work but Dyce Sombre supplied the specific documents he wanted included, inserted his own footnotes and commentary on them, as well as identified passages from the original texts that he wanted deleted or otherwise modified. The arguments Dyce Sombre made in *Refutation* reflected his thinking at the time of its completion, 25 August 1849.

The book consisted of an autobiographical sourcebook that justified all he had been contending over his years in Europe. Dyce Sombre selectively narrated his heroic family history, particularly that of Reinhardt and the Begum, building his case for his own distinguished lineage and respectable youth. He openly declared what his own lawyers had been consistently denying: 'calling me a native of India does not annoy me in the least, but I only wish it to be understood: I was certainly born in India, but I consider myself not Indian, which according to the late meaning of the word, required one of the parents of the party to have been entirely native of India. My grandfather was a Scotchman; my father, his son, was married to a lady whose grandfather was a German; her mother was half French; this therefore could not be taken either in law or in reality to be the case of a native of India.'[62]

Much of the text consisted of key selections from the correspondence, many affidavits, and other documents that he had accumulated during his many struggles in Chancery. Despite his own understanding of their significance, not all of the included documents actually advanced his cause for an outside reader. Nor does a comparison with the originals show that he was scrupulous about including all passages from all of these documents. Indeed, Dyce Sombre's own footnotes contest some of the evidence that he included. Overall, he conceded none of his long-held contentions: he was totally sane; he had been unjustly persecuted by almost everyone around him, particularly the immoral Mary Anne, Solaroli, and two Lord High Chancellors; Georgiana was illegitimate; and that these documents and his own logic would convince all readers of his ultimate vindication and the unmitigated evil of his persecutors. He also expressed his frustration: 'Dead men are never heard, otherwise they would be taken for ghosts; and such is the case with Chancery Lunatics. I am a dead man, according to the existing law.'[63]

The most passionately phrased passages come in *Refutation*'s twelve page conclusion, which Montucci later admitted writing anonymously in order to articulate his own understanding of Dyce Sombre's position as representative of the unjust treatment of all legal lunatics by the British judicial and medical systems. It begins:

My own painful example must convince every impartial mind, that personal liberty, so jealously guarded in England by the law, is liable to be infringed with the greatest ease on the mere plea of lunacy... The mere word of a physician, supported no doubt by petitions and affidavits, was sufficient to restrain me from the exercise of my liberty, me, who had committed no crime nor illegality, without so much as a question being addressed to me by any responsible person in office, while a thief, a pickpocket or a burglar cannot be kept 24 hours in custody, even when caught in the act, without being examined by a magistrate![64]

After many stirring passages, the book concludes:

Thus it is, that by the combined efforts of intrigue, ignorance and misrepresentation, and by the defective state of the English law as regards lunatics, I am debarred from personal liberty in my mother-country, the management of my property is withheld from me, while it is wasted through negligence and cupidity, and myself cast out as far as possible from the society of reasonable men, a lunatic among the sane, by the mere dictum of a few men who openly profess to set their wisdom against that of the rest of the world.

And all this in a country which prides itself on being the only one in the world where personal liberty is fairly understood, where a pickpocket or murderer will meet with all the tenderness of the law, but where, alas! there is no law for the presumed lunatic, when there are interested parties whose wishes are that he should remain so.[65]

This autobiographical account by a legal lunatic (in England although not in France) piqued the interest of many, including not only his legal opponents and supporters but also the popular press throughout the British Empire, including the *Nelson Examiner and New Zealand Chronicle* as well as professional journals for alienists, including *Journal of Psychological Medicine and Mental Pathology*.[66]

Before Dyce Sombre published this massive and, he felt assured, revelatory and persuasive tome, however, he uncharacteristically paused to consult the solicitor he had at hand. As he received the proofs of this book from the printer, Joseph Privitera, Dyce Sombre passed on some of them to solicitor Desborough, who was currently in Paris completing the will. Even on the basis of this partial reading, Desborough strongly recommended against publication as libellous and unhelpful in persuading the world, and the Lord Chancellor in particular, of Dyce Sombre's sanity at this crucial time of the signing of his will.[67] Temporarily heeding this advice, Dyce Sombre instead turned his attention to an even more libellous personal attack dishonouring Solaroli in particular, a man he thought of as 'the Italian Brigand' working conspiratorially with his many enemies, and even his alleged friends, including by bribing some of his lawyers.[68]

Dyce Sombre himself wrote a pamphlet asserting a catalogue of accusations against Solaroli.[69] Among other charges, this pamphlet claimed: young Solaroli had murdered his father; he had served as a cook and a footman before fleeing to India; after Solaroli had reached Sardhana, he had treacherously wormed his way into the misplaced trust of the Begum, but proved himself incompetent, corrupt, and sadistic once in office there; since Solaroli's wife, Georgiana, was only the daughter of a concubine by George Dyce, thus Dyce Sombre's illegitimate half-sister, she and her husband had no legal claim on the Begum's or Dyce Sombre's estate despite their false pretensions. The pamphlet concluded that Solaroli was currently abusing Georgiana's gratuitous but generous gifts from the Begum and from Dyce Sombre in order to buy his way into the nobility, army, and court of the King of Sardinia (where Solaroli had by that point risen to the ranks of Baron and Major General).

Dyce Sombre then paid Montucci to translate this pamphlet into French and Italian. While Montucci had been largely persuaded by the material in *Refutation*, he saw evidence in this pamphlet that Dyce Sombre 'was credulous', easily subject to manipulation by designing people.[70] Nonetheless, Montucci completed the translations. Dyce Sombre was foresightful enough to keep the scurrilous pamphlet anonymous. He had a hundred copies in each of the three languages produced. His usual printer, Joseph Privitera, would not accept this job but M. Emile Briére did so, soon coming to regret this undertaking.

In order to do the most damage to Solaroli's burgeoning career and personal reputation, Dyce Sombre traveled to Italy in Autumn 1849. There, he carefully placed this libelous pamphlet throughout the hotels through which he knew Solaroli would pass. Solaroli was currently on duty escorting the funeral cortège of the late King Charles Albert, so his exact itinerary was public knowledge. Dyce Sombre's ordered his valet to place one copy of the pamphlet between each plate in the public dining room of Hotel Feder in Turin, Sardinia, for example, just before Solaroli arrived there.[71]

Solaroli took this slander badly. He successfully sued M. Emile Briére, the pamphlet's printer, in Paris, but he could not gain a conviction against Dyce Sombre himself, even though Brière testified Dyce Sombre had been the anonymous author.[72] Further, Solaroli only received a token 200 Francs in damages, only 1% of what he sought (and that on the technicality that the French-language edition pamphlet had not been registered with the French government). In addition, however, the printer was sentenced to publish repudiations of all the pamphlet's libels in six French newspapers of Solaroli's selection. The printer also lost out when Dyce Sombre's cheque for the production costs, 500 Francs, bounced. Nor did Dyce Sombre reimburse the printer for the court and retraction costs of 1,500 Francs more.[73] Dyce Sombre defended his actions in private letters to his friends and lawyers as an issue of freedom of expression, that Solaroli had offended him, and that all the improbable charges were true.

On his return to Paris, Dyce Sombre decided to proceed with the publication of his magnum opis, *Refutation*, despite Desborough's advice.[74] He had the entire manuscript proof-read, with an errata page added to correct typographical flaws. Then, he paid the printer, Joseph Privitera, 4,000 francs to make 2,000 copies of *Mr. Dyce Sombre's Refutation of the Charges of Lunacy in the Court of Chancery* (Paris: Dyce Sombre, 1849). Over the next nine months, Dyce Sombre made strenuous efforts to distribute this book extensively, sending copies to various officials in England and elsewhere around the world. For instance, he dispatched 250 copies for free distribution by Galignani's Subscription Library in Paris and another 250 copies to the Oriental Club in London so each member could have one gratis. Solaroli did what he could to suppress the book, including successfully threatening to sue the Oriental Club should they actually distribute it. Nonetheless, *Refutation* was received by people and institutions far and wide and advertised by Dyce Sombre in prominent newspapers as well. A score of copies still exist, enshrined in libraries in Britain and the United States.[75]

In receipt of a comfortable income but barred from any resolution of his legal status, Dyce Sombre amused himself in other ways both in Paris and also elsewhere on the continent. At some point, he acquired two huge half-bred Newfoundland dogs, which some visitors found overwhelming (after his death these dogs would become the newsworthy objects of complex judicial cases, with cross-charges of dog-napping and breach of contract).[76] He read widely, keeping a substantial library in English, Persian, and Urdu poetry and prose with him, even during his travels. Apparently giving up on distinguishing among European women on the streets, he solicited females promiscuously until he happened upon one who would sell him sex.[77] He also collected diverse works of art, reflecting his particular tastes.

In Paris, where he spent most of his time, he adorned his rented apartments with works of unconventional art, including erotic ones, that he found attractive although many visitors found them fascinatingly offensive. A locksmith, Jean Francois Ranchet, whom he patronised, was simultaneously proud that he was summoned to serve a 'Prince' but also disconcerted by what he considered Dyce Sombre's especially indelicate taste in art and behaviour. In particular, this locksmith found shockingly memorable an 30 cm. by 46 cm. oil-painting in Dyce Sombre's bedroom. Five years later, this Parisian artisan still recalled this art 'of the most disgusting kind, viz. a naked woman [lying]... and a man in an ecclesiastical dress, with spectacles on, inspecting her private parts, the woman's legs being stretched open'.[78] Several physicians whom Dyce Sombre hired to examine his mental condition and then swear to his sanity remarked strongly (but shrank from describing) another erotic figure that he displayed prominently on his sitting room mantel. While these doctors concurred the sculpture was remarkable, one described it as a 'filthy piece', while another conceded 'as a work of art it is of distinguished merit, and though not fit to be left about on a chimney-piece, it is probably to be found in many collections'.[79] Paris abounded, however, in differences over avant-garde and erotic art so Dyce Sombre's personal aesthetic tastes were not at issue, although they certainly affected his personal relationships there.

Dyce Sombre also collected popular art. One of his pastimes was selecting, cutting out, and pasting into his large scrapbooks etchings of aristocrats and celebrities of the day, many of whom he knew personally, from the *Illustrated London News* and comparable journals [many of the illustrations in this book are reproduced from the same source].[80] Since his scrapbooks have, to our knowledge, not survived, we cannot assess how his selection and arrangement reflected his attitudes toward these noblemen and women.

Another of Dyce Sombre's constant activities was collecting affidavits to his sanity. For example, he asked Madame Sophie de Grefuille, the landlady of the apartments where he lived periodically for years in Paris, for such an affidavit. She had willingly provided one on 10 July

1847, denying ever seeing in him 'the least symptom of mental aberration' rather swearing: he was 'a man enjoying quite fully his intellectual faculties'.[81] Dyce Sombre included this affidavit in his book
Refutation. Yet, three years later, this same woman provided another
paid affidavit to Dyce Sombre's opponents, repudiating her earlier one
and instead attesting that Dyce Sombre is 'quite mad, and out of his
senses, and that he is even at certain times a very dangerous lunatic'.[82]
In this latter testimony, she catalogued his sins including striking her
and her servants, bringing women 'even of the lowest class' into his
rooms, urinating on her carpets, drinking, gambling, breaking her
furniture, and owing her money. Dyce Sombre behaviour may have
changed over these years but perhaps a more significant explanation of
these contradictory affidavits stemmed from the fact that, as Madame
Grefuille admitted, Dyce Sombre compensated her for the first and his
opponents for the second affidavit.[83] Dyce Sombre, indeed, while con-
ceding that he had broken furniture, dismissed her second affidavit in
a private letter to Prinsep as 'from the Landlady where I have lived for
the last two years, and who was advised to impose upon me for broken furniture, and who also has given affidavits in my favor before...
of course 10 francs each would produce hundreds more like them'.[84]
Yet, the many agents for the various lawyers complained about the rising cost of obtaining such affidavits, specifically including those from
Madame Grefuille.[85] Purchasable as such affidavits were, they became
legal evidence once submitted to the Lord Chancellor, with every
phrase pored over, parsed, and cited by the respective lawyers as precise evidence of Dyce Sombre current condition.

Undisputed was consistent and continuing evidence from several
parties that Dyce Sombre frequently indulged himself with prostitutes,
contracting various venereal diseases. Strikingly, he trained some of
them in the full-body therapeutic massage, shampooing, that he desired
and other Parisians found incomprehensibly deviant, including some
of Dyce Sombre's servants whom he also directed to do it, as well as
visitors to his apartments who inadvertently observed it.[86] Since his
uniquely infamous situation made him game for scrutiny and assessment by everyone around him, people's attitudes toward the 'oldest
profession' and the public display of indulgence in it by a rich gentleman, were reflected in their respective moral judgments.

Similarly, Dyce Sombre's sartorial practices also proved controversial, whatever he did. When he dressed according to European high

fashion, some bystanders stared at him for a costume they considered incongruous with his complexion. Even one of Dyce Sombre's sympathetic doctors characterised his anomalous public appearance as 'that of a corpulent Asiatic, dressed in the fashion of a young English gentleman'.[87] When Dyce Sombre instead incorporated items of Indian clothing as he occasionally did, for instance, an 'Indian cap embroidered with gold', this also drew critical attention from passersby as disharmonious with the European dress around him.[88] Unlike Dyce Sombre, some other Indian gentlemen in Europe during this period wore wholly Indian-style clothing but this collected crowds, whose mass blocked their progress and even drove them to refuge in shops (even some of these shops had their windows broken by the press of the gawkers).[89] Some Muslim Indians tried using Ottoman costumes, considering this a cultural half-way house. Dyce Sombre, however, rightly felt himself being scrutinised hostilely and, given his notorious career, commented upon conspiratorially, by the surrounding society no matter what he wore.

In his apartments, he often relaxed in a long-tailed shirt, especially in the hot Parisian summer, but this shocked visitors or deliverymen when Dyce Sombre opened the door wearing only that and no trousers, or nothing at all; a wine dealer recalled his own response: 'out came Mr Dyce Sombre as absolutely naked as when he was born. I was positively frightened at the sight of his large swarthy figure. I exclaimed, "You blackguard!"'[90] Further, the degree of acceptable public urination and defecation by males varied across classes and societies, with customs differing in Britain, the Continent, Turkey, Egypt, and India. Several Europeans condemned Dyce Sombre for practising this to a degree they found excessive, considering the context and his status. Some European servants, after leaving his employ, testified critically about his personal hygiene.[91] Again, Dyce Sombre dismissed such negative affidavits as 'none of them are of the least importance, not one of them being from a gentleman or a lady—one is from a discharged servant, who had given more than one before in my favor'.[92]

The Paris police also found Dyce Sombre troublesome but profitable. In addition to public spats with men of his own class like Ventura, he also became entangled in scuffles with lower class people, including cab drivers and street-walkers. As did most wealthy gentlemen, he took items on credit from shops and art galleries. However, when Dyce Sombre later refused to pay, the purveyor had to either physically repossess, have policemen seize, or bring small-claims-court cases.[93] Further, given his muddled financial situation, sometimes his cheques bounced or his promissory notes were refused because Larkins or Mahon unexpectedly repudiated them. However, for the cost of a generous tip to the local gendarme or an often substantial fine at the local police station or court, he escaped any more meaningful punishment. His vast fortune and his sense of his apparent inevitable inability to gain acceptance by certain groups in society combined to free him of the normative constraints of bourgeois society. As he philosophically concluded: 'Where would I have been today if I had not money to encounter all these unjust acts? But they say misfortunes never come alone and so I find them.'[94] London, Paris, and the continent generally, had whole sets of wealthy and anomalous men, untied to immediate family, who indulged in a comparable bohemian lifestyle.

To some in high Parisian society, Dyce Sombre's exotic appeal faded over time. He never achieved the fluency in the French language that marked a worthy resident of Paris.[95] Instead, he tended to circulate among the British expatriate community there, where many noblemen and women had enemies among the same political factions in London that he did. Some disingenuously swore that Dyce Sombre never gambled or became intoxicated or the least loud; many continued to invite him to their social affairs, seeing him made more distinctive by his reputation. One Anglo-Irish gentlelady, the daughter of a clergyman, wrote:

[He was] uniformly received and treated as a man of sound mind, the same as any other visitor, excepting only that his history, which was well known, made him an object of more curiosity. It was a matter of notoriety that he was declared Lunatic in England, but he was not so considered here. He was peculiar, as an Asiatic in colour; he was reserved, rather absent, and might be considered eccentric, nothing more—rather odd: his habits and manners were out of the ordinary style, but no one, I believe, ever thought him more than that.[96]

Many leading British expatriates in Paris swore affidavits that concurred.

Occasionally, Mary Anne herself traveled to Paris, but secretly under the name 'Mrs Sinclair'. In her interviews with men who knew Dyce Sombre there, she eagerly sought information about his condition and doings. As one of Dyce Sombre's doctors, Olliffe, recalled, during a routine medical consultation:

She talked very much about Abd-el-Kader, for whose liberty she expressed great anxiety. She then asked me if I had heard of another celebrated character, Mr Dyce Sombre. I answered in the affirmative... She interrupted me by saying, 'I may as well tell you before you go further that I am his Wife,' and she requested that I would make her a promise not to divulge that, as she was remaining in strict incognito.[97]

She continued to do what she could to reestablish her personal relationship with Dyce Sombre, although her amateur detective work produced little of help to her.

Meanwhile, Mary Anne's high-society life in London flourished as she regained her reputation as impulsive, despite her advance toward middle age. The controversial Sir Charles Napier, just back from annexing and ruling Sindh, boasted in August 1848 how, in Brighton with the Duke of Wellington, poet Samuel Rogers, and other dignitaries, 'after dinner Mrs Dyce Sombre came in, and a very agreeable madcap she is, with the most beautiful voice I ever heard, I could listen to her singing forever: she sung the '*Beau*' delightfully'.[98] Benjamin Disraeli savoured a similar evening with her, Wellington, and Rogers the next year at a select soirée, complete with her singing, in her suite in the Clarendon where she was living with her aging father.[99]

Mary Anne's Trustees (Lords Combermere and Lowther, recently retitled Lonsdale) and Larkins sought, not always successfully, to maneuver her wedding settlement and the rest of Dyce Sombre's estate through the challenging new world of investment capitalism. Late in 1849, for example, their speculation in London and Birmingham, Great Western, and Grand Junction railroad stocks hit a significant snag when they had to meet substantial margin calls or lose their investments entirely. They proposed selling £16,000 of other stock in Dyce Sombre's estate in order to meet these calls. Even as the Lord Chancellor was ruling on the subtleties and contradictions of Dyce Sombre's mental condition, he also had to supervise such intricate investment decisions. From his bench, he chided Larkins and the trustees of Mary Anne's settlement for not selling these railway stocks for a profit four years earlier as he himself had advised.[100] Now, Cottenham caviled with the lawyers for Dyce Sombre's estate as to whether the consequent loss would be £3,000 (as he initially estimated), or only £670 (as the trustees hoped), finally supposing that the loss would be £2,000. Since the figures were beyond Cottenham's expertise, all these complex accountings were referred to the Master of

Rolls to determine how much of Dyce Sombre's money had really been lost by this mismanagement.

During Dyce Sombre's periods of aimless life in Paris, he considered his future. If he could only clear himself to live in England, he unrealistically confided to Prinsep in March 1849, he 'would not mind taking a Seat in Parliament' again.[101] As things stood, however, he feared that if he returned to India, or travelled anywhere else in the British empire, he would be seized. As he stated in August 1849, for example, having just completed his *Refutation* and written his will but having to wait before repetitioning the Lord Chancellor again, 'I am heartily sick of these proceedings & remaining so long in one place, without having anything to do'.[102] He made short pleasure trips to resorts in Belgium and the German states. While he was impressed by the quality of his fellow visitors, he nonetheless felt anomalous in each of the spas he toured: 'there were not many of my sort there, so I did not stay long'.[103] Thus, he dreamed up more distant travels once he was at liberty to travel freely. He planned a journey across Turkey and Iran to India.[104] As his guide and travelling companion, he offered £500 to Joseph Wolff, the impoverished but still celebrated explorer, a former Jew and former Catholic who was currently Anglican Vicar of Ile Brewers in Somerset. Dyce Sombre knew Wolff, having hosted him in Sardhana in 1835. Although the money would have doubled Wolff's meager assets, he detested travel for its own sake rather than for evangelism and declined.[105] In anticipation of Dyce Sombre's arrival in India, he tried to elevate his reputation there by getting his contentions published in newspapers. But editors largely refused to comply.

To accelerate his legal case by bringing his plight directly to the attention of Parliament, in August 1849 Dyce Sombre had personally composed a twelve page pamphlet entitled *Petition to Lords Temporal and Spiritual and to the Commons* (Paris: Dyce Sombre, 1850). This, he felt confident, 'will shame the Govt... As for the pamphlet... no one can find fault with it—it is so very simple even the Hon'ble Court of Directors can not say much against it tho' I have not spared them as to their intentions... taking all in all it is enough to hang 20 Chancellors instead of 2.'[106] But not until nine months later, in April 1850, after he had submitted his next petition for reexamination in London before the Lord Chancellor, did he have Joseph Privitera print 1,200 copies: 1,000 he sent to the Houses of Parliament and the rest to other influential men in London.[107] This *Petition* extracted material from his

Refutation, occasionally referring for further elaboration to specific pages in that book. Taken alone, it was not a particularly coherent argument; overall, it and *Refutation* evidently did not persuade any in Parliament to alter their opinions concerning Dyce Sombre's sanity.

Sixth and Final Petition for Supercedas in London

Early in 1850, Dyce Sombre finally convinced lawyer Shadwell to submit his sixth petition for supercedas to Cottenham, vowing to give this Chancery process one last chance before he appealed above the Lord Chancellor to the Queen's Privy Council.[108] Dyce Sombre felt tethered by the continuing irresolution of his case and need to remain near at hand for any sudden opportunity: 'I should wish to be out of Paris if I knew when I will be required [in London]. I hope everything will be finished before June, for I have a long journey before me, & I cannot avoid the snowy season before reaching the capital of Persia.' Yet, by late April, he despaired to Shadwell of much progress from Cottenham. At this time, Cottenham himself was on trial in the House of Lords for corruption, which raised rumours of his retirement. Nonetheless, Dyce Sombre despaired: 'I don't see any change of the Lord Chancellors sitting at Court for some time to come & I scarcely know what to do'.[109]

Lord Cottenham, however, did not have to face the next round of hearings about Dyce Sombre. On 27 May 1850, he abruptly resigned as Lord Chancellor, his health worn out, including in modest measure by Dyce Sombre's apparently interminable case. Cottenham's removal raised Dyce Sombre's hopes that he would receive a new and more sympathetic hearing under the next Lord Chancellor, whomever he might prove to be. After much uncertainty, Dyce Sombre received news that one of his old employees had been selected.

On 15 July 1850, Thomas Wilde, who had half-a-dozen years earlier been paid by Dyce Sombre to represent him, but then had been fired, took the Lord Chancellor's seat as Baron Truro. Wilde's colleagues attributed his elevation primarily to his late, second marriage to the Duke of Sussex's daughter.[110] Dyce Sombre, assuming that his past employment of Wilde would soon sway him favourably, over the next few weeks sent Wilde personally three separate packets of papers. Instead of expressing gratitude or surreptitious compliance as Dyce Sombre hoped, Wilde openly chided this personal approach as

Lord Chancellor Sir Thomas Wilde, Baron Truro

'unpleasant and improper' and never unsealed these packets.[111] Since Wilde was nonetheless required *ex-officio* to sit in judgment on Chancery Lunatic Dyce Sombre, Wilde had his Vice Chancellor, Sir James Lewis Knight-Bruce, join him in ruling on Dyce Sombre's sixth petition for supercedas.[112]

As another hopeful sign, Dyce Sombre's strong supporter, Prinsep, finally won election to the Court of Directors in August 1850, after many failed attempts. Dyce Sombre felt firmly that his ally was now in even more in a position to aid him.[113] Indeed, Prinsep became one of the most influential of the Directors and remained so well after Dyce Sombre's death. All this put him into renewed hopes of an early and positive resolution of his situation. Yet, it was a hope to be long frustrated since Wilde delayed ruling on Dyce Sombre's latest petition for seven months.

Anxious to travel yet fearing being away or out of touch too long, Dyce Sombre spent much of 1850 crisscrossing Europe. From Vienna, instead of going again to more distant Constantinople as he had intended, he circled down through Italy, keeping in regular communication with his advocates in London. When he reached Marseilles, an outbreak of cholera in Algiers dissuaded him from a planned north African tour.[114] Instead, he headed north, late in 1850, to Copenhagen, then to Stockholm and the royal city of Christiana (now called Oslo). Seeing larger significance in all that he did, he noted to several correspondents, 'by a strange coincidence I arrived at [Christiana] the last capital in Europe which I had not visited before, on the very day I left Sirdhana 14 years before (namely the 3rd October 1836)'.[115]

Meanwhile, lawyers for his opponents used Dyce Sombre's absence and the inevitable delays in communication as he travelled to suggest hypocritically 'there was great difficulty in ascertaining where the unfortunate lunatic now was. He had not been heard of for eight weeks, and it was a matter of doubt whether he was dead or alive, which of course had caused great anxiety.'[116] Only the eventual resumption of correspondence from Dyce Sombre revived unproductive but expensive sparring among the lawyers before the Lord Chancellor.

Dyce Sombre's case and many travails formed the basis for debate by lawyers, doctors, and diplomats globally. Some legal commentators regarded his dogged persistence as proof that the British legal system provided opportunities for falsely accused lunatics to regain their freedom. But few legal lunatics succeeded since most lacked Dyce Sombre's resources, especially his wealth and exceptional position outside of the actual power of the Lord Chancellor to confine and control him. But many commentators recognised the problems with the extant system that his case revealed. English doctor Forbes Winslow highlighted Dyce Sombre (whom he had personally declined to examine) in his article on the 'Defects of the English Law of Lunacy' in his influential *Journal of Psychological Medicine*. Further, others recognised how undependable was legally acceptable medical evidence. The *London Medical Recorder* editorialised, referring to Dyce Sombre, 'it is possible, by the aid of substantial fees, and the exertions of a clever legal man of business, to procure certificates that the person is sane, and that the facts upon which the other members of the family rely, are really not indications of insanity'.[117] Washington's *National Daily Intelligencer* and New York's *Journal of Commerce*, for example, both endorsed an essay by the American consul in Paris arguing that the legal value any of medical testimony was nil since 'Mr. Dyce Sombre, the Anglo-Indian nabob... had been uniformly pronounced *compos mentis* on this side of the Channel, and *non compos* on the other'.[118] Similarly, dozens of other newspapers globally frequently featured his case; the *Times* alone

311

would eventually publish more than one hundred often critical articles about him while the London *Satirist or, the Censor of the Times* published three dozen articles, which became increasingly sympathetic over time toward him and his plight.

As time went on, Dyce Sombre came to fear that his next hearing might be delayed further by extraneous events in London such as the elaborate festivities and ceremonies of the Great Imperial Exhibition ('The Crystal Palace'). He confided to Prinsep in January 1851: 'you rightly say that late the London season will commence and on account of the Exhibition (tho' I hope I will be allowed to see it for a week or two) but the Town will be crowded and perhaps the Lord Chancellor himself will not have time to sit at Court'.[119] Since Wilde still had not reached the point of scheduling Dyce Sombre's next examination, despite his unorthodox direct personal appeals and the more orthodox motions by his lawyers, Dyce Sombre made another loop across the continent in early 1851, touring through Germany before returning to Paris to await his long-anticipated London visit.

As the months rolled by, Dyce Sombre anxiously found Shadwell's frequent but inconsequential assurances ever less satisfactory: 'The 15th April has also passed by, and my case has not been heard, therefore I will stand it no longer'.[120] Dyce Sombre, to spur Shadwell on, threatened to expose his incompetence and irregular and unprofessional behaviour: 'unless you send me a satisfactory reply to this by return of post, I mean to publish copies of all your letters to me from January 1849 up to this period in one of the public papers which will I think not add much to your professional respectability'. Working for Dyce Sombre might be lucrative but it also entailed untoward menaces.

In Paris, Dyce Sombre also encountered celebrated women who lived as unconventionally as himself. Among them, Lola Montez (born Elizabeth Gilbert, later married as Mrs Thomas James) had a comparably notorious reputation. Dyce Sombre had known her mother and step-father, Elizabeth and Patrick Craigie, well in Sardhana, Meerut, and Calcutta. In May 1851, after she had been elevated to the Bavarian peerage as Countess Landsfeld and then had her brief bigamous marriage with the young and wealthy George Trafford Heald, Dyce Sombre took her out for a Paris dinner. Even he found her something of an implausibly constructed character:

You must have heard a great deal about Mrs James, or the Lolla Montès... but she is no more Mrs J. than I am Mr James, for you know I knew her mother

Lola Montez

and step-father, Major & Mrs Craigie, at Meerut; I therefore made my acquaintance with her, and asked her to dine with me. She... talked so foolishly about India, and her mother and step-father, that I soon found out that it was all a hoax; in fact, I ought to have known that from her looks, for she has a little idiocy in her looks... [T]he King of Bavaria... was obliged to abdicate the throne as a fool, for her sake. Then, you know, she married a Mr Heald, an officer of the Guards, a rich, foolish, young man. What kind of marriage that was, it was their affair to know, for her supposed husband was still alive. He has left her now too, and now she is living in the Rue du Faubourg St Honoré, gives soirées, and seems to be comfortable, as far as money goes, speaks Hindustani too, but receives all kind of society. I cannot make out who she is—beyond this, certainly the King of Bavaria was very fond of her, and still allows her £600 a-year.[121]

Significantly, in this assessment that Dyce Sombre wrote to Joseph Skinner, his mixed ancestry classmate from Meerut, he highlighted her boldness, chequered marital career, and current inscrutable identity and excessive pretensions. Rather than acknowledge their common characteristics, Dyce Sombre deprecated her as slightly idiotic and something of a fraud. Conversely, she in her (ghost-written) autobiography narrated a somewhat garbled account of Dyce Sombre's family.[122] At this point in her notorious career, Ms Montez was looking for yet another rich male patron; Dyce Sombre, however, did not find her as fascinating as some other men did.

Dyce Sombre's irregular lifestyle had been taking its toll on his enfeebled body. He was frequently impotent from his recurrent venereal diseases; as his regular doctor stated: 'Quite latterly he had ceased to possess the power of gratification. Vice at times, survives passion, but in his case it was disease.'[123] He lost the power to concentrate on one of his favorite pastimes: solving mathematical puzzles. Some friends noted a 'vacant stare' at times. After yet another rotten tooth was extracted, his gums proved incapable of mending.[124] In December 1850, following an evening of imbibing, he passed out while lounging before a blazing fire and blistered the soles of his feet. Over the early months of 1851, as he continued to wander Europe, these blisters suppurated.[125] Subsequently, infections appeared on his legs and persisted despite his prescribed special sulfur baths in his rooms. By mid-June 1851, doctors diagnosed Erysepelas (*Streptococcus* bacterial infection) and advised amputation of the worst of his diseased toes, but Dyce Sombre resisted surgery.[126]

As his health deteriorated badly, his sixth petition revived. Since the procedure by this point had become routine, all the contending lawyers made their usual arguments before agreeing that Dyce Sombre should be allowed safe passage to London for yet another rehearing.[127] The question of which doctors should examine him, however, proved particularly vexed.

Trying to secure a sympathetic, or at least neutral, panel, Dyce Sombre objected strenuously to the Lord Chancellor against 'those corrupt & lying physicians, Drs. Southey and Bright, who have so disgraced themselves in every examination they have made in my case'.[128] Unwilling to face Dyce Sombre's abuse again, Southey and Bright removed themselves from consideration. Dyce Sombre also objected to Sir James Clark, having no hope that anything he could do would convince Clark to reverse his long-held opinion.

Not until May 1851 did Wilde complete arrangements for Dyce Sombre to come and face reexamination.[129] As many popular newspapers and medical journals around the Anglophone world recounted, Wilde inclined toward approving Dyce Sombre's petition for supercedas. In open court, Wilde mocked as lawyerly tricks the heartrending pleadings of Mary Anne's lawyer, Bethell.[130] In particular, the new Lord Chancellor explicitly determined to give Dyce Sombre a fresh start by appointing doctors who had never examined him before and vowed not to consult their many court-appointed predecessors.[131] Finally, Wilde found two physicians, Henry Jeaffreson and Benjamin Guy Babington, who met his criteria and were willing to take on this complex and controversial case. Yet, Dyce Sombre vainly objected that Babington was hostile due to Dyce Sombre's past conflicts with his (inaccurately) supposed relatives, Charles Trevelyan and Thomas Babington Macaulay.[132] Wilde rejected Dyce Sombre's incorrect objection and sent on to Jeaffreson and Babington the vast collection of diagnoses, judgments, and supporting documents necessary for them to master prior to examining Dyce Sombre. Babington had published scholarship about India and brought Orientalist orientations along with his medical training.

Finally ready to face these new doctors, Dyce Sombre rushed from Paris to London despite his spreading infections and other debilities. He arrived on 30 May, settled into his usual Mivart's Hotel but was clearly very ill. Shadwell offered to summon Mary Anne but Dyce Sombre vociferously opposed this: 'Mrs Dyce Sombre! Why, Mr Shadwell, you must be out of your senses to propose such a thing. No, impossible… No! if all the money of the Begum were offered me, I would not see her. She is in a conspiracy; a deep conspiracy. No!'[133] Nonetheless, informed of his perilous condition, she wrote her last letter to him on 14 June: 'My Dearest Friendy, I hear you are ill, and write to say how much I am concerned, and if I can be of any use or comfort to you, I am ready at any moment to go to you. [My maidservant] Lake and myself are waiting close by, so that if you will see us, or either of us, now, please to send a verbal answer by the servant who takes this, and is waiting. Believe me, yr affectionate, M. A. Dyce Sombre.'[134]

Adamantly rejecting this overture, Dyce Sombre replied, 'Madam, Had you gone on and acted on those expressions of kindness which you now do… there would not have been any need for a separation. But it is too late now, and if you really consult my comfort and your own reputation, is what I have always advised you to look to, and that is to take a divorce. I remain, Madam, Dyce Sombre.[135] This was his final word to her in life.

By the end of June, Dyce Sombre demanded that he be moved to the Hyde Park Hotel but the attending physicians informed the Lord Chancellor that he was too weak and Wilde blocked the move.[136] Finally, Mahon and the other doctors had him put in a sedan chair and

Kensal Green Cemetery, London

taken to the nearby infirmary of Dr Eugene Detkins at 8 Davies Street, Berkeley Square. There, Dyce Sombre quickly succumbed to the spreading infection and died on 1 July, ending his final struggles in London.

Even his corpse created problems. His will directed that his body be returned to Sardhana and Begum Sombre. Instead, the Lord Chancellor and Mary Anne concurred it should be interred in London's newly fashionable Kensal Green Cemetery. According to that cemetery's records, his body remains there undisturbed today. Yet, the Sardhana basilica's records indicate that in 1867 his body was transported there, where it—or perhaps only its heart—allegedly lies entombed, adjacent to Begum's body as he had desired. While his life had ended, his death did not end the repercussions of it.

13

LEGACIES

Dyce Sombre left behind countless unresolved issues, reams of contradictory evidence, and endless controversies. His death immediately inspired international commentators to reappraise his life's many facets, but they did so in light of their own outlook. His vehement critics, and their implacable foes who supported him, continued to spar over his reputation in society, the public press, as well as Parliament. His gossiped about widow, contentious brothers-in-law, acquisitive executors, and the imperious East India Company (succeeded by the British Government) all launched fleets of lawyers into battle over his vast wealth and various legacies. For another two decades, several trials about his will and claims to Badshahpur and the Sardhana armaments ground out in courts in India and England. Until today, would-be heirs step forward. Medical men and jurists still draw on precedents generated by the challenges he presented to their professions. Popular writers of fiction continue to evoke the Begum's fortune which he controlled. Overall, his complexity reveals the constructed and contingent nature of legal, medical, social, and cultural categories including nationality, normality, class, gender, and race or ethnicity in both Asia and Europe, in his day and our own.

Postmortem

Many newspapers and journals throughout the Anglophone world posthumously recapitulated Dyce Sombre's life with diverse degrees of sympathy, disrespect, and accuracy, according to their own perspective on what they presumed he represented. Auckland's *New Zealander* anticipated news of his expected passing as an internationally newsworthy event. Upon his demise, the fashion-conscious *Illustrated London News* respectfully represented him as a gentleman, complete with coat of arms, who bore his afflictions with 'great fortitude'. Papers including London's *Daily News* and Calcutta's *Bengal Catholic Herald* portrayed 'Poor Dyce Sombre!' as a 'simple' soul, a 'young half-caste Croesus' out of his depth in sophisticated and avaricious London society and driven out of his mind by it. Uncreative editors just reprinted another publication's article, word for word. Less generous newspapers—including Britain's *Annual Register*, *Examiner*, *Gentleman's Magazine*, and *News of the World*, Tasmania's *Hobart Town Courier* and New Zealand's *Nelson Examiner and New Zealand Chronicle*—treated him as undistinguished and unaccomplished 'except [for] his pedigree and his wealth', both of which had deeply immoral Oriental implications.[1] Some ambivalent newspapers ran two separate articles, with differing information and interpretations of his origins, putative lunacy, huge estate, and life's larger significance.

Few journalists actually investigated or reported precisely his inordinately challenging history, being more concerned with sensationalizing him with easily comprehended stereotypes to fascinate their readers. Most published obituaries garbled his complex genealogy, particularly his unfamiliar relationship to Begum Sombre and hers to Reinhardt, the original Sombre—with disparate colourful summations of their notorious careers. However, accounts unanimously highlighted Dyce Sombre's 'almost fabulous wealth', although its stated size and expected beneficiaries varied considerably.

Dyce Sombre's mental condition and race, endlessly debated during his lifetime in popular discourse and by contending medical and legal theorists, provoked continued controversy. Some commentators considered the lunacy charges against him completely concocted. Agnostic authors simply mentioned the lunacy judgment without venturing to accept or deny its validity. Other, more assertive writers assumed his lunacy was real but diagnosed its causes variously. Professional physicians used him to prove one fashionable medical theory about insanity after another; in the decades after his death, 'hysteria' displaced 'monomania' almost entirely as the prevalent diagnosis of people who acted like him.[2] Bigoted British officials in India, like Sir Robert Hamilton who supervised the annexation of Sardhana, disparagingly recalled Dyce Sombre as 'the greatest of cowards, a thoroughly low-minded native'.[3] The most humane eulogy was by Dr Drever, who pleaded fruitlessly for postmortem respect and maintained, as he had consistently in Britain, that Dyce Sombre was well-meaning but had simply gone insane, and now should be left to rest in peace.[4]

Yet, the Dyce Sombre story was too tempting and susceptible to tendentious interpretation to sink away immediately. In particular, Dyce Sombre's unconventional relationship with Mary Anne received diverse but passionate postmortem assessments. Cautious writers characterised his marriage neutrally as 'ill-starred', without attributing blame.[5] Some populist sympathisers portrayed him as a naïve and innocent Indian victim, seduced and looted by manipulative, gold-digging English aristocrats; a few suggested he had been murdered by Mary Anne's family or driven to suicide so they could grab his money. Conservative writers used him to demonstrate the decline from purity of the English peerage due to the rise of callous commerce. They portrayed the St Vincents as corrupted by Dyce Sombre's Oriental money. Typical of this view, the London *Age* blamed the St Vincents for being willing to 'sacrifice the daughter of an illustrious family to mere wealth and show, and procure a rich husband at any cost, and no matter how low, vulgar, and immoral a one he may be... Surely the diamonds and the gold were dearly bought when a name which should have been pure as the diamond and far more precious than all the gold of Hindostan was bandied about in the law reports, and connected with the filthiest charges by the husband's lips!'[6] Thus, editors and reporters used him to confirm agendas they had long advocated and interests they already sought to advance.

Factional and personal conflicts within the English peerage that had coalesced around Dyce Sombre during his lifetime persisted after his death. Prominent among other noblemen who used his memory to attack each other, Viscount St Vincent repeatedly assaulted Viscount Combermere verbally in the House of Lords, blaming him for everything that had gone wrong in the marriage.[7] This provoked even more vituperative attacks in the public press by factions aligned against St Vincent:

There is an old and homely proverb about stirring up dirty puddles which Lord St Vincent would have done well to remember last night before he invoked [in the Lords] the swarthy and licentious spirit of Dyce Sombre to appear again on earth... As soon as [Dyce Sombre] arrived in this country, he was fastened upon... The manners and known disposition and character of the man went for nothing. He had what they wanted—gold... this Hindoo monster... with Hindoo notions in his head.[8]

This account crudely bashed St Vincent by making Dyce Sombre simultaneously dark-skinned, prey, immoral, opulent, Hindu, and bestially Oriental.

Across America, journalists continued for a half-century to play upon their readers' familiarity with striking images of Dyce Sombre. White Protestant newspapers in particular evoked his example to denounce the perverted horrors of racial and cultural promiscuous intercourse: 'his mixture of European and Asiatic blood, and European and Asiatic habits,—the combination of the Romanist faith with a Mahomedan life', producing a bizarre 'Eurasian millionaire'.[9] In such racist editorialising, Dyce Sombre often appeared animalised: 'a gorilla', 'an orang-outang', 'a pariah not on account of his conduct, but by reason of his birth', 'educated—or rather not educated—in a state of false and depraved Oriental semi-civilization, into which entered, in no inconsiderable degree, the worst vices of the Western World'. A decade after his death, Boston's *The New England Farmer: a Monthly Journal, Devoted to Agriculture, Horticulture, and Their Kindred Arts and Sciences* assumed its rural readers would still know well the stereotype of Dyce Sombre, using him to describe the utterly black complexion of an Alabama slave on the auction block, whose 'skin was as dark as that of the late Mr. Dyce Sombre'.[10] Among the most salacious columns during the late nineteenth century about Dyce Sombre and his 'interracial' marriage came from a New York woman syndicated gossip-monger who pretended to be a French aristocrat: 'Marquise de Fontenoy'.[11] Hence, various lurid images of him long persisted in the American popular press.

Newspapers, like the law courts, became the arena where various parties staked out their claims to his huge estate from the moment of his demise. One repeated, but inaccurate, newspaper assertion—apparently instigated by his brothers-in-law Solaroli and Troup—was that they would inherit everything, including widow Mary Anne's jointure on her death. Many papers republished this claim, including New York's *American International Monthly Magazine of Literature, Science, and Art* and London's *Bell's Life in London and Sporting Chronicle*. In contrast, other newspapers, including New York's *Albion, A Journal of News, Politics and Literature*, repeatedly lauded Dyce Sombre's admirable bequest in his last few wills, which the East India Company adamantly supported, to devote his money to pay for Indian education at Sumroo's College.

Indeed, his final, 1849 will provoked five years of vitriolic litigation. Prinsep and the other East India Directors, with the approval of the Board of Control, marshalled the Company's substantial economic and political resources in defense of Dyce Sombre's will, just as he had intended.[12] The core of their case was (as Dyce Sombre had been maintaining for years) that he was sane and Georgiana was illegitimate so Solaroli deserved nothing. In addition, the Company's phalanx of lawyers supported the Orientalist position, which Dyce Sombre had never accepted: his un-British actions resulted from his Asiatic birth and 'black blood' but were completely in accord with Indian customs. The Directors consistently argued that their sole motivation in defending his will was to enable the creation of Sumroo's College, as he proposed, 'for the education of the natives of India'; that the Directors would be personally enriched by the will was irrelevant to their defense of it. Nonetheless, rather than be embroiled in this heated case, co-executors Elphinstone and Elliot declined serving, therefore forfeiting Dyce Sombre's bequest of £7,500 each in cash and jewels.

Opposing Prinsep and the other Directors were their political enemies, including a later President of the Board of Control from another political faction. In Parliament and public fora, they accused the Directors of acting corruptly for their own aggrandisement, squandering over £30,000 of Indian taxpayers' money to defend the will.[13] But Prinsep led the Directors to continue the fight.

Also aligned against the Directors and the validity of the will were the many lawyers of Mary Anne plus those of Solaroli and Troup. They concomitantly asserted that Dyce Sombre had died intestate since he had been mentally, and therefore legally, incompetent for seven years before signing the will. Mary Anne and Troup supported Solaroli's further claim that Georgiana was Dyce Sombre's full-sister. Thus, Mary Anne and the brothers-in-law contended they should divide his estate, half and half, as next of kin.[14]

The expensive trial over the will lasted nearly five years, frequently reported by journals in Britain—ranging in London alone from the *Times* to the *New Sporting Magazine* to the *Indian News*. Likewise, this trial was featured over the years by newspapers throughout the Anglophone world including New Zealand's *New Zealand Spectator and Cook's Strait Guardian*, Australia's *Perth Gazette, Maitland Mercury and Hunter River General Advertiser* and *Hobarton Mercury* and America's *Charleston* [South Carolina] *Mercury, Lowell* [Massachusetts]

Daily Citizen and News, the New York *Herald*, and the San Francisco *Daily Evening Bulletin*. Some papers, including New York's *Harpers Weekly Magazine: A Journal of Civilization* and London's *Times*, proclaimed the case a '*cornucopia* to lawyers' since 'All the leading members of the [London] bar hold briefs on one side or the other, and have received fees of 500 guineas each... [plus] there are two consultations daily, one in the morning and the other in the evening, each time a fee of 30 guineas being paid to every counsel so consulting'. Indeed, advocates for legal reform in Britain and the U. S. cited the vast total costs on all sides of this single case (£80,000) to argue for streamlined judicial procedures for proving wills.[15]

The Directors, Dyce Sombre's will, and Sumroo's College finally lost in 1856. Sir John Dodson of the Privy Council's Judicial Committee revisited all the medical evidence and decided that Dyce Sombre had in fact been insane since 1842. Consequently, he was incompetent to sign his will in 1849. Unusually, Dodson charged all the court costs not to the estate but to the losing defenders of the will, concluding that Prinsep and the other Directors had acted improperly in so improbably claiming Dyce Sombre to have been competent. But this did not end the controversy as various contending popular newspapers and legal and medical professional journals featured and dissected Dodson's four-hour summation.[16]

Running concurrently with the will trial, and lasting even longer, other twin legal campaigns continued over Badshahpur and the Sardhana armaments seizures by the Company in 1836 (the matter of the Sardhana pensioners eventually being deemed non-justiciable). Here, hosts of lawyers on all sides swarmed over the case, although the principals kept shifting over the decades before it was settled. On one side, working to protect Indian revenue-payers from the massive compensation demanded by Dyce Sombre's estate, was the East India Company and, after its termination in 1858, the British Government. On the other side, ownership of Dyce Sombre's estate remained moot until after the 1856 decision on his will. Thereafter, Mary Anne claimed half the estate; after her remarriage (8 November 1862) to her old friend Cecil Weld Forester, he took possession of this half of the claim (she also settled a £4,000 annual allowance on him, exactly the same amount that Dyce Sombre had given to her). The other half of the estate was claimed by the Troups and Solarolis. But the childless death of John Troup (1862) and Ann May Troup (1867) left their share to the Solarolis. When Georgiana died (1867), Solaroli and their descendants inherited this claim. Coast-to-coast across America and as far as the New Zealand and Australia, newspapers evoked the endless and fruitless trial in Dickens' *Bleak House* to describe these cases by titling, their articles 'Jarndice vs. Jarndice'.[17]

Repeatedly, Mary Anne and her second husband tried to use all their personal connections and considerable political influence to convince the British Government to drop its defense and submit. A leading member of the Privy Council (which would ultimately rule in these cases) was Mary Anne's former lawyer Bethell, now Baron Westbury, her 'old friend' and continued dinner companion.[18] Following her marriage to Cecil Forester, he wrote and published a politely accusatory book in 1865, *Heirs of Mr Dyce Sombre v. The Indian Government; The History of a Suit during Thirty Years between a Private Individual and the Government of India*; a British official of the Government of India was

Judicial Committee of the Privy Council

assigned to refute this book point-by-point.[19] Another set of lawyers for the Solaroli-Troup combine usually supported the Foresters.

These cases ranged back and forth over the decades through various levels of courts in Delhi, Punjab, Agra, and London. Multiple disputes arose over the validity of the documentation supplied by each side (many records having been destroyed during the 1857 'Mutiny' fighting). The cases had only been filed by Larkins, acting as Committee of Dyce Sombre's Estate, after the twelve year statue of limitations had lapsed (as discussed above). When this particular issue rose to the Privy Council in 1857, it ruled against the Company's time-limit, based on Dyce Sombre's legal incompetence when the limit had expired.[20]

A further crucial question was the Begum's political status. If she were sovereign, which the Company now argued, her Badshahpur *jagir* and/or armaments were state property, not privately owned. Thus, they had been legally confiscated according to her 1805 treaty. Further, state-to-state matters could not be decided by municipal courts, where Larkins had originally filed the suits. When this issue rose to the Privy Council in 1858, it equivocally decided that the Begum was 'nominally at least, a kind of small Sovereign'.[21]

Finally, in 1872, the cases rose a third time to the Privy Council which decided both cases in favour of the Estate. But the Privy Council decreed differing consequences. The seizure of Badshahpur had been illegal but, since the Government claimed it was a 'political action', this annexation was irreversible and without the estimated £500,000 compensation. Further, this lawsuit should have been originally filed in the Calcutta Supreme Court not Delhi municipal court. Thus, Dyce Sombre's Estate won a symbolic but empty judgement, despite decades of legal struggles and fees. The Privy Council, however, ruled the East India Company's seizure of the Sardhana armaments to have been an illegal confiscation of the Begum's personal property—as such, compensation was due. However, much additional negotiation was still needed to determine what the cash value of those armaments had been in 1836. Only in 1873 (37 years after the event) was the case finally closed with a payment by the British Government of India (thus, indirectly, by Indian taxpayers) to the Estate of £30,000 plus 12% interest (not compounded), totaling £163,318 and 7 shillings.[22] This finally closed Dyce Sombre's legal legacy, but resounding echoes of him and his fortune persists till today.

Aftermath

Over the decades following Dyce Sombre's death, many individuals have claimed his legacy and the authority to speak for him. Mary Anne eventually inherited not only much of his fortune but also many of his associations with Sardhana. As his widow, she evoked his exotic appeal by appearing occasionally in English high social circles wearing Indian-style clothing, graciously accepting the epithet 'The Begum'. Further, she used Dyce Sombre's wealth (in addition to properties inherited from her natal family) to make substantial donations in Sardhana (as well as patronizing many popular causes in England). In a more socially acceptable manner than her first husband, she also communicated with spirits: as a devotee of fashionable séances, often hearing child spirits produce 'thick clusters of little round sounds like the dropping of sudden rain'.[23] So well known in British popular culture had she become that Arthur Conan Doyle used her specifically as a named character in 'The Sign of the Four' and other Sherlock Holmes stories.[24] She died childless in 1893, still well-known across the Anglophone world primarily for her first marriage to Dyce Sombre and enriched by the Begum's wealth; she left about half her £570,000 fortune to charity and the other half to the Forester family of her childless second husband.[25]

But other putative heirs, tracing their claims back to Walter Reinhardt continue to appear. The British Government still irregularly receives demands from supposed descendants for access to documents that would prove them entitled to the Reinhardt-Sombre millions.[26] Concomitantly, diverse swindlers have preyed on the avarice and credulity of these would-be heirs to bilk them. The most famous of these frauds was Baron Alexander von Pawel-Rammingen, a distant relation to the British royal family and sometime Chamberlain to the Pope. As publicised in Britain and India, and even across America (in the *Booklyn Daily Eagle* and the *Milwaukee Sentinel* among other papers), in 1883 he was convicted and sentenced in Austria to seven years imprisonment with revocation of his status as a nobleman for deceiving gullible would-be heirs to the Sombre fortune.[27]

The legendary legacy, enhanced by the Begum's and Dyce Sombre's dramatic lives, has continued to inspire authors of many other kinds of fiction as well. The prolific German author, Hermann Goedsche, using the alias Sir John Retcliffe, wrote and published (1858–65) an extremely popular and racist three volume novel, *Nena Sahib oder die Empörung in Indien*, celebrating Germanic virtues, in which the Begum, Dyce Sombre, and their fortune play crucial roles. Conversely, Frenchman Jules Verne's 1877 novel, *Les Cinq cents millions de la Bégum* portrays Dyce Sombre's fortune as the foundation for a racial struggle in which noble Frenchmen who pursue virtuous science defeat Germans (based in California) who aggressively industrialise.

Dyce Sombre, however, has not appeared in the national narratives of either India or Britain. Begum Sombre has inspired many romantic accounts and popular histories of the transitional period from the Mughal to the British Empires. But Dyce Sombre presents too many questions and problems for him to be similarly celebrated. Further, most authors and politicians who wish to highlight Indians who rose to prominence in Britain select Dadabhai Naoroji as the 'first Indian' elected to Parliament.[28] As a true Indian nationalist hero, Naoroji articulates well the successful struggles of progressive Indians in Britain. Britons can also point to their election of Naoroji as proof that race was not an insurmountable barrier in England. Neither Dyce Sombre (elected to Parliament half a century earlier) nor even Sir Mancherjee Merwanjee Bhownaggree (who followed Naoroji by a few years there, but was a Conservative) can be used to make these Indian or British nationalist arguments.

Nor do European political, social, or cultural histories, including the history of medicine, include Dyce Sombre. He and his anomalous deeds presented, and continue to present, unsettling problems. Widely regared as 'Black' and 'Oriental', he bought election to the British Parliament, only to have his English constituency disenfranchised for corruption. A Catholic from India, he married into the Anglican aristocracy, only to have some of its factions battle others over his immorality versus that of his wife. Even successors of Foucault ignore Dyce Sombre's case in their analyses, interjecting as it does complicating Orientalist and racial factors. His example certainly shows the effects of power and cultural constructions in how European authorities incarcerated and otherwise dealt with the alleged insane. But the imperial French and Russian states defended Dyce Sombre's liberty and sanity, while the imperial British state sought to confine him. Further, those authorities who judged him essentially 'Oriental' found him sane, while those who identified him as 'European' decreed him lunatic. Additionally, his many trials publicised the internal contradictions among physicians and jurists, and also provided him with fora for his own self-representations rather than suppressed his voice.

Dyce Sombre's inordinate history, therefore, continues unresolved. This book does not seek to produce a definitive reading of Dyce Sombre's strange life in Asia and Europe. Rather, it strives to make available to readers the manifold ways that he challenged culturally constructed categories wherever he went. Rather than closing questions about the many meanings of his life, it hopes to open them for further consideration.

NOTES

INTRODUCTION: QUESTIONING CATEGORIES

1. Dhingra, *Managing Multicultural Lives*.
2. Bhabha, *Location of Culture*.
3. Yet, Hawes attributes David Dyce Sombre's problems in London to his personal flaws, not his Anglo-Indian race. Hawes, *Poor Relations*, p. 191n67.
4. Foucault, *Madness and Civilization*; Eigen, *Witnessing Insanity*; Jay, *Air Loom Gang*; Porter, *Mind-forg'd Manacles*; Scull, *Most Solitary of Afflictions* and *Museums of Madness*; Suzuki, *Madness at Home*; Walker, *Crime and Insanity in England*, vol. 1.
5. Shreeve *Dark Legacy*; *From Nawab to Nabob*; *Indian Heir*.

PART ONE: ASIA

1. THE STATE OF DAVID'S ORIGINS

1. Archer, *Tours of Upper India*, vol. 1, pp. 137–42; Bacon, *First Impressions*, vol. 2, p. 35; Compton, *Particular Account*, p. 403; Dyer, 'Begam of Sardhana'; Higginbotham, *Men Whom India Has Known*, pp. 406–8; Keene, *Hindustan*, p. 76; Charles Metcalfe to Auckland 4 May 1836, IPC 23 May 1836, no. 66; Sleeman, *Rambles*, pp. 594–95. Among of the best biographies are Mahendra Sharma, *Life and Times* and Lall, *Begum Samru*.
2. Among the many popular histories, dramas, and novels are: Bell, *Foreigner*; Bond, 'Lady of Sardhana'; Chandra, *Red Earth and Pouring Rain*; Vera Chatterjee, *All This is Ended*; Colland, *La Begom Sombre*; Hockley, 'Natch'; Hutchinson, *European Freebooters*, pp. 57–61; 80–86; Keene, 'Women'; Larneuil, *Roman de la Begum Sombre*; Malleson, *Recreations*, pp. 438–59; Nair, *Sardhana*; Ranganath, *Sardhana ki Begham*; Shamsuddin, *Loves of Begum Sumroo*; Partap Sharma, *Begum Sumroo*; Sher, *Begam Samru*; Umashankar, *Dil par Ek Dagh*.
3. He has variously been identified, including as an Alsatian from Strasbourg, a German from Trier/Trèves in Rhineland Palatinate, an Austrian from Salzburg, a German Swiss, and a gypsy. Keene, *Hindustan*, pp. 16–17;

North-Western Provinces, *Gazetteer*, vol. 3, p. 96; Noti, *Das Furstentum Sardhana*; National Archives of India, *Fort William-India House Correspondence*, vol. 4, pp. 132–134, 258, 263, 313–14; Polier, *Shah Alam*, pp. 45, 93–6; Qanungo, *History*, vol. 1, *passim*; Reinhardt, *Wegweiser*; Weber, *Maharadscha Reinhardt*.

4. Seid Khan, *Seir*, vol. 2, pp. 505–6, and translator's footnote; Sleeman, *Rambles*, p. 597.

5. de Tassy, *Auteurs Hindoistanis*, pp. 17–18; Saksena, *European and Indo-European Poets*, pp. 86–94.

6. Even in 1834, Sardhana's revenues were 1,020,992 Rupees and expenditures were 1,025,311 Rupees. Diary 9 Oct. 1834, 5 April 1835.

7. Powell, "Artful Apostasy?'; Vannini, *Hindustan-Tibet Mission*, p. 245. See also Viswanathan, *Outside the Fold*.

8. Some British Christians lamented the annexation, arguing Sardhana would have been a model Christian state under David Dyce Sombre. M.T., 'Christianity in India'.

9. Ghosh, *Sex and the Family*, pp. 147–63.

10. Francklin, *Military Memoirs*, pp. 161–2.

11. See: Richards, *Mughal Empire*; Irvine, *Later Mughals*.

12. India. Imperial Record Department, *Calendar of Persian Correspondence*, vol. 9, letters 1650, 1651, 1721; vol. 10, letters 175, 176, 487, 511, 1115; vol. 11, letters 389, 463, 475, 578, 626.

13. In the keeping of Monsieur Joseph Even, a fellow Frenchman who had earlier served in the Begum's army but had retired to British territory. Diary, 5 June 1836, 21 Dec. 1836; Sleeman, *Rambles*, pp. 603–9; India. Imperial Record Department, *Calendar of Persian Correspondence*, vol. 11, letters 1141–42.

14. Francklin, *Military Memoirs*, pp. 58–60; National Archives of India, *Fort William-India House Correspondence*, vol. 18, p. 262.

15. Stafford County Record Office, D1798/398/2/19.

16. Diary, 26 May 1834; 28 May 1835.

17. Begum's orders to her army (10 Nov. 1803) to obey British, reprinted in *Times* 10 Nov. 1871.

18. Mahendra Sharma, *Life and Times*, pp 103–30; Aitchison, *Collection of Treaties*, vol. 4, p. 42.

19. Diary 12 May 1834. See also Thorn, *Memoir*, pp. 331–32.

20. IPC 23 May 1836, no. 71.

21. The Company claimed no 'fully authenticated' list of pensioners was on file. India and Bengal Dispatches, 8 Nov. 1837–28 Feb. 1838, E/4/753, ff. 649–62, BL.

22. George Henry Hewett (1791–1862) son of Sir George Hewett. Hewett, *Private Record*, p. 56n.

23. Prior, 'Role of English'; Spear, *Twilight*, pp. 167–93.

24. Diary 13 Feb. 1837.

25. [Deane], *Tour*, pp. 148–75. The evening after her memorable imperial audience, Ms Deane and the Begum met at a formal dinner at the British Resident's mansion.

26. [Deane], *Tour*, pp. 159–60. For news reports of the Begum's frequent interactions with the Emperor as well as the British Resident see Pernau, *Information*.

27. Spear, *Twilight*, pp. 39, 62.

28. [Deane], *Tour*, p. 159; Aitken, 'Pardah and Portrayal'.

29. [Deane], *Tour*, pp. 148–75.

30. Nugent, *Journal*, vol. 2, pp. 51–54.

31. Diary 20 Nov. 1830; Cotton, *Sardhana Pictures*; Francklin, *Military Memoirs*, p. 92; Sleeman, *Rambles*, p. 614.

32. Hingorani, 'Artful Agency'.

33. Bacon talks about staying in one of her Delhi houses near Raj Ghat and she also owned a garden near Kashmiri Gate. Bacon, *First Impressions*, vol. 2, p. 217. See also Hosagrahar, *Indigenous Modernities*.

34. Pernau, *Information*, p. 263.

35. Will of Joanna Sombre 16 Dec. 1831, DS, *Refutation*, pp. 373–5 and Privy Council, *In the Privy Council*, pp. 42–44.

36. Fanshawe, *Delhi Past and Present*, p. 49 n; Mainodin in Charles Metcalfe, *Two Native Narratives*, pp. 185–86.

37. Thomas Metcalfe, *Delhi Book*, reproduced in Kaye, *Golden Calm*, p. 110. For a map see Ehlers and Krafft, *Shahjahanabad/Old Delhi*, frontispiece.

38. [Deane], *Tour*, pp. 178–79.

39. Mirza Babar, a younger son of Emperor Akbar Shah, had built his own European-style palace in the Red Fort. Losty, 'Delhi Palace in 1846'.

40. Sleeman, *Rambles*, p. 504.

41. See Dalrymple, *White Mughals* and *Last Mughal*.

42. Thomas Metcalfe, *Delhi Book*, reproduced in Kaye, *Golden Calm*, p. 181.

43. Sir David Ochterlony's son by one of his Indian concubines, Roderick Peregrine Ochterlony, married Sarah Nelley, the daughter of Lt Col John Nelley, apparently with an Indian woman, so Sir Charles Metcalfe Ochterlony had half British and half Indian ancestry.

44. Dyce to Meerut Commissioners 2 March 1836, IPC 23 May 1836, no. 79; Charles Trevelyan deposition 19 August 1852, *DSAT*, vol. 2, p. 53; Hodson, *List*, vol. 2, p. 111.

2. THE CHILDLESS BEGUM'S POSSIBLE HEIR

1. Chand, 'Zeb-ut-Tawarikh', MS ADD 25,830, BL, and *History of Zeb-ul-Nissa*; Bullock, 'Some Soldiers of Fortune'; Kincaid, 'Indian Bourbons'; Mahendra Sharma, *Life and Times*, pp. 154–57; Vibart, 'Sepoy Revolt'.

2. Tupper, *Indian Political Practice*, vol. 3, pp. 233–43.

3. Wolff, *Travels and Adventures*, vol 2, pp. 125–6; Wolff, *Researches*, p. 243.

4. Diary 7–8 Nov. 1835.

5. Diary 11 Dec. 1834, 28–29 March 1835; Archbishop of Canterbury letter 16 July 1834, Catholic Bishop of Madras letter 15 Oct. 1835, D1798/398/2/2–3, Stafford County Record Office; Compton, *Particular Account*, p. 410; DS, *Refutation*, p. 401; North-Western Provinces, *Gazetteer*, vol. 3, p. 295; Mahendra Sharma, *Life and Times*, pp. 185–6; Sleeman, *Rambles*, p. 612.

6. Surprised Anglican authorities were skeptical and wary but were delighted with the money. Bateman, *Life of the Right Rev. Daniel Wilson*, vol. 1, pp. 354–56.

7. Dalrymple, *Last Mughal*, p. 67.

8. Ibid., p. 239. See also Bailey, 'Architectural Relics'. For earlier accounts see: Keene, *Hindustan*, p. 192; Minturn, *From New York to Delhi*, p. 196.

9. Bishop of Amartanta (on Cyprus not actually under Catholic control). Diary 8 April 1835; Keene, *Hindustan*, p. 196; Sleeman, *Rambles*, pp. 594–95.

10. Sherwood, *Life*, pp. 346–7; *Littell's Living Age* 27 June 1896; Sherer, 'Bishop in Partibus'.

11. Samuel Enderby deposition 11 August 1854, *DSAT, vol. 2*, p. 304.

12. Diary 16 March 1834.

13. Sherwood, *Life*, p. 483.

14. Dyce Sombre to Peter Solaroli 14 Jan. 1838, *DSAT*, vol. 1, pp. 859–62.

15. Diary 1 August 1834, 10 August 1834, 20 Oct. 1835, 3 June 1838.

16. Reghellini had joined the Begum's service in 1810. She had arranged his marriage soon thereafter, making a three year old son likely. Nugent, *Journal*, vol. 2, pp. 52–3; Antonio Reghellini to Henry Prinsep recd 18 March 1836, IPC 8 Feb. 1836, no. 99.

17. Will of Joanna Sombre 16 Dec. 1831, DS, *Refutation*, pp. 373–5 and Privy Council, *In the Privy Council*, pp. 42–44; Juliana John Thomas alias Sohagun Begum letter 27 March 1845 to Graham, D1798/398/2/9 Stafford Record Office. Keene, *Hindustan*, pp. 192ff; Leach, *Mughal and Other Indian Paintings*, vol. 2, pp. 788–95; *Times* 31 July 1847.

18. Diary 28 May 1835; Chamberlain, *Memoirs*; [Grant], 'Memories'; Anonymous, 'Story of Our Missions'; *Missionary Register* vol. 3, no. 34 (Oct. 1815), pp. 564–65.

19. Heber, *Narrative*, vol. 2, pp. 274, 277–80; Joseph Skinner deposition 10 Jan. 1853, *DSAT*, vol. 2, pp. 292–93.

20. Diary 28 Sept. 1837.

21. Ibid., 20 Dec. 1836.

22. Ibid., 7 Oct. 1837, 15 Jan. 1838, 18–21 Feb. 1838.

23. Sleeman interviewed Agha Avanis, father-in-law of John Thomas, who remembered the incident from his boyhood and whose mother owned one of the executed slaves. Sleeman, *Rambles*, p. 602.

24. Heber, *Narrative*, vol. 2, pp. 277–80; Bacon, *First Impressions*, vol. 2, p. 76; Jacquemont, *Letters*, vol. 2, pp. 246–8; Sleeman, *Rambles*, p. 567.

25. Dr Louis Jule Béhier deposition, *DSAT*, vol. 2, p. 141.

26. Diary 20 Feb. 1834, 12 Jan. 1835 5 Jan. 1834.

27. Charles Metcalfe to Auckland 19 Oct. 1836, IPC 21 Nov. 1836, no. 18.

28. In 1835, Combermere sent a painting of Christ bound by soldiers allegedly by Rembrandt dated 1649. Diary 15 Nov. 1835; Lord Combermere deposition 3 July 1852, *DSAT*, vol. 2, pp. 40–45.

29. James Rodgers deposition 7 Dec. 1853, *DSAT*, vol. 2:, pp. 516–21; Creighton, *Narrative of the Siege and Capture of Bhurtpore*.

30. Metcalf to Governor General 3 Dec. 1825, in Mahendra Sharma, *Life and Times*, Appendix D.

31. Diary 7 August 1834; 28 May 1835.

32. This according to one of David's schoolmates, Joseph Skinner (himself of mixed ancestry and sensitive to racial gradations). Joseph Skinner deposition 10 Jan. 1853, *DSAT*, vol. 2, pp. 292–93.

33. Charles Trevelyan affidavit 22 Dec. 1843, L/L/65 (451), BL.

34. Solaroli fled his homeland due to politics, taking various jobs in India, including managing an indigo plantation. He came to Sardhana early in 1831, reportedly to marry the daughter of fellow Italian and courtier of the Begum, Major Antonio Reghellini. Instead, the Begum recruited Solaroli as a husband for Georgiana within ten weeks of his arrival. Antonio Reghellini deposition 31 Dec. 1852, Peter Solaroli deposition 17 Nov. 1853, *DSAT*, vol. 2, pp. 172–83, 496–504.

35. Fort William Political Letters 1 August 1831, no. 12, 15 Dec. 1831, nos. 27–33, Board Collection 55482, F/4/1401, BL; Foreign Political Proceedings, Consultation 24 June 1831, no. 32, BL; Hodson, *List*, vol. 4, pp. 310–11.

36. Troup came from the Scottish Presbyterian gentry. At seventeen, he had married Englishwoman Caroline Georgiana Stopford in Dacca, but she soon died. Troup's skills in Urdu language gained appointments as official interpreter in the successive native infantry regiments. He had served under Combermere at Bharatpur when the Begum was present there. Ann May Troup deposition 10 Feb. 1854, *DSAT*, vol. 2, pp. 530–32.

37. Dyce Sombre to Peter Solaroli 10 August 1837, *DSAT*, vol. 1, pp. 856–57; Diary 25 April 1837, 8 August 1837, 6–15 April 1838; Begum to Resident Delhi Jan. 1829, Brown to Craigie 26 Dec. 1828, Extract Political Letter from Bengal 9 Oct. 1830, Board Collection 52470, F/4/1324, BL.

38. Diary 25 May 1834, 27 March 1835.

39. Hamilton to Commissioner Meerut 12 March 1836, IPC 23 May 1836, no. 73.

40. See Fisher, *Counterflows*.

41. Diary 18 Dec. 1833, 24 April 1834.

3. HEIR APPARENT TO A DOOMED PRINCIPALITY

1. The surviving sections of his diary include a daily journal and then a Private Memorandum (3 October 1836 until his arrival in England) plus a terser pocket calendar book kept on his tour of the Mediterranean for 1847–48. These survived only due to his virtually all-encompassing legal entanglements later in life. The courts had a transcription printed. PROB 37/1700, National Archives of the United Kingdom and L/L/63–65, British Library. *Times* 7 March 1857. These have been partly transcribed in Shreeve, *From Nawab to Nabob* and *Indian Heir*.
2. Diary 1 Nov. 1837.
3. Ibid., 12 May 1834.
4. Ibid., 21 Nov. 1837.
5. Ibid., 27 Sept. 1834.
6. Ibid., 5 Feb. 1835.
7. Ibid., 27–28 June 1835.
8. Ibid., 16 July 1834.
9. Ibid., 21 Jan. 1834.
10. Ibid., 12 August 1835.
11. Ibid., 5 May 1837.
12. Ibid., 5 August 1835, 31 March 1834, 21 May 1837, 1 June 1834.
13. Ibid., 15 July 1835.
14. Ibid., 25 May 1834, 29 June 1834.
15. Ibid., 16 Sept. 1834.
16. Ibid., 21 March 1834.
17. Ibid., 5 April 1835.
18. Ibid., 29 April 1834.
19. Ibid., 24 May 1835, 25 May 1835, 7 June 1835.
20. Fraser letter 17 July 1834, L/PJ/5/399, BL.
21. Everest letter 23 Dec. 1835 in McMahon, *Badshapoor Suit*, p. 15.
22. Diary 7 Jan. 1836.
23. Sleeman, *Rambles*, p. 545.
24. Mahendra Sharma, *Life and Times*, p. 123; Keene, *Hindustan*, p. 103.
25. Diary 21–22 June 1834.
26. Ibid., e. g., 13 April 1835, 10 May 1835.
27. Ibid., 27 June 1834.
28. Ibid., 14 June 1834.
29. Ibid., 30 May 1834.
30. Ibid., 29 June 1834.
31. Ibid., 4 July 1834.
32. Ibid., 8 Nov. 1834.
33. Ibid., 14 Dec. 1834.
34. Ibid., 2 Dec. 1834.
35. Skinner had asked for 350,000 Rupees. Ibid., 30 April 1835, 25 July 1835.

36. Ibid., 30 April 1835, 25 July 1835, 1 Nov. 1836, 26 March 1837.
37. Louis-Philippe, Emperor of the French to Most Illustrious, Most Excellent and Most Magnificent Simrou Begum, Princess of Sardana, 27 Oct. 1835, L/L/64 (438); PROB 37/1700, PRO.
38. Diary 30 Sept. 1834.
39. Ibid., 1 Oct. 1834.
40. Ibid., 3 Oct. 1834.
41. Ibid., 14 Nov. 1834, 15 Dec. 1834, 15 Jan. 1836, 31 Dec. 1836, 24 Jan. 1837, 4 March 1837, 21 April 1838.
42. Ibid., 23–28 Dec. 1834; Comte Ventura deposition 22 Oct. 1853, *DSAT*, vol. 2, pp. 472–79; *Bombay Times* 23 Jan. 1839 quoted in *Freemasons' Quarterly Review*, vol. 1839, p. 376.
43. Diary 22 Dec. 1837.
44. Ibid., e. g., 21–24 March 1834.
45. E. g. Rajah Sohun Lall and Humed Buckshi. Ibid., 29 Dec. 1835.
46. Ibid., e. g., 16 Dec. 1834.
47. Ibid., 30–31 Dec. 1835; Losty, 'Delhi Palace in 1846'.
48. Bacon, *First Impressions*, vol. 2, p. 54.
49. Diary 24–31 Dec. 1833. Dyce Sombre took a similar attitude toward other Mughal princes visiting Sardhana: Diary 27 Feb. 1834, 25–28 Nov. 1834, 23–27 Dec. 1834, 17 March 1835.
50. Ibid., 26–28 Nov. 1834 16–24 Dec. 1834, 17 March 1835.
51. Ibid., 24 Dec. 1834.
52. Ibid., 5 July 1835.
53. Ibid., 14 August 1835.
54. Ibid., 28 August 1835, 2 Sept. 1835, 16 Sept. 1835, 22 Sept. 1835.
55. Ibid., 25 Oct. 1835.
56. Ibid., 24 Jan. 1837.
57. Charles Trevelyan affidavit 19 Feb. 1849, DS, *Refutation*, pp. 16–18; Charles Edward Trevelyan deposition 19 August 1852, *DSAT*, vol. 2, pp. 45–47.
58. DS, *Refutation*, p. 18.
59. Spear, *Twilight*, pp. 182–93.
60. Diary 23–25 March 1835.
61. Bacon, *First Impressions*, vol. 2, pp. 32, 45, 51–3, 203, 217–18. See also Skinner, *Excursions*, pp. 79–84.
62. Diary 2 Nov. 1835, 10 Nov. 1835.
63. Samuel Enderby deposition 11 August 1854, *DSAT*, vol. 2, p. 304.
64. Diary 20 Dec. 1835; Charles Trevelyan letter 19 August 1843, DS, *Refutation*, p. 8.
65. Ibid., e. g., 23 Oct. 1835.
66. Ibid., 29 Sept. 1835; 'Records of Lodge Hope, No. 296', Freemason's Library, London; *Freemasons' Quarterly Review*, vol. 1836, p. 546; Firminger, *Early History of Freemasonry in Bengal*; Gupta, *Freemasonic Movements in India*; Hamill, *Craft*.

67. Lodge Hope, *Bylaws*, p. 27. See also Rich, *Elixir of Empire*.
68. Diary 5 Oct. 1835.
69. *Freemasons' Quarterly Review*, vol. 1840, pp. 533, 537; Harland-Jacobs, *Builders of Empire*, pp. 220–39.
70. Diary 31 July 1834.
71. Ibid., 2 April 1835.
72. Ibid., 7 July 1835.
73. Indeed, General Ramsay supported the British annexation of Sardhana, yet he subsequently asked Dyce Sombre for a personal loan, which the latter refused (although his sister's husband, Troup, provided it). Diary 1–2 Dec. 1837.
74. Ibid., 23 Oct. 1835.
75. Ibid., 20 Oct. 1835.
76. Ibid., 25 Dec. 1835.

4. MADE ROOTLESS

1. Ibid., 5 Jan. 1834; 20 Feb. 1834.
2. *Agra Moofussil Akbar*, quoted in Diary 8 April 1834.
3. Diary 25 July 1835.
4. Ibid., 6 April 1835.
5. Ibid., 5 April 1834.
6. Ibid., 16 April 1834.
7. Ibid., 13 Dec. 1834 to 4–5 Feb. 1835.
8. Ibid., 26 Nov. 1835.
9. Ibid., 8 Feb. 1835.
10. Keene, *Hindustan*, p. 103; Bacon, *First Impressions*, vol. 2, p. 59; Sleeman, *Rambles*, p. 610.
11. Hamilton in *Notes and Queries*, 8th Series, vol. 7 (20 April 1895), p. 309.
12. Diary 12 Feb. 1837.
13. McMahon, *Badshapoor Suit*, pp. 15–16.
14. Charles Metcalfe to Auckland 19 Oct. 1836, IPC 21 Nov. 1836, no. 18.
15. E.g., *Times* 2 August 1836; *Niles' Weekly Register* 22 Oct. 1836.
16. After a ten week gap following the death of the Begum, the diary recommences with his departure from Sardhana on this trip. This quotes come from his memory of his departure a year earlier. Diary 5 April 1836, 2 Oct. 1837.
17. Diary 13 April 1836.
18. Ibid., 28–29 April 1836.
19. Ibid., 11 Jan. 1837.
20. Ibid., 11–14 June 1834, 29 March 1835. David insisted that Fisher take out a life insurance policy on himself to ensure repayment. Henry Fisher letters 4 Jan., 17 Jan. 1838, D1798/398/2/5–6, Stafford County Record Office.

21. Ibid., 12 Feb. 1837.
22. Ibid., 9 Oct. 1836.
23. Ibid., 15 July 1835.
24. Keene, 'Sardhana', p. 458; Hodson, *List*, vol. 4, p. 579.
25. Diary 14 Oct. 1836.
26. Dyce Sombre to Peter Solaroli 14 Oct. 1836, *DSAT*, vol. 1, pp. 851–2.
27. Charles Metcalfe to Auckland 19 Oct. 1836, IPC 21 Nov. 1836, no. 18.
28. Diary 16 Dec. 1836.
29. Ibid., 21 Dec. 1836.
30. Ibid., 6 Jan. 1837.
31. Ibid., 30 Nov. 1837–7 Dec. 1837.
32. Ibid., 30 Nov. 1836.
33. Ibid., 9 Dec. 1836.
34. Ibid., 18 Jan. 1837.
35. Ibid., 19 Jan. 1837.

5. THE LAST OF ASIA

1. Ibid., 23 Jan. 1837.
2. Ibid., 30 Jan. 1837.
3. Ibid., 5 July 1837.
4. Soon after David left Calcutta, St Leger was replaced by a more concilia-tory Vicar Apostolic with greater experience in Asia and sensitivity to diversity within the Church. Stephen, *History of Christianity in India*, pp. 282–85.
5. Diary 25 Jan. 1837.
6. Ibid., 27 Jan. 1837.
7. Ibid., 27 Jan. 1838.
8. Ibid., 24 Jan. 1837.
9. Ibid., 25 Jan. 1837, 21 March 1837.
10. Ibid., 25 Jan. 1837.
11. Letter 8 Feb. 1836 in Macaulay, *Letters*, vol. 3, p. 169; Dyce Sombre to Lord Chancellor, 20 May 1851, Dyce Sombre, *In Lunacy*, pp. 201–3.
12. Diary 5 May 1837.
13. Henry Prinsep deposition 7 Sept. 1854, *DSAT*, vol. 2, pp. 65ff.
14. Diary 26 Jan. 1837.
15. Ibid., 1 Feb. 1837.
16. Ibid., 7 Feb. 1837.
17. Ibid., 21 Feb. 1837.
18. Ibid., 6 June 1837.
19. Ibid., 28 June 1837.
20. Ibid., 27 April 1837.
21. Ibid., 2 Feb. 1838.
22. *Annual Register* (1834), Law Cases (19 July 1834), pp. 305–9.

23. Diary 4 July 1837.

24. Ibid., 26 April 1837.

25. Ibid., 13 Feb. 1837, 6 March 1837.

26. Ibid., 8–13 Nov. 1837.

27. Bacon, *First Impressions*, vol. 2, p. 48.

28. Diary 28 Dec. 1837.

29. Ibid., 15 May, 20 May 1837.

30. Ibid., 7 Feb. 1837.

31. His Highness Prince Gholam Mahumed deposition 7 July 1854, *DSAT*, vol. 2, pp. 306–8; Fisher, *Counterflows*, pp. 305–9, 406–10.

32. Diary 15 Jan. 1838.

33. Ibid., 8 April 1837.

34. Ibid., 28 Jan. 1837.

35. Ibid., 1 Jan. 1838; see also Ibid., 10 June 1837, 21 Jan. 1838.

36. Ibid., 16 May 1837.

37. Ibid., 25 March 1837.

38. Ibid., e. g., 17 May 1837, 19–21 June 1837.

39. Ibid., 18–20 Jan. 1838.

40. Ibid., 30 Jan. 1838.

41. Ibid., 7 Feb. 1838.

42. Ibid., 9 Feb. 1837.

43. Ibid., 11 June 1837.

44. Ibid., 4 June 1837.

45. Ibid., 16, 28 June 1837.

46. Ibid., 28 June 1837.

47. Ibid., 17–27 July 1837.

48. Charles Trevelyan deposition 19 August 1852, *DSAT*, vol. 2, pp. 45–47; Diary 17–27 July 1837.

49. DS, *Refutation*, p. 19.

50. Diary e.g., 29 Jan. 1837.

51. Ibid., 8 March 1837.

52. Ibid., 5 April 1834.

53. Ibid., 14 August 1837.

54. Ibid., 25 Feb. 1837.

55. Ibid., 28 Feb. 1837.

56. Ibid., 11 March 1837.

57. Ibid., 25 April 1837.

58. Ibid., 7 Oct. 1837.

59. Ibid., 25 Feb. 1837.

60. Ibid., 26 March 1837.

61. Ibid., 30 March-18 May 1837.

62. Ibid., 11–13 Feb. 1837.

63. Ibid., 23 Feb.-28 April 1837.

64. Ibid., 7 May 1837–3 July 1837, 9 June 1837.

65. Ibid., 12–14 August 1837.

66. Ibid., 17 August 1837.
67. Ibid., 16 August 1837.
68. Ibid., 30 August 1837.
69. Ibid., 12–15 Sept. 1837.
70. Ibid., 8 Oct. 1837.
71. Ibid., 28 August 1837.
72. Ibid., 7 Sept. 1837.
73. Ibid., 21–22 Sept. 1837. He had previously written his second will while travelling across north India. Ibid., 19 Dec. 1836.
74. Ibid., 7 Sept. 1837.
75. Ibid., 8 Sept. 1837.
76. Ibid., 19 Sept. 1837.
77. Ibid., 15 Oct. 1837.
78. Ibid., 25 Oct. 1837.
79. Dyce Sombre to Peter Solaroli 14 Jan. 1838, *DSAT*, vol.'1, pp. 859–62.
80. Diary 3–5 Dec. 1837.
81. Ibid., 17–22 Dec. 1837.
82. Ibid., 21 Nov., 13 Dec. 1837.
83. Ibid., 17–22 Dec. 1837; William Spencer letter 30 Sept. 1837, D1798/398/2/4 Stafford County Record Office.
84. Diary 3–5 Dec., 21 Dec. 1837, 1–12 Jan. 1838.
85. Ibid., 24 Dec. 1837, 5–11 Jan. 1838.
86. Dyce Sombre to Peter Solaroli 14 Jan. 1838, *DSAT*, vol. 1, pp. 859–62.
87. Diary 9–10 Jan. 1838; Dyce Sombre to Antonio Reghellini 6 Nov. 1844, L/L/64 (438), BL; Syed Oodeen alias Sheik Edoo deposition 6 Jan. 1853, *DSAT*, vol. 2, pp. 291–2.
88. Diary 21 Dec. 1837.
89. Ibid., 1 Jan. 1838.
90. Ibid., 11 Jan. 1838.
91. Ibid., 13–19 May 1838.
92. Dyce Sombre to Drever 8 Feb. 1838, *DSAT*, vol. 1, pp. 862–63.
93. Diary 7 August 1837; Deed of Settlement by David Ochterlony Dyce Sombre, Mss Eur C318/1–2, BL; Answers of Ann May Troup 2 Sept. 1851, *DSAT*, vol. 1, pp. 101–17.
94. Dyce Sombre to Drever 8 Feb. 1838 and 17 Feb. 1838, *DSAT*, vol. 1, pp. 862–65.
95. Dyce Sombre to Drever 17 Feb. 1838, *DSAT*, vol. 1, pp. 864–65.
96. Diary 10 Jan. 1838.
97. Thompson, *Life of Charles, Lord Metcalfe*, pp. 101–2, 340–54.
98. *Oriental Herald and Colonial Intelligencer*, vol. 2 (1838), p. 487; Diary 31 Jan. 1838.
99. Dyce lies buried in North Park St Burial Ground, Calcutta, see F/4/1324/ 52471; Burial N/1/52 f.55, BL; George Craigie deposition 7 Sept. 1852, *DSAT*, vol. 2, pp. 168–69.

100. Colonel George A. D. Dyce estate, *DSAT*, vol. 1, pp. 492–512. Dyce's intestate estate, by that point 44,559 Rs., was paid to his children in 1841. *London Gazette* 7 Feb. 1843.

101. *DSAT*, vol. 1, pp. 522–27.

102. Diary 22 Feb. 1837.

PART TWO: EUROPE

6: TO BRITAIN

1. Dyce Sombre took only one hired servant with him, about whom we know virtually nothing. Nowhere in his diary does Dyce Sombre even mention his name or any deed.

2. Diary 18–21 March 1838.

3. Ibid., 28 May 1838.

4. Ibid., 26–31 March 1838, 21 April 1838.

5. Ibid., 22 Feb. 1838.

6. Ibid., 17 Feb. 1838.

7. Ibid., 18–21 March 1838.

8. Ibid., 13–19 May 1838.

9. Ibid., 26–31 March 1838.

10. Ibid., 25 Feb. 1838.

11. Ibid., 28 May 1838.

12. Ibid., 25 Feb. 1838.

13. Ibid., 11 March 1838.

14. Ibid., 20, 21 April 1838.

15. Ibid., 5 June 1838.

16. Charles Metcalfe, *Life and Correspondence*, vol. 2, pp. 222–223n. www.measuringworth.com.

17. Diary 5 June 1838.

18. Ibid., 5 June 1838.

19. Ibid., 5 June 1838.

20. Ibid., 7 June 1838.

21. Grindlay and Co., *Overland Circular*; Tyson, *100 Years of Banking*.

22. According to the retail price index. It is worth over £15 million using average earnings. www.measuringworth.com

23. In technical terms: Quarterly, 1st and 4th, Or [gold], two chainshots, the one in chief and the other base Sable [black], for SOMBRE; 2nd and 3rd, per chev. embattled Or and Gules [red] in chief two bombs fired Proper [natural color] in base two battle axes in saltire Argent [silver], for DYCE. RESTS: 1st, for SOMBRE: the "Chatti" or Parasol of State of Sirdhana, Or; 2nd, DYCE: Out of an Eastern crown Or, a demi tiger issuant Vert [green], striped gold, holding between the paws a flagstaff Proper thereon hoisted a banner per bend embattled Argent and of the second, charged

with a scymitar in bend sinister also Proper pommel and hilt of the first. *Illustrated London News* 12 July 1851.

24. *United Service Journal and Naval and Military Magazine* (1838) part 2, p. 417.
25. Jamh ood-Deen however generated complaints from fellow members for removing his shoes and sitting with his feet on the sofa. Forrest, *Oriental*, p. 88; Oriental Club Candidate Books, 1824–58, LMA/4452/04/01/001–2 and Miscellaneous Letters to Oriental Club Secretary LMA/4452/08/01/008, London Metropolitan Archives; Wheeler, *Annals of the Oriental Club*; Riches, *History of the Oriental Club*.
26. See Sinha, 'Britishness, Clubbability, and the Colonial Public Sphere'.
27. He was elected 11 Nov. 1843 to this status, above Novice Esquires and mere Knights but below Grand Cross Knights. Grand Conclave, *Statutes*.
28. George Sigmond depositions 28 July 1851, 6 April 1852, *DSAT*, vol. 1, pp. 68–72, 686. See also Fisher, *Counterflows*, Chapters 7–10.
29. Dyce Sombre to Peter Solaroli 2 June 1839, *DSAT*, vol. 1, p. 867.
30. See Eaton, 'Critical Cosmopolitanism'.
31. Combermere, *Memoirs and Correspondence*, vol. 2, pp. 220–22.
32. Combermere, *Memoirs and Correspondence*, vol. 1, p. 354; 'Accounts of Slave Compensation Claims', Great Britain, Parliamentary Papers, Commons, 1837–38 (215), vol. 48, pp. 1–79, List A, Jamaica.
33. This amount was equivalent to over 60% of Combermere's net wealth. Lord Combermere deposition 3 July 1852, *DSAT*, vol. 2, p. 40–45; Mrs Dyce Sombre deposition 20 Feb. 1849, L/L/65 (451), BL; *Times* 1 March 1849.
34. Diary 7 June 1838. These were the last words in the surviving part of his diary.
35. See Political Department, Home Correspondence, L/PS/3/106, ff. 23–4, 50–53; L/PS/3/107, ff. 83, 105–7, BL; DS, *Refutation*, pp. 438–42, 445–46.
36. Dyce Sombre to Peter Solaroli 11 May 1839, *DSAT*, vol. 1, pp. 865–66.
37. Combermere, *Memoirs and Correspondence*, vol. 2, p. 294; Lord Combermere affidavit 2 March 1844, Dyce Sombre, *In Lunacy*, Appendix 1, pp. 7–10; Lord Combermere deposition 3 July 1852, *DSAT*, vol. 2, pp. 40–45.
38. *Oriental Herald and Colonial Intelligencer*, vol. 3, (1839), p. 390.

7. A VISCOUNT'S DAUGHTER

1. Owen, *Life of Lord St Vincent*, pp. 239ff.
2. Lady Elizabeth Jane nonetheless remarried less than a year later, to the Reverend Richard Brickenden. *Times* 12 March, 23 Jan. 1799; Gill, *New Volume*, vol. 2, pp 175–209; Society of Gentlemen of the Middle Temple, *Counsellor's Magazine*, pp. 191–5.
3. Clarey, 'Lady Forester', p. 373.

4. *Times* 1, 2 Oct. 1829; Suzuki, *Madness at Home*, p. 107.

5. Suzuki, *Madness at Home*, p. 22.

6. England and Wales, Commissioners in Lunacy, *Report of the Metropolitan Commissioners*, pp. 115–16.

7. Suzuki, *Madness at Home*, p. 37. See also Porter, *Mind-forg'd Manacles*, p. 112.

8. *Times* 1, 2 Oct. 1829.

9. *Times* 10, 12 Dec. 1829.

10. Mary Anne lived in Paris in 1833 and 1836–37. For excerpts from her Paris diary of 1836–37 see Clarey, 'Lady Forester', pp. 78–104 and original in William Salt Library. Wellington letter 11 August 1838, Maxwell, *Life of Wellington*, vol. 2, p. 376.

11. Her published music includes: '*shall This Pale Cheek; a Ballad*'; '*La Partenza*'; '*Two Italian Duetts and One Song*'; '*Blow, Blow, Thou Winter Winde*' from *As You Like It*. See also Greenhill, *List*, pp. 4–5.

12. *Morning Post* 27 June, 8 July 1831; Clarey, 'Lady Forester', p. 71.

13. 'Genealogical Memoir of the Hon. Miss Jervis', *Court Magazine and Belle Assemblee*,vol. 4 (May 1834), pp. 162–4.

14. Benjamin Disraeli to Sarah Disraeli 19 June 1833, Disraeli, *Letters*, vol. 1, no. 279.

15. Derby, *Disraeli*, p. 348.

16. Mary Ann Jervis, 'Diary' (1836), William Salt Library, quoted in Cleary, 'Lady Forester', pp. 99–100. For similar sentiments see Shelley, *Diary*, p. 405; Arbuthnot, *Journal*, vol 2, p. 257.

17. Greville, *Memoirs*, vol. 1, pp. 186–7, 192–94; vol. 2, p. 339.

18. Other Asians also used the status of women to compare the morality of their culture with Europe. See Fisher, 'Representing "His" Women'.

19. 'Inventory of Dyce Sombre's effects', 9 August 1845, L/L/65, (452), BL.

20. Marchioness of Salisbury, 'Diary', 30 Oct. 1833, 7 Nov. 1836, Salisbury MSS, quoted in Oman, *Gascoyne Heiress*, pp. 94, 218, 224.

21. Wellington to Lady de Ros, 17 August 1837, quoted in Maxwell, *Life of Wellington*, vol. 2, p. 376.

22. Anonymous letter 27 Sept. 1837, Wellington MSS in possession of Duke of Wellington, quoted in Longsford, *Wellington*, pp. 297–98.

23. Moore, *Journal*, vol. 5, pp. 1899–2073.

24. Taylor, *Correspondence*, pp. 91–2.

25. Wellington letter 11 August 1838, quoted in Maxwell, *Life of Wellington*, vol 2, pp. 376ff.

26. Parker Jervis Collection, William Salt Library, quoted in Clarey, 'Lady Forester', p. 109.

27. Maxwell, *Life of Wellington*, vol. 2, pp. 249–50.

28. Lord St Vincent Speech, 9 June 1828 in Great Britain, Parliament, *Parliamentary Debates*, 2nd series, vol. 19, 1188–89; Holland, *Holland House Diaries*, p. 55.

29. E. g., G. Bobson, 'Letter to T. Smith', *Blackwood's Edinburgh Magazine*, vol. 59, no. 367 (May 1846), pp. 534–42; *Agra Ukhbar* 14 August 1841 reproduced in *Friend of India* 2 Sept. 1841; *Satirist* 10 March 1849; *Saturday Evening Post* 29 Sept. 1860; Neuman, *Diary*, vol. 2, pp. 164–65; *Le Siècl* 21 March 1844.

30. *Anti-Slavery Reporter and Aborigines' Friend*, ser. 3, vol. 9 (1861), p. 143.

31. Lord St. Vincent speeches, 5 Feb. 1807, 17 April 1826, 4 June 1833 in Great Britain, Parliament, *Parliamentary Debates*, 1st series, vol. 8, p. 669; 2nd series, vol. 15, p. 264; 3rd series, vol. 18, pp. 299, 360–362, 1171–74. See also Higman, 'West India "Interest" in Parliament'.

32. Forester, 'Notes on the Jervis Pedigree', ff. 26–27.

33. Lord Combermere affidavit 2 March 1844, Dyce Sombre, *In Lunacy*, Appendix 1, pp. 7–10.

34. Edward Ricketts deposition 20 Sept. 1853, *DSAT*, vol. 2, pp. 373–74.

35. Forester, 'Notes on the Jervis Pedigree', ff. 26–27.

8. ENCOUNTERING THE EUROPEAN ARISTOCRACY

1. Mary Anne Dyce Sombre affidavit 25 June 1844, Dyce Sombre, *In Lunacy*, pp. 1–25.

2. Reverend Thomas Farr deposition 20 Jan. 1844, L/L/65 (451), BL; Dyce Sombre, *In Lunacy*, Appendix 1, pp. 5–6; DS, *Refutation*, pp. 95–97.

3. Wellington to Lady Wilton, 8 Sept. 1840, in Wellington, *Wellington and His Friends*, pp. 143–44.

4. *Observer* reprinted in *Times* 26 Feb. 1839; Benjamin Disraeli to Mary Anne Lewis 20(?) Dec. 1838 and Benjamin to Sarah Disraeli 6 Feb. 1839, Disraeli, *Letters*, vol. 3 nos. 855, 879; George Forester affidavit 27 August 1853, *DSAT*, vol. 2, p. 365.

5. Neuman, *Diary*, vol. 2, p. 162.

6. *Gagliani's Messenger* reprinted in *Times* 23 Oct. 1838.

7. Sebastian Felix Feuillet de Conches deposition 22 May 1852, *DSAT*, vol. 2, pp. 155–59.

8. Broadley, *History of Freemasonry in the District of Malta*, pp. 23–24.

9. Dyce Sombre to Peter Solaroli 11 May 1839, *DSAT*, vol. 1, pp. 865–66.

10. Dyce Sombre to Antonio Reghellini 6 Dec. 1838 and 16 Jan. 1839, *DSAT*, vol. 2, pp. 183–85.

11. Dyce Sombre to Peter Solaroli 11 May 1839 and 27 Dec. 1841, *DSAT*, vol. 1, pp. 865–66, 868–69; D1798/398/2/5–6, Stafford County Record Office.

12. Gladstone, *Diaries*, vol. 2, pp. 558, 567, 569; Joseph Olliffe deposition 7 April 1852, *DSAT*, vol. 2, pp. 73–84; George Chichester deposition 3 Jan. 1849, L/L/65 (451); DS, *Refutation*, pp 493–95.

13. Reverend Thomas Farr deposition 20 Jan. 1844, L/L/65 (451), BL; Dyce Sombre, *In Lunacy*, Appendix 1, pp. 5–6; DS, *Refutation*, pp. 95–97.

14. Manavit, *Esquisse historique sur le cardinal Mezzofanti*, pp. 100–1; Murray, *Handbook of Rome*, p. 269.

15. Dyce Sombre to Peter Solaroli 11 May 1839, *DSAT*, vol. 1, p. 867.

16. Dyce Sombre to Antonio Reghellini 16 Jan. 1839, *DSAT*, vol. 2, p. 183.

17. Keegan, *Sardhana and its Begam*, pp. 55–64.

18. Dyce Sombre to Peter Solaroli 2 June 1839, *DSAT*, vol. 1, p. 867.

19. *Morning Chronicle* 8 July 1839; *Charter* 14 July 1839.

20. Hannah Matheson deposition 20 Jan. 1854, *DSAT*, vol. 2, pp. 526–28.

21. Wellington to Lady Wilton 8 Sept. 1840, in Wellington, *Wellington and His Friends*, pp. 143–44.

22. Reverend Thomas Farr deposition 20 Jan. 1844, L/L/65 (451), BL; Dyce Sombre, *In Lunacy*, Appendix 1, pp. 5–6; DS, *Refutation*, pp. 95–97.

23. Lord Combermere deposition 3 July 1852, *DSAT*, vol. 2, pp. 40–45. For her version of these events see: Answers of Mrs Dyce Sombre 2 Sept. 1851, *DSAT*, vol. 1, pp. 92–100.

24. Dr. Edward Monro deposition 18 August 1853, *DSAT*, vol. 2, pp. 354–55.

25. Dyce Sombre Marriage Settlement, D1535 Box 4, Stafford County Record Office.

26. This letter was quoted in court and many newspapers. E. g., *Times* 16 July 1844.

27. Helen Cleary suggests that this was the cause of her illness; personal communication, 24 Dec. 1996.

28. Dyce Sombre to Antonio Reghellini 31 Oct. 1840, *DSAT*, vol. 2, pp. 182, 204.

29. Dyce Sombre to Antonio Reghellini 2 Oct. 1842, *DSAT*, vol. 2, pp. 205–6.

30. Mary Anne Dyce Sombre affidavit 25 June 1844, Dyce Sombre, *In Lunacy*, pp. 1–25.

31. Neuman, *Diary*, vol. 2, pp. 164–65; Geary, *Musical Education*, p. 40.

32. Mary Anne Dyce Sombre affidavit 25 June 1844, Dyce Sombre, *In Lunacy*, pp. 1–25.

33. Dyce Sombre to Peter Solaroli 1 May 1841, *DSAT*, vol. 1, p. 868; James Rodgers deposition 7 Dec. 1853, *DSAT*, vol 2., pp. 516–21.

34. Mary Anne Dyce Sombre affidavit 25 June 1844, Dyce Sombre, *In Lunacy*, pp. 1–25.

35. Dyce Sombre to Peter Solaroli 27 Dec. 1841, *DSAT*, vol. 1, pp. 868–69.

9. DYCE SOMBRE IN BRITISH PARLIAMENT

1. John Stewart, Esq., who owned a small sugar plantation on Antigua, represented Lymington (1832–47) as a Conservative. He, too, reportedly purchased his election. *Notes and Queries* quoted in *Littell's Living Age* 11 July 1857, p. 82; *Saturday Evening Post* 29 Sept. 1860, p. 6.

2. Charles Trevelyan deposition 19 August 1852, *DSAT*, vol. 2, p. 56.

3. Obituary of James Coppock, *Times* 21 Dec. 1857; *Gentleman's Magazine* (Feb. 1858), pp. 222–23.

4. Quoted in Boyd, *Reminiscences*, pp. 183–86.

5. Dod, *Electoral Facts*, pp. 298–99; Berry, *Bribery!*.

6. Dickens, *Posthumous Papers*, vol. 1, pp. 165–83; Bagenal, *Life of Ralph Bernal Osborne*, pp. 43–44, 182–83.

7. *Ipswich Journal* 26, 3 July 1841.

8. Disraeli, *Coningsby*, p. 273.

9. Parry, 'Benjamin Disraeli'.

10. A silk-merchant based in London but with business connections with Sudbury, Andrew Peacock, also helped the Sudbury delegation in their search. Great Britain, Parliament, *Report of the Commissioners*, pp. 6ff.; Reform Club, *Rules*; John Stuart Mill to Harriet Mill 22 Feb. 1855, Mill, *Collected Works*, vol. 14, pp. 341n, 342; 'Surity for Frederick Villiers Meynell' 23 Oct. 1857, J117/99, PRO; Bulwer, *Life*, pp. 330–32.

11. Great Britain, Parliament, *Journals of the House of Commons*, vol. 90, 25–6 Feb. 1835, 12 March 1835, 24 March 1835, 26 March 1835, 8–9 April 1835, 26 May 1835; Dod, *Electoral Facts*, p. 46.

12. Dod, *Electoral Facts*, pp. xlvii-xlviii.

13. Bentham, *Works*, p. 66.

14. Peter Solaroli deposition 17 Nov. 1853, Neil Baillie deposition 11 Feb. 1854, *DSAT*, vol. 2, pp. 496–504, 532–35.

15. *Times* 26 May 1846; Gash, *Politics in the Age of Peel*, pp. 130–1, 431.

16. Dickens, *Posthumous Papers*, vol. 1, pp. 165–83.

17. Great Britain, Parliament, *Minutes of Evidence on Second Reading of Bill, 'Act to exclude Borough of Sudbury'*.

18. Aydelotte, 'House of Commons in the 1840s'.

19. *Ipswich Journal* 3 July 1841.

20. Cox, *Law and Practice of Registration and Elections*, p. 136.

21. 'Poll Book for Sudbury, 1841', Institute for Historical Research, London.

22. *Times* 27 April 1842, reprinted 27 April 1942.

23. *Times* 5 July 1841.

24. Salop CRO 1224/31, quoted in Cleary, 'Lady Forester', p. 241.

25. *Who's Who of British Members of Parliament*, pp. 356, 392.

26. Kemp, 'General Election of 1841'.

27. Great Britain, Parliament, *Parliamentary Debates*, 3rd Series, vols. 59–63 (1841–42).

28. He was later MP for Carmarthenshire in his native Wales, 1862–68.

29. Dod, *Electoral Facts*, pp. lxiii-lxiv.

30. Barron and Austin, *Reports of Cases of Controverted Elections*, p. vi.

31. Woodbridge, *Reform Club*.

32. Troup deposition 25 Nov. 1853, *DSAT*, vol. 2, pp. 504–12.

33. DS, *Refutation*, pp. 447–58.

34. *Ipswich Journal* 25 June 1842.

35. Khan, *Siyahat Namah*, pp. 130, 174–75, 192, 229; Fisher, *Counterflows*, Chapter 8.

36. See Fisher, *First Indian Author.*

37. *DSAT*, vol. 1, p. 45.

38. Johan Furhberg, Amede, and Christopher Smith depositions 8 Oct. 1853, Joseph Privitera deposition 14 Oct. 1853, *DSAT*, vol. 2, pp. 405–22.

39. Dyce Sombre to Peter Solaroli 2 June 1839 and 1 May 1841, *DSAT*, vol. 1, pp. 867–68; Dyce Sombre to Antonio Reghellini 1 May 1841 and 30 Dec. 1842 PROB 37/1700, PRO.

40. Dyce Sombre to Peter Solaroli 27 Dec. 1841, *DSAT*, vol. 1, pp. 868–69.

41. Dyce Sombre to Peter Solaroli 4 April 1842, *DSAT*, vol. 1, pp. 871–72.

42. Dyce Sombre to Antonio Reghellini 2 Oct. 1842, *DSAT*, vol. 2, pp. 205–6.

43. Fallon, *New Hindustani-English Dictionary*, p. 527b, s.v. 'charna'.

44. Hawes, *Poor Relations.*

45. Cumming did not know Dyce Sombre personally and so repeated British oral tradition about him in Meerut. Cumming, *Six Year's Diary*, p. 136.

46. *Agra Ukhbar* 14 August 1841 reproduced in *Friend of India* 2 Sept. 1841.

47. *Atlas* quoted in *Daily National Intelligencer* 17 May 1842; *Times* 27 Dec. 1841; Fane, *Five Years in India*, vol. 1, pp. 105–7.

48. Mary Anne Dyce Sombre affidavit 25 June 1844 and Sir James Clark affidavit 21 June 1844, Dyce Sombre, *In Lunacy*, pp. 1–25, 41–6; *Times* 2 August 1843; Cardigan, *My Recollections*, pp. 41–46.

49. Thomas Drever deposition 24 June 1844, *DSAT*, vol. 2, pp. 31–40.

50. Mary Anne Dyce Sombre affidavit 25 June 1844, Dyce Sombre, *In Lunacy*, pp. 1–25.

51. Dyce Sombre letter to Drever 11 Jan. 1842, quoted in Thomas Drever deposition 24 June 1844, *DSAT*, vol. 2, pp. 31–40.

52. Thomas Drever deposition 24 June 1844, *DSAT*, vol. 2, pp. 31–40; *Times* 2 August 1843.

53. Lord Combermere deposition 2 March 1844, Dyce Sombre, *In Lunacy*, Appendix 1, pp. 7–10.

54. Thomas Drever deposition 24 June 1844, *DSAT*, vol. 2, pp. 31–40.

55. Dyce Sombre to Peter Solaroli 31 Jan. 1842, *DSAT*, vol. 1, pp. 870–71.

56. *Age* 13 Feb. 1842.

57. Barron and Austin, *Reports of Cases of Controverted Elections*, pp. 237–52.

58. *Times* 31 July 1847, 22 Jan. 1848.

59. *Times* 8, 9 April 1842.

60. Thomas Drever deposition 24 June 1844, *DSAT*, vol. 2, pp. 31–40.

61. Barron and Austin, *Reports of Cases of Controverted Elections*, pp. 240–41.

62. Great Britain, Parliament, Select Committee on the Sudbury Election Petition, p. 847; Great Britain, Parliament, *Parliamentary Debates*, 3rd series,

vol. 63, p. 343–51; *Times* 15 April 1842; *Westminster Review*, vol. 50 (Oct. 1848–Jan. 1849), pp. 34–60.

63. Great Britain, Parliament, *Parliamentary Debates*, 3rd series, vol. 76, pp. 587–90; Gash, *Politics in the Age of Peel*, pp. 135–36, 159–64.

64. Dod, *Electoral Facts*, pp. xxxvii n. 2, 298–99.

65. *Punch*, vol. 2 (Jan.-June 1842), pp. 202, 250.

66. *Bury Post* reprinted in *Times* 27 April 1842.

67. *Ipswich Journal*, 16 April 1842; Great Britain, Parliament, *Parliamentary Debates*, 3rd series, vols 63–76 (1842–44); Hobhouse Papers, Add 36471, ff.203, 436, BL; Southgate, *Passing of the Whigs*, p. 93n2.

68. *Times* 15, 27 April 1842, 21 May 1842, 3 August 1843.

10. LUNACY

1. India Board to Dyce Sombre 14 June 1842, *Refutation*, pp. 461–62.

2. Dyce Sombre to Edward Drummond 2 August 1842, Peel Papers, Add 40513, ff 48–49, BL.

3. Mary Anne Dyce Sombre affidavit 25 June 1844, Dyce Sombre, *In Lunacy*, pp. 1–25.

4. Lewis, *Horace Walpole's Library*, p. 52; Smith, 'Hunting for Manuscripts', *Atlantic Monthly*, vol. 160 (July-Dec., 1937), pp. 92–98.

5. Joseph Olliffe deposition 7 April 1852, *DSAT*, vol. 2, pp. 73–84.

6. Thomas Drever deposition 24 June 1844, *DSAT*, vol. 2, pp. 31–40.

7. Comte Ventura deposition 22 Oct. 1853, *DSAT*, vol. 2, pp. 472–79; *Times* 2 August 1843.

8. Dyce Sombre to Peter Solaroli 4 June 1842, *DSAT*, vol. 1, pp. 871–2.

9. Dunsford, *Pathogenetic Effects* and *Practical Advantages of Homeopathy*.

10. Nicholson, *Trial at Full Length*.

11. Mrs Dyce Sombre to Dyce Sombre 1 Dec. 1842, *DSAT*, vol. 2, pp. 207–8; Mary Anne Dyce Sombre affidavit 25 June 1844, Dyce Sombre, *In Lunacy*, pp. 1–25.

12. Scull, 'John Conolly' and 'Victorian Alienist: John Conolly'; Showalter, *Female Malady*.

13. John Conolly deposition 7 Sept. 1853, *DSAT*, vol. 2, pp. 365–67.

14. John Conolly affidavits 9 Feb. 1844 and 21 June 1844, Edward Monro affidavits 12 Feb. 1844 and 21 June 1844, Dyce Sombre, *In Lunacy*, pp. 47–53.

15. Dyce Sombre letter to Drever 4 Feb. 1843, quoted in Thomas Drever deposition 24 June 1844, *DSAT*, vol. 2, pp. 31–40.

16. Wellington to Lady Priscilla Burghersh 27 March 1843, Burghersh, *Correspondence*, pp. 146–47.

17. Sir James Clark affidavit 21 June 1844, Dyce Sombre, *In Lunacy*, pp. 41–46.

18. *Times* 2 August 1843.

19. Dyce Sombre to Lady Marcus Hill 2 April 1843, *DSAT*, vol. 1, p. 874.

20. Dyce Sombre to Mrs Dyce Sombre 5 April and 8 April 1843, *DSAT*, vol. 1, pp. 875–76.

21. Elmes, Metropolitan Improvements, p. 50; Samuel, *Villas in Regent's Park*, pp. 18–21; Saunders, *Regent's Park*, pp. 9ff, 118–19.

22. Dyce Sombre to Bartle Frere 5 July 1843, PROB 37/1700, PRO; Dyce Sombre to Sir James Clark 5 July 1843, *DSAT*, vol. 1, p. 877.

23. Jones, *Lunacy, Law and Conscience*, pp. 145–47, 170ff.; Suzuki, *Madness at Home*.

24. Perceval, *Narrative of the Treatment*; McCandless, 'Dangerous to Themselves and Others'.

25. *Spirit of the Times* 20 May 1843.

26. Dyce Sombre's unattested will of 10 May 1843, *DSAT*, vol. 1, pp. 42–45.

27. 'Journal or Report of the Medical Council of St Petersburgh' 17 Dec. 1844, Dyce Sombre, *In Lunacy*, pp. 19–21.

28. E.g., Millingen, *Aphorisms*, pp. 148–49.

29. Mary Anne Dyce Sombre affidavit 25 June 1844, Dyce Sombre, *In Lunacy*, pp. 1–25.

30. Lord Combermere affidavit 2 March 1844, Dyce Sombre, *In Lunacy*, Appendix 1, pp. 7–10.

31. Thomas Drever deposition 24 June 1844, *DSAT*, vol. 2, pp. 31–40.

32. Orlich, *Travels in India*, vol. 2, pp. 204–9.

33. 5&6 Vict, c. 84 of 1842 created, under Lord Chancellor, two 'Commissioners in Lunacy'. Jones, *Lunacy, Law and Conscience*, p. 222.

34. *Annual Register* 3 July 1843, Chronicle, pp. 83–4. For the Cheetham family, see Burke, *Genealogical and Hereldic History*, vol. 4, pp. 602–3. See also Ernst, *Mad Tales of the Raj*, pp. 72–3, 137–38.

35. Dyce Sombre to Bartle Frere 5 July 1843, PROB 37/1700, PRO; Dyce Sombre to Sir James Clark 5 July 1843, *DSAT*, vol. 1, p. 877.

36. *Annals of Our Time* 31 July 1843; *Annual Register* 31 July 1843, Chronicle, pp. 101–2; *John Bull* 5, 7 August 1843; *Spirit of the Times* 2 Sept. 1843, p. 324; DS, *Refutation*, p. 31n.

37. *Times* 2 August 1843.

38. Dudley-Ward, *Romance of the Nineteenth Century*, p. 169.

39. *Times* 17 July 1844; Elliotson, 'Accounts of More Painless Surgical Operations', p. 59n.

40. Charles Trevelyan to J. C. Melville 19 August 1843, DS, *Refutation*, pp. 8–9.

41. Pagan, *Medical Jurisprudence of Insanity*, esp. pp. 120ff, pp. 198–99; England and Wales, Commissioners in Lunacy, *Report of the Metropolitan Commissioners,*, pp. 102–13; Goldstein, *Console and Classify*, pp. 153ff.

42. Quoted in Scull, *Museums of Madness*, p. 237. In 1843, the M'Naughten Rules tried to bring system and definition to criminal cases concerning

lunacy and the insanity plea. The juridical principle became the mental capacity of the defendant to distinguish between right and wrong. Smith, *Trial by Medicine*; Eigen, *Witnessing Insanity*.

43. Pagan, *Medical Jurisprudence of Insanity*, p. 2.
44. Clark, *Memoir of John Conolly*, p. 184.
45. Quoted in Pagan, *Medical Jurisprudence of Insanity*, p. 2.
46. Millingen, *Aphorisms*, p. 151n.
47. Pagan, *Medical Jurisprudence of Insanity*, p. 15.
48. Lennox, *Fifty Years' Biographical Reminiscences*, vol. 2, pp. 230–45.
49. *Westminster Review*, vol. 49 (April 1848–July 1848); Burnett, *Insanity Tested by Science*.
50. Parry-Jones, *Trade in Lunacy*, p. 69; Lyndhurst, *Memoir*, pp. 46–47.
51. Elmer, *Outline of the Practice in Lunacy*, pp. 58–62; Phillips, *Law Concerning Lunatics*, pp. 278–9.
52. Clarke, *Memoir of John Conolly*.
53. Charles Trevelyan deposition 19 August 1852, *DSAT*, vol. 2, p. 47.
54. Charles Trevelyan to J. C. Melville 19 August 1843, DS, *Refutation*, pp. 8–9.
55. Charles Trevelyan letter 6 Sept. 1843, Minutes of the Court of Directors 13 Sept. 1843, B/206, f. 545, BL.
56. Charles Trevelyan to Lord Chancellor 26 Jan. 1849, Dyce Sombre, *In Lunacy*, p. 165; Charles Trevelyan affidavit 19 Feb. 1849, DS, *Refutation*, pp. 16–18; Charles Trevelyan affidavit 27 Feb. 1849, L/L/64 (438), BL.
57. James Martin affidavit 24 June 1844, Dyce Sombre, *In Lunacy*, pp. 55–6; Martin, *Influence of Tropical Climates*; Ernst, *Mad Tales of the Raj*, p. 119.
58. Drever to St. Vincent 23 August 1843 and reply 27 August, DS, *Refutation*, pp. 70–71.

11. LUNATIC ONLY IN ENGLAND, SANE ELSEWHERE

1. Among other newspapers: *Illustrated London News* 30 Sept. 1843; *Times* 28 Sept., 2 Oct. 1843; *Ipswich Journal* 30 Sept. 1843; *Bristol Mercury* 30 Sept. 1843.
2. Gabriel Delessert affidavit 13 May 1852 and Henry Martin affidavits 4 Jan. 1844 and Feb. 1844, L/L/64 (438), BL.
3. Mary Anne Dyce Sombre affidavit 25 June 1844, Dyce Sombre, *In Lunacy*, pp. 1–25.
4. Dyce Sombre to Mrs Dyce Sombre Paris 24 Sept. 1843, *DSAT*, vol. 1, pp. 878–82; Dyce Sombre to Mrs Dyce Sombre 20–28 Oct. 1843, quoted in Mary Anne Dyce Sombre affidavit 25 June 1844, Dyce Sombre, *In Lunacy*, pp. 1–25.
5. Dyce Sombre to Antonio Reghellini 3 Oct. 1843 and 3 Nov. 1843, *DSAT*, vol. 2, pp. 208–9; Dyce Sombre to Antonio Reghellini 6 Dec. 1843, L/L/64 (438), BL.

6. Dyce Sombre to Mrs Dyce Sombre 12 Oct. 1843, quoted in Mary Anne Dyce Sombre affidavit 25 June 1844, Dyce Sombre, *In Lunacy*, pp. 1–25.

7. Felix Feuillet de Conches affidavit 1 Feb. 1844, DS, *Refutation*, pp. 47–50.

8. Dr. Louis Jule Béhier deposition 22 May 1852 and Sir Robert Chermside deposition 20 May 1852, *DSAT*, vol. 2, pp. 140–41, 160–61.

9. Charles Okey deposition 16 Sept. 1853, *DSAT*, vol. 2, pp. 369–72.

10. Mrs Dyce Sombre to Dyce Sombre 28 Sept., 3 Nov., 16 Oct., 21 Oct., 24 Oct. 1843, 8 Jan. 1844, *DSAT*, vol. 2, pp. 276, 281–85.

11. Dyce Sombre to Mrs Dyce Sombre 24 Sept., 21 Nov. 1843, *DSAT*, vol. 1, pp. 878, 883; 12 Oct. to 7 Dec. 1843, quoted in Mary Anne Dyce Sombre affidavit 25 June 1844, Dyce Sombre, *In Lunacy*, pp. 1–25.

12. *Times* 18 July 1844.

13. Great Britain, Parliament, 'Report from the Select Committee on Dog Stealing', p. 327; Sarah Lake deposition 29 August 1853, *DSAT*, vol. 2, pp. 359–62; Dyce Sombre to Mrs Dyce Sombre 25 Nov. 1843, quoted in Mary Anne Dyce Sombre affidavit 25 June 1844, Dyce Sombre, *In Lunacy*, pp. 1–25.

14. Mary Anne Dyce Sombre affidavit 25 June 1844, Dyce Sombre, *In Lunacy*, pp. 1–25; Affadavit of John Newing 6 Jan. 1844, DS, *Refutation*, p. 111.

15. Dowbeggin, 'Degeneration and Hereditarianism in French Mental Medicine'.

16. Dyce Sombre to Troup 10 Dec. 1843; Dyce Sombre to Mrs Dyce Sombre 2 Dec. 1843, quoted in Mary Anne Dyce Sombre affidavit 25 June 1844, Dyce Sombre, *In Lunacy*, pp. 1–25.

17. Peter Solaroli to Minister of Interior of France 5 Oct. 1843, PRO 37/1700 part II; Dyce Sombre to Mrs Dyce Sombre 7 Dec. 1843, quoted in Mary Anne Dyce Sombre affidavit 25 June 1844, Dyce Sombre, *In Lunacy*, pp. 1–25; Peter Solaroli deposition 17 Nov. 1853 and Thomas Fraser deposition 29 Nov. 1853, *DSAT*, vol. 2, pp. 496–504, 512–14; *Times* 30 March, 17 April 1846.

18. Solaroli was not punished for accusing Frere of offering him a bribe because the Lord Chancellor judged Solaroli's imperfect knowledge of English explained his mistaken understanding of events. Hence, being non-Anglicized excused what would be a crime in an Englishman or someone more Anglicised. Lord Lyndhurst judgement 8 August 1844, Dyce Sombre, *In Lunacy*, pp. 57–92.

19. Joseph Olliffe deposition 7 April 1852, *DSAT*, vol. 2, pp. 73–84.

20. Louis Lassieur Breguet affidavit 30 Jan. 1844, DS, *Refutation*, p. 106.

21. Alexandre Vallor affidavit 6 Jan. 1844, DS, *Refutation*, p. 105.

22. Louis Francois Schrader affidavit 27 Jan. 1844, DS, *Refutation*, p. 110.

23. *Suffolk Herald* quoted in *Times* 2 May 1844.

24. Johan Furhberg deposition 8 Oct. 1853, *DSAT*, vol. 2, pp. 405–7; *Le Siècle* 21 March 1843.
25. *Punch*, vol. 6 (Jan.-June 1844), p. 139; Charlotte Stuart deposition 13 May 1852 and Dyce Sombre to Antonio Reghellini 6 April 1844, *DSAT*, vol. 2, pp. 128–29, 214.
26. Burrows, 'Lewis Goldsmith'.
27. Lewis Goldsmith affidavits 8 Jan. and 29 Jan. 1844, DS, *Refutation*, pp. 89–94; Mrs Dyce Sombre deposition 29 July 1846, Dyce Sombre, *In Lunacy*, pp. 98–99.
28. *Times* 23 Jan., 15, 19 Feb., 23 Nov. 1844.
29. 'Order of Committee of the Estate, John Larkins' 8 April 1850, D1798/398/2/12, Stafford County Record Office.
30. Dyce Sombre to Mrs Dyce Sombre 20–28 Oct. 1843, quoted in Mary Anne Dyce Sombre affidavit 25 June 1844, Dyce Sombre, *In Lunacy*, pp. 1–25; *Times* 28 March 1844, 15 June 1847.
31. Rolt, *Memoirs*, pp. 135–36.
32. *Times* 30 March 1844.
33. Rolt, *Memoirs*, pp. 139–40, 147–49; Nash, *Life of Richard Lord Westbury*, vol 1, pp. 77–79.
34. *Times* 4, 27 May, 16, 29 July 1844.
35. Her mother's English family, that of Lord Sherborne, petitioned for a Commission of Lunacy 21 Dec. 1843 but her Russian half-brother, Prince Bariatinski, sought to control her treatment and properties. The Commission was held in Canonbury Tavern, Islington. *Times* 22 Dec. 1843, 16 Jan., 25, 30, 31 May, 9 August, 5 Dec.1844, 21 Feb. 1846, 30 Dec. 1867.
36. Dyce Sombre to Peter Solaroli 1 May 1841, *DSAT*, vol. 1, p. 868; Dyce Sombre letter 2 Oct. 1843 and reply 12 Oct. 1843, Political Department Home Correspondence, L/PS/3/107, BL.
37. Arbuthnot, 'Henry Tholby Prinsep'.
38. Henry Thoby Prinsep affidavits 15 July 1846 and 9 Jan. 1849, L/L/65 (451), BL.
39. *Dharma Shastra*, or the *Laws/Institutes of Manu*, is a third century Brahmanic text which, while taken by European Orientalists as authoritative for Indian society, actually had virtually no bearing on Dyce Sombre's culture. *Times* 22, 27 June, 1, 4, 12, 17, 18 July 1844; *Annals of Our Time* 8 July 1844.
40. Lord Combermere affidavit 2 March 1844, Dyce Sombre, *In Lunacy*, Appendix 1, pp. 7–10.
41. Mary Anne Dyce Sombre affidavit 25 June 1844, Dyce Sombre, *In Lunacy*, pp. 1–25; Answers of Mary Anne Dyce Sombre 2 Sept. 1851, *DSAT*, vol. 1, pp. 92–100.
42. Thomas Drever deposition 24 June 1844, *DSAT*, vol. 2, pp. 31–40.
43. *Times* 15 July 1844; Responsive Allegation by Townsend for Mary Anne Dyce Sombre 30 March 1853, *DSAT*, vol. 1, pp. 136–46.

44. *Annals of Our Time* 8 July 1844; *Annual Register* 11 July 1844, Chronicle, p. 74; *Atlas* quoted in *Nelson Examiner and New Zealand Chronicle* 21 Dec. 1844.
45. Lutfullah, *Autobiography*, pp. 248–60, 367ff., 436.
46. Scull, *Museums of Madness*, pp. 164ff.
47. Using Dyce Sombre's case to prove the unreliability of medical determinations of lunacy was *Littell's Living Age*, vol 5, no. 51 (3 May 1845), pp. 206–7.
48. *Times* 31 May, 1, 10, 13 June, 25 July 1844.
49. Brunonianism was developed by John Brown in the late 18th century, based on a theory of excitation. Andrews, 'John Bright'.
50. England and Wales, Commissioners in Lunacy, *Report of the Metropolitan Commissioners*.
51. The fees of advocates and their clerks depended on the length of their paperwork, hence adding to the notorious cumbersomeness of the Chancery process. Manchester, *Modern Legal History of England and Wales*.
52. Palmer, *Memorials*, vol. 1, p. 372; Rolt, *Memoirs*, pp. 84–88.
53. Lord Chancellor Lyndhurst speech in House of Lords 30 March 1851, *Times* 31 March 1852.
54. Mrs Dyce Sombre deposition 29 July 1846, Dyce Sombre, *In Lunacy*, pp. 98–99.
55. Lawrence affidavit cited in *Times* 9 August 1844.
56. Report of Bright and Southey to Chancellor 24 June 1844, Dyce Sombre, *In Lunacy*, pp. 56–7.
57. John Conolly affidavits 9 Feb. and 21 June 1844, Edward Thomas Monro affidavits 12 Feb. and 21 June 1844 Dyce Sombre, *In Lunacy*, pp. 47–54.
58. *Satirist* 7 July 1844.
59. *Illustrated London News* 20 July 1844.
60. *Times* 13 July 1844.
61. Nash, *Life of Richard Lord Westbury*, vol. 1, pp. 77–79.
62. 'Othello', Letter to Editor, *Times* 13 July 1844, and reply from 'Desdemona', 15 July 1844, p. 8.
63. *Dolman's Magazine*, vol. 2, no. 4 (1 August 1845), pp. 195ff.
64. *Times* 31 July 1844.
65. Bennet, *Select Biographical Sketches*, p. 215; *Illustrated London News* 10 August 1844; Lamington, 'In the Days of the Dandies'; *Littell's Living Age* 29 March 1890; *New York Times* 13 April 1890; *Legal Observer or Journal of Jurisprudence*, vol. 29 (Nov. 1844 to April 1845), pp. 25–29, 50–53; *Times* 9 August 1844.
66. Ball, *Justices' Justice*, p. 31.
67. *Times* 25 July 1844.
68. *Observer* quoted in *Times* 19 August 1844.
69. *Globe* quoted in *Times* 27 August 1844.
70. DS, *Refutation*, p. 53.

71. British lawcourts accepted that Dyce Sombre wrote this poem, but may have been a parody by the *Satirist*'s editors. *Satirist* 1 Sept. 1844; *DSAT*, vol. 2, pp. 213–14.

72. Dyce Sombre to Antonio Reghellini 3 Oct. 1844, L/L/65 (450), BL.

73. Dyce Sombre to Antonio Reghellini 6 Nov. 1844, L/L/64 (438), BL.

74. Brown, 'Psychiatrists and the State in Tsarist Russia'.

75. Dyce Sombre to Antonio Reghellini 6 Nov. 1844, L/L/64 (438), BL.

76. 'Journal or Report of the Medical Council of St. Petersburgh' 17 Dec. 1844, Dyce Sombre, *In Lunacy*, pp. 19–21.

77. Letter Dyce Sombre to Antonio Reghellini 6 Nov. 1844, L/L/64 (438), BL.

78. *Hamshire Telegraph and Sussex Chronicle* 18 March 1893.

79. Dyce Sombre to Cecil Forester 14/26 March 1845, *DSAT*, vol. 1, p. 891; Mrs Dyce Sombre affidavit 29 July 1846, Dyce Sombre, *In Lunacy*, pp. 98–9.

80. Dyce Sombre to Antonio Reghellini 13 Nov. 1844, L/L/64 (438), BL.

81. Dyce Sombre to Prinsep 6 April 1845, *DSAT*, vol. 1, p. 892; John Warwick affidavit 18 Nov. 1846, Dyce Sombre, *In Lunacy*, pp. 93–98.

82. These doctors included: Dr Vleminckx (Inspector General of the Service of Health of the Belgian Army; President of the Royal Academy of Medicine of Belgium); Louis Seutin (Head Surgeon of the Hospital St Pierre, Brussels; Physician to His Majesty the King of the Belgians; Professor of the University at Brussels; President of the Medical Commission at Brabant); Joseph Guislain (Director of the Public Establishment for the Insane at Ghent; Professor of the Faculty of Medicine of the University of Ghent; Member of the Royal College of Medicine of Belgium); Constant Crommelinch (Doctor of Medicine, Director and Proprietor of an Invalids and Insane Establishment of Brussels); Pinkstan Blackwood (Surgeon of the Royal North Down Regiment, now practicing at Brussels); Anthony Mahon, M.D. (Late Surgeon in the Royal Artillery). Doctors' Reports, Brussels, 17, 21, 22 June 1845, L/L/65 (452), BL.

83. Dr Jean Francois Vleminckx deposition 13 July 1854, *DSAT*, vol. 2, pp. 298ff.

84. Dyce Sombre to Antonio Reghellini 2 Oct. 1842, *DSAT*, vol. 2, pp. 205–6; Dyce Sombre to Antonio Reghellini 16 Sept. 1847, L/L/64 (438), BL.

85. E.g., Affidavit of Edward De Porre, Banker in Brussels 17 July 1845.

86. Richard Stegg affidavit 17 July 1845, L/L/65 (452), BL.

87. Reconfirmed in writing, Anthony Mahon to Dyce Sombre 29 July 1845, *Refutation*, p. 513.

88. For example, Mahon paid Dr David M'Manus £170 to travel to Paris to examine Dyce Sombre and swear his affidavit of 22 Jan. 1846. Anthony Mahon to Dyce Sombre 23 August 1845, *DSAT*, vol. 1, pp. 892–94.

89. Pinkstan Blackwood deposition 18 July 1854, *DSAT*, vol. 2, pp. 334–38.

90. Comte Ventura deposition 22 Oct. 1853, *DSAT*, vol. 2, pp. 472–79.

91. *Satirist* 7 June 1846; *Spirit of the Times* 11 July 1846.

92. Warwick interviewed Ventura in August 1845. John Warwick affidavit 18 Nov. 1846, Dyce Sombre, *In Lunacy*, pp. 93–98.

93. *Times* 21 August 1845.

94. Dyce Sombre to Lord Aberdeen 18, 19 August 1845, Aberdeen Papers, Add 43244, ff.333–36, BL; Dyce Sombre to Sir Robert Peele 6 Dec. 1845 and reply, Peel Papers, Add 40580, ff.290–92, BL; Dyce Sombre to Sir Robert Peele 6 April 1846, Peel Papers, Add 40589, ff.171–72, BL.

95. Palmer, *Memorials*, vol. 1, pp. 371–72; Rolt, *Memoirs*, p. 90.

96. *Times* 1 August 1846.

97. Sherer, 'Bishop in Partibus', p. 468.

98. James Copland deposition 26 March 1852, *DSAT*, vol. 2, pp. 31–34; W. Sankey affidavit 1 April 1849, DS, *Refutation*, pp. 545–46; James Copland affidavit 22 Sept. 1846, L/L/65 (451), BL; Moore, 'James Copland'.

99. Anthony Mahon to Dyce Sombre 11 Sept. 1846 and Dyce Sombre to Cottenham 9 March 1847, DS, *Refutation*, pp. 211, 229–30.

100. Second Report of Southey and Bright 26 Sept. 1846, Dyce Sombre, *In Lunacy*, pp. 101–3.

101. Phillips, *Reports of Cases*, vol 2, pp. 242–44, 855.

102. Lord Combermere to Dyce Sombre 22 Sept. 1846, L/L/64 (438), BL.

103. *Times* 23 Dec. 1845; Dyce Sombre Marriage Settlement, D1535 Box 4, Stafford County Record Office.

104. Drever letter of 16 March 1846, quoted in Mrs Dyce Sombre affidavit 9 July 1846, L/L/65 (451), BL.

105. Dyce Sombre to Troup 10 Oct. 1846, L/L/65 (451), BL; Dyce Sombre to Prinsep 10 Oct. 1846, *DSAT*, vol. 1, p. 898.

106. Dyce Sombre to Antonio Reghellini 26 Nov. 1846, *DSAT*, vol. 2, pp. 233–34.

107. Lord Combermere to Dyce Sombre 14 Oct. 1846, *DSAT*, vol. 2, pp. 258–59.

108. *Times* 4, 11 Nov., 7, 24 Dec. 1846, 15, 16, 18, 19 Jan., 12, 15 July 1847.

109. *English Reports*, vol. 47, pp. 880–81.

110. *Times* 26 May 1846.

111. *Times* 15 July 1847.

112. Dyce Sombre to Lord Chancellor Cottonham 9 March 1847, Dyce Sombre, *In Lunacy*, pp. 107–8.

113. *Times* 19 July 1847.

114. Lord Combermere to Dyce Sombre 14 July 1847, *DSAT*, vol. 2, p. 247.

115. Lord Combermere to Dyce Sombre 31 August 1846, L/L/64 (438), BL.

116. Reprinted in *Daily News* 28 Jan. 1856.

117. *Standard* quoted in *Times* 17 July 1847.

118. Third Report of Southey and Bright 5 August 1847, Dyce Sombre, *In Lunacy*, pp. 109–10.

119. DS, *Refutation*, p. 237.

120. England and Wales, Commissioners in Lunacy, *Report of the Metropolitan Commissioners*, pp. 169ff.
121. Lord Chancellor's Order 8 Sept. 1847, *DSAT*, vol. 1, pp. 88–89.
122. *Times* 16 June 1848.
123. *Atlas* quoted in *Times* 8 Nov. 1847.
124. Sophia Culpin deposition 26 Sept. 1853 and Thomas Bartholomew 21 Dec. 1853, *DSAT*, vol. 2, pp. 382–83, 391–92.
125. *Times* 26 May 1846, 22 Jan. 1848.
126. E. g., *Times* 28 Dec. 1847.
127. Dyce Sombre to Cottenham 12 Jan. 1849, DS, *Refutation*, pp. 500–8; Bartle Frere to Richard Jenkins 17 Feb. 1849 and reply 26 Feb. 1849, *DSAT*, vol. 2, pp. 173–76.
128. In the Privy Counsel, In Appeal from the Sudder Dewanny Adawlut, North Western Provinces, Agra, Badshapore Suit, L/L/63 (433) and Revenue, Judicial, & Legislative Committee L/PJ/5/399, BL.
129. Daniel McCarthy affidavit 15 April 1852, L/L/64 (438), BL.
130. Helena Mornington to Dyce Sombre 22 July 1847, *DSAT*, vol. 2, p. 272.

12. TRAVELLING, PUBLISHING, CHALLENGING AND EXPIRING

1. August Kastenbein affidavit 17 June 1848, L/L/65 (451), BL.
2. Dyce Sombre to Troup, Constantinople 10 Oct. 1847, L/L/65 (451), BL; Diary 6 Dec. 1847, PROB 37/1700, PRO.
3. Thus, he started writing with the printed section for August 1846 to describe his setting out on 31 August 1847 and, on reaching the end of the book, continuing on the pages printed for January until April 1846 to record his doings from January until April 1848.
4. Diary 4–16 Oct. 1847, PROB 37/1700, PRO.
5. Dyce Sombre to Antonio Reghellini 25 Oct. 1847, *DSAT*, vol. 2, p. 237; Diary 22 Oct.-6 Nov. 1847, PROB 37/1700, PRO.
6. Letter Dyce Sombre to Antonio Reghellini, Rome 7 Feb. 1848, *DSAT*, vol. 2, pp. 187–88.
7. Diary 24 Nov. 1847, PROB 37/1700, PRO.
8. Reverend Thomas Grant deposition 16 Dec. 1853 and Dyce Sombre to Cardinal Franzoni 10 Feb. 1848, *DSAT*, vol. 2, pp. 397–98, 913–4; Diary 10 Feb. 1848, PROB 37/1700, PRO.
9. Diary 4 Jan. 1848, PROB 37/1700, PRO.
10. Ibid., 20 Dec. 1847–18 Feb. 1848, PROB 37/1700, PRO; Dyce Sombre to John Larkins 26 Feb. 1848, *DSAT*, vol. 2, p. 915; *Times* 13 Jan. 1848. The cenotaph remained a continuing logistical problem until it reached Sardhana.
11. Diary 18/2–23 March 1848, PROB 37/1700, PRO.
12. Ibid., 28 March 1848.

13. Ibid., 2 April 1848.
14. Henry Prinsep to Dyce Sombre 26 June 1848, *DSAT*, vol. 2, p. 924.
15. Dyce Sombre to Antonio Reghellini 26 June 1848, 2 April 1849, *DSAT*, vol. 2, pp. 189–194.
16. Dyce Sombre to Prinsep 20 May 1848, L/L/65 (451), BL; Johan Furhberg deposition 8 Oct. 1853, *DSAT*, vol. 2, pp. 405–7.
17. Catherin Montucci affidavits 13 June 1848 and 16 April 1852, L/L/ Box 65 (438 and 451), BL; *DSAT*, vol. 2, pp. 123–24.
18. Dyce Sombre to Henry Prinsep 2 June 1848, L/L/65 (451), BL.
19. Anthony Mahon letter to arbiters, quoted in DS, *Refutation*, p. 514 and *Times* 8 March 1849.
20. Charles Shrimpton deposition 5 June 1848, *DSAT*, vol. 2, p. 84.
21. *Times* 26 Feb. 1849.
22. Dyce Sombre to Lord John Russell 18 June 1848, *DSAT*, vol. 1, p. 923.
23. *Times* 12 March 1849.
24. Dyce Sombre to Henry Prinsep 14 August 1848, L/L/65 (451), BL.
25. Dyce Sombre to Charles Shadwell 6 Oct. 1849, L/L/65 (451), BL.
26. James Martin affidavit 20 Feb. 1849, DS, *Refutation*, pp. 538–42.
27. James Martin affidavit 20 Feb. 1849, Dyce Sombre, *In Lunacy*, pp. 176–8.
28. Mary Anne Dyce Sombre affidavit 20 Feb. 1849, L/L/65 (452), BL; DS, *Refutation*, pp. 508–12, 532.
29. *English Reports*, vol. 47, pp. 1419–1425; DS, *Refutation*, pp. 464–65; *Times* 10 August 1848.
30. Fourth Report of Bright, Southey, Clark, and Martin 18 Nov. 1848 and Lord Chancellor Cottonham's Judgment 20 April 1849, Dyce Sombre, *In Lunacy*, pp. 156–7, 181–91; *Times* 23 Dec. 1848, 12 Jan. 1849; Phillips, *Law Concerning Lunatics*, p. 362.
31. Lord Combermere to Anthony Mahon 8 Dec. 1848, DS, *Refutation*, p. 554.
32. *Times* 5 March 1849; Reports of Drs John Ayrton Paris, Thomas Mayo, Alexander Morison, James Copland, Robert Ferguson, William Costello, DS, *Refutation*, pp. 468–86 and *DSAT*, vol. 2, pp. 15–21, 27–37, 66–70.
33. Dyce Sombre to Henry Prinsep 14 August 1848, L/L/65 (451), BL.
34. Alexander Morison deposition 25 March 1852, *DSAT*, vol. 2, pp. 27–29.
35. Thomas Mayo depositions 22 March and 27 March 1852, *DSAT*, vol. 2, pp. 15–18.
36. Thomas Mayo, 'Correspondence', *London Medical Gazette*, n.s. vol. 11 (1850), pp. 123–24.
37. Mayo, *Medical Testimony*, pp. 29–32.
38. Henry Prinsep affidavit 8 Sept. 1854, DS, *Refutation*, pp. 308–12.
39. *Globe* 26 Dec. 1848.
40. Edward Mivart affidavit 8 Jan. 1849, DS, *Refutation*, pp. 490–91.

41. Lord Combermere and other noblemen to Lord Chancellor 18 Jan. 1849, Dyce Sombre, *In Lunacy*, pp. 164–5.

42. Charles Trevelyan affidavit 19 Feb. 1849, DS, *Refutation*, p. 489.

43. Cottonham's Judgment 20 April 1849, Dyce Sombre, *In Lunacy*, pp. 181–91; *Morning Post* 26 Feb. 1849; *Times* 17 Feb. 1849; DS, *Refutation*, pp. 535–36, 548–65; Ray, *Treatise on the Medical Jurisprudence of Insanity*, p. 384n1; Hall and Twells, *Reports of Cases*, vol. 1, pp. 285–300.

44. Dyce Sombre to Chancellor 12 Jan. 1849, Dyce Sombre, *In Lunacy*, pp. 158–63; DS, *Refutation*, p. 513.

45. Dyce Sombre to Queen Victoria 24 Jan. 1849, DS, *Refutation*, pp. 519–20.

46. Secretary of Lord John Russell to Dyce Sombre 6 Dec. 1848 and Lord Auckland to Dyce Sombre 1 Nov. [sic] 1848, DS, *Refutation*, p. 499.

47. *Times* 27 Feb. 1849; Thomas Brett affidavit 20 Feb. 1849, DS, *Refutation*, p. 256; John Warwick also wrote about his former patient in the *Water Cure and Hygienic Magazine*, 18 (Jan. 1849), pp. 186–7.

48. Henry Prinsep to Dyce Sombre 17 Feb. 1849, DS, *Refutation*, pp. 546–48.

49. David Reid affidavit 20 Dec. 1849, DS, *Refutation*, pp. 497–98.

50. *New York Evening Post* quoted in *Littell's Living Age* 28 April 1849; Brougham, 'On Partial Insanity'; *Courier* (Hobart, Tasmania, 25 August 1849).

51. *Times* 5 March 1849.

52. *Times* 1 March 1849.

53. *Times* 3 March 1849.

54. Lord Chancellor Cottenham Order in Chancery 20 April 1849, *DSAT*, vol. 1, p. 90; Dowling and Lowndes, *Reports of Cases*, vol. 3, p. 357; Hall and Twells, *Reports of Cases*, vol. 1, pp. 285–300; Phillips, *Law Concerning Lunatics*, pp. 5, 7, 8, 247, 279, 285, 292, 347, 355, 359–62.

55. *Times* 1–10 March 1849; Combermere Affidavit 8 March 1849, L/L/65 (451), BL.

56. *Times* 15 Nov. 1849; Sir John Dodson Judgment 26 Jan. 1856 in Henry Tholby Prinsep v. the Hon. Mary Anne Dyce Sombre, from Prerogative Court of Canterbury, L/L/63 (435), BL and PCAP 3/21, PRO.

57. Cottonham's Judgment 20 April 1849, Dyce Sombre, *In Lunacy*, pp. 181–91; *Times* 21 April 1849; *DSAT*, vol. 1, pp. 90ff; DS, *Refutation*, pp. 548–65; *English Reports*, vol. 47, pp. 1419–25; Phillips, *Law Concerning Lunatics*.

58. Henry Prinsep deposition 7 Sept. 1854 and Henry Prinsep to Anthony Mahon 20 Dec. 1848, *DSAT*, vol. 2, pp. 65–7, 171–2.

59. Lawrence Desborough Sr deposition 17 March 1852 and Lawrence Desborough Jr deposition 18 March 1852, *DSAT*, vol. 2, pp. 1–2, 6–13.

60. Dyce Sombre Will 25 June 1849 with drafts and codicil 13 August 1849, *DSAT*, vol. 1, pp. 2–32.

61. Depositions of Drs Charles Shrimpton, Daniel McCarthy, Joseph Olliffe, and George Sigmond 6–15 April 1852, *DSAT*, vol. 2, pp. 68–85, 117–18; George Sigmond Report 28 July 1851, *DSAT*, vol. 1, 686.
62. DS, *Refutation*, p. 19.
63. DS, *Refutation*, p. 244.
64. DS, *Refutation*, p. 571.
65. DS, *Refutation*, p. 582.
66. *Nelson Examiner and New Zealand Chronicle* 30 Nov. 1850; *Journal of Psychological Medicine and Mental Pathology* 2 (1849), pp. 323–9; 628.
67. Lawrence Desborough Jr deposition 18 March 1852, *DSAT*, vol. 2, pp. 6–13.
68. Dyce Sombre to Henry Prinsep 14 May 1849, *DSAT*, vol. 1, p. 951.
69. 'Memoir', Dyce Sombre, *In Lunacy*, pp 105–7.
70. Deposition of Catherin Montucci 16 April 1852, *DSAT*, vol. 2, pp. 123–24.
71. Peter Solaroli deposition 17 Nov. 1853 and Johan Furhberg deposition 15 Oct. 1853, *DSAT*, vol. 2, pp. 496–504, 552; Dyce Sombre to Charles Shadwell, 22 March 1850, L/L/65 (450), BL; Dyce Sombre to Henry Prinsep 18 Nov. 1849, L/L/65 (451), BL.
72. John Troup affidavit 11 Dec. 1846 and John Troup and Peter Solaroli affidavit 7 Sept. 1847, Dyce Sombre, *In Lunacy*, pp. 103–4, 111–12.
73. Emile Briére deposition 21 Oct. 1853, *DSAT*, vol. 2, pp. 541–42.
74. Catherin Montucci deposition 16 April 1852, Joseph Privitera deposition 14 Oct. 1853, and Henry Ancot deposition 22 Oct. 1853, *DSAT*, vol. 2, pp. 126, 413–14, 471–2; Henry Haverfield to Charles Shadwell 5 July 1850, L/L/64 (438), BL.
75. Plus a translation into German by Kurt Reinhardt: *Mr. Dyce Sombre's Widerlegung der Beschuldigung geisteskrank zu sein, die gegen ihn erhoben* (Dellfeld: T. Reinhard, 1995).
76. John Hoffe deposition 28 Oct. 1853, *DSAT*, vol. 2, pp. 481–82; *News of the World* 10 August 1851; *Daily News* 11 August 1851.
77. Jean Bailly deposition 11 Oct. 1853 and Leon Courtignon deposition 1 Nov. 1853, *DSAT*, vol. 2, pp. 539–40, 560; Charles Cundy affidavit 6 May 1851, L/L/65 (452), BL.
78. Jean Ranchet depositions 31 Oct. 1853 and 2 Jan. 1853, *DSAT*, vol. 2, pp. 559–61.
79. Daniel McCarthy affidavit 15 April 1852, L/L/64 (438), BL.
80. John Hoffe depostion 28 Oct. 1853 and Dugald Campbell deposition 15 Nov. 1853, DSAT, vol. 2, pp. 384–84, 481–82.
81. Sophie de Grefuille affidavit 10 July 1847, DS, *Refutation*, pp. 235–36.
82. Sophie de Grefuille affidavit 11 Oct. 1850, Dyce Sombre, *In Lunacy*, pp. 192–96; M. Grefuille to Court and reply 4–8 Oct. 1851, Revenue, Judicial, & Legislative Committee, L/P&J/1/3 Reference 306 of 1851, BL.
83. Baron Palm testified to this landlady's purchased inconsistency in his own 1851 affidavit about how much Dyce Sombre had improved and moder-

ated his habits over these same years. Joseph Baron Palm affidavit 22 March 1851, L/L/65 (451), BL.

84. Dyce Sombre to Henry Prinsep 14 Feb. 1851, PROB 37/1700, PRO.

85. Charles Cundy affidavit 6 May 1851, L/L/65 (452), BL.

86. Jean Ranchet depositions 31 Oct. 1853 and 2 Jan. 1853, *DSAT*, vol. 2, pp. 559–61.

87. Robert Ferguson affidavit 25 March 1852 *DSAT*, vol. 2, pp. 21–23.

88. Comte Ventura deposition 22 Oct. 1853, *DSAT*, vol. 2, pp. 472–79.

89. See Fisher, *Counterflows*, Chapter 7.

90. Johan Furhberg deposition 8 Oct. 1853 and Alexander Arthur deposition 24 Oct. 1853, *DSAT*, vol. 2, pp. 405–7, 479–80.

91. Johan Furhberg affidavit 27 Jan. 1851, Dyce Sombre, *In Lunacy*, pp. 196–201.

92. Dyce Sombre to Henry Prinsep 14 Feb. 1851, PROB 37/1700, PRO.

93. Louis de Ligneville deposition 11 Oct. 1853, *DSAT*, vol. 2, p. 540; Dyce Sombre to Henry Prinsep 26 March 1849, *DSAT*, vol. 1, p. 949; Dyce Sombre to Henry Prinsep 10 Dec. 1849 and Dyce Sombre to Charles Shadwell 28 March 1850, L/L/65 (450–51), BL.

94. Dyce Sombre to Henry Prinsep 1 Feb. 1849, L/L/65 (451), BL.

95. Adam, Prince Czartoryski affidavit 21 March 1851, L/L/65 (451), BL; Adam, Prince Czartoryski deposition 12 April 1852, James Butler deposition 10 April 1852, and Camille Marechal deposition 21 April 1852, *DSAT*, vol. 2, pp. 91–93.

96. Catherine Simpson, wife of Pierce Simpson of Clonclorick Castle, deposition of 14 May 1852, *DSAT*, vol. 2, pp. 130–32; Lord Sussex Lennox affidavit 15 April 1851, L/L/65 (452), BL.

97. Joseph Olliffe deposition 7 April 1852, *DSAT*, vol. 2, pp. 73–84.

98. Napier, *Life and Opinions*, vol. 4, p. 105.

99. Benjamin Disraeli to Sarah Disraeli 4 August 1849, Disraeli, *Letters*, vol. 5, no. 1861; *Times* 18 July 1849.

100. *Times* 23 Dec. 1845, 24 Nov. 1849, 14 Dec. 1850, 27 March 1851.

101. Dyce Sombre to Henry Prinsep 7 March 1849, L/L/65 (451), BL.

102. Dyce Sombre to Henry Prinsep 10 August 1849, L/L/65 (451), BL.

103. Dyce Sombre to Henry Prinsep 12 Sept. 1849, *DSAT*, vol. 1, pp. 960–61.

104. Dyce Sombre to Henry Prinsep 10 August 1849, L/L/65 (451), BL.

105. Dyce Sombre to Joseph Skinner 28 Oct. 1850, *DSAT*, vol. 2, pp. 296–97; Joseph Wolff to Royal Geographical Society 30 March 1850, RGS/CB3/819, Joseph Wolff collection, Royal Geographical Society; Carlyle, 'Joseph Wolff'.

106. Dyce Sombre to Henry Prinsep 10 August 1849, L/L/65 (451), BL.; Dyce Sombre to Henry Prinsep 12 Sept. 1849, *DSAT*, vol. 1, pp. 960–61.

107. Joseph Privitera deposition 14 Oct. 1853 and corrected page proofs for *Petition*, *DSAT*, vol. 2, pp. 413–22.

108. Dyce Sombre to Charles Shadwell 28 March 1850, L/L/65 (450–51), BL; Dyce Sombre to Antonio Reghellini 11 Jan. 1850, *DSAT*, vol. 2, p. 199.

109. Dyce Sombre to Charles Shadwell 22 April 1850, L/L/64 (438), BL.
110. Palmer, *Memorials*, vol. 2, p. 130.
111. *Times* 6 August 1850, 8 May 1851.
112. *Daily News* 3 May 1851.
113. Dyce Sombre to Henry Prinsep 7 August 1850, L/L/65 (451), BL.
114. Dyce Sombre to Charles Shadwell 28 March 1850, L/L/65 (450–51), BL.
115. Dyce Sombre to Henry Prinsep 15 Jan. 1851, L/L/65 (451), BL; Dyce Sombre to Joseph Skinner 7 Oct. 1850, *DSAT*, vol. 2, p. 295.
116. *Times* 14 Dec. 1850.
117. *London Medical Recorder: A Monthly Review of the Progress of the Medical Sciences at Home*, n.s. vol 10 (1850) p. 201n.
118. Robert Walsh in *Journal of Commerce* reprinted in *Daily National Intelligencer* 15 July 1851.
119. Dyce Sombre to Henry Prinsep 15 Jan. 1851, L/L/65 (451), BL.
120. Dyce Sombre to Charles Shadwell 21 April 1851, L/L/65 (450), BL.
121. Dyce Sombre to Joseph Skinner 21 May 1851, *DSAT*, vol. 2, p. 294. See also Seymour, *Lola Montez*.
122. Montez, *Lectures*, pp. 31–4.
123. Daniel McCarthy affidavit 15 April 1852, L/L/64 (438), BL.
124. John Hoffe deposition 28 Oct. 1853, *DSAT*, vol. 2, pp. 481–82.
125. Johan Furhberg affidavit 27 Jan. 1851, Dyce Sombre, *In Lunacy*, pp. 196–201; Dyce Sombre to Charles Shadwell 12 Dec., 31 Dec. 1850, L/L/65 (450), BL; Camille Marechal deposition 21 April 1852, *DSAT*, vol. 2, pp. 91–93.
126. Dyce Sombre to Mrs Dyce Sombre 15 June 1851, *DSAT*, vol. 1, p. 991; Forbes Winslow deposition 26 June 1854, *DSAT*, vol. 2, p. 61; Forbes Winslow, *Journal of Psychological Medicine and Mental Pathology*, vol. 9 (1856), p. lxii.
127. *Times* 7, 8 August 1850.
128. Dyce Sombre to Lord Chancellor 18 March, 28 April 1851, *DSAT*, vol. 1, pp. 981–85.
129. *Times* 8, 14 May 1851.
130. Bell, *Justices' Justice*, p. 38.
131. *Daily News* 8, 14 May 1851; *Weekly Dispatch* 18 May, 1851; *London Medical Gazette*, n.s. vol. 12 (1851), pp. 438–39.
132. Dyce Sombre to Lord Chancellor 20 May 1851, Dyce Sombre, *In Lunacy*, pp. 201–3; Macaulay, *Letters,*, p. 169.
133. *DSAT*, vol. 1, p. 147.
134. Mrs Dyce Sombre to Dyce Sombre 14 June 1851, *DSAT*, vol. 1, p. 990.
135. Dyce Sombre to Mrs Dyce Sombre 15 June 1851, *DSAT*, vol. 1, p. 991.
136. Sir Benjamin Brodie, Caesar Henry Hawkins, and Henry Holland to Lord Chancellor in *DSAT*, vol. 1, p. 161.

13. LEGACIES

1. *Annual Register* 1851 Deaths, p. 303–4; *Examiner* 5 July 1851 quoted in *Nelson Examiner and New Zealand Chronicle*, 6 Dec. 1851, p. 163; *Gentleman's Magazine* vol. 190 (May-Aug. 1851), pp. 201–202; p. 330; *News of the World* 6 July 1851, p. 6; *Hobart Town Courier* 5 Nov. 1851.
2. Goldstein, *Console and Classify.*
3. Hamilton in *Notes and Queries*, 8th series, vol. 7 (20 April 1895), p. 309.
4. *Times* 8 August 1856.
5. *International Monthly Magazine of Literature, Science, and Art* 1 August 1851.
6. E. g., *Age* 13 Feb. 1852.
7. St Vincent speech 30 March 1852, Great Britain, Parliament, *Parliamentary Debates*, 3rd series, vol. 120, pp. 353–54; *Times* 26 July 1856; *News of the World* 3 August 1856.
8. Newspaper clipping 26 July 1856, glued in *DSAT*, vol. 1, frontispiece, ORB 40/4, BL; *Albion* 26 July 1856.
9. *Weekly News and Courier* 6 Oct. 1897; *News of the World* 6 July 1851; *Daily Picayune* 24 Oct. 1895.
10. *The New England Farmer* July 1861, p. 342 among many other newspapers, quoting letter from W. H. Russell on attending a slave auction in Montgomery, Alabama.
11. Mrs Marguerite (de Godart) Cunliffe-Owen (1859–1927) of New-York, known as Marquise de Fontenoy or Countess du Planty. [Cunliffe-Owen] Fontenoy, *Revelation of High Life within Royal Palaces*; Marquise de Fontenoy, 'Behind the Scenes', *Daily Picayune* 4 April 1893, 2 Jan., 24 Oct. 1895.
12. *Times* 16 Feb. 1852; *Albion* 7 July 1855.
13. Arthur John Otway, Henry Danby Seymour, and Sir James Hogg speeches 14 March 1856, Great Britain, Parliament, *Parliamentary Debates*, 3rd series, vol. 141, pp. 172–8; *Daily News* 27 Feb., 7, 31 March 1856; *Times* 19 April 1856.
14. They inconsistently dismissed his previous wills, signed when he was not yet legally lunatic, as irrelevant since he had repudiated them with this 1849 will.
15. *Harpers Weekly Magazine*, 28 Feb. 1857; *Times* 4, 7 Dec. 1856.
16. E. g., *Daily News* 28 Jan. 1856; *Journal of Psychological Medicine and Mental Pathology*, 9 (1856), p. lxii.
17. *Daily Evening Bulletin* 9, 11 Dec. 1871; *Daily Southern Cross*, 9 May 1865; *Evening Post* 9 May 1865; *New York Times* 27 Nov. 1871.
18. Nash, *Life of Richard Lord Westbury*, vol. 2, p. 151. John Motley to Mrs Motley 11 July 1858, Motley, *Correspondence*, vol. 1, p. 296.
19. Denis Fitzpatrick, I.C.S., Simla, Foreign Department, Judicial, 16 June 1865, no. 8, BL.
20. 'On Appeal from the sudder Dewanny Adawlut of Agra', Sutherland, *Weekly Reporter*, vol. 4, pp. 111–13.

21. Judgement of Judicial Committee of the Privy Council 2 Feb. 1858, L/PJ/5/399, BL.
22. Privy Council ruling 11 May 1872, L/PJ/5/407, BL; Queen's Report 5 Feb. 1873 based on Privy Council Report 30 Jan. 1873, L/AG/50/5/8, BL; *Times* 7 Nov. 1871–May 13, 1872, *passim*; *New York Times* 27 Nov. 1871; *Daily Evening Bulletin* 9, 11 Dec. 1871; *Daily Telegraph* 13 Nov. 1871.
23. Lytton to Brownings 7 Jan. 1854, Lytton, *Letters*, p. 57.
24. Doyle, 'Sign of Four'; Leavitt, "Who was Cecil Forrester?'.
25. *Times* 15 April 1853; 7 April 1860; 26 Sept. 1860; *Spirit of the Times* 1 Oct. 1859; *Leeds Mercury* 8 June 1893; *Otago Witness* 3 May 1862; *Staffordshire Advertiser* 11 March 1893; *Daily Picayune* 4 April 1893; Bowers and Clough, *Researches into the History of Stone*, pp. 125–30.
26. For various claims see L/PJ/6/88, 80, 89, 373, 398, 408, 416, 621–2, BL; *Times* 22 March 1876.
27. *Brooklyn Daily Eagle* 1 April 1883; *Milwalkee Sentinel* 2 April 1883; *Daily Evening Bulletin* 11 April 1883; *Calcutta Review* (Oct. 1880), p. 371.
28. Ralph, *Naoroji*.

BIBLIOGRAPHY

LIBRARIES AND ARCHIVES USED

British Library, London (BL).
Freemason's Library, London.
Institute for Historical Research, London.
London Metropolitan Archives, London.
National Archives of India, New Delhi (NAI).
National Archives of the United Kingdom, Kew (PRO).
Royal Geographical Society, London.
Stafford County Record Office, Stafford.
Wellcome Library, London.
William Salt Library, Stafford.

JOURNALS AND NEWSPAPERS CITED

Age (London).
Albion, A Journal of News, Politics and Literature (New York).
American International Monthly Magazine of Literature, Science, and Art
    (New York) .
Annals of Our Time (London).
Annual Register (London).
Anti-Slavery Reporter and Aborigines' Friend (London).
Atlantic Monthly (Boston).
The Belfast News-Letter (Belfast).
Bell's Life in London and Sporting Chronicle (London).
Bengal Catholic Herald (Calcutta)
Bengal Past and Present (Calcutta).
Blackwood's Edinburgh Magazine (Edinburgh).
Bristol Mercury (Bristol).
Brooklyn Daily Eagle (New York).
Calcutta Review (Calcutta).
Catholic Telegraph (Cincinnati).
Charleston Mercury (Charleston).
The Charter (London).

Cincinnati Weekly Herald and Philanthropist (Cincinnati).
The Courier (Hobart).
Court Magazine and Belle Assemblee (London).
Daily Evening Bulletin (San Francisco).
Daily National Intelligencer (Washington).
Daily News (London).
Daily Picayune (New Orleans).
Daily Southern Cross (Auckland).
Daily Telegraph (London).
Dolman's Magazine and Monthly Miscellany of Criticism (London).
Eclectic Magazine of Foreign Literature (New York) .
Emancipator and Weekly Chronicle (Boston).
Evening Post (Wellington).
Freemasons' Quarterly Review (London).
Friend of India (Calcutta).
Gentleman's Magazine (London).
Glasgow Herald (Glasgow).
Globe (London).
Hamshire Telegraph and Sussex Chronicle (Portsmouth).
Harpers Weekly Magazine: A Journal of Civilization (New York).
Hobart Town Courier (Hobart).
Hobarton Mercury (Hobart).
Illustrated London News (London).
Indian News (London).
International Monthly Magazine of Literature, Science, and Art (New York).
Ipswich Journal (Ipswich).
John Bull (London).
Journal of Psychological Medicine and Mental Pathology (London).
Leeds Mercury (Leeds).
Legal Observer or Journal of Jurisprudence (London).
Littell's Living Age (Boston).
London Gazette (London).
London Medical Gazette or Journal of Practical Medicine (London).
London Medical Recorder: A Monthly Review of the Progress of the Medical Sciences at Home (London).
Lowell Daily Citizen and News (Lowell).
Maitland Mercury and Hunter River General Advertiser (New South Wales).
Milwaukee Sentinel (Milwaukee).
Missionary Register (London).
Morning Chronicle (London).
Morning Post (London).
Nelson Examiner and New Zealand Chronicle (Nelson).
The New England Farmer: a Monthly Journal, Devoted to Agriculture, Horticulture, and Their Kindred Arts and Sciences (Boston).
New Sporting Magazine (London).

New York Herald (New York).
New York Spectator (New York).
New York Times (New York).
New Zealand Spectator and Cook's Strait Guardian (Wellington).
News of the World (London).
Niles' Weekly Register (Washington.).
Notes and Queries (London).
Oriental Herald and Colonial Intelligencer (London).
Otago Witness (Otago).
The Perth Gazette (Perth).
Punch (London)
Raleigh Register and North-Carolina Gazette (Raleigh).
Satirist; or, the Censor of the Times (London).
Saturday Evening Post (Philadelphia).
Le Siècle (Paris).
Spirit of the Times: A Chronicle of the Turf, Agriculture, Field Sports, Literature, and the Stage (New York).
Staffordshire Advertiser (Stafford).
Standard (London).
Sydney Gazette and New South Wales Advertiser (Sydney).
Times (London).
United Service Journal and Naval and Military Magazine (London).
Vermont Chronicle (Bellows Falls).
Water Cure and Hygienic Magazine (London).
Weekly Dispatch (London).
Weekly Herald (New York).
Weekly News and Courier (Charleston).
Westminster Review (London).

BOOKS AND ARTICLES CITED

Aitchison, C. U., *Collection of Treaties, Engagements, and Sanads*, 3rd edn, Calcutta: Superintendent of Government Printing, 1892.

Aitken, Molly Emma, 'Pardah and Portrayal: Rajput Women as Subjects, Patrons, and Collectors, *Artibus Asiae*, 62, 2 (2002), pp. 247–80.

Andrews, Jonathan, 'John Bright', *NDNB*.

Anonymous, 'Story of Our Missions', *Missionary Magazine* (November 1871), pp. 1–10.

Arbuthnot, A. J., rev. R. J. Bingle, 'Henry Tholby Prinsep', *NDNB*.

Arbuthnot, Harriet, *Journal of Mrs Arbuthnot, 1820–1832*, 2 vols, London: Macmillan, 1950.

Archer, Major, *Tours in Upper India*, 2 vols, London: Richard Bentley, 1833.

Archibiugi, Daniele, ed., *Debating Cosmopolitics*, London: Verso, 2003.

Aydelotte, W. O., 'House of Commons in the 1840s', *History* 39, 137 (October 1954), pp. 249–62.

Bacon, Thomas, *First Impressions and Studies from Nature in Hindostan*, 2 vols, London, W. H. Allen, 1837.

Bagenal, Philip Henry, *Life of Ralph Bernal Osborne, M. P.*, London: Richard Bentley, 1884.

Bailey, Gauvin Alexander, 'Architectural Relics of the Catholic Missionary Era in Mughal India', in Rosemary Crill, Susan Stronge, Andrew Topsfield, eds, *Arts of Mughal India*, Ahmedabad: Mapin, 2004, pp. 146–50.

Ball, Robert James, *Justices' Justice, a Satire*, London: Effingham Wilson, 1845.

Ballantyne, Tony, *Orientalism and Race*, Houndmills: Palgrave, 2002.

Banerji, Brajendra Nath, *Begam Samru*, Calcutta: M. C. Sarkar, 1925.

Barron, Arthur, and Alfred Austin, *Report of Cases of Controverted Elections*, London: S. Sweet, 1844.

Bateman, Josiah, *Life of the Right Rev. Daniel Wilson, D.D., Late Lord Bishop of Calcutta*, 2 vols, London: J. Murray, 1860.

Bell, Eva Mary, *Foreigner*, London: Hodder and Stoughton, 1928.

Bennet William Heath, *Select Biographical Sketches from the Note-books of a Law Reporter*, London: G. Routledge and Sons, 1867.

Bentham, Jeremy, *Works*, ed. John Bowring, New York: Russell and Russell, 1962.

Berry, Allan W., *Bribery!: Sudbury Elections of the Past*, Colchester: A. W. Berry, 1991.

Bhabha, Homi K., *The Location of Culture*, London: Routledge, 1994.

Bond, Ruskin, 'Lady of Sardhana', *Strange Men, Strange Places*, Bombay: Pearl, 1969, pp. 12–20.

Bowers, W. H., and J. W. Clough, *Researches into the History of Stone*, Birmingham: Midland Educational Company, 1929.

Boyd, Mark, *Reminiscences of Fifty Years*, New York: D. Appleton, 1871.

Broadley, A. M., *History of Freemasonry in the District of Malta*, London: George Kenning, 1880.

Brougham, Lord, 'On Partial Insanity', *Journal of Psychological Medicine and Mental Pathology*, 2 (1849), pp. 323–9.

Brown, Julie Vail, 'Psychiatrists and the State in Tsarist Russia', in Stanley Cohen and Andrew Scull, eds, *Social Control and the State*, New York: St. Martins, 1983, pp. 267–87.

Bullock, Major H., 'Some Soldiers of Fortune: Four Sardhana Officers', *Bengal Past and Present*, 51, 1 (1936), pp. 7–8.

Bulwer, Edward, *Life, Letters and Literary Remains*, ed. Edward Robert Bulwer-Lytton, London: Kegan, Paul, Trench, 1883.

Burghersh, Lady, *Correspondence of Lady Burghersh with the Duke of Wellington*, ed. Lady Rose Weigall, New York: E. P. Dutton, 1903.

Burke, John, *Genealogical and Hereldic History of the Commoners of Great Britain and Ireland*, 4 vols, London: Henry Colburn, 1838.

Burnett, M. D., *Insanity Tested by Science, and Shown to be a Disease Rarely Connected with Permanent Organic Lesion of the Brain*, London: Highley, 1848.

Burrows, Simon, 'Lewis Goldsmith', *NDNB*.

Cardigan and Lancastre, Countess, *My Recollections*, New York: John Lane, 1910.

Carlyle, E. I., rev. Todd M. Endelman, 'Joseph Wolff', *NDNB*.

Chamberlain, John, *Memoirs*, ed. William Yates, London: Wightman and Cramp, 1826.

Chand, Lalla Gokul, 'Zeb-ut-Tawarikh', ADD 25,830, BL; *History of Zeb-ul-Nissa: The Begum Samru of Sardhana*, ed. Nicholas Shreeve, Crossbush: Bookwright, 1994.

Chandra, Vikram, *Red Earth and Pouring Rain*, Boston: Little, Brown, 1995.

Chatterjee, Partha, *Princely Impostor?: The Strange and Universal History of the Kumar of Bhawal*, Princeton: Princeton University Press, 2002.

Chatterjee, Vera, *All This is Ended: The Life and Times of H.H. The Begum Sumroo of Sardhana*, New Delhi: Vikas, 1979.

Clarey, Helen, 'Lady Forester—A Woman of Wealth', MA diss., Keele University, 1986.

Clark, James, *Memoir of John Conolly, M.D.*, London: John Murray, 1869.

Colland, Henri, *La Begom Sombre: Drame en 5 Actes et 6 Tableaux*, Paris: Barnier Freres, 1855.

Combermere, Viscountess, and William Wallingford Knollys, *Memoirs and Correspondence of Field-Marshall Viscount Combermere*, 2 vols, London: Hurst and Blackett, 1866.

Compton, Herbert, *Particular Account of the European Military Adventures of Hindustan, from 1784 to 1803*, London: T. Fisher Unwin, 1893.

Coppock, James, *Elector's Manual; or, Plain Directions by Which Every Man May Know His Own Rights, and Preserve Them*, London: W. Buck, 1835.

Cotton, Evan, *Sardhana Pictures at Government House, Allahabad*, Allahabad: Superintendent, Printing and Stationery, U.P., 1934.

Cox, Edward W., *Law and Practice of Registration and Elections*, 5th edn, London: Law Times Office, 1847.

Creighton, J. N., *Narrative of the Siege and Capture of Bhurtpore*, London: Parbury, Allen, 1830.

Cumming, James Slator, *Six Years' Diary*, London: Martin and Hood, 1847.

Cunliffe-Owen, Marguerite [alias Marquise de Fontenoy], *Revelation of High Life within Royal Palaces*, U.S.: Edgewood, 1892.

Dalrymple, William, *Last Mughal: The Fall of a Dynasty, Delhi, 1857*, New York: Alfred A. Knopf, 2007.

———, *White Mughals*, London: HarperCollins, 2002.

Davis, Natalie Zemon, *The Return of Martin Guerre*, Cambridge: Harvard University Press, 1983.

[Deane, Mrs Ann] A. D., *Tour through the Upper Provinces of Hindostan*, London: C. and J. Rivington, 1823.

Derby, Edward Henry Stanley, Earl of, *Disraeli, Derby and the Conservative Party: Journals and Memoirs*, ed. J. R. Vincent, Hassocks: Harvester Press, 1978.

Dhingra, Pawan, *Managing Multicultural Lives: Asian American Professionals and the Challenge of Multiple Identities*, Stanford: Stanford University Press, 2007.

Dickens, Charles, *Bleak House*, Ware: Wordsworth Classics, 1993.

———, *Posthumous Papers of the Pickwick Club*, 2 vols, London: Chapman and Hall, 1837.

Disraeli, Benjamin, *Coningsby or the New Generation*, London: Longmans, Green, 1928.

———, *Letters*, ed. J. A. W. Gunn et al., 5 vols, Toronto: University of Toronto, 1982–93.

Dod, Charles R., *Electoral Facts from 1832 to 1853*, ed. H. J. Hanham, Hassocks: Harvester Press, 1972.

Dowbeggin, Ian, 'Degeneration and Hereditarianism in French Mental Medicine, 1840–90', in William Bynum, Roy Porter, and Michael Shepherd, eds, *The Anatomy of Madness: Essays in the History of Psychiatry*, 3 vols, London: Tavistock, 1985, vol. 1, pp 188–232.

Dowling, Alfred and John James Lowndes, *Reports of Cases Argued and Determined in the Queen's Bench*, 7 vols, London: S. Sweet, 1845–51.

Doyle, Arthur Conan, 'Sign of Four', *Lippincot's Monthly Magazine* (February 1890), pp. 147–223.

Dudley-Ward, C. H., *Romance of the Nineteenth Century*, New York, D. Appleton, 1923.

Dunsford, Harris F., *Pathogenetic Effects of Some of the Principal Homoeopathic Remedies*, London, Baillière, 1838.

———, *Practical Advantages of Homeopathy*, London, Baillière, 1841.

Dyce Sombre, David Ochterlony, *Humble Petition of David Octerlony Dyce Sombre Addressed to the Lords Temporal, Spiritual and Commoners assembled in Parliament*, Paris: Author, 1850.

———, *In Lunacy: In the Matter of David Ochterlony Dyce Sombre, a Person Found to Be of Unsound Mind*, London: Hansard, 1851.

———, *Mr. Dyce Sombre's Refutation of the Charge of Lunacy Brought against Him in the Court of Chancery*, Paris: Dyce Sombre, 1849; tr. Kurt Reinhardt, *Mr. Dyce Sombre's Widerlegung der Beschuldigung geisteskrank zu sein, die gegen ihn erhoben*, Dellfeld: T. Reinhard, 1995.

Dyce Sombre, Mary Anne, *Dyce Sombre against Troup, Solaroli (Intervening) and Prinsep and the Hon. East India Company (also Intervening) in the Goods of David Ochterlony Dyce Sombre, Esq., Deceased, in the Prerogative Court of Canterbury [DSAT]*, 2 vols, London: Seyfand 1852.

Dyer, A. Saunder, 'Begam of Sardhana', *Calcutta Review*, 98 (April 1894), pp. 310–26.

Eaton, Natasha, 'Critical Cosmopolitanism: Gifting and Collecting Art at Lucknow, 1775–1797', in *Art and the British Empire*, eds, Tim Barringer, Geoff Quilley, and Douglas Fordham, Manchester: Manchester University Press, 2007, ch. 11.

Ehlers, Eckart, and Thomas Krafft, eds, *Shahjahanabad/Old Delhi: Tradition and Colonial Change*, Delhi: Manohar, 2003.

Eigen, Joel Peter, *Witnessing Insanity: Madness and Mad-Doctors in the English Court*, New Haven: Yale University Press, 1995.

Elliotson, John, 'Accounts of More Painless Surgical Operations', *Zoist: A Journal of Cerebral Physiology and Mesmerism, and their applications to Human Welfare*, 4, 13 (March 1846 to January 1847), pp. 1–59.

Elmer, Joseph, *Outline of the Practice in Lunacy*, London: V. R. Stevens and G. S. Norton, 1844.

Elmes, James, *Metropolitan Improvements: or London in the Nineteenth Century*, London: Jones, 1827–28.

England and Wales, Commissioners in Lunacy, *Report of the Metropolitan Commissioners in Lunacy to the Lord Chancellor, presented to both Houses of Parliament by Command of Her Majesty*, London: Bardbury and Evans, 1844.

English Reports, 176 vols, London: Stevens, 1900–1930.

Ernst, Waltraud, *Mad Tales of the Raj: The European Insane in British India, 1800–1858*, London: Routledge, 1991.

Fallon, S. W., *New Hindustani-English Dictionary with Illustrations from Hindustani Literature and Folk-lore* (London, Trübner, 1876).

Fane, Henry Edward Hamlyn, *Five Years in India*, 2 vols, Patiala: Department of Languages, 1970.

Fanshawe, H. C., *Delhi Past and Present*, London: John Murray, 1902.

Firminger, Walter Kelly, *Early History of Freemasonry in Bengal and the Punjab*, Calcutta: Thacker, Spink, 1906.

Fisher, Michael H., *Counterflows to Colonialism: Indian Travellers and Settlers in Britain, 1600–1857*, Delhi: Permanent Black, 2006.

———, *First Indian Author in English: Dean Mahomet in India, Ireland, and England*, Delhi: Oxford University Press, 1996.

———, 'Representing "His" Women: Mirza Abu Talib Khan's 1801 "Vindication of the Liberties of Asiatic Women",' in *Indian Economic and Social History Review* 37, 2 (2000), pp. 215–37.

Forester, George Cecil Weld, *Heirs of Mr Dyce Sombre v. The Indian Government. The History of a Suit during Thirty Years between a Private Individual and the Government of India*, Westminster: T. Brettell, 1865.

Forester, Mary Ann, 'Notes on the Jervis Pedigree by Lady Forester, Insbruck, August 1892' copied by William Bowers, 34/17/68, William Salt Library, Stafford.

Forrest, Denys, *Oriental: Life Story of a West End Club*, London: B. T. Batsford, 1968.

Foucault, Michel, *Madness and Civilization: A History of Insanity in the Age of Reason*, tr. Richard Howard, New York: Random House, 1965.

Francklin, William, *History of the Reign of Shah-Aulum, the Present Emperor of Hindostaun* Lucknow: Pustak Kendra, 1973.

———, *Military Memoirs of Mr George Thomas*, Calcutta: author, 1803.

Fraser, J. Baillie, *Military Memoir of Lt.-Col. James Skinner*, 2 vols, London: Smith, Elder, 1851.

Gash, Norman, *Politics in the Age of Peel*, London: Longmans Green, 1953.

Geary, Eleanor Margaret, *Musical Education*, London: D'Almaine, 1841.

Ghosh, Durba, *Sex and the Family in Colonial India: The Making of Empire*, Cambridge: Cambridge University Press, 2006.

Gill, R., *New Volume; A New and Complete Collection of the Most Remarkable Trials for Adultery, 1799–1802*, London: Gill, 1802.

Gladstone, William Ewart, *Diaries*, 14 vols, ed. M. R. D. Foot, Oxford: Clarendon Press, 1968.

Godesche, Hermann (alias Sir John Retcliffe), *Nena Sahib oder die Empörung in Indien* (Berlin: Verlagsgesellschaft, 1858–65).

Goldstein, Jan, *Console and Classify: The French Psychiatric Profession in the Nineteenth Century*, Cambridge: Cambridge University Press, 1987.

Grand Conclave, *Statutes of the Religious and Military Order of the Temple, as Established in Scotland*, Edinburgh: Grand Conclave, 1843.

[Grant] Octogenarian, 'Memories of Life in India', *Outlook* (17 September 1898), pp. 179–84.

Great Britain, Parliament, *Journals of the House of Commons.*

——, *Minutes of Evidence on Second Reading of Bill, 'Act to exclude Borough of Sudbury from sending Burgesses to Parliament, brought from Lords 29 May 1843*, ordered printed 12 May 1843.

——, *Report of the Commissioners appointed under the Act of the 6th and 7th Victoria, chap. 97 to inquire into the existence of Bribery in the Borough of Sudbury*.

——, Report from the Select Committee on Dog Stealing (Metropolis), *Sessionals*, 1844, 14, pp. 291–349.

——, *Parliamentary Debates*, London: Hansard, 1812–56.

——, *Parliamentary Papers Relating to the Slave Trade 1837–38*, vol. 87, Shannon: Irish University Press, 1969.

——, Select Committee on the Sudbury Election Petition, Minutes of Proceedings and Evidence, chair Sir Thomas Nicholas Redington, House of Commons Papers; *Reports of Committees* (paper 176), vol. 7, no. 847 ordered by House of Commons to be printed 15 April 1842.

Greenhill, James, Rev. W. A. Harrison, and F. J. Furnivall, eds, *List of All the Songs and Passages in Shakspere: Which Have Been Set to Music*, London: New Shakspere Society, 1884.

Greville, Charles C. F., *Memoirs: A Journal of the Reigns of King George IV and King William IV*, ed. Henry Reeve, 3 vols, 3rd edn, London: Longmans, Green, 1875.

Grindlay and Co., *Overland Circular: Hints for Travellers to India*, London: Smith, Elder, 1847.

Gupta, G. S., *Freemasonic Movements in India*, New Delhi: Indian Masonic Publication, 1981.

Hall, Frederick James, and Philip Twells, *Reports of Cases Argued and Determined in the High Court of Chancery, During the Time of Lord Chancellor Cottenham*, 2 vols, London: W. Maxwell, 1849–51.

Hamill, John, *Craft: A History of English Freemasonry*, Great Britain: Crucible, 1986.

Harland-Jacobs, Jessica, *Builders of Empire: Freemasons and British Imperialism, 1712–1927*, Chapel Hill: University of North Carolina Press, 2007.

Hawes, Christopher J., *Poor Relations: the Making of a Eurasian Community in British India*, London: Curzon, 1996.

Heber, Reginald, *Narrative of a Journey through the Upper Provinces of India, from Calcutta to Bombay, 1824–1825*, 3 vols, London: John Murray, 1827.

Hewett, George, *Private Record of the Life of the Right Honorable General Sir George Hewet*, Newport: W. W. Yelf, 1840.

Higginbotham, J. J., *Men Whom India has Known*, London: Richardson, 1870.

Higman, Barry, 'West India "Interest" in Parliament, 1807–1833', *Historical Studies*, 13, 49 (October 1967), pp. 1–19.

Hingorani, Alka, 'Artful Agency: Imagining and Imaging Begam Samru', *Archives of Asian Art*, 53 (2002), pp. 54–70.

Hockley, William B., 'Natch', *English in India and Other Sketches*, 2 vols, London: Longman, Rees, Orme, Brown, Green, and Longman, 1835, pp. 159–77.

Hodson, V. C. P., *List of the Officers of the Bengal Army*, 4 vols, London: Constable, 1927–47.

Holland, Henry Richard Vassall, *Holland House Diaries 1831–1840*, ed. Abraham D. Kriegel, London: Routledge and Kegan Paul, 1977.

Hosagrahar, Jyoti, *Indigenous Modernities: Negotiating Architecture and Urbanism*, London: Routledge, 2005.

Hutchinson, Lester, *European Freebooters in Moghul India*, London: Asia, 1964.

India. Imperial Record Department, *Calendar of Persian Correspondence*, vols 9–11, Calcutta, Superintendent Government Printing, 1911–49.

Irvine, William, *Later Mughals*, ed. Jadunath Sarkar, 2 vols, New Delhi: Oriental, 1971.

Jacquemont, Victor, *Letters from India*, 2 vols, Karachi: Oxford University Press, 1979.

Jay, Mike, *Air Loom Gang: The Strange and True Story of James Tilly Matthews and His Visionary Madness*, New York: Bantam, 2003.

Jervis, Hon. Mary Anne, *Aure amiche, Aria*, London: Willis, 1836.

———, *La Partenza*, London: Willis, n.d.

———, *Shall This Pale Cheek; a Ballad*, words by Rt. Hon. Lady Dacre, London: Willis, 1831.

———, *Two Italian Duets and One Song*, London: Willis, 1836.

Jones, Kathleen, *Lunacy, Law, and Conscience, 1744–1845*, London: Routledge and Kegan Paul, 1955.

Kaye, M. M., ed., *Golden Calm: An English Lady's Life in Moghul Delhi, Reminiscences by Emily, Lady Clive Bayly, and her Father, Sir Thomas Metcalfe*, New York: Viking, 1980.

Keegan, W., *Sardhana and its Begam*, Agra: St Peters College, 1932.

Keene, H. G., *Hindustan under Free Lances, 1770–1820*, London: Brown, Langham, 1907.

———, 'Sardhana: The Seat of the Sombres', *Calcutta Review*, 70 (1880), pp. 445–64.

———, 'Women of Indian History', *Eclectic Magazine of Foreign Literature*, 44, 6 (December 1886), pp. 820–27.

Kemp, Betty, 'General Election of 1841', *History*, 37, 130 (June 1952), pp. 146–57.

Khan, Karim, Nawab, 'Siyahatnama', Urdu MSS OR 2163, British Library; *Siyahat Namah*, ed. 'Ibadat Barelvi, Lahore: Majlis-i Isha'at-i Makhtutat, 1982.

Khan, Seid Gholam Hossein, *Seir Mutaqherin, or, Review of Modern Times*, 4 vols, tr. Nota Manus, Lahore: Sheikh Mubarak Ali, 1975.

Kincaid, W., 'Indian Bourbons', *Littell's Living Age* (19 February 1887), pp. 493–98.

Lall, John, *Begam Samru: Fading Portrait in a Gilded Frame*, New Delhi: Roli, 1997.

Lamington, Lord, 'In the Days of the Dandies', *Blackwood's Magazine* (1890), p. 316.

Larneuil, Michel, *Roman de la Begum Sombre*, Paris: A. Michel, 1981.

Leach, Linda York, *Mughal and Other Indian Paintings from the Chester Beatty Library*, vol. 2, London: Scorpion Cavendish, 1995.

Leavitt, Robert Keith, 'Who was Cecil Forrester?', *Baker Street Journal*, 1, 2 (April 1946), pp. 201–4.

Lennox, William Pitt, Lord, *Fifty Years' Biographical Reminiscences*, 2 vols, London: Hurst and Blackett, 1863.

Lewis, Wilmarth Sheldon, *Horace Walpole's Library*, Cambridge: Cambridge University Press, 1958.

Limbird, John, *Picturesque Guide to The Regent's Park*, London: John Limbird, 1829.

Lodge, Edmund, *Peerage, Baronetage, Knightage and Companionage of the British Empire*, 72nd edn, London: Kelly's Directories, 1903.

Lodge Hope, *Bylaws*, Calcutta: P. M. Cavenburgh and Jas. R. Rogers, 1865.

Longsford, Elizabeth, *Wellington: Pillar of State*, New York: Harper and Row, 1972.

Losty, J. P., 'Delhi Palace in 1846: A Panoramic View by Mazhar 'Ali Khan', in Rosemary Crill, Susan Stronge, Andrew Topsfield, eds, *Arts of Mughal India*, Ahmedabad: Mapin, 2004, pp. 286–302.

Lutfullah, *Autobiography*, ed. Edward B. Eastwick, New Delhi: International Writer's Emporium, 1987.

Lyndhurst, Lord, *Memoir*, ed. William Sidney Gibson, London: Butterworths, 1869.

Lytton, Robert, Earl of, *Letters from Owen Meredith (Robert, First Earl of Lytton) to Robert and Elizabeth Barrett Browning*, ed. Aurelia Brooks Harlan and J. Lee Harlan, Waco: Baylor University, 1936.

M. T., 'Christianity in India by One Long Resident in India', *Fraser's Magazine*, 16, 93 (September 1877), pp. 306–19.

Macaulay, Thomas Babington, *Letters*, ed. Thomas Pinney, vol. 3, Cambridge: Cambridge University Press, 1976.

McCandless, Peter, 'Dangerous to Themselves and Others: the Victorian Debate over the Prevention of Wrongful Confinement', *Journal of British Studies*, 23, 1 (Fall 1983), pp. 84–104.

McMahon, C. A., *Badshapoor Suit, Hon. Mrs Forester, Mary Anne Troup and Mary [sic] Solaroli vs the Secretary of State for India*, Roorkee: Thomason Civil Engineering College Press, 1865.

Macnaghten, Steuart, and Alexander Gordon, *Reports of Cases Argued and Determined in the High Court of Chancery during the Time of Lord Chacellor Cottenham*, London: Stevens and Sons, 1860.

Malleson, George B., *Recreations of an Indian Official*, London: Longmans Green, 1872.

Manavit, Augustin, *Esquisse historique sur le cardinal Mezzofanti*, Paris: Sagnier et Bray, 1853.

Manchester, A. H., *Modern Legal History of England and Wales, 1750–1950*, London: Butterworths, 1980.

Martin, James Ranald, *Influence of Tropical Climates in Producing the Acute Endemic Diseases of Europeans*, London: John Churchill, 1855.

Martin, Theodore, *Life of Lord Lyndhurst*, London: John Murray, 1883.

Maxwell, Herbert, *Life of Wellington*, 2 vols, London: Sampson Low, Marston, 1899.

Mayo, Thomas, *Medical Testimony and Evidence in Cases of Lunacy Being the Croonian Lectures Delivered before the Royal College of Surgeons in 1853*, London: John W. Parker, 1854.

Metcalfe, Charles, *Two Native Narratives of the Mutiny in Delhi*, Westminster: Archibald Constable, 1898.

Metcalfe, Charles Theophilus, *Life and Correspondence*, ed. John William Kaye, 2 vols, London, Smith, Elder, 1858.

Metcalfe, Thomas, *Delhi Book*, in M. M. Kaye, ed., *Golden Calm: An English Lady's Life in Moghul Delhi, Reminiscences by Emily, Lady Clive Bayly, and her Father, Sir Thomas Metcalfe*, New York: Viking, 1980; BL Add. Or. 5475.

Mill, John Stuart, *Collected Works*, vol. 14, ed. Francis E. Mineka and Dwight N. Lindsay, Toronto: University of Toronto Press, 1972.

Millingen, J. G., *Aphorisms on the Treatment and Management of the Insane*, London: John Churchill, 1840.

Minturn, Robert B., *From New York to Delhi*, 3rd edn, New York: D. Appleton, 1859.

Montez, Lola, *Lectures*, ed. Charles Chauncey Burr, New York: Rudd and Carleton, 1858.

Moore, Norman, rev. Anita McConnell, 'James Copland', *NDNB*.

Moore, Thomas, *Journal*, ed. Wilfred S. Dowden, New Jersey: Associated University Presses, 1984.

Motley, John Lothrop, *Correspondence*, 2 vols, ed. George William Curtis, New York: Harper and Brothers, 1889.

Murray, John, *Handbook of Rome and Its Environs*, London: John Murray, 1864.

Nair, Bishop Patrick, *Sardhana: Its Begum, Its Shrine, Its Basilica*, Meerut: Prabhat Press, 1963.

Napier, William, *Life and Opinions of General Sir Charles James Napier*, 4 vols, London: John Murray, 1857.

Nash, Thomas Arthur, *Life of Richard Lord Westbury*, 2 vols, London: Richard Bentley, 1888.

National Archives of India, *Fort William-Indian House Correspondence*, vols 4, 18 New Delhi: National Archives of India, 1949–79.

Neuman, Philipp von, *Diary*, 2 vols, ed. and tr. E. Beresford Chancellor, Boston: Houghton Mifflin, 1928.

Nicholson, Mr, *Trial at Full Length, of Major-General Sir Robert Thomas Wilson, Michael Bruce, Esq. and Captain John Hely Hutchinson*, London: Sherwood, Neely, and Jones, 1816.

North-Western Provinces, *Gazetteer*, Allahabad, North-Western Provinces and Oudh Government Press, 1875.

Noti, Severin, *Das Furstentum Sardhana: Geschichte eines deutschen Abenteurers und einer indischen herrscherin*, Freiburg: Herdersche Verlagshandlung, 1906.

Nugent, Lady Maria, *Journal*, 2 vols, London: Author, 1839.

Oman, Carola, *Gascoyne Heiress: The Life and Diaries of Frances Mary Gascoyne-Cecil, 1802–39*, London: Hodder and Stoughton, 1968.

Orlich, Leopold von, *Travels in India*, tr. H. Evans Lloyd, 2 vols, Delhi: Usha, 1985.

Owen, Aubrey Sherrard, *Life of Lord St Vincent*, London: G. Allen and Unwin, 1933.

Oxford Dictionary of National Biography, Oxford: Oxford University Press, 2004– [*NDNB*].

Pagan, J. M., *Medical Jurisprudence of Insanity*, London: Ball and Arnold, 1840.

Palmer, Roundell, *Memorials*, 2 vols, London: Macmillan, 1896.

Parry, Jonathan, 'Benjamin Disraeli', *NDNB*.

Parry-Jones, William Llewellyn, *Trade in Lunacy, A Study of Private Madhouses in England in the Eighteenth and Nineteenth Centuries*, London: Routledge, Kegan Paul, 1971.

Perceval, John, *Narrative of the Treatment Experienced by a Gentleman During a State of Mental Derangement*, London: Effingham Wilson, 1840.

Pernau, Margrit and Yunus Jaffery, eds, *Information and the Public Sphere: Persian Newsletters from Mughal India*, Delhi: Oxford University Press, 2009.

Phillips, Charles Palmer, *Law Concerning Lunatics, Idiots, and Persons of Unsound Mind*, London: Butterworths, 1858.

Phillips, T. J., *Reports of Cases Argues and Determined in the High Court of Chancery during the Time of Lord Chancellor Cottenham*, vol. 2, London: William Benning, 1849.

Polier, Antoine Louis Henri, *Shah Alam II and His Court*, Calcutta: Asiatic Society, 1989.

Porter, Roy, *Mind-forg'd Manacles: A History of Madness in England from the Restoration to the Regency*, Cambridge: Harvard University Press, 1987.

Powell, Avril, 'Artful Apostasy? A Mughal Mansabdar among the Jesuits', in Peter Robb, ed., *Society and Ideology*, Delhi: Oxford University Press, 1993, pp. 72–96.

Prinsep, Henry T., *History of the Political and Military Transactions in India during the Administration of the Marquess of Hastings*, London: J. Murray, 1820.

Prior, Katherine, Lance Brennan, and Robin Haines, 'Role of English, Persian and other Esoteric Tongues in the Dismissal of Sir Edward Colebrooke as Resident of Delhi in 1829', *Modern Asian Studies*, 35, 1 (2001), pp. 75–112.

Qanungo, Kalika-Ranjan, *History of the Jats*, vol. 1, Calcutta: M.C. Sarkar, 1925.

Ralph, Omar, *Naoroji, the First Asian MP: A Biography of Dadabhai Naoroji, India's Patriot and Britain's MP*, St. John's, Antigua: Hansib, 1997.

Ranganath, Tivari, *Sardhana ki Begham*, New Delhi: Radhakrishna, 2005.

Ray, Isaac, *Treatise on the Medical Jurisprudence of Insanity*, 3rd edn, Boston: Little, Brown, 1853.

Reform Club, *Rules and Regulations*, London: T. Brettell, 1840.

Reinhardt, Kurt, *Wegweiser zu den Quellen der Geschichte des deutschen Nabobs von Sardhana in Indien Walter Reinhardt genannt Sombre*, Völkingen: Selbstverlag, 1993.

Rich, Paul J., *Elixir of Empire: The English Public Schools, Ritualism, Freemasonry, and Imperialism*, London: Regency Press, 1989.

Richards, John F., *Mughal Empire*, Cambridge: Cambridge University Press, 1993.

Riches, Hugh, *History of the Oriental Club*, London: Oriental Club, 2000.

Roberts, R. Ellis, *Samuel Rogers and His Circle*, London: Methuen, 1910.

Rolt, John, *Memoirs of The Right Honourable Sir John Rolt, Lord Justice of the Court of Appeal in Chancery, 1804–1871*, London: Inner Temple, 1939.

Saksena, Ram Babu, *European and Indo-European Poets of Urdu and Persian*, Lucknow: Nevil Kishore, 1941.

Samuel, Enid C., *Villas in Regent's Park and their Residents*, London: St Marylebone Society, 1959.

Saunders, Ann, *Regent's Park: A Study in the Development of the Area from 1086 to the Present Day*, Newton Abbot: David and Charles, 1969.

Scott, Caroline, Lady, *Marriage in High Life*, 2 vols, ed. Lady Charotte Bury, London: H. Colburn, 1828.

Scull, Andrew T., 'John Conolly', *NDNB*.

——, *Most Solitary of Afflictions: Madness and Society in Britain*, New Haven: Yale University Press, 1993.

——, *Museums of Madness: The Social Organization of Insanity in Nine-teenth-Century England*, New York: St Martins, 1979.

——, 'Victorian Alienist: John Conolly', in *Anatomy of Madness*, vol. 1, eds William Bynum, Roy Porter, and Michael Shepherd, London: Tavistock, 1985, pp 103–50.

Seymour, Bruce, *Lola Montez: A Life*, New Haven: Yale University Press, 1995.

Shamsuddin, *Loves of Begum Sumroo and Other True Romances*, Delhi: Hind Pocket Books 1967.

Sharma, Mahendra Narain, *Life and Times of Begam Samru of Sardhana*, Sahibabad: Vibhu Prakashan, 1985.

Sharma, Partap, *Begum Sumroo: A Play in Three Acts*, New Delhi: Rupa, 2004.

Shelley, Frances, Lady, *Diary*, ed. Richard Edgcumbe, New York: Charles Scribner's Sons, 1913.

Sher, Amita, *Begam Samru, the Most Beloved*, Lahore: Sang-e-Meel, 1993.

Sherer, J. W., 'Bishop in Partibus', *Gentleman's Magazine*, 280 (January-June 1896), pp. 459–69.

Sherwood, Mrs [Mary Martha Butt], *Life of Mrs Sherwood, Chiefly Autobio-graphical*, ed. Sophia Kelly, London: Darton, 1867.

Showalter, Elaine, *Female Malady: Women, Madness, and English Culture: 1830–1980*, New York: Penguin, 1985.

Shreeve, Nicholas G., *Dark Legacy*, Arundel: Bookwright, 1996.

——, *From Nawab to Nabob: The Diary of David Ochterlony Dyce Som-bre, 1833–8*, Crossbush: Bookwright, 2000.

——, *Indian Heir*, Arundel: Bookwright, 2001.

Sinha, Mrinalini, 'Britishness, Clubbability, and the Colonial Public Sphere', *Journal of British Studies*, 40, 4 (October 2001), pp. 489–521.

Skinner, Captain Thomas, *Excursions in India*, 2nd ed, 2 vols, London: Rich-ard Bentley, 1833.

Sleeman, William Henry, *Rambles and Recollections of an Indian Official*, 2 vols, Karachi: Oxford University Press 1973.

Smith, Logan Pearsall, 'Hunting for Manuscripts', *Atlantic Monthly*, 160 (July-December, 1937), pp. 92–8.

Smith, Roger, *Trial by Medicine: Insanity and Responsibility in Victorian Trials*, Edinburgh: Edinburgh University Press, 1981.

Society of Gentlemen of the Middle Temple, *Counsellor's Magazine*, London: W. and J. Stratford, 1796.

Southgate, Donald, *Passing of the Whigs, 1832–1886*, London: Macmillan, 1962.

Spear, Percival, *Twilight of the Mughuls: Studies in Late Mughul Delhi*, Cambridge: Cambridge University Press, 1951.

Stephen, Neill, *History of Christianity in India: 1707–1858*, Cambridge: Cambridge University Press, 2002.

Sutherland, D., ed., *Weekly Reporter, Appellate High Court*, vol. 4, Calcutta: Law-Publishing Press, 1891.

Suzuki, Akihito, *Madness at Home: The Psychiatrist, the Patient, and the Family in England, 1820–1860*, Berkeley: University of California Press, 2006.

Tassy, M. Garcin de, *Auteurs Hindoistanis et Leurs Ouvrages*, Paris: de Dubuisson, 1855.

Taylor, Henry, *Correspondence*, ed. Edward Dowden, London: Longmans, Green, 1888.

Thompson, Edward, *Life of Charles, Lord Metcalfe*, London: Faber and Faber, 1937.

Thorn, William, *Memoir of the War in India*, London: T. Egerton, 1818.

Tupper, C. L., *Indian Political Practice: A Collection of the Decisions of the Government of India in Political Cases*, 4 vols, Calcutta: Superintendent of Government Printing, 1895.

Tyson, Geoffrey, *100 Years of Banking for Grindlay's Bank*, London: Bank, 1963.

Umashankar, *Dil par ek Dagh*, Cawnpur: Pariwar Prakashan, 1965.

Vannini, Fulgentius, *Hindustan-Tibet Mission*, New Delhi: Vishal, 1981.

Verne, Jules, *Les Cinq cents millions de la Bégum* (Paris : J. Hetzel, 1877); *Begum's Fortune*, tr. I. O. Evans, Westport: Associated Booksellers, 1958.

Vibart, E., 'Sepoy Revolt', *Eclectic Magazine of Foreign Literature* (January 1898), pp. 45ff.

Viswanathan, Gauri, *Outside the Fold: Conversion, Modernity*, Princeton: Princeton University Press, 1998.

Walker, Nigel, *Crime and Insanity in England*, vol. 1, Edinburgh: Edinburgh University Press, 1968.

Warren, Samuel, *Passages from the Diary of a Late Physician*, 2 vols, Edinburgh: W. Blackwood and Sons, 1832.

Weber, Peter, *Maharadscha Reinhardt, Feldherr des Grossmoguls*, Berlin: Propyläen, 1943.

Wellington, Arthur Wellesley, Duke of, *Wellington and His Friends*, London: Macmillan, 1965.

Wheeler, Stephen, ed., *Annals of the Oriental Club, 1824–1858*, London: Author, 1925.

Who's Who of British Members of Parliament: a Biographical Dictionary of the House of Commons, vol. 1, Hassocks: Harvester, 1976.

Wolff, Joseph, *Researches and Missionary Labours*, Philadelphia: Orrin Rogers, 1837.

———, *Travels and Adventures*, 2nd edn, 2 vols, London: Saunders, Otley, 1861.

Woodbridge, George, *Reform Club, 1836–1978: A History from the Club's Records*, New York: Reform Club, 1978.

www.measuringworth.com, accessed 10 January 2008.

Yates, William, *Memoirs of John Chamberlain, Late Missionary in India*, London: Wightman and Cramp, 1826.

INDEX